Television Regulation and Media Policy in China

Since the late 1990s, there has been a crucial and substantial transformation in China's television system involving institutional, structural and regulatory changes. Unravelling the implications of these changes is vital for understanding the politics of Chinese media policy-making and regulation, and thus a comprehensive study of this history has never been more essential.

This book studies the transformation of the policy and regulation of the Chinese television sector within a national political and economic context from 1996 to the present day. Taking a historical and sociological approach, it engages in the theoretical debates over the nature of the transformation of media in the authoritarian Chinese state; the implications of the ruling party's political legitimacy and China's central-local conflicts upon television policy-making and market structure; and the nature of the media modernization process in a developing country. Its case studies include broadcasting systems in Shanghai and Guangdong, which demonstrate that varied polices and development strategies have been adopted by television stations, reflecting different local circumstances and needs.

Arguing that rather than being a homogenous entity, China has demonstrated substantial local diversity and complex interactions between local, national and global media, this book will be of interest to students and scholars of Chinese media, politics and policy, and international communications.

Yik Chan Chin is a Research Assistant Professor at Hong Kong Baptist University, working in the areas of media and communication policy, regulation and law, new media and governance and media policy-making and politics.

Routledge Contemporary China Series

144 Media Power in Hong Kong
Hyper-marketized media and
cultural resistance
Charles Chi-wai Cheung

145 The Identity of Zhiqing
The lost generation
Weiyi Wu and Fan Hong

146 Teacher Management in China
The transformation of
educational systems
*Eva Huang, John Benson and
Ying Zhu*

**147 Social Entrepreneurship in the
Greater China Region**
Policy and cases
Yanto Chandra

**148 China's Approach to Central
Asia**
The Shanghai Co-operation
Organisation
Weiqing Song

**149 China's Peasant Agriculture
and Rural Society**
Changing paradigms of farming
*Jan Douwe van der Ploeg and
Jingzhong Ye*

150 China's Changing Economy
Trends, impacts and the future
Edited by Curtis Andressen

151 China's Energy Security
A multidimensional perspective
*Edited by Giulia Romano and
Jean-François Di Meglio*

**152 Chinese Muslims and the
Global Ummah**
Islamic revival and ethnic
identity among the Hui of
Qinghai Province
Alexander Blair Stewart

**153 State Propaganda in China's
Entertainment Industry**
Shenshen Cai

**154 Assessing the Balance of Power
in Central-Local Relations in
China**
Edited by John Donaldson

**155 Television Regulation and
Media Policy in China**
Yik Chan Chin

**156 Space, Politics, and Cultural
Representation in Modern
China**
Cartographies of revolution
Enhua Zhang

**157 The Occupy Movement in
Hong Kong**
Sustaining decentralised protest
Yongshun Cai

Television Regulation and Media Policy in China

Yik Chan Chin

LONDON AND NEW YORK

First published 2017
by Routledge
2 Park Square, Milton Park, Abingdon, Oxon OX14 4RN

and by Routledge
711 Third Avenue, New York, NY 10017

First issued in paperback 2018

Routledge is an imprint of the Taylor & Francis Group, an informa business

© 2017 Yik Chan Chin

The right of Yik Chan Chin to be identified as author of this work has been asserted by her in accordance with sections 77 and 78 of the Copyright, Designs and Patents Act 1988.

All rights reserved. No part of this book may be reprinted or reproduced or utilized in any form or by any electronic, mechanical, or other means, now known or hereafter invented, including photocopying and recording, or in any information storage or retrieval system, without permission in writing from the publishers.

Trademark notice: Product or corporate names may be trademarks or registered trademarks, and are used only for identification and explanation without intent to infringe.

British Library Cataloguing in Publication Data
A catalogue record for this book is available from the British Library

Library of Congress Cataloging in Publication Data
Names: Chin, Yik Chan, author.
Title: Television regulation and media policy in China / Yik Chan Chin.
Description: Abingdon, Oxon ; New York, NY : Routledge, 2017. |
Series: Routledge contemporary China series ; 155 | Includes
bibliographical references and index.
Identifiers: LCCN 2016009917 | ISBN 9780415490832 (hardback) |
ISBN 9780203798751 (ebook)
Subjects: LCSH: Television broadcasting policy–China. | Mass media
policy–China. | Television broadcasting–China.
Classification: LCC HE8700.9.C6 C45 2017 | DDC 384.550951–dc23
LC record available at https://lccn.loc.gov/2016009917

ISBN 13: 978-1-138-60671-5 (pbk)
ISBN 13: 978-0-415-49083-2 (hbk)

Typeset in Times New Roman
by Wearset Ltd, Boldon, Tyne and Wear

Contents

List of figures	vi
List of tables	vii
Acknowledgment	viii
List of abbreviations	ix

1	Introduction	1
2	The political system and economic transition	19
3	Broadcasting authority in China	40
4	State legitimacy and administration according to law for broadcasting	59
5	China's television in the 1990s	79
6	China's television policy between 1996 and 2003	87
7	China's television policy between 2004 and 2015	110
8	Public service broadcasting	124
9	Shanghai television: from state institution to enterprise	147
10	Guangdong: the role of local in China's media policy-making process	171
11	A reconsideration of national, local and global relationships	191

Appendix I: laws, regulations and documents	211
References	219
Index	254

Figures

2.1	Organization of the Chinese Communist Party	21
2.2	Structure of the Chinese Government	22
3.1	Organizational structure of SAPPRFT (2015d)	45
7.1	China's national networks distribution	113
7.2	Division of labor between SAPPRFT and MIIT	114
9.1	Three channels' revenue in 2003 and 2005 (in million yuan)	159

Tables

3.1	Broadcasting related laws in China	50
5.1	TV broadcasting in China (1981–1996)	80
5.2	Growth of advertising revenue in China (1981–1996)	81
5.3	Growth of Chinese television stations (1983–1996)	83
6.1	China's service export and share of the world total (1985–2001)	105
8.1	Income of Chinese broadcasters in 2009 (billions, yuan, %)	138
9.1	The important stages of Shanghai's television development before 1996	150
9.2	The major institutions under the Shanghai Culture, Radio, Film and TV Bureau in 2000	153
9.3	The major entities of the Shanghai Media Group (SMG) in 2002	154
9.4	Shanghai TV market in 2000	156
9.5	TV channels in Shanghai, 2000 (before conglomeration)	156
9.6	TV channels in Shanghai in January 2002 (after conglomeration)	156
11.1	China's political economy and television policy from the late 1990s	194

Acknowledgment

Chapter 8 in this book draws from previously published research. I would like to thank Nordicom for permission to reuse material from Yik Chan Chin and Matthew Johnson (2012) Public Service: New Paradigms of Policy, and Reform in China, in: *Regaining the Initiative for Public Service Media*, edited by Gregory Ferrell Lowe and Jeanette Steemers, Gothenburg: NORDICOM, 149–166. Copyright 2012; and Yik Chan Chin (2012) Public Service Broadcasting, Public Interest and Individual Rights in China, *Media, Culture & Society* (34) 7: 898–912. Copyright 2012.

Chapter 10 in this book draws from previously published research. I would like to thank SAGE for permission to reuse material from Yik Chan Chin (2011) Policy Process, Policy Learning, and the Role of Provincial Media in China, *Media, Culture & Society* (33) 2: 193–210. Copyright 2011.

Abbreviations

AOL	American Online
BAR	Broadcasting Administrative Regulations
BBC	British Broadcasting Corporation
BIA	Beijing Internet Association
BJTV	Beijing Television Station
CASS	Chinese Academy of Social Science
CBN	China Broadcasting Network Limited (when referring to company)
CBN	China Business Network (when referring to network)
CC	Central Committee
CCP	Chinese Communist Party
CCPIT	China's Council for the Promotion of International Trade
CCPLRO	Literature Research Office of Chinese Communist Party Central Committee
CCTV	China Central Television
CCYL	Chinese Communist Youth League
CDM	China DTV Media Incorporated Limited
CDMA	Code Division Multiple Access
CEO	Chief Executive Officer
CESCR	Committee on Economic, Social and Cultural Rights
CETV	China Entertainment Television
CG	Computer Graphics
CITVC	China International Television Corporation
CMC	China Media Capital
CMCC	China Mobile Communications Corporation
CMCDI	China Merchants China Direct Investments Limited
CNBC	Consumer News and Business Channel
CNN	Cable News Network
CNR	China National Radio
COD	Central Organization Department
CPD	Central Propaganda Department
CPPCC	Chinese People's Political Consultative Congress
CPRS	Central People's Radio Station
CPS	Cultural Public Service

x *Abbreviations*

CRAO	Central Radio Administrative Office
CRI	China Radio International
CVP	Connected Village Project
DBS	Direct Broadcasting Satellite
DBTA	Departments or agencies in charge of Broadcasting and Television Administration
DPP	Democratic Progressive Party
DTH	Direct-To-Home
DTvP	Digital Television Policy
EU	European Union
GAPP	General Administration of Press and Publication
GATS	*General Agreement on Trade in Services*
GBB	Guangdong Broadcasting Bureau
GDP	Gross Domestic Product
GDTV	Guangdong Television
GE	General Electrics
HDTV	High-Definition Television
ICCPR	*International Covenant on Civil and Political Rights*
ICESCR	*International Covenant on Economic, Social and Cultural Rights*
IOS	The Information Office of the State Council
IP	Internet Protocol
IPTV	Internet Protocol Television
ISP	Internet Service Providers
JSLLC	Joint-Stock Limited Liability Company
KBS	Korean Broadcasting System
LLC	Limited Liability Company
MASTV	Macau Asia Satellite Television
MBC	Mico Broadcasting Corporation
MCP	Ministry of Central Propaganda
MFN	Most Favored Nation
MII	Ministry of the Information Industry
MIIT	Ministry of Industry and Information
MPT	Ministry of Post and Telecommunications
MRFT	Ministry of Radio, Film and Television
MTV	Music Television
NDRC	National Development and Reform Commission
NGO	Non-Governmental Organization
NPC	National People's Congress
NVOD	Near-Video-on-Demand
OTV	Shanghai Oriental Television Station
OTvC	Overseas Television Channel
PCS	Public Culture Service
PI	Public Interest
PL	Policy Learning
PRC	People's Republic of China

PSB	Public Service Broadcasting
PSM	Public Service Media
RD	Radio Department
R&D	Research and Development
ROC	Republic of China
RTS	Radio and Television Shanghai
SAIC	State Administration for Industry and Commerce
SAIL	Shanghai Alliance Investment Limited
SAPPRFT	State Administration of Press, Publication, Radio, Film and Television
SARFT	State Administration of Radio, Film and Television
SARS	Severe Acute Respiratory Syndrome
SASAC	State-owned Assets Supervision and Administration Commission
SCT	Shanghai Cable Television
SGAPP	State General Agency of Press and Publications
SMEG	Shanghai Media & Entertainment Group
SMG	Shanghai Media Group
SNS	Social Networking Site
SOE	State-Owned Enterprise
SSC	State Security Committee
SST	Shanghai Symphony Telecommunications Corporation Limited
STAR TV	Satellite Television Asian Region Limited
STB	Set Top Box
STS	Southern Television Station
STV	Shanghai Television Station
SZE	Special Economic Zone
TNC	Transnational Corporation
TV	Television
TXP	Tibet-Xinjiang Project
UN	United Nations
USA	United States of America
VOD	Video-On-Demand
WTO	World Trade Organization
XNA	Xinhua News Agency
XNCR	Yanan Xinhua Radio Station

1 Introduction

This book studies the transformation of the policy and regulation of the Chinese television sector within a national political and economic context from 1996 to 2015. The study also engages in the theoretical debates over the nature of the transformation of television broadcasting in the transitional Chinese state, the nature of the implication of the central-local tension upon the policy-making, regulation and the structure of China's television sector, and the nature of the television broadcasting modernization process in a developing country.

At the national level, the study investigates China's national television regulatory policy and structural changes from 1996 to 2015 and the reasons for the changes, because since 1996, a substantial transformation has been ongoing in China's television broadcasting system, involving institutional, structural and regulatory changes. Theoretical accounts developed in the former communist Eastern European context to explain the nature of transformation of Chinese TV broadcasting are contested.

At the national-local level, it investigates the changes in practices and market structures in the local Shanghai television broadcasting system, and the television policy-making and implementation process in Guangdong. China is not a homogeneous entity; it is a large country with diverse local cultures with different dialects, lifestyles, traditions and customs. The uneven economic development between regions has led to differentiation in the structure of the market and different priorities in development policy. It is important for researchers to recognize this regional segmentation, and investigate its impact upon the local media (Ciu and Liu, 2000). Second, the tension between central and local governments observed in China's economy has also become increasingly apparent in the television sector: how does this central-local nexus influence policy-making, regulation and the transformation of the television sector? This is a very important issue that cannot be ignored in a study that aims to understand the complex reasons for the changes. Three interpretations of the implication of the central-local tension upon the existing political structure are contested.

This research adopts the case study method for the investigations on local-central tension and local diversity. The identification of the case studies is based on the degree of relevance of the case to the theoretical concerns of this study,

2 Introduction

the economic and political significance of the case study and the accessibility of the data. The case studies chosen are two local broadcasting systems – those of Shanghai and Guangdong.

By drawing evidence from the investigations above, the study then moves on to analyze the major theoretical issue – the nature of the modernization process in developing countries in international communication studies. Three arguments conceptualizing the nature of China's modernization process – the development paradigm, political economy and Chinese modernity – are also contested against the evidence.

Outline of the book

The book consists of 11 chapters. In Chapter 1, the aims and theoretical framework of the study are introduced.

In Chapter 2, China's culture, political structure, the central-local relationship and economic and political reform are reviewed, with particular focus on the period from 1996 to 2015. This chapter serves the purpose of setting up the general background for the research, covering significant issues and tendencies observed in the field.

In Chapter 3, the historical development of China's broadcasting regulator – SAPPRFT – is examined as is the supervisory mechanism used by the State Council and the Party's propaganda department to control the regulator. The command-based regulatory methods of SAPPRFT are then studied in detail, and the chapter suggests that the Chinese state's broadcasting regulation is shifting from heavily relying on legal rules and normative documents to a combination of command and consensus building mechanisms.

In Chapter 4, how the change in the Chinese Communist Party's political legitimacy has affected the functions of broadcasting regulation in China is explored, and it is argued that the political legitimacy of the Chinese Party-State shapes the discourse of the rule of law and the country's broadcasting regulatory strategies and structure.

In Chapter 5, the structure and major features of China's television system are reviewed, and the issues and problems that emerged from the interaction between the Chinese state, its local media and foreign satellite TV channels from the 1980s to mid-1990s are explored. The conflicts between the local and national government and the media, caused by the disjunction of each other's interests, are set out. This chapter also introduces the beginning of the substantial and significant restructuring of China's television since 1996.

In Chapters 6 and 7, China's national TV policies and structural changes from 1996 to 2015 are studied, and the underlining reasons for the changes in relation to domestic political and economic factors are investigated. The initial implications of the process of the changes are set out.

Having examined the historical development of China's national broadcasting regulatory policy and structure, in Chapters 8, 9 and 10 in-depth cases studies on three topics are conducted: public service broadcasting; Shanghai broadcaster's transformation from state institution to enterprise; and the role of local broadcaster in national media policy-making process.

Chapter 11, the conclusion chapter, summarizes the research findings, contests the arguments and theories and spells out the theoretical implications of the findings upon the study of Chinese television in general and its regulatory policy in particular.

Theoretical framework

In this section, the issues and arguments concerning the transformation of the broadcasting media in a one-party state, and the relationship between global influence and local media in media and international communication studies are examined. In this way it aimed to establish a coherent theoretical approach to analyzing the research subject. The section is organized according to different topics of discussions. First, it examined the theoretical accounts developed to explain the nature of social and media transformation in the former communist Eastern European countries, and suggested that these models could also be used as an analytical framework to discuss the nature of the television policy changes in the one-party state China.

Second, amid the decentralized television network structure and the emergence of localism in China, the study reviewed three major arguments concerning the nature of the central-local tensions observed in the country's economic transformation, and points out the significance and essence of studying this central-local nexus for understanding the complex reasons for the development of Chinese television policy, regulation and structure.

Beyond these local and national levels of study, the nature of the media modernization or development process in developing countries, was identified as important subject for discussion in this research. This section examines the arguments of three different core paradigms developed in the Euro-American context and China, and proposes to contest them with evidences drawn from China's television restructuring process.

The final part of the section introduces the normative requirement of the fulfilment of the political and socio-cultural functions of the media serving as a starting point for the discussion of the implications of Chinese TV broadcasting's transformation.

The nature of transformation in the communist state

In his study of Eastern European former communist media systems, Colin Sparks points out that, as the media is a social organization, its structure in any country is constrained and influenced by three factors: the external pressures from the economic and political structure of an increasingly globalized world economy; internal pressures from different dissident groups; and divisions within the ruling group or bureaucracy[1] itself as to the future of the society they ruled (Sparks, 1998: 65).

4 *Introduction*

Despite the variety of communist media systems, they share some common features and practices. First, in order to protect their leading positions in society, the ruling class seeks to make mass media directly subordinate to their political goals via the direct supervision of the political elite over the daily workings of the mass media, and economic force plays a marginal and secondary role. The media are the mechanism through which the ideology of the ruling class is disseminated and generalized for the maintenance of the regime. Second, the media does not work with a commercial dynamic but is primarily determined by the political interests of the Party. It is run according to the logic of a centrally planned economy to ensure that there is not enough economic benefit that could make the mass media risk their political duties. Third, the socio-cultural function of the mass media is to organize and mobilize the masses to support the construction of socialism and defend their country via news reports. Its content production is not motivated by considerations of audience maximization. Most interestingly, Sparks observes that, "the basic aim of the media was didactic enlightenment rather than diversion." In other words, the media is to "improve the morale and the consciousness" of the masses by providing information, education and entertainment rather than pure entertainment content and infotainment. There is no real competition; the mass media's volume, channels and nature are subjected to planning. The mass media is financed by State subsidy rather than advertisements (Sparks, 1998: 44).

After the fall of communist political rule and the collapse of the command economy in the region in 1989, many theoretical accounts were developed to explain the nature of the transformation of these societies and their mass media. Amongst these Sparks identified two groups of approaches: the first group looks at the discontinuous nature of the changes while the second stresses the continuity of systems before and after 1989. In conjunction with these, he establishes four models to analyze the nature and role of communist television broadcasting in transformation[2] – total transformation, social revolution, political revolution school and what revolution models (Sparks, 1998).

In the context of one-party state China, as Sparks observes, the order of economic and political transformations differed profoundly between the formerly communist Eastern European countries and communist party ruled China, especially in the mass media arena. In the former, the collapse of political rule decided economic changes while, in the latter, the economic changes preceded the end of communist political control. Despite this difference in sequential logic, Sparks argues that the underlying social logic is the same in both cases, the typical feature of transformation is about to transform "the collective ruling class of the communist epoch into the individualized rulers of a private capitalist economy" (1998: xv). In other words, it is about two things, one is the transformation of the socialist state economy into a private capitalist economy; the other is the transformation of the old communist political ruling class into the new capitalist economic elite, or in the Chinese critic He Qinglian's words, it is a process of "marketization of power" (2002: 26). For Sparks, the transformation of the Eastern European countries could exemplify typical features of China. In Sparks' later article (2008), he explicitly argues that there is no correlation between marketization and democratization: despite the rapid marketization in China, authoritarian control has not been relaxed but political control has increased. The transformation in China in general and in its media in particular is a political process: it is the transformation of the way in which the country is governed, but not a fundamental change of social order and elite composition in media or the state machine (Sparks, 2008: 10). Not only did the political institution survive the changes, but there was also continuity amongst the elite personnel in the media sector and throughout the society, which demonstrated a shift from political to economic power. In other words, it is the shift from state control of productive property to private control of productive property and the direct introduction of market relations into the internal working of the economy. In his 1998 book, Sparks called this the capitalization process. That is, the process of transforming the older socialist economy and the ruling elite group into a free enterprise and market capitalist system and true capitalist class respectively, in which the state sets the rules for privatization while the formal political processes that are required in democratic government are absent. While the shift to individualized private capital could create a pluralization of power in the society, it does means that this will automatically translate into a democratic impulse (Sparks, 2008).

In this book, the explanatory power of Sparks' model will be assessed, with empirical evidence drawn from the development of Chinese broadcasting policy and the local Shanghai Media Group's transformation since the 1990s.

The central-local relationship in China

In contemporary China, the Party and State's power are integrated and the realization of the State's authority is tied to the Party's Central Committee (CC). The state government is the representative of the CCP's authority and the executive body of the principles and policies of the CCP. The CCP's CC, or its correspondent party committees in local areas, appoint people to the key government and social organization positions (*People's Daily Online*, 2002; Saich, 2001; Xian, 2002; Yang, 2002). The Party, state and social organization are thus fused under the control of the Central Committee – a tiny elite group. In terms of formal institutions, China has constitutionally remained a unitary state whereby all local governments are subordinate to the Central Government. China's Constitution defines the principle of the territorial distribution of power, and, according to this, all provincial governments are local state administrative organs and they must accept the unified leadership by the State Council, implement administrative measures, regulations and decisions by the State Council, and be responsible and report to the State Council (Constitution of the PRC, 1982). On the other hand, the State Council can define the specific functions and powers of the local governments, nullify their decisions, impose martial law in the localities and direct its auditing agencies to conduct financial inspections. Similarly,

6 *Introduction*

while the Provincial People's Congresses have the right to make local laws, the Standing Committee of the National People's Congress can annul this legislation if it conflicts with national laws. There is also no clear demarcation regarding the scope and content of the respective legislative authority between the Central and Provincial Congresses (Zheng, 2006).

China's economic reform since 1978 has changed the country fundamentally. Economically, it resulted in the transformation of a centrally planned economy to a quasi-market economic system (Ma and Chao, 2002; Saich 2001; Xian, 2002). Socially, it helped to alter the Party's hegemony over society and public discourse, partially by the Party's will and partially by default (Ma, 2000; Tang *et al.*, 2000).

Alongside economic and social changes, the existence of the "inhabited center" to Chinese political authority is observed. Because of the decentralization of fiscal and administrative power that devolved part of these powers from the Central Government to the local governments, and the shift of emphasis from political movement to economic development between the 1980s and 1990s, there was a more complicated center-peripheral relationship. In this relationship, the objectives and interests of the CCP and the State are not always synonymous and the Party can no longer count on State organs for automatic policy support.

It is argued that, after 20 years of economic reform, there is no specialized state institution existing in China that serves to provide public goods exclusively. However, various local governments and organizations have used or abused power to pursue their own ends rather than performing the functions of State institutions (Li, 2002). In order to pursue their own interests, local governments may adopt policies that are in conflict with or against Party policy. They warn that this tendency to regionalism or localism and the growing power of the provinces could cause a crisis in Central Government's authority (Li, 2002; Tang *et al.*, 2000).

On the other hand, Zheng Yongnian (2006) points out that although China does not have a federalist system of government – it has neither constitutional division of power between the different levels of government nor the separation of power within the branches of government – the political system existing in China is, de facto, federalism.[3] The central-local relationships are becoming increasingly like federalism, not at a formal institutional level but at an actual practice and behavioral level, so that power is divided between the central and local actors. In a behavioral sense, China's de facto federalism can be defined as follows:

> A relatively institutionalized pattern which involves an explicit or implicit bargain between the center and the provinces, one element in the bargain being that the provinces receive certain institutionalized or ad hoc benefits in return for guarantees by provincial officials that they will behave in certain ways on behalf of the center.
>
> (Zheng, 2006: 107)

China's central-local relationship is de facto federalism because:

1   It is a hierarchical political system in which central and local government has some activities on which it makes final decisions.
2   The increased institutionalization of inter-governmental decentralization means that it is becoming difficult, if not impossible, for the national government to unilaterally impose its discretion on the provinces and alter the distribution of authority between governments.
3   The provinces have primary responsibility over the economy and, to some extent, over politics within their jurisdictions.

Instead of seeing de facto federalism as a force weakening the central authority's power, and calling for recentralization and political innovations to reconstruct central-local relations in order to maintain national unity,[4] Zheng, amongst others, suggests institutionalizing de facto federalism. Moving from de facto to de jure federalism can promote political stability by reducing the tension between the central and local actors and protecting local autonomy from arbitrary interference by Central Government and thus sustain the country's rapid development.

Kenneth Lieberthal (1997) presents an alternative interpretation of the central-local relationship. He observes that the Chinese Party-State is politically highly centralized, and economically it is a dynamic official-entrepreneurship with massive state intervention. First, despite the tendency towards substantial decentralization, the nature of it differs fundamentally from a federal system. In China, what lower level officials can bargain for – for example, flexibility or preferential policies – is conditional, and not based on the Constitution. This has resulted in conflicts concerning resource and privileges being sorted out through a variety of negotiations within the bureaucracy itself. Although ample room has been given by the higher level of the political system to those on the lower level to achieve economic growth within their own localities, the former still retain powers to intervene massively in the operation of the latter. Besides this, the prerequisite of local economic pursuit is to sustain political and social stabilities. Lieberthal argues that until the 1990s, the Chinese political system was still centralized and extraordinarily disciplined.

In order to secure the support of local officials for moving away from the planned economy towards a quasi-market economy, the Party-State at the center has permitted local officials to participate in, and directly benefit from, the economic reform. These officials have actually become entrepreneurs and utilized political power to promote economic growth beneficial to their localities and themselves. Lieberthal sees this system as decentralized state capitalism with "official entrepreneurship" (1997: 18).

Lieberthal agrees that economic reform has brought unprecedented individual freedoms to the Chinese people. As long as the pursuit of freedom does not actively challenge the political power of the Party-State itself, the Party-State is willing to, in his words, "[leave] most people alone politically" (1997: 19).

8 *Introduction*

He predicates that economically a true free market economy is unlikely to be adopted in China in the short term. The Party-State has tried to learn from the Japanese and South Korean economic models where the state continues to play a major role in shaping economic development, with strong polices and substantial administrative intervention. However, a more fully market-driven system, characterized by an improved legal system, is developing at a slow pace in China.

In the case of the broadcasting television system in China, the four-tier mixed coverage decentralization policy led to the structural diversity of Chinese television within the Party-State system. This happened along with the redistribution of power from the center to the different local state organizations. With the rise of localism television was, thus, also localized and used to promote local interests (Wu, 2000) and this made the control and monitoring of local stations increasingly difficult.

Thus, the central-local tension has not only been observed in the country's economic and political arenas, but has also become increasingly apparent in the broadcasting sector. How does this central-local contest influence media policy and regulation in China? What kind of central-local relationships are found, the increasingly de facto federalism or centralized central-local? These are two questions that cannot be ignored in a study that aims to understand the complex reasons for the changes in China's broadcasting and media regulation and policy-making.

Chapters 7 and 10 of this book explore the impact of central-local tension upon broadcasting policy and policy-making.

The modernization debates

Scholars of Chinese studies have long debated the nature of China's modernization process, while in international communication research, the discussion of modernization in developing countries began with the emergence of the development paradigm. The central concern of the debate is the nature of the modernization or development process in developing countries.

The concern of this book is: what is the nature of the modernization or development process of the media industry in developing countries? This book approaches this question by examining the following three explanations with evidence drawn from China's broadcasting policy and the modernization process of the local Shanghai media.

Essential Westernization – the development paradigm

From the 1940s to the 1960s development theorists argued that the Western-style capitalist model was the essential path for the development of Third World countries (Lee, 1980; Melkote, 1991; Reeves, 1993; Thussu, 2000).

Daniel Lerner, in his influential book *The Passing of Traditional Society* (1958) claims that modernization was essentially Westernization, but for diplomatic convenience, people chosen the neutral term "modernization" rather than "Westernization." "For Middle Easterners more than ever want the modern

Introduction 9

package but reject the label 'made in the U.S.A'.... We speak, nowadays, of modernization" (Lerner, 1958: 45). He criticizes the ideology of national self-development as "extreme nationalism" and "passionate xenophobia":

> [What they] wanted are modern institutions but not modern ideologies, modern power but not modern purpose, modern wealth but not modern wisdom, modern commodities but not modern cant.
>
> (Lerner, 1958: 47)

He asserts that the Western model of development provides "the most developed model of societal attributes (power, wealth, skill, rationality)" and "exhibits certain components and sequences whose relevance is global" and is the most effective way for developing society to become modern (Lerner, 1958: 46 and 47). This development model is criticized for its linear evolution and Eurocentric nature. It assumes that the earlier stage of the history of developing countries parallels the same period of western European nations. It predicts that all nations will inevitably go along the same Western modernization path, i.e., nation-state formation, capitalist industrialization, rationalization of government and the political participation of the masses. It takes the Western democracy and liberal model for granted, imposing it as the political model for developing countries. Countries that failed to subscribe to this model were categorized as underdeveloped (Melkote, 1991).

By the mid-1970s, Everett Rogers proclaims that:

> it seemed safe to conclude that the dominant paradigm had "passed," at least as the main model for development in Latin America, Africa and Asia [...]. It would still be followed enthusiastically in some nations, but even then with certain important modifications.
>
> (1976: 131)

"Decentered" and "disorganized" globalization

Since the 1980s other theorists have attempted to redefine international relations from a structural perspective, to a paradigm emphasizing the decentered but complex connectivity of the world. They suggest a process of rapid intensification of interconnections and interdependence between societies, cultures, institutions, individuals and so on, in the world as globalization (Featherstone, 1990; Giddens, 1990; Tomlinson, 1997). As Anthony Giddens proclaimed in BBC Radio 4's 1999 Reith Lectures:

> globalization today is only partly Westernization. Globalization is becoming increasingly decentered not under the control of any group of nations, and still less of the large corporations. Its effects are felt as much in Western countries as elsewhere.
>
> (1999: 31)

10   *Introduction*

His argument is seen as changing the terms of reference of the global-local debate, because it shifts the center of the debate from the "modern versus traditional" model of modernization and the center-periphery model to the "decentered" and "disorganized" process of globalization and conceptualizes it as a process that transforms both developed and developing countries alike (Curran 2002: 171).

Giddens formulates the process of globalization as the consequence of modernity. It is the global expansion of four institutional dimensions of modernity from their origins in seventeenth century Europe: the capitalist economy; industrialism; surveillance, i.e., the nation-state system; and military order (Giddens, 1990). Despite this skepticism about the Westernization of globalization, Giddens' formulation of global modernity is criticized for playing down the unevenness of the globalization process, the Western-centric theories of modernity and the ignorance of the distinct forms of non-Western modernity (see Tomlinson, 1999). Although Giddens defends this by arguing for a dialectical formulation of power relations in which, instead of merely looking at the expropriating nature of global modernity, local agencies actively engage in this process and actively appropriate or resist global modernity. Critics challenge him by saying that first, the patterns of appropriation still follow some family line of social division; and second, that the resources of local resistance in the face of globalizing forces cannot be presumed to exist simply by theoretical faith, but need empirical evidence.

John Tomlinson also argues that despite the plural formulations of modernities, the central nature, i.e., the deep-structural transformation of modernity, has been observed in all other societies. Thus, he tends to see modernity not as a Western project but as inheriting some universally applicable elements (Tomlinson, 1999). Without denying the occurrence of the modernization process in the world, Tomlinson's argument avoids some fundamental questions. First, how and in what context did this modernity emerge in different societies? Second, what is the dynamic driving this deep-structural transformation? These are vital questions to achieve an understanding of the nature of modernization in developing countries and the global spread of modernity.

Modernization: Chinese conceptualization and interpretations

Looking back at China's history, various schools of modern Western thought have influenced the intellectual discourse on the pursuit of modernity, or the search for the modernization of China. Western influence dates back to the Self-strengthening Movement in the middle to late nineteenth century and the later May Fourth Movement which began in 1919. In both cases, modern science, European Enlightenment, reasoning and democracy were assumed to be the core values of modernity and were used by Chinese intellectuals to challenge the traditional Confucianism that had dominated Chinese society for 2,000 years (Lin, 1999).

Introduction 11

In the 1990s, influenced by postmodernism and post-colonialism, a more critical reflection on China and Chinese cultural tradition, the power relationship between the self and different others and the global hegemony of Western culture and intellectual discourse, made Chinese intellectuals rethink the issue of China's cultural reconstruction and the search for modernity. So, a more sophisticated perspective, including the double critique of "cultural essentialism" and "Western centralism" has gradually replaced the 1980s totalitarian adoption of an "advanced" Western conceptual framework (Lin, 1999).

Chinese intellectuals seriously questioned the universality and superiority of Western thoughts, produced with relative ignorance of non-Western culture and society. They criticize the Western version of modernity as reflecting a dualist notion of the West versus China, and modern versus traditional, and as suffering from a linear view of history. They argue that China's intellectuals have internalized this linear view of history over the past 150 years. However, they also reject the idea of the purity of Chinese culture and assert that there is no pure, authentic, pre-modern Chinese culture waiting to be revived, but rather that Chinese culture and the way of thinking have been irreversibly influenced by Western culture and ideas. For them, contemporary Chinese culture and intellectual discourse is cross-cultural and a hybrid.

By applying Paul Gilroy's concept of "double consciousness," Lin Min argues that the Chinese intellectuals' pursuit of a hybridized culture based on dialogue with, and critiques of, the West is not narrow-minded cultural nationalism, but transcends "the boundaries of ethnicity and nationalism to proclaim a considerably more generous 'double consciousness'" (Gilroy in Lin 1999: 199). It is within this context that some Chinese intellectuals have begun to advocate a Chinese version of modernity, which synthesizes national cultural identity and modern rationality.

In the 1990s, by drawing essential inspirations from different intellectual strands including liberalism, nationalism, conservatism and postmodernism, a hybrid Chinese theory of modernity was shaped and accepted by a number of intellectuals. The principles of this Chinese version of modernity include:

- the market economy, private property, the priority of economic development and the inevitability of integration in the global system;
- individual legal rights and autonomy, the acceptance of the particularity of "self";
- greater participation in the political process and the institutionalization of state governance;
- social justice and equality, the state has a role in providing social welfare, education, health care and infrastructure;
- formation of a new national identity based on interaction between Chinese cultural tradition and global civilization; a powerful and wealthy state with national dignity;
- social stability, law and order, a peaceful evolutionary transition and orderly development;

12 *Introduction*

- development of a critical awareness of the inner dilemmas and contractions inherent in Enlightenment modernity; a new global consciousness based on the understanding of the complex relationship between the West and the developing world within a historical context.

(Lin, 1999: 32–33)

However, there are logical inconsistencies and contradictions between the various objectives of this conceptualization and there is substantial disagreement about how these objectives should be integrated. It is therefore a fragile consensus. Meanwhile, the criticism of Western modernity may lead to the exclusion of some positive values, such as democracy and liberty, that are essential to China's modernization (Lin, 1999).

During the same period, Chinese neo-conservatism, which epitomizes the Chinese conceptualization of modernity, appeared in the Chinese intellectual discourses (Xie, 2001). The objective of neo-conservatism is a market economy and China's future democracy. It approves the discourse of the continuation of history, including China's contemporary history and the socialist tradition and that the idea of China's modernization must be based on respect of the existing order, i.e., the historical continuation of the CCP's leadership. (Xie, 2001: 106). The key slogans associated with the neo-conservatives are "China's unique national conditions" and the negative example of radical social change in the former Soviet Union, the economic success of the "Four Little Asian Dragons" in modernization and "an organic synthesis of tradition and modernity" (Zhongguo qingnianbao lilunbu in Lin, 1999: 25). Unrest in the former Soviet Union and the uniqueness of China, including its huge population, the low educational level of this population, the lack of a democratic consciousness and the underdeveloped economy, have been used to justify the pursuit of a non-Western modernization model and a gradual reform process.

Politically, it prescribes an evolutionary approach towards a smooth and peaceful social transformation from a backward to a modern society and supports a strong authoritarian political system like the government of Singapore (Qi in Lin, 1999; Yuan in Lin, 1999; Xie, 2001). It emphasizes the authority of state, and law and order at the expense of individual political rights and freedoms to achieve a peaceful transition to a civil society. Neo-conservatives believe that revolutionary reform will lead to chaos and instability in China (Xu in Lin, 1999). For many neo-conservatives, the ultimate goal is an open and democratic political system, but China needs to pass through several transitional stages to reach this goal (Wang Yuechuan, 1999; Yuan in Lin, 1999; Xie, 2001).

The other main ideological features of neo-conservatism include:

- opposing both liberalism and radical anti-traditionalism; advocacy of a revitalization of Chinese tradition and national self-strengthening based on a vision of inevitable conflicts between China and the Western powers (He in Lin, 1999);
- opposing cultural fundamentalism which rejects any change in national tradition (Xiao in Lin, 1999);

- adoption of Western rationalist philosophy that "advocate[s] proof, instrumental reason, order and gradualism [and is] opposed to romanticism and violence, irrationalism, disorder, anti-social and anti-cultural behavior" (Zhongguo qingnianbao lilunbu in Lin, 1999: 27);
- incorporation of John Dewey's pragmatism to pursue rationality at the expense of ideological purity. In other words, the cornerstone of its ideology is the highly pragmatic assumption of "what works" rather than "what is ultimately or transcendently justifiable in a grand, coherent theory" (Lin, 1999: 28).

Professor Xie Wujun at the Party School of the Central Committee of the CCP, considers that because of the similarities in the basic principles and reform objectives and strategies between neo-conservatism and the Chinese Communist Party, neo-conservatism compared to the other "idea," would be easier to incorporate in China's actual political operation (Xie, 2001: 107). Meanwhile, the non-radical, compromising and pragmatic approach of neo-conservatism is the key element for its strong appeal to many Chinese intellectuals and large numbers of people (Lin, 1999). Others criticize neo-conservatism as being authoritarianism characterized by economic liberalism and political anti-democracy and as bureaucratic capitalism resulting from the convergence of the market and power. It lacks of elements of liberalism and the socialist principles of equality and fairness. It is argued that neo-conservatism could become a serious obstacle to China's market economy and democratization reform (Wang Sirui, 1999; Wang Yuechuan, 1999).

Practically, the search for a Chinese model of modernization is being pursued continuously. As observed by Zhao Suisheng (2010) that instead of following the Washington-Consensus style modernization model characterized by a free market economy, the limited role of the state and liberal democracy, China's development path has demonstrated a unique model even though it is a transitional not a stable model. The China model, in Zhao's opinion, has three features. First, it is driven by a pragmatic and experimental approach, not by any ideologies or principles. Reform has been executed in a piecemeal and gradual manner, implemented in selective sectors or regions and in less controversial policy areas. Second, it is led by a strong state capable of maintaining an overall stable political and macroeconomic environment. Third, the Chinese Party-State has selectively learned from liberal Western models, including the role of market, globalization and entrepreneurship. It has rejected or modified other aspects of the liberal democracy, for instance, reducing the state's role, multi-party electoral democracy and the protection of civil and political rights. Meanwhile, it proposes or utilizes the instrumental aspects of democracy to maintain social order and harmony, such as the proposal of a consultative rule-of-law regime to improve the rule of the Chinese Communist Party within the single party system. Zhao (2010: 431) observed that amid this context, political reform in China has mainly been undertaken in four ways: institutionalization of the decision-making system in the Party and State Council to avoid the rule of man

14   *Introduction*

in the decision-making process; making government officials and cadre more accountable for their bad performance by installing institutions, such as legislative oversight committees, Party discipline committees, administration reconsideration procedures, administrative law, and judicial review; building a rule by law system; and reforming the Communist party through changing the Party. This non-ideological, pragmatic and experimental China modernization model has spurred "both social stability and economic growth while not compromising the Party's authority to rule." Nevertheless, Zhao criticizes the China model's pragmatic approach: guided neither by a set of values or principles, it has failed to deliver a moral appeal. Its appeal to other developing countries has been entirely based on the tangible economic and political benefits. Partly because of this issue, the China model is a transitional model of development, and logically it would progress to include legal reforms, democratization and constitutionalism after achieving high levels of economic growth (Zhao, 2010).

Opponents of the China model argue that China's modernization path is informed and constrained by the dominant modernization paradigm. Chinese officials and academics perceive such a paradigm as the only correct path to development, subsuming Chinese development experiences under those of the West within a hierarchical view of the world, contrasting "traditional" China to the "developed" countries (Barabantseva, 2012). China's development agenda has been characterized by the prioritization of science as the source of pragmatic knowledge and absolute truth. Since the late 1970s the official ideology of the Chinese Communist Party on China's development has evolved from revolution, class struggle and anti-imperialism to market reforms, science and technology, the rule of law, institutional reforms, gradual economic reform and the production of verifiable "scientific" knowledge. The "Scientific Development" concept, proposed by the former Chinese President Hu Jingtao, was particularly criticized for its dichotomist position between China and Western countries and between traditional China and developed countries. As Guo Baogang observes, "some traditional beliefs will fade as modernization renders them obsolete [...]. Confucian norms and concerns with preservation of harmony and obligation and general orientation toward family and community are likely to survive" (Guo, 2010: 87–88). Despite Scientific Development's emphasis on people-centered approaches to development and social harmony, in contrast to stressing economic growth, it is argued that the official development strategies still prioritize the material base for spiritual advancement and GDP growth as the principal economic target (Barabantseva, 2012: 66). Elena Barabantseva (2012: 66) points out that:

> Since the start of the reforms, the Chinese government has systematically consulted and emulated Western ideas and socio-economic models to solidify its political priorities of social cohesion, harmony and unity. The stress on modern, managerial skills and innovation central to the debates on "scientific development" is also evident in the changes taking place in [...] state propaganda techniques.

Despite the different perceptions of China's modernization path by Zhao Suisheng and Elena Barabantseva, they both, along with others (Du, 2013), agree that China has (selectively) adopted some typical elements of Western modernization in its development path, including: market forces, globalization and entrepreneurship, science and technology, the rule of law, and institutional reforms. China's leader Deng Xiaoping (1994) once justified China's learning from the Western modernization by saying that:

> learning some good things from capitalist countries, including methods of operations and management, is not equivalent to implementing capitalism. This is socialism exploiting such methods to develop the productive forces. By treating it as a method, it will have no impact on socialism as a whole and is not a return to capitalism.

Since China's productive forces were still far behind those of the developed countries, it was necessary for China to learn from global modernization, and exploiting the existing achievement of capitalism was the most direct path (Du, 2013: 50).

To some extent, the intellectual and practical pursuit of Chinese modernization also resembles and accommodates the Party-State's objective of strengthening its governing capacity through institution building, rule by law and administrative reform. One of the keys to the CCP's continuous monopoly of political power, even though the Party has decayed and ideologically-based social solidarity has eroded, is the Party-State's institution building, which is aimed at enabling China's leadership to cope with the rapid pace of change (Chen, 2006: 12). Institution building in China includes the processes of institutionalization and new institution building (Chen, 2006: 11). Institutionalization is a means to stabilization and of perpetuating a particular order (Cox and Sinclair, 1996). The objective of institutionalization can be ideas, concepts, or spaces, such as social and political spaces (Sweet, Sandholtz and Fligstein, 2001). Samuel Huntington (1973: 5) has explained stability from a modernist perspective, and argued that rapid socio-economic change "undermines traditional sources of political authority and political institutions," thus incurring political instability. Therefore, institutions must change. Political stability is a function of "institutionalization" and "participation" (Huntington, 1968). When political organizations are institutionalized to accommodate political participation, political stability will be achieved. Thus, China's leadership has consistently stressed the need for institutionalization or legalization as a way to build political stability, which is a critical precondition for continuous economic growth (Lee, 2010).[5] To enable the institutionalization of the organization of the Party-State's power and policy decision-making, the Party-State must: act within the framework of the Constitution and laws; establish administration according to law to standardize the administrative power; and build a legal system providing guidance for all aspects of social life (Chen, 2006: 29). In fact, rule by law (*yifa zhiguo*, 依法治国) is an important aspect of China's political institutionalization (Lee, 2010). The Party incorporated the statement: "No organization or

16 *Introduction*

individual is privileged to be beyond the Constitution or other laws" into the Chinese Constitution of 1982. The National People's Congress (NPC) in 2000 promulgated the *Legislation Law* to promote more institutionalization of the legislation-making process and make the *Legislation Law* a central piece of the Chinese legal system. The supervisory role of the national and local people's congresses has been enhanced, and legalization has also increased. The NPC, its standing committees and the State Council introduced more legal and administrative regulations. Administration according to law (*yifa xingzheng*, 依法行政) aiming to institutionalize state department's and agency's decision-making is consistently stressed by Chinese leaders such as Hu Jintao and Xi Jinping: "The State respects and preserves human rights" was also enshrined in the Chinese Constitution in 2004's Amendment to the Constitution of the People's Republic of China (NPC, 2004).

Meanwhile, in the Chinese literature on law, legal modernization is a dominant theme. Many describe China's legal reforms since the nineteenth century as part of China's modernization process (see Du, 2010: 17); the rule of law, both as a concept and as a practice, is often seen as a hallmark of Western legal traditions (Peerenboom, 2002; Tamanaha, 2004). The discourses on the rule of law, with its increasing emphasis on human rights and the oversight of the People's Congress, is seen as an example of the rise of Western ideas and the decline of traditional Chinese concepts.

Chapter 4 of this book examines how the Party-State appeals to the rule of law in order to institutionalize and legitimize its broadcasting media regulation.

Discussion – the normative requirements of the broadcasting media

The basic normative elements of broadcasting's political and socio-cultural functions include political independence from government and private monopoly; accountability to society and audiences; freedom; "universal service"; information quality; "diversity and representatives of content in political, social and cultural terms"; choice; social cohesion and solidarity, and a "non-profit goal" (van Cuilenburg and McQuail, 1998: 66).

Although Denis McQuail highlights that these normative requirements only "summarise[s] the most commonly accepted idea" in the Western democratic capitalist countries,[6] it is by no means presented as a consensus in any society on what the media ought to do, or not do, in the name of public interest. The application of any principle should be established in a relevant political situation before it has much weight and consequence. He also agrees that these sets of commonly accepted ideas of the political, socio-cultural functions of the media provide a starting point for researchers' criticism and discussion (McQuail, 2000: 179 and 166).

Despite the differentiation of the political systems of China and Western European countries, if we accept the universal relevance of some basic functions of the media, e.g., to serve audiences as citizens rather than merely as consumers, then it is reasonable for a researcher to ask questions about how these political and socio-cultural functions have served in connection with the economic pursuits of broadcasting organizations in China. Chapter 8 of this book explores the emergence of the concept of public service (*gonggong fuwu*, 公共服务) and public service media in China, identifies its features and evaluates its functions in relation to the normative debates of broadcasting media.

Summary

Through examining and drawing together theories and arguments developed in both global and national contexts, this chapter has established a multi-level theoretical framework to analyze the transformation of China's broadcasting regulatory policy and system.

The level of analysis is divided into three parts. At the national level, based on Sparks' argument (1998 and 2008) on the common social logic of social and media transformations in communist states, it will test the compatibility of the theoretical models established to explain the nature of social and media transformations in China. China's broadcasting restructuring from 1996 to 2015 is used as the case study, in light of the country's economic and political changes. Second, at the national-local level, three approaches are developed to explain the nature of the central-local relationship in China. They will be contested against the central-local tensions observed in the development of Chinese national broadcasting policy and policy-making. The first approach argues that rising regionalism or localism and the growing power of the provinces will cause a crisis in Central Government's authority. The second suggests that China is politically de facto federalism. The third supports the still highly centralized political system due to the lack of unconditional and constitutionalized conflict negotiating measures and the subordination of the economic elite to the political power.

At the global-local level, it will test different global and Chinese theoretical models of the interpretations and conceptualization of the nature of the modernization process in developing countries and in China, with case studies of China's national broadcasting policy and the transformation of local Shanghai broadcasters.

This chapter concludes by pointing out that, despite different political systems in China and Western Europe, some basically normative requirements for the media, such as an emphasis on the citizenship of audiences, rather than merely seeing them as consumers, have universal relevance in both types of society. These normative requirements for the fulfillment of the political and socio-cultural functions of the media, as McQuail (2000) suggests, will serve as the starting point for a normative discussion of China's broadcasting regulatory policy and structural transformation.

In the next chapter, China's culture, political structure, intra central-local relation and economic and political reform from 1997 to 2015 is reviewed. It sets up the general background for the whole research and presents the significant issues and tendencies observed in the field.

18 *Introduction*

Notes

1 Here Sparks refers to the bureaucracy as a tiny minority within the ruling party, they occupy the highest positions in the Party (Sparks, 1998).
2 Sparks refers to the social aspects of television as issues related to finance, organization and regulation, while the political aspects involve areas of executive personnel and government broadcasting policies (Sparks, 1998).
3 Federalism is often regarded as a form of government that differs from unitary forms of government in terms of the distribution of power between central and sub-national governments, the separation of powers within the government, and the division of legislative powers between national and regional representatives. (Zheng, 2006: 102).
4 Wang Shaoguang and Hu Angang are two Chinese scholars who have been known for their calls for recentralization and political innovations (Zheng, 1999: chapter 2).
5 According to Lee (2010: 561), the ideal path of political development would be a sequence of "institutionalization" leading to "participation" leading to "contestation."
6 Sparks (1998) considers that the characteristic of the capitalist democracies or in the classic terminology, "bourgeois democracies" is the clear distinction between political life and economic life. The former is concerned with common interest and public good, and political power is gained through success in free and competitive elections. Economic life is concerned with the pursuit of private interest and only takes the common interest into consideration when it affects its private pursuits. Economic power is embodied in the ownership of productive property.

2 The political system and economic transition

Introduction

To understand China's media, it is essential to know about the nation's culture, political-economic structure and the relationship between the center and regions' intra central-local relations, as each of them are closely linked with, and influence, the overall direction of media development.

This chapter reviews China's culture and political power structures, and the country's economic reform after 1978, and their effect on society and politics. The chapter emphasizes the prominence of regional disparities and the increasing tension between the central authority and local governments as a result of the country's economic reform and fiscal decentralization. Despite the continuity of an economic liberalization and political authoritarian governing mode, the chapter reveals how the Party-State gradually adjusted its economic and social policy in responding to its international interdependence and domestic social discontent.

An overview of China

China is the world's most populous country with approximately 1.4 billion people as of 1 July 2014, which is equivalent to 19.24 percent of the total world population; 54 percent of China's population is urban[1] (Wordometers, 2015). There are 56 ethnic groups within China, the Han people amounting to more than 91 percent of the country's total population (*Xinhua News Agency*, 2011). Besides the official language, Mandarin (*Putonghua*, Beijing dialect), Chinese people speak a large variety of local dialects, for instance, *Yue* (Cantonese), *Wu* (Shanghaiese), *Minbei* (Fuzhou) and *Minnan* (Hokkien-Taiwanese).

Administratively, China has 31 provinces (*sheng,*省), five autonomous regions (*zizhiqu,* 自治区), four municipalities (*zhixiashi,*直辖市)[2] – Beijing, Shanghai, Tianjin and Chongqing – and two special administrative regions (SARs) – Hong Kong and Macau. The highest legislative body is the National People's Congress (NPC). Its members are selected by local people's congresses and are responsible for electing the state President and Vice President. The highest administrative institution is the State Council, led by a Premier, nominated by the state President

20 Political system and economic transition

and confirmed by the NPC (Yang, 2002). The People's Republic of China (PRC) was established by the Chinese Communist Party (CCP), which took over the Republic of China (ROC) government in 1949. Since then, the socialist CCP regime that instituted state ownership has been China's only ruling party.[3]

For 30 years (1949–1979) China experienced enormous chaos and destruction, including socialist reconstruction (the "Greater Development") from 1957 to 1966 and the ten-year "Cultural Revolution" (1966–1976). As a result, not only was it politically isolated from the Western world, but it was also economically backward compared to industrialized countries in East Asia. The transition of political power within the CCP led to economic reform and the opening up of China to the rest of the world in 1978. Its economic model began to move from a Soviet-style, centrally planned economy to a more market-oriented system. The leader of the CCP, Deng Xiaoping, defined the country's market economic system as "socialism with Chinese characteristics":

> to domesticate freewheeling capitalism through state control and to drive home the Deng logic that socialism will use capitalism for increasing the power of the Chinese nation-state ("it doesn't matter whether the cat is black or white as long as it catches mice").
>
> (Ong, 1997: 175)

Since 1978, economic development has become the government's focus and China has become one of the fastest growing economies in the world.

The Chinese Communist Party's organization

The CCP has been the sole ruling power in China since 1949. Its dominant status is a complex historical and cultural tradition, but the absence of equivalent political powers in China to challenge the CCP fundamentally guarantees its monopoly of political power (Yang, 2002).

The Party's organizational pattern is highly hierarchical and pyramidical. At the top are the Party's core bodies in Beijing. These include the Party Central Committee (CC), CC's Politburo, the Standing Committee of the Politburo, CC's Secretariat and other executive units. By the end of 2011, the Party had over 82 million members (Liang and Yao, 2013), and at the bottom were 3.8 million primary party organizations based in work-units, public organizations, towns and villages in rural areas (Institute of Party Building, 2011). Between these layers there are networks of Party organizations in most local and Central Government institutions (see Figure 2.1). In addition, the Party's cells also exist in bureaus, economic and cultural organizations, and public societies (Saich, 2001; Xian, 2002).

The Party statutes define democratic centralism as the basic principle of its organization. It demands individual subordination to the organization, the minority subordinated to the majority, the lower level subordinated to the higher level, and organization and party members subordinated to the national party

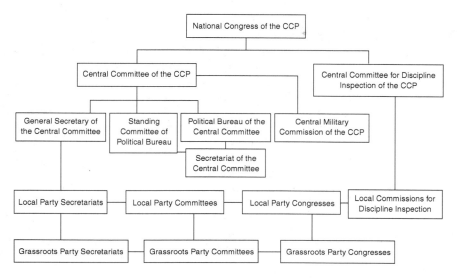

Figure 2.1 Organization of the Chinese Communist Party (source: 1. Organization Chart of the Eighteenth CCP Central Leadership. Available at: http://english.cpc.people.com.cn/206972/207121/index.html [accessed 22 February 2016]; 2. China's Political System: The Party in Power. Available at: www.china.org.cn/english/Political/26151.htm [accessed 22 February 2016]).

congress and the Central Committee (Saich, 2001; Yang, 2002). It emphasizes collective leadership in order to avoid power concentration in the hands of one person and the protection of different Party members' voices (Yang, 2002). Nevertheless, both Party norms and internal discipline do not follow this rule. Instead, a continual tendency towards personal rule over institutionalized rule is observed (Saich, 2001: 81).

In China, personal power and personal relationships (*guanxi*) with powerful political figures are decisive not only in politics but also in society. This feature has led to the formation of networks and factions in line with individual, institutional or regional interests within the Party. It is said that over-dependence on individual power relationships has essentially destabilized the Party's leadership (Saich, 2001).

The Party-State power structure

A "horizontal seven and vertical five" (*hengqi zongwu*, 横七纵五) two-dimensional structure constitutes the Chinese state's political power system. At the core of power is the CCP's Central Committee. Horizontally, functionally related bureaucracies are grouped together under the same "system" (*xitong*, 系统)[4] where the CCP system exerts a leadership relationship over the other six systems (Xian, 2002).

22 Political system and economic transition

Vertically, a five-level administrative network is organized from top to bottom according to hierarchy. At the top are the central authorities in Beijing, i.e., Central Government and the CCP's CC. At the second level are the local authorities of the 22 provinces, five autonomous regions, four municipalities and two SARs. Below this, there are three more local networks (see Figure 2.2). The entire network is highly centralized. The higher-level units control its lower levels. The central authorities, therefore, are the source of all powers and they make all important political, social-economic and cultural decisions. Lower administrations are expected to act as the implementing agents of their policies (Xian, 2002).

Meanwhile, the Party's committees at each level enjoy authority, coordinating the activities of the units within their geographic jurisdiction. Thus, there is a dual rule that a lower level unit has to report to higher corresponding departments and to the Party's committee at the same level (Saich, 2001).

The State Council, or Central Government, is the executive body of the National People's Congress and the highest organ of state administration. In theory, it has absolute power over its affiliated institutions and governments at the non-central levels (*People's Daily Online*, 2004). However, realization of the State Council's authority has been closely tied to the operation of the CCP's CC because of the Party's penetration into state affairs. In China, the distinction between state and Party power is blurred and, for most of the time, integrated. Chinese people call this an "authorization and representation relationship with Chinese Characteristics." In other words, the state government has been

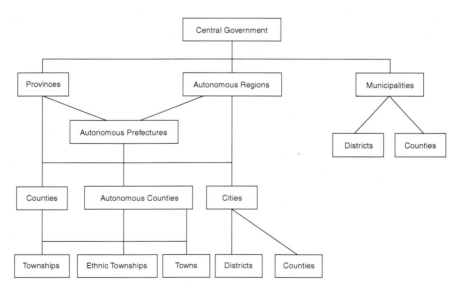

Figure 2.2 Structure of the Chinese Government (source: China's Political System: The Local Administrative System. Available at: www.china.org.cn/english/Political/28842.htm [accessed 22 February 2016]).

Political system and economic transition 23

identified as the representative of the CCP's authority (Xian, 2002: 7) and is "responsible for carrying out the principles and policies of the Communist Party of China" (*People's Daily Online*, 2004).

Although the NPC has been the highest organ of state power since 1954, there is no doubt that the CCP is the real political power. Not only is its dominance found in every aspect of social life, from control of the Legislature and Executive to the dictation of the nation's moral and ethical values, but also the Party's leadership has been written into the State Constitution (Yang, 2002).

In the Western academic tradition, this Party-State power structure is categorized as a totalitarian regime that is characterized (Sparks, 1998), by the fusion of different sections of the ruling class, or different elites, so that other elite groups are directly subordinated to the political elite. It is also characterized by the ruling class's control and organization of the subordinate class or general population's life as much as possible. Independent political and economic organizations are destroyed because they may become the source of independent thought, values and oppositions that do not fit into the status quo and they are replaced by institutions that, more or less directly, represent the Party-State.

At the same time, the economic reform started in 1978 has fundamentally transformed China (Zhang, 2000). It led to the relaxation of the Party's control over the country's economy, society and public discourse, partially by the Party's will and partially by default. First, the increase of social space has resulted in the appearance of heterodox ideas and beliefs. Second, due to the serious corruption of its officials and the close links between business and the Party, the CCP has found it increasingly difficult to hold on to its legitimacy.

Moreover, over the last decade, with the shift of emphasis to economic development, the objectives and interests of the state and Party are not always synonymous. This has been reflected in a more complicated center-local relationship where the Party can no longer depend on state organs for automatic policy support. In order to pursue their own interests local government may adopt policies that conflict with the Party's policy, or even run counter to it (Saich, 2001). However, this central-local tension has drawn great academic interest. Some scholars suggest that the growing power of the provinces could undermine the Central Government's ruling capacity and even lead to the country's disintegration (see Li, 2002: 1).

Regional disparities

Contrary to popular belief that it is a homogeneous entity, China is "a conglomeration of markets" segmented by factors such as the uneven level of economic development, industrial priority and local culture (Cui and Liu, 2000: 58). Substantial differences exist between the country's regions. Since the launch of economic reform in 1978, regional inequality has increased. Less developed areas, such as the northwestern and southwestern parts of China, have gained very little (Kanbur and Zhang, 1999 in Diao *et al.*, 2003: 333; Lu, 2002).

24 Political system and economic transition

If measured by Gross Domestic Product (GDP), the eastern, northern and southern coastal areas are China's most-developed regions. In 2009, China's 12 coastal provinces (out of a total of 31 provinces) accounted for 65 percent of the country's GDP, and had a collective per capita GDP 50 percent higher than the national average (Chovanec, 2011), while the coastal share of population has remained steady in the low 40 percent range (Orenstein, 2014). Residents of these three coastal areas have more purchasing power and have been the primary interest to economists and Western industrialists when they look at China's market (Huang and Green, 2000).

Moreover, due to geographical and socio-economic conditions, the degree of openness varies significantly across regions (Diao, Fan and Zhang, 2003). Coastal provinces and municipalities, like Guandong, Fujian, Shanghai and Zhejiang, were the first to open up to international investment. They have also gained the most from the Central Government's economic policy (Yeung and Hu in Giu and Liu, 2001).

However, this regional disparity is not only manifested in the country's economy, but is also reflected in the diversity of regional cultural patterns, embodied in the variations of dialect, lifestyle, tradition and custom (Cui and Liu, 2000). For instance, dialect is one of the most important symbols of regional uniqueness. While Cantonese is the dominant spoken language in Guangdong province, people in Shanghai still prefer to speak in Shanghaiese.

The central–local relationship

China's vast territorial size and regional diversity have been both assets and liabilities for the country. On the one hand, they are regarded as huge geographic and cultural resources. On the other, Central Government has to take vast disparities in regions into consideration and to respond to local requests when formulating national policies.

In China, before economic reform, there was a highly centrally planned economy. Central Government had built up a centralized system of resource allocation and material circulation. Resources were allocated to the government ministries on an annual basis (Zhao and Kwan in Li, 2000). Local governments had less influence on Central Government's policy-making (Li, 2000).

Despite this, processes taking place at the center largely shape local conditions. This does not mean that the role of the local is ignored. It has been suggested that, regardless of the subordinate position of local to Central Government:

> the legitimacy and stability of the center, to a large extent, are built upon the many resource and services that it provides to and the support that it obtains from the various localities or regions. Reciprocity is a necessity.
>
> (Tang, Li and Kwok, 2000: 8)

This was especially the case after fiscal reform introduced by the state in 1982, which gave local government and enterprises much greater powers to organize and decide on local economic activities.

By the mid-1980s, provincial governments had built up alliances with local enterprises so that they could take measures to prioritize local interests, even at the expense of national interests. "Policies on the top, and counter measures down below" (*shangyou zhengce, xiayou duice*, 上有政策,下有对策) is said to be "a vivid description" of central-local relations (Li, 2000: 171). Even the content and implementation methods of the state's policies, planned to be applied equally to the entire country, could be significantly modified to accommodate local needs. "Local cadres, an important component in the state-society relation, have played a significant role in [police] implementation," and Central Government's policies were filtered through a complicated network of administrative hierarchy (Tang in Tang, Li and Kwok, 2000: 8). Sometimes, local authorities may have a more decisive role. For instance, many measures that were either legally uncertain or in conflict with state policies were first launched by local authorities, then accepted and applied to the entire country by Central Government (See Li, 2000).

Alongside the growing autonomy of the localities was the emergence of regional protectionism or the formation of a "dukedom economy" (Jiang in Li, 2000, 171; Shen and Dai in Li, 2000, 171). In order to utilize local resources and foster local industries within their respective administrative regions, each province has set up a variety of protectionist measures, such as restrictions on using capital goods produced by other provinces. This regional protectionism is criticized for having damaged the formation of a unified national market and reduced economic efficiency and economies of scale (Li, 2000). It is warned that this tendency to "regionalism" or "localism" could cause a crisis in Central Government's authority (see Li, 2000).

Li Qiang (2002) moves beyond this regionalism concern and points out that the authority crisis in China is much deeper. The real crisis is the decline of public authority in general. In other words, after 20 years of economic reform, there is no specialized state institution to serve the provision of public goods exclusively to China. Instead, various local governments and organizations use or abuse power to pursue their own benefits. The CCP, from another point of view, "has abandoned its desire for ideological correctness" and "[...] has become a network of bureaucratic elites whose primary purpose is to retain power to protect their own interests" (Zhao in Saich, 2001: 105).

China's economic transition since 1978

China's economic reform started in 1978 and has gone through four stages. In December 1978, the CCP announced that economic modernization would be the focus of the country's future work. This began the transition of China's highly centrally planned economy to a more market-oriented one. The period from 1978 to 1984 is usually identified as the initial stage of the marketization of the country's economy (Ma and Chao, 2002; Xian, 2002). During this stage, no comprehensive economic blueprint was in place, Central Government's policy resulted from a response to policy innovation or experiment at the local level. This kind

26 *Political system and economic transition*

of policy-making process is referred to as "Crossing the River by Feeling the Stones." Meanwhile, the central authority also began to redistribute its power to local authorities and to open up the country to the outside world to attract foreign investment, technology and consumer goods through the formation of special economic zones (Saich, 2001).

Another stage took place from 1984 to 1992. The announcement of the *Decisions on the Reform of Economic Institution* by the CCP's CC in 1984 marked the beginning of the marketization process touching the cornerstone of transformation, i.e., establishing a market system. The Party's Thirteenth National Congress in 1987 declared China's economy to be a "planned commodity economy" (*youjihuade shangpin jingji*, 有计划的商品经济). In December 1992, the Party again announced that the objective of China's economic reform was to establish a "socialist market economic system" (Jiang and Qian in Xian, 2002: 99). Thus, market mechanisms were officially recognized as the most important forces in resource allocation.

The announcement of the Third Plenary of the Fourteenth National Party Congress' crucial decision on the *Establishment of Social Market Economy* in November 1993 indicated that China's economic reform had moved to another stage. Between 1992 and 1997, the government removed a wide range of restrictions on foreign investment, village, township and private enterprises. A large number of village and township enterprises were privatized. The stock market was further expanded to accelerate capital accumulation. In 1994, the government also started to address the organizational and managerial problems of state-owned enterprises (SOEs) and their property rights (Saich, 2001).

China's economy, state-owned enterprises reform and politics from 1997 to 2003

The 1997 Fifteenth National Congress of the CCP made a clear commitment to a mixed economy with the dominance of the non-state-owned sector. The State economy was declared to no longer occupy the dominant position in China's economic system.

The Party CC's *Decision on Important Issues of the Reform and Development of SOEs* in 1999, further encouraged SOEs to pull out of certain sectors of the national economy, opening them to a variety of non-state capital, including private and collective capital (Ma and Chao, 2002). It allowed the conversion of small and medium-size SOEs into shareholding companies. In other words, these enterprises could be transformed into non-state, shareholding or private firms through bankruptcies, expansion of shareholding system, joint ventures, or by selling state-owned shares to other interested parties (Ma and Chao, 2002; Tylecote and Cai, 2004; Xian, 2002).

Despite this, privatization is still a very sensitive issue in China, as under the name of defining property rights and withdrawing state capital, many kinds of privatization of small state-owned enterprises have been carried out (Wu, 2002: 8). A number of local officials have seen this as a great opportunity to get rich at

Political system and economic transition   27

the expense of the State's assets. Official figures indicate that the State lost US$6 billion a year from 1986 to 2001 because of "spontaneous privatization" which diverted State assets into individual pockets (Hughes in Saich, 2001: 234).

For large SOEs, the decision was not to privatize them but to transform them into "modern enterprise corporations," mainly as limited liability companies (LLCs) or joint-stock limited liability companies (JSLLC),[5] the state retaining at least a majority stake. As of 2000, 70 percent of these SOEs had completed this transformation and some are also listed on the stock exchange (Tylecote and Cai, 2004).

Tylecote and Cai (2004) consider that from the mid-1990s, China's SOE reform began to borrow the Western experience of corporate governance[6] to address problems such as the lower performance of the SOE's management and lower productivity. The difference between corporate governance in the West and in China is that the former is "based on relationships among various participants (shareholders, the board of directors, managers, employees, customers, supplies, creditors and communities), which determine the direction and performance of a corporation" while the latter "mainly focus on its formal legal and structural aspects" (Tylecote and Cai, 2004: 65). They quote a Chinese definition of corporate governance to illustrate this difference:

> Corporate governance is a company's system of organisation and system of management. A scientific and regularised system of organisation consists of shareholder's meetings, board of directors, executive arms staffed by senior managers and board of supervisor.
>
> (Qin and Li cited in Tylecote and Cai, 2004: 65)

The state also requested these large SOEs to form Japanese *keiretsu* or South Korean *chaebols*[7] similar to conglomerates through market mechanisms. The privately owned *chaebol* is seen as a successful example, combining capitalism and state intervention. In China's context, the difference is that the Chinese state apparently prefers to use state-owned enterprises as its vehicle for such policies (Tylecote and Cai, 2004). The industry's enormous surplus productivity and the impending entry into the World Trade Organization (WTO) are said to be underlying reasons. The Chinese government wants to build up a certain number of world-class, major media conglomerates to compete with their counter players in the global media economy. "The dream of being in the Fortune 500 list seems irresistible!" (Saich, 2001: 235). It is also believed that the government's desire for continuous substantial intervention in the country's economic development (Lieberthal, 1997) and the Party's imperative in maintaining social stability and avoiding further social unrest caused by the privatization of SOEs, are other crucial reasons.

The Party's report[8] delivered at the Sixteenth Party National Congress on 8 November 2002 reiterates the importance of diverse forms of ownership to stimulate economic growth in the country. It commits to additional liberalization of market areas for domestic non-governmental capital access and to introduce

28 *Political system and economic transition*

measures to encourage fair competition (Jiang, 2002). The then Premier, Zhu Rongji said in the *People's Daily*, 6 March 2002:

> to further resolve the structural conflicts and institutional barriers that constrain economic development is a fundamental measure for accelerating the continuing growth of the economy, to raise economic quality and competitive power. [We] must forcefully push the economic-structure adjustment and persistently deepen economic system reform.[9]

Accompanying this, the massive industry restructuring and the downsizing of SOEs to improve efficiency and profitability, is the widening gap of income inequality and the increasing unemployment rate. The State Statistic Bureau's figures state that, from 1997 to 2001, the state sector cut more than 34 million jobs or 30.8 percent of its total employment (Yang, 2002). This has resulted in a substantial increase in social tension. Meanwhile, serious corruption and the rent-seeking behaviors of local government officials, combined with widespread materialism nurtured by economic reform, have sapped the CCP's political legitimacy as the defender of China's social revolution. On the one hand the government has tried to ease this tension through policies such as opening up to international markets, increasing government spending on welfare and launching new reforms. On the other hand, it has employed a hardline stance towards different voices and tightened control over the media (Saich, 2001; Yang, 2003). It has been described as a "combination of economic liberalization and political authoritarianism" (Yang, 2003: 1).

Although the Party announced that they would strengthen the quality of the rule of law and improve the "scientific and democratic basis" of the decision-making mechanism (Jiang, 2002), to promote ideological and ethical correctness is declared continuously as being the prerequisite of the cultural industries' development. "[P]ress, publishing, radio, film and television must give correct guidance to the public" (Jiang, 2002). So maintenance of social stability and unity continued to be of overriding importance to CCP's rule in China and all kinds of reforms and improvements needed to both underpin and uphold CCP's leadership (Yang, 2003).

This "stability overwhelms everything else" policy was criticized as a way of justifying the CCP's political authority: e.g., its control of public opinion, repression of outspoken media and independent critical intellectuals and journalists and suppression of social organizations' activities. It was anticipated that after China's accession to the WTO, its political and economic ruling groups would converge with foreign entrepreneurs to achieve the continuous accumulation of the domestic monopoly capital and support the political status quo by combining the powers of local and international capital. This might result in a situation where political, economic interest groups and foreign capitalists come together to exercise their rule in China (He, 2002). Consequently, it is not surprising that in 2000, the then CCP leader, Jiang Zemin, proposed a new idea of the "Three Represents" upheld at the 2002 Sixteenth Party National Congress as the new guidance of the Party's work: "the CCP must always represent developmental trends in China's advanced productive forces, the orientation of China's advanced culture and the fundamental interests of the overwhelming majority of the Chinese people" (*BBC News*, 2002a). This putting forward of the "Three Represents" was regarded as the CCP's official invitation to Chinese entrepreneurs: in other words, to invite the capitalists to become party members. More significantly, this was widely interpreted by both domestic and foreign commentators as an indicator of the Party's re-positioning from a working class party to a party representing both the working class and middle classes *(BBC News*, 2002b). Later in 2004, at the Tenth National People's Congress, private ownership and "Three Represents" were enshrined into the Chinese state's Constitution (*BBC News*, 2004).

The internationalization of China's economy

Since its economic reform started in 1978 China has depended, and is increasingly expected to depend, on foreign investment to encourage its economic growth. Its WTO accession also made the country more interdependent with global economic markets. It was believed that mounting independence would broaden the issues that the Chinese state considered to be in its national interest and subsequently would increase China's need for political power. On the other hand, the country's economic capability and growing influence in the world economy and markets has also become a powerful political tool that the country "is only now learning how to use" (Perritt and Clarke, 1998: 395).

The Chinese economist, Zhang Yongjin, regards the internationalization of China's economy and the responses of the Chinese state to the globalization of world economy as "nothing other than China's adaptation to harmonizing economic policies and practices with those widely practiced in the global economy, and to learning to adopt general norms of 'correct' economic behavior" (Zhang YJ, 2003: 22). In the late 1980s and early 1990s, the question of how to "make the Chinese economic system compatible with the world economy"(与世界经济接轨, *yu shijie jingji jiegui*) in principle and in practice was at the center of intellectual and policy discussion in China.

Economists in the West, predominantly in the USA, embraced the economic reform led by political figures like Zhu Rongji and Li Ruihuan, who were associated with "Western ideology, democracy, capitalism, and freedom of speech" (Hart, 1997: 81). These economists admitted that China has made substantial progress towards a market-driven economy and emerged as a major economic and trade power (Hart, 1997; Holliday, 1997). On the other hand, they criticized the governance practiced in China as being by good people but not by good laws. They urged that, in order to cater for China's role in the international marketplace, the country's commercial and legal policy should be governed by the rule of law[10] to ensure that the rules of the commercial and legal environment are transparent and consistently applied (Perkins, 1997; Perritt and Clarke, 1998). Some of them were concerned that Chinese nationalists, embedded in their

30 *Political system and economic transition*

anti-American and Western sentiment, and the Beijing hard-liners, would resist and reject policies made by the pro-Western-style reformers who were in power. They promised the Western policy makers that a cordial relationship with the Chinese government would remain to avoid the revival of the conservative political power in China, in both political security and commercial interests. They tended to agree that economic forces from both inside and outside China were driving domestic social transformation and suggested that the increased participation of China in international forums could reduce the country's threat to the world (Hart, 1997). From their points of view, allowing China to join international organizations such as the WTO would put pressure on the government to be more open to foreign trade and investment, to adhere to international standards, resulting in greater market access with more transparent rules for foreign exports, and to further support internal market liberalization (Hart, 1997; Holliday, 1997).

China's economy and politics under the Hu-Wen administration

Since the new Hu-Wen administration came to power in the fall of 2002, it has been noted that the government adopted more egalitarian and populist policies in terms of China's economic development (Brandt and Rawski, 2008), and it began to reverse some of Deng Xiaoping's reforms in 2005 (Derek, 2009).

Equality and social harmony have been the consistent themes of the Hu-Wen administration. In the report given by Hu Jintao (2007) at the Seventeenth National Congress of the Communist Party of China on 15 October 2007, he stressed that the government must make the resolution of issues concerning agriculture, rural areas and farmers a top priority in the work of the whole Party as this will have an overall impact on building a moderately prosperous society in all respects. In addition to the "Three Rural Issues" (agriculture, rural areas and farmers; 三农; *san nong*), the leadership also promised to strive for equal access to basic public services and guide a rational flow of factors of production between regions in order to narrow the gap in development among regions. These commitments were once regarded as mere rhetorical differentiations from the Jiang administration, however, as the Hu-Wen administration found its feet, actual decisions on resource allocation turned out to have increasingly followed this egalitarian and populist bent. Polices were made to be more favorable to rural-to-urban migrants, farmers, and human development. Increased policy-making attention and budgetary resources have been allocated to pensions, health care, and education (Brandt and Rawski, 2008). On the other hand, according to some analysts, the conservative Hu-Wen administration began to reverse some of Deng Xiaoping's reforms through halting privatization and making the privileged state sectors become large "national champions" so that they could compete with large foreign corporations. During 2006 alone the number of individuals who owned businesses fell by 15 percent to 26 million, and in the following two years, the truly private companies contributed less than

Political system and economic transition   31

10 percent of national tax revenues during the first nine months of 2007 and that figure dropped in the first part of 2008 (Derek, 2009). Therefore, although the annual percentage growth rate of GDP of China during 2006 and 2010 remained positive at around 9 percent to 14 percent (The World Bank, 2015), the growth was interpreted as "explicitly led by the state, fueled by investment by state-owned entities, and accompanied by powerful regulatory steps meant to ensure the state's dominance of the economy – all measures that contrast sharply with prior reforms" (Derek, 2009).

Tightened political control and administrative reform

The government tightened their political control across the whole country. Like their predecessors, Hu and Wen were aware that political reforms were needed, however they still took the view that they should be implemented gradually to keep things in check. Besides, dissenting voices were muted to ease policy implementation. Controls were tightened on the Internet and media; new limits were imposed on speech and other civil liberties (Hays, 2008).

The Hu-Wen leadership tightened control over societal elements that could destabilize society, such as public intellectuals, universities and non-governmental organizations (NGOs). With the rapid development of the Internet in China, regulation of the Internet was also tightened for the same reason. The Ministry of Industry and Information Technology (MIIT) issued a directive requiring the content filtering and control software called "Green Dam" (Chinese: 绿坝; Pinyin: *lvba*) to be installed on all personal computers. This was originally intended to take effect in July 2009, and although the project failed because of public outrage, it clearly showed the government's determination to control the public voice in the Internet era (Chao, 2009).

Tightening political control across the whole society on the one hand, the Hu-Wen government also held an ambiguous attitude towards the political and administrative reform. China's reform and opening up, together with the impact of globalization, make Hu and Wen, and fourth generations of China's leadership, more concerned about the international environment. Although Hu and Wen still insist on communist ideology officially, they are inevitably influenced by the widespread democratic waves around the world (Feng and He, 2012).

Moreover, in order to counter pressures from radical leftist and rightist camps, Hu re-emphasized further economic and social reforms and the reform of the Chinese Communist Party (CCP) leadership in 2008. In a conference held at the Great Hall of the People in Beijing on 18 December 2008, Hu Jintao cautioned the Party and the Chinese people to remain realistic by pointing out the problems faced by China, including a low level of industrial innovation, a weak agricultural foundation, less-developed rural areas and deficiencies with Party and government work. "Given the current world situation, especially the escalation and spread of the international financial crisis, China must continue to firmly focus on economic development," Hu said. Hu also listed ten "musts" that the Party had been doing and should continue to do: one of them was to emphasize reform

32 *Political system and economic transition*

and social stability equally; another "must" was to continuously push forward political reform so as to provide a system and legal guarantee for China's reform and modernization drive (International Department, 2008).

Within the Party, Hu has made a concerted effort to enhance its governing capacity. In January 2005, the CCP launched a new campaign to "maintain the advanced nature of the Party" (保持党的先进性, *baochi dangde xianjinxing*), as part of its broader effort to strengthen the "governing capacity" of the Party – the primary theme of the Fourth Plenary Session of the Sixteenth Central Committee in September 2004 (Joseph, 2005). Party members, from the rank and file to senior personnel, have had to participate in educational activities to improve their quality of work and better serve the people. At the same time, a great effort to re-examine or redefine Marxism was called for and became popular with Party members across the whole country, making it more consistent with the rising capitalist realities in Chinese society.

Besides the reform inside the Party, to keep its advanced nature, for the Central Government, administration reforms could also be found throughout Hu's governance. A government report in 2006 (Wen, 2006), stated that five new ministries, namely the Ministry of Industry and Information Technology, the Ministry of Environmental Protection, the Ministry of Human Resources and Social Security, the Ministry of Housing and Urban–Rural Construction, and the Ministry of Transport, were established, through merging relevant ministries and commissions. Also, the importance of accountability was also stressed.

An accountability system (问责制, *wenze zhi*) was put forward by the Hu-Wen government to make government officials and cadres more responsive to society demands and more accountable for poor performance. The account-ability system was primarily triggered by the Severe Acute Respiratory Syn-drome (SARS) crisis in 2003 after a whistleblower exposed lies about the outbreak of SARS. The Chinese people started to demand their basic rights to information, and the WTO and foreign media also clamored for accountability (Zhao, 2014). To counter both domestic and international pressure, in April 2004, the CCP Central Committee issued a *Provisional Regulation on the Party and Government Resignation*, stipulating that officials who make serious mis-takes and produce serious consequences should take responsibility for their behaviors and resign from their posts. This regulation provided a legal base for accountability, and introduced resignation for responsibility (引咎辞职, *yinjiu cizhi*) into the accountability system for the first time (Zhao, 2011). Earlier that year, China's national legislature passed the *Law on Supervision*, giving local legislatures the power to check local governments. Later that year, through the implementation of the *Law on Civil Servants*, as well as several Party regulations in 2006, the accountability system finally settled down. Then in 2007, the Party showed its tendency to allow more political participation, transparency and accountability, thus the accountability system was further developed (Lai, Wang and Tok, 2006). The political report given by Hu to the Party Congress guaran-teed the people's right to know about important information, to participate in government decision-making, to be heard, and to oversee the work of the

Political system and economic transition 33

government. This meant that the CCP attempted to combine its accountability reform with citizens' rights, indicating that the government's top echelon was gradually adopting a more liberal political mindset.

Scientific development and the idea of a harmonious society

Hu Jintao's administration philosophy is epitomized by the proposal of the "Scientific Development" idea and the harmonious society concept.

Since 2005 the Hu-Wen administration had emphasized balanced and sustainable development, which was the so-called "Scientific Development" idea. This was a notion fostered by the Hu Jintao leadership that development policy-making must not only pursue high-speed economic growth but also take due account of social, environmental, and other consequences of growth (Miller, 2008). Hu's vision of a "harmonious society," and its attendant slogan of "people-oriented" (以人为本, *yi ren wei ben*), was to look beyond raw numbers of national GDP growth, and pursue more balanced and equally distributed economic development intended to promote a "Socialist Harmonious Society" by the year 2020 (John, Zhao and Taffer, 2012). By the end of 2005, "Harmonious Society" had become a catchphrase in China's political discourse. At the Fifth Plenum in October 2005, "building a Harmonious Society" was formally endorsed as the guiding principle of China's Eleventh Five-Year Plan. In the report given by Hu Jintao at the Seventeenth National Congress of the CCP in October 2007, he pointed out that, for "Scientific Development," development is the essence, putting people first is the core, comprehensive, balanced and sustainable development is the basic requirement, and overall consideration is the fundamental approach. He also mentioned that, to deepen "Scientific Development," the government should follow and insist on the path of "one central task and two basic points:" one central task refers to economic development, and two basic points refer to the reform and opening up and the "Four Cardinal Principles" (*Xinhua News Agency*, 2007). In 2007, Hu Jintao further consolidated his power by bringing his trusted officials into the Political Bureau and having his "Scientific Development" concept incorporated into the Party constitution's preamble (Miller, 2008).

As a proposal for equitable, balanced and sustainable development (Zheng, Wang and Lye, 2005), the "Harmonious Society" idea was born in a context when the Chinese government had to manage the unintended consequences of more than two decades of uneven reform and development: relative poverty, income disparity, regional development gaps, rising social discontent, deteriorating work safety, government incompetence and corruption and environmental degradation, among others. Based on such a societal context, ensuring equitable and well-rounded development was the foremost task of the Hu-Wen leadership. With the guidance of the "Harmonious Society" concept, Hu Jintao and Wen Jiabao put more energy into the interests of ordinary people and disadvantaged groups, such as peasants and migrant workers.

At the Sixth Plenum of the Central Committee in October 2006, the Party formally adopted "Harmonious Society" as its supreme goal in governance. The

34 *Political system and economic transition*

proposal of "Harmonious Society" stresses the "comprehensive building of a moderately well-off society" to improve the wellbeing of ordinary people; "comprehensively implementing Scientific Development" to achieve balance and sustainability; "building a new socialist rural society" to improve farmers' income and living standards; and to better conserve resources and protect the environment (Lai, Wang and Tok, 2006). The Sixth Plenum of the Central Committee in October 2006 was also the first time in 25 years that a plenary session devoted itself specifically to the study of social issues. This move signaled the Chinese policymakers' shift from no-holds-barred growth to a more sustainable model of development that would boost social and economic equality, and would enable underprivileged and low-income groups to have more access to education and employment, primary health care and social security (Bell, 2007). In the following year, at the Seventeenth National Congress of the CCP in October 2007, Hu Jintao again mentioned: "To thoroughly apply the Scientific Outlook on Development, we must work energetically to build a harmonious socialist society." Social harmony was regarded as an essential attribute of socialism with Chinese characteristics. A series of livelihood policies were published in line with the "Harmonious Society" idea, the policies have included efforts at every level of society, such as the rural problem, education, health, social insurance, land and personal property, with the aim of sustaining social equity.

The Xi Jinping and Li Keqiang administration

In 2012 Xi Jinping came to the helm of the Party, and, unlike his predecessor, Xi took all key Party titles immediately. Xi Jinping was a political leader with a distinctive style. He and his premier Li Keqiang, were considered to be running quite a different government compared to their predecessors Hu Jintao and Wen Jiabao. They were commonly seen as a tougher leadership with stricter policies on certain areas, such as Central Government's role, anti-corruption and sustainable development.

China's economy under the Xi-Li administration

Xi Jinping took office as the Chinese Communist Party's General Secretary and Military Commander-in-Chief in November 2012. The *Decision on Several Major Questions About Deepening Reform* ("the Decision" hereafter) passed at the Third Plenum of the CCP's Eighteenth Congress in 2013 (CCP, 2013), together with the summary communiqué issued right after the Third Plenum (*Xinhua News Agency*, 2013a), and the explanatory note on the Decision given by Xi (2013a) all indicated the top leadership's ambitious agenda to reconstruct the roles of the government and the market. This indication was also supported by an authoritative interview with Yang Weimin, the Vice Office Director of the Party's Leading Group for Financial and Economic Affairs, the highest body for coordination and discussion on issues related to the economy in China (Yang 2013 in Xu, 2013). The crucial parts of the Xi–Li administration's economic reform included: (1) China was still at a stage where pursuing economic development was the primary task; (2) the core principle of the current economic reform was that market forces should play a "decisive" role in resources allocation while the previously the market had a "basic" role in allocating resources; (3) consequently, the government should transfer from its powerful role in allocating resources to a role that provides macroeconomic regulation, market supervision, public service provision, social management and environmental protection (Kroeber, 2013).

However, in 2015 it remains to be seen whether the Xi-Li administration would eventually deliver on these policy goals, as critics still see tight control towards the economy, and some even hold the opinion that the Chinese government under Xi Jinping is more obsessed with control than its predecessors. Such control is not only employed in politics but also in the economy, for example, in the 2015 Shanghai stock exchange crisis, the government poured state funds in to keep stock prices artificially high (*Guardian*, 2015). Besides, in terms of SOEs, the Decision and the communiqué both made clear that state ownership must still play a "leading role" in the economy, although SOEs might face more competition and tighter regulation compared with the Hu-Wen era (Kroeber, 2013).

Faced with the doubt on the leadership's commitment to the economic reform that promised to let the market play a "decisive" role, while the stock market rescue and other actions revealed the government's intervention to the contrary, Xi's response was "that means we need to make good use of both the invisible hand and the visible hand" (Hutzler, 2015). After Xi's four-day visit to Britain in October 2015, he said in written answers to questions put by Reuters that the leadership did have concerns about the Chinese economy and they were also worried about the sluggish world economy. The solution, he said, was to open up the Chinese economy to more foreign investment and to encourage the country's firms to invest overseas (Phillips and Goodley, 2015). Again, whether Xi's prescription will cure China's mounting social and economic ills remains to be seen.

The Chinese Dream

Since Xi Jinping took office as the Party's General Secretary and Military Commander-in-Chief in November 2012, he has promoted the concept of "the Chinese Dream", a term that first appeared in Xi's high-profile visit to the National Museum of China next to Tiananmen Square on 29 November, two weeks after his appointment (*The Economist*, 2013a). Since then, from the National People's Congress annual meeting to his international trips, Xi (2013b) has stressed the Chinese Dream as a main theme in most of his public speeches. In addition, the CCP's propaganda machine has used its various resources to promote the narrative. Obviously the Chinese Dream has become the signature ideology for Xi's term, thus understanding the Chinese Dreams is critical to understanding Xi Jinping's administration and China's future policy orientation (Wang, 2014).

36 *Political system and economic transition*

Xi summarized his political idea, the Chinese Dream, as "national rejuvenation, improvement of people's livelihoods, prosperity, construction of a better society and a strengthened military" (Osnos, 2013). More specifically, the grand goal of the great rejuvenation of the Chinese nation was to achieve "two 100s," referring to China becoming a well-off society by 2021 (the one-hundredth anniversary of the Chinese Communist Party) and China becoming a socialist developed country by 2049 (the one-hundredth anniversary of the founding of the PRC) (Chen, 2014).

Critics have discussed interpretations of this term, the Chinese Dream, and its relationship with the American Dream. The majority of the conclusions show that the American Dream underlines individuals and families bettering their situations through their own efforts, while the core of Chinese Dream is a vision of national rejuvenation (Wasserstrom, 2015). Although Xi has sometimes referred to individual and family betterment as part of the Chinese Dream, he has always presented the state as a natural ally and an essential promoter of this process. For example, the alleviation of poverty is usually attributed to the CCP's great emphasis on rural problems instead of the poor's own efforts in pulling themselves out of poverty. Xi also urged the Chinese young people to "work assiduously to fulfill the dreams and contribute to the revitalization of the nation" (*Xinhua News Agency*, 2013b), which again indicates that national rejuvenation outweighs individual improvement in the official discourse of the Chinese Dream. Thus, critics pointed out the potential danger of the Chinese Dream in aggravating nationalism and in handing more power to the Party than to the people (*The Economist*, 2013b).

In order to achieve his political idea of the Chinese Dream, a series of policies have been considered by Xi Jinping. In late 2015 the most recent one was the publication of the *Thirteenth Five-Year Plan of China* (十三五计划; *Shisanwu Jihua*). In line with the Third Plenum, during which the Party set 2020 as the deadline for achieving "decisive results," the date continues a time frame set in 2006 at the Sixth Plenary Session of the Sixteenth Central Committee of the Communist Party of China that set the goal to achieve "a harmonious socialist society" and the conclusion of the *Thirteenth Five-Year Plan* (2016–2020) (Brunswick Group, 2013).

Deepen the reform with no political priority

Since taking charge the leadership team has recognized that the growth model that has driven the country over the last 35 years is not sustainable and is causing significant challenges. Therefore, reform, which was a crucial agenda for each Chinese government leadership team, is still the top priority for the government to sustain the economic momentum and unleash the power of the market. Nonetheless, reviewing the past three years, 2013–2015, such reform, though it deepened over the years, was not politically motivated, that is, political liberalization was not a priority, but rather it was economically motivated.

In Premier Li Keqiang's first Government Work Report delivered at the Second Session of the Twelfth National People's Congress on 5 March 2014, he explicitly stated that reform was the top priority for the government. The Twelfth National People's Congress (NPC) together with Chinese People's Political Consultative Congress (CPPCC) in 2014, commonly known as *Lianghui* (two sessions; 两会), showed that the government attempted to deepen economic liberalization and enhance the role of market forces by reducing bureaucratic red tape and gradually shifting away from a planned economy towards a one based on market forces (Li, 2014). Though the market is expected to play an increasingly decisive role in the allocation of resources and pricing, the reform was essentially not political motivated as the Party remained as the overriding decision maker. Instead, a review of the three years since Xi and Li took charge clearly shows their tendency to strengthen the power of the Central Government, and their increased emphasis on media regulation, in order to control the news flows and quell the spread of rumors (Ash, 2014).

During Xi Jinping's first year at the helm, he made ongoing efforts to strengthen control over political power (Buckley, 2013). In addition to the establishment of the new State Security Committee (SSC) at the Third Plenum of the Eighteenth Chinese Communist Party's Central Committee, the Eighteenth CCPCC also established several so-called "Central Leading Small Groups" (中央领导小组; *zhongyang lingdao xiaozu*) to further centralize power. A report published by the Beijing News, a state-owned newspaper, stated that there were 22 central leading small groups by 2015, covering six different categories altogether: organization and personnel; propaganda, culture and education; politics and law; finance and economics; foreign affairs; and party building. Some of the leading groups have had a history of 60 years, while five of them were newly established after the Eighteenth CCPCC. Xi Jinping is the leader of four groups, including the Central Leading Group for Comprehensive Deepening of Reform, the Central Leading Group for Internet Security and Information, the Leading Group for National Defense and Military Reform of the Central Military Commission, and the Leading Group for Financial and Economic Affairs (Wang, 2015).

Moreover, certain measures to improve the administration have been introduced, with the intention of changing the role of the government. The Xi and Li office believes the role of the government in the development of society and the economy must adapt to match the development position of the country. They intended to reduce bureaucratic red tape and improve coordination between the center and the provinces with the support of fiscal and taxation reform. At the same time, they streamlined government departments. For instance, the new SAPPRFT (State Administration of Press, Publication, Radio, Film and Television) was established in 2013, merging the former GAPP (General Administration of Press and Publication) and SARFT (State Administration of Radio, Film and Television). The intention was to improve the administration by rationalizing the overlapping jurisdictions of the various authorities involved in the regulation and supervision of certain areas of China's media and publication industry (Hogan Lovells, 2013).

38 *Political system and economic transition*

Summary

Hardly a homogeneous entity, China has a huge population, a complex local governance structure and substantial regional disparities both in terms of economies and cultural patterns.

The CCP has monopolized the country's political power since 1949. The CCP installed a totalitarian party-state rule and a centrally planned and state-owned economic model before the launch of economic reform in 1978. Economic reform has fundamentally transformed the country. First, the decentralization of the fiscal system, introduced in 1982, has led to the growing autonomy of local government and enterprises and they have sought to prioritize their own interests at the expense of national interests. State policies are filtered and may even be significantly modified to cater to local needs. Regional protectionism has emerged in order to best utilize local resources and foster local industries. Could this regionalism possibly cause a crisis in the Central Government's authority?

Second, the trajectory of China's economic development over the last four decades has demonstrated a transformation from the centrally planned and state-owned economy to a quasi-market and mixed ownership economic model. In recent years, the tendency towards the prominence of the non-state-owned economy has become particularly evident in the country with the wave of privatization of small and medium-size SOEs since the late 1990s. This private economy is further protected by the CCP's acceptance of party members being capitalists and the legislation of private property in the state's Constitution in the early 2000s.

Accompanying the process of economic transition and privatization is the serious corruption of local government officials, widespread materialism, the substantial intensification of social tension and the weakening of the CCP's political legitimacy. The Party has adopted a hardline stance towards different voices and the media, while also shifting its GDP-dominated economic policy to one seeking balanced and sustainable development. The CCP has appealed to ideas of equality and national rejuvenation to gel support for the Party and government. The Party's present domestic policy is conceived as economic liberalization and political authoritarianism.

Internationally, it is anticipated that the country will become more interdependent on global markets. Subsequently, this will increase the state's imperative for political influence on the global stage to protect its broader national interests.

So, has this economic transformation made an impact on China's social organization, and, more precisely, on China's media? If so, in what ways? In the following chapters, the historical progress of China's television sector from the 1980s to 2015 shows the changing relationship between the Chinese media and the economic-political structures of the country.

Notes

1 Three regions – Hong Kong, Macao and Taiwan – are excluded from all figures.
2 The municipalities are directly under Central Government administration, and have similar status to the provinces.
3 From here on the term "China" refers to the People's Republic China or Mainland China (that is, Mainland China, excluding Hong Kong, Macau and Taiwan).
4 These include the CCP, the National People's Congress, the State Government, the People's Liberation Army, the People's Courts, the People's Procuratorates and the Chinese People's Political Consultative Conference (CPPCC).
5 In 1993, the National People's Congress passed the Company Law to help SOEs to build modern enterprise systems. Four organizational forms are allowed for transformation: limited liability companies (LLC), joint-stock limited liability companies (JSLLC), employee shareholding cooperatives, and private enterprises. The Company Law defines the organizational structure of LLC and JSLLC as comprising of shareholders, a Board of Directors and a Supervisory Board. The Board of Directors is set up at a meeting of the shareholders. The Supervisory Board includes representatives of shareholders and an appropriate proportion of employee representatives (Tylecote and Cai, 2004).
6 The theory of corporate governance has been mainly associated with the principal-agent approach. The owner(s) of an asset or enterprise is defined as the principal(s), and the top manager(s) as the agent(s). The main purpose of corporate governance is defined as being "to secure as far as possible that managers act in shareholders' interests, assumed to be the maximization of their wealth through some kind of long-run profit maximization" (Tylecote and Cai, 2004: 60). In China's case, the owners or principals of SOEs are the Chinese people or the State, the government is the first-order agent, and top management is the second-order agent.
7 South Korea's has been seen a successful example of combining capitalism and state intervention through the privately owned *chaebol*. Their experience has been of great interest in the Chinese context (See Tylecote and Cai, 2004).
8 Considered to be an outline of the blueprint for the country's political, economic and social development in the twenty-first century.
9 Published in the People's Daily, 6 March 2002. Citied in an internal document published by the Management and Science Research Institute of China in Beijing (2003: 282).
10 Henry H Perritt, Jr. and Randolph R Clarke state that, in most practical international relations discussions, the rule of law means procedural transparency and decisional rationality (1998: 398).

3 Broadcasting authority in China

History of broadcasting authority

The State Administration of Press, Publication, Radio, Film and Television of The People's Republic of China (SAPPRFT) is the current administrative department in charge of regulating China's press and broadcasting media. The PRC's broadcasting authority began in December 1940 with the establishment of the Chinese Communist Party's radio station – Yanan Xinhua Radio Station (XNCR). The XNCR was set up during the Japanese military invasion of China in the Second World War, and used by the CCP as a war time propaganda machine to "disseminate news of anti-Japanese war by Chinese armies and people, and to educate and encourage Chinese people in the occupied area" (Xu, 2003a: 2). Before 1949, the CCP's Xinhua News Agency's (XNA) audio broadcasting team ran the XNCR. The XNA was started in November 1931 as the Red China News Agency and changed to its current name in 1937. The XNA was the first media organization set up by the CCP and was responsible for running and managing the Party's newspaper, press agency and radio stations. It was also important in mobilizing public opinion for the CCP's "national revolution struggle" during the anti-Japanese war and the civil war against the nationalist party (Xinhau Net, 2006). After the end of the Second World War, XNCR was continuously used as propaganda machine by the CCP.

In 1948, the XNA was reformed, and a Radio Administration Department was set up to prepare for the establishment of a national radio administration organization. One year later, in June 1949, amid the victory of the CCP in the civil war and with the increasing need for broadcast media, the CCP announced that the radio broadcasting department of XNA was to be expanded to become the Central Radio Administrative Office (CRAO, 中央广播事业管理处), managing national broadcasters owned by the CCP. In terms of organizational structure, the office was under the leadership of the CCP's Department of Central Propaganda. The CRAO and the Propaganda Department were both responsible for the supervision of the CCP's broadcast media. After the establishment of the PRC, in October 1949, the CCP controlled the media through multifunctional roles: propaganda, industrial development and sector administration. The CRAO was renamed the Radio Department (RD, 广播事业局) in October 1949. The duties of the RD included leading the nation's radio broadcasters; directly leading the Central People's Radio Station (CPRS); expanding broadcasting nationwide; and fostering and training broadcasting officials (SARFT, 2007a). It was under the supervision of the Central People's Government's Executive Council (政务院) (renamed the State Council in 1954). From 1952, the RD was under the supervision of the Executive Council's Cultural and Education Committee (文化教育委员会), and its propaganda functions were under the supervision of the CCP's Ministry of Central Propaganda (MCP). From 1954, the RD became a constitutional department of the State Council, which supervised its technical and administrative functions, while its propaganda function was still under the control of the MCP. Local governments at provincial and city level were requested to establish local radio departments, which were responsible for constructing rural broadcasting networks, and for administering local radio stations. The provincial broadcasting departments usually worked together with the provincial radio stations, sometimes under the same person's leadership (局台合一, *Ju Tai Heyi*). Local broadcasting departments were under the leadership of the RD (Xu, 2003a: 11–12). Local radio stations were direct organizations of the local people's committee, and under the leadership of the local committee and the local RD.

During the Cultural Revolution (1966–1976), martial law (军事管制) was imposed from 1967 to 1972, the RD was renamed the Central Broadcasting Department (CRD) and was under the direct control of the CCP's Central Committee until 1976. After the massively destructive Cultural Revolution ended in 1976, the State Council regained its supervisory power over the CRD while the MCP resumed its leadership over the CRD's propaganda functions (SARFT, 2007b). The CRD was upgraded to become the Ministry of Radio and Television (MRFT) following the 1982 CCP Twelfth National Congress in which the CCP leader, Deng Xiaoping, announced the construction of socialism with Chinese characteristics in China and initiated the open door economic reform policy, and the institutional reform of the State Council. Local radio departments were also upgraded to broadcasting bureaus.

The Chinese broadcasting institution was reshaped at the 1983 Eleventh National Broadcasting Working Meeting. The central theme of the meeting was to re-establish the propaganda function among the Chinese broadcasters' reforming goals. The meeting not only set up the "four-tier broadcasters and mix coverage" policy goal (Yu, Jiang and Guo, 2003), more importantly, Wu Lengxi, then head of the national broadcaster regulator, MRFT, announced at the meeting (Xian, 1983) that broadcasters serve the public by providing them with: (1) all kinds of information (news and government policy being the highest priority); (2) education, cultural and scientific knowledge; (3) arts, entertainment and other services. He also said that propaganda is the core function of the broadcasters. In conjunction with this, the Party's Central Committee issued the significant 1983 No. 37 document *Circular on the Outline of the Report on Broadcasting Work* (CCP [1983] No. 37), which underpins the guiding principle of broadcasting development (Yu, Jiang and Guo, 2003). The document explicitly affirms the

42 *Broadcasting authority in China*

new leadership structure of the Chinese broadcasting sector. Chinese broadcasters were under the leadership of both the government's broadcasting department and the Party committee at the same administrative level. The Party is responsible for broadcasters' propaganda and the government department is responsible for the organization's development. The national regulatory MRFT supervise all broadcasters in the country. This core principle of the administrative structure had not been reshaped since the 1980s, despite the commercialization and institutional reform of the Chinese broadcasting sector over three decades. Similarly, local broadcasting authorities are subject to the dual supervision of the broadcasting authority at the higher administrative level and the Party committee at the same administrative level.

This document was regarded as highly significant in China's broadcasting history for its long-lasting impact on the role of the broadcasting media. Xu Guang Chun,[1] said that "it is the first time in China's broadcasting history that the Central Committee issued such a long formal circular in responding to the broadcasting department's working report."

> The Central Committee's circular not only confirms the fundamental nature and objective of broadcasters, [...] but also emphasizes the features and functions of broadcasters, requiring party committees at all levels to strengthen and improve their leadership of broadcasters, and the Party and government department will learn of how to "use" the broadcasting media.
>
> (2003: 219)

The No. 37 document clearly defined the nature and function of broadcasting bureaus, which were designed as both propaganda and administrative departments with propaganda being their core function. The document restructured the broadcasting sector to a "four-tier, mixed coverage" hierarchy, and requested "that different propaganda departments shall follow the Party's guiding principle, [...] utilizing different measures to serve socialist modernization" (Xu, 2003a: 217).

> Party and government departments need to learn to use (or manipulate) broadcasting media for propaganda and to mobilize the masses [...] via broadcasting media, [the departments] can directly disseminate Party and government's policy, performance and missions to the masses and swiftly mobilize them.
>
> (Xu, 2003a: 218)

It also stated that the local Party Committee and the MRFT would guide the local broadcasting bureau's propaganda work; and that the organizational administration would be under the dual leadership of local government (the main leader) and the MRFT. This principle also applied to lower levels.

In 1997, the State Council promulgated the first broadcasting administrative regulation, *Broadcasting Administrative Regulations (BAR)*, which formally legalized the aforementioned leadership and administrative system. Article 5 of BAR states that:

> The department of broadcasting and television administration under the State Council shall be responsible for broadcasting and television administration across the country. The departments or agencies in charge of broadcasting and television administration (hereinafter the DBTA) of local people's governments at or above the county level shall be responsible for broadcasting and television administration within their respective administrative areas.
>
> (*Broadcasting Administration Regulation*, 1997)

The DBTA's functions include:

1 Formulation of a national development plan for nationwide broadcasters, including total number of stations, their distribution and structure (Article 8);
2 Examination and approval of broadcaster licenses (Article 12);
3 Construction of broadcasting and transmission networks including transmitting stations, relay stations, broadcasting satellites, satellite up-link stations, satellite reception and relay stations, microwave stations, monitoring stations and cable networks (Article 17);
4 Designation and allocation of channel frequencies (Article 18);
5 Regulation enforcements including imposing financial penalties; suspension of programs, channels or broadcasters; revoking of broadcasting licenses (Articles 47–52).

From 1998 to 1999, institutional reform was launched in China to slim down the bureaucratic structure of both central and local governments. Together with others, MRFT was downgraded from a constitutional ministry of the State Council to the State Administration of Radio, Film and Television (SARFT), a state bureau directly subordinated to the State Council. In 1998, a new chief – Tian Congming – replaced Sun Jiazheng to lead the bureau. This was a period characterized by institutional and structural adjustments not only within MRFT but also throughout the entire government. The transition was moving towards "simpler administration," "consolidation," "convergence," "concentration" and "improvement of quality" but was no longer concerned with its economic viability.[2]

In January 2003, National Broadcasting and Film Working Conference, the separation of the institutional and enterprise natures of broadcasting were brought forward. In late 2003, the *Opinions on Experimental Works of the Cultural System's Institutional Reform*, formulated by the Party, clearly divided the cultural sector into two parts – cultural institutions serving the "public good" and cultural industries pursuing commercial interests. In terms of the television sector, it requested the establishment of a market and public service system. The

44 Broadcasting authority in China

Party chose some cities and television stations to test the model so that it could learn from the trial. A government monitoring system was also put into place to secure an organized transformation. Under this system, the government's central and local broadcasting authorities no longer ran television or radio stations, but functioned as administrators and regulators, and had policy- and regulation-making functions. They employed both legislative measures, such as the law and rules, and administrative means, such as instructions and notices, to guide operations, penalize violations and so on (Xu, 2003a).

SAPPRFT

In 2013, following the decisions of the CCP's Eighteenth National Congress, the State Council (2013a) announced the reform plan for its departmental structure and functions at the first sessional meeting of the Twelfth National People's Congress. The Council stated that the purposes of this institutional reform were to "simplify administration and devolve power," "increase administrative efficiency" and "enhance the market economy". It also aimed to equip the Council with clear rights and duties, a reasonable division of functions, and with the rule of law.

According to the State Council General Office's *Notice on Dividing the Tasks for Implementation of the Plan for Institutional Reform and Functional Transformation of the State Council* (State Council, 2013b), the Chinese government was planning to complete the State Council reform in three to five years, and build a more civilian friendly government by accelerating the optimization of the institutional structure of the government and improving the effectiveness of the civil service. As a result, the reform in the media administration reflected the spirit of the State Council reform. Many trivial responsibilities were abandoned or given to the provincial or the much lower grass-root units, and the focus of its work was also shifted from supervision to a more macro-scoped industrial guidance (2013a). One reform measure was to merge SARFT and GAPP (General Administration of Press and Publication) to a "Mega Department" (SAPPRFT) (Phoenix Net, 2013). This was not a Cabinet-level department constituting the State Council, but a ministerial level administrative department directly under the State Council. The new SAPPRFT consisted of 22 internal divisions including a General Office, the Television Drama Division, the Internet Audio-visual Program Management Division, the Import Management Division and so on. Thirteen of the Administration Heads were Chinese communist party members. Among them, there was one General Head and seven Vice Heads, one Team Leader of the Discipline Inspection Commission and three General Heads of the state's television stations – China Central Television (CCTV), China Radio International (CRI) and China National Radio (CNR). Matters concerning press, publication, radio, television, film and the Internet audio-visual channels across the whole country are all subject to SAPPRFT plans and decisions.

In 2013, the State Council (2013c) issued a normative notice to formally announce the functions and organizational structure of the newly formed SAPPRFT. According to the notice, SAPPRFT's main duties were to include:

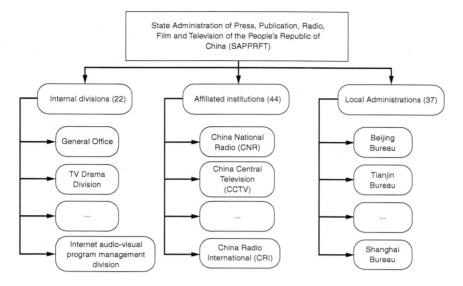

Figure 3.1 Organizational structure of SAPPRFT (2015d).

1 Formulating media policy, and upholding correct guidance of public opinions and creation;
2 Formulating media and copyright law and regulations, enacting departmental rules and industry standards, and responsibility for their implementation and enforcement;
3 Organizing public interest projects, and supporting impoverished and remote regions' media development and construction;
4 Promoting, implementing and supervising technological convergence, formulating technological development plans, policies and industry standards;
5 Advancing the media sector's institutional reform;
6 Supervising media organizations, their business and media content, implementing an administrative licensing system according to law. Investigate illegal activities and supervise broadcasters' advertisements;
7 Supervising the digital publications of online and mobile contents. Supervising and examining the content and quality of online audio-visual programs and public audio-visual carriers;
8 Responsibility for importing audio-visual products and the "going out" project;
9 Directly controlling state-owned media at the national level including CCTV, CNR and CRI.

Some aspects of the responsibilities were emphasized to be reinforced in the upcoming years (State Council, 2013a), such as the media's public service role; the integration of the media industry; institutional reform in media sphere; digital

46 *Broadcasting authority in China*

broadcasting; copyright protection; the regulatory role of the market, social supervision and the industry's self-regulation. In addition, as the new name SAPPRFT suggested, the merger has expanded its regulatory fields. Press and publication were newly added into the scope of the administration, and the whole regulation system included press, publication, radio and television broadcasting and the film industry. Copyright protection, Internet television, online audiovisual production, and especially the integration of the three networks, i.e., the Internet, telecommunication network and the television cable network, are the areas of most focus by SAPPRFT.

Meanwhile, 20 administrative approval and managerial functions of SAPPRFT were either retracted or abolished including the power to censor television drama and movie scripts, and the evaluation of the quality of newspapers and periodicals. The State Council delegated the responsibility of the latter to industry associations, i.e., the Chinese Press Association and Chinese Periodical Association. Seven functions were devolved to local media regulators at the provincial level, mainly those concerning minor administrative responsibilities such as the approval of setting up satellite television channels receiving equipment and the approval of national film festivals.

Control of the Central Propaganda Department and State Council

SAPPRFT is supervised by both the State Council and the Ministry of Central Propaganda. The Central Propaganda Department is the most important institution for monitoring media personnel and controlling the content of media. It oversees the Propaganda and Education System (宣教系统, *xuanjiao xitong*) which consists of three connected parts: the state-run culture, education, sport, science and technology sector, the health sector and the media sector in China. It also oversees the network of propaganda cadres and offices installed in party branches at all levels of organizations in both the state bureaucracy, as well as in Chinese and foreign-run private enterprises with CCP branches (Brady, 2006). It controls SAPPRFT through the *nomenklatura* system of appointments (Esarey, 2006). The principal mechanism for forcing media authority and organizations to comply with the CCP is the vertically organized *nomenklatura* system of appointments granting the Party power to hire and fire party leaders and state officials including those in charge of the media industry and top media managers (Esarey, 2006: 3). The Central Organization Department (COD) and Central Propaganda Department directly appoint the senior officials of national media authorities, and senior managers of national media, such as the SAPPRFT, Ministry of Culture, and the national television station, CCTV and the People's Daily. Since the early 1980s, the system of appointments for the broadcasting authority has officially been a "one-level down" system. At the upper level, the COD and MCP confirm the broadcasting authority's appointments at the central level and the head of propaganda department at the provincial level. One level down, the provincial party committee and propaganda department approves the provincial broadcasting authority's appointments and the city level propaganda department's appointment. Lastly, the city level oversees broadcasting authority appointments at the same level and propaganda cadres' appointments at the county level (CCP, 2014).

The Central Propaganda Department is supervised by the Propaganda Leading Small Group, made up of the most senior officials of the leading Party and State institutions in the propaganda sphere (Brady, 2006). The senior leader currently responsible for the propaganda and ideological sphere is Liu Yunshan, who is the Politburo Standing Committee member. The head of the Central Propaganda Department is Liu Qibao.

The Party's Propaganda Department is responsible for:

1   Leading public opinion, guiding and coordinating the national media's propaganda;
2   Supervising the creation and production of cultural products;
3   Planning and arranging national ideology thought work, educating the Party's cadres and producing educational materials;
4   Working together with departments of the CCP to supervise the cadres and leaders of the propaganda and culture organizations including SAPPRFT, the Xinhua News Agency, the People's Daily, the Ministry of Culture, and the Chinese Academy of Social Science (CASS);
5   Initiating the guiding principles of propaganda and cultural systems, guiding the policy and law-making of propaganda and culture organizations; coordination between different departments; organizing, coordinating and guiding the monitoring of public opinion for the Central Committee's leaders to facilitate their decision-making;
6   Responsibility for the institutional reform of the culture system including conducting research and proposing policy recommendations.

The Central Propaganda Department's guidance on various topics is issued in the form of written or verbal instructions, such as normative documents, and the Party leader's speeches and written comments. The State Council and its departments, such as the SAPPRFT, the Ministry of Culture, Party and non-Party newspapers, and state owned television stations (Brady, 2006) undertake the actual task of implementing the policy advice given by the Central Propaganda Department. Since the SAPPRFT is a department that is directly under the State Council, the State Council can adjust the broadcasting regulator's internal structure, and also directly encourage the regulator to embark on certain policy goals. For example, the general office of the State Council issued a document in 1994 *Notice on the issuance of the MRFT's function, organization and staffing* (State Council, 1994) and in 1998 *Notice on the issuance of the SARFT's function, organization and staffing* (State Council, 1998a). These documents, when combined with the *Decision of the First Session of the Twelfth National People's Congress on the Plan for State Council Restructuration and Function Transformation* (NPC, 2013), the *Notice of the General Office of the State Council on*

48 *Broadcasting authority in China*

Dividing the Tasks for Implementation of the Plan for Institutional Reform and Functional Transformation of the State Council (State Council, 2013b) and *Notice on the Issuance of the SAPPRFT's Function, Organization and the Staffing* (State Council, 2013c) in 2013, reflected the State Council's role in the staffing, internal structure, and focus of the work of the regulator.

SAPPRFT's regulatory instruments

Regulatory instruments can be classified into five types according to the underlying behavior that is to be controlled: command, competition, consensus, communication and code (or architecture) (Morgan and Yeung, 2007). The Chinese state regulates the country's broadcasting mainly through a command mechanism. Command-based mechanisms for regulating behavior involves state promulgation of legal rules prohibiting specified conduct, underpinned by coercive sanctions (civil and criminal in nature) if the prohibition is violated. In the Chinese context, it also involves administrative authority and party issuing of normative documents and written comments, underpinned by administrative penalties and party discipline.

International law

China has signed several international treaties, which cover media and expression freedom and human rights, including the *International Covenant on Economic, Social and Cultural Rights* (ratified in 2001, by the NPC's Standing Committee) and the *International Covenant on Civil and Political Rights* (ICCPR) (not ratified). These international treaties function to some extent as a legal framework for the Chinese government's media policy-making. For instance, the NPC's ratification of the *International Covenant on Economic, Social and Cultural Rights* (ICESCR) in 2001, binds the PRC legally to the obligations enshrined therein. In 2005 the UN Committee on Economic, Social and Cultural Rights (CESCR) published its concluding observations on China's implementation of ICESCR (E/C.12/1/Add.107, 13 May 2005), highlighting its concerns over income inequalities between rich and poor and urban and rural areas, and over adequate standards of living. It urged the Chinese government to allow freedom of information, that all Chinese may take part in cultural life and enjoy the benefits and applications of scientific progress. In response to the CESCR's concerns, the State Council published its *Outline of Cultural Development for the Eleventh Five-Year Plan* in September 2006. This important policy document championed "cultural public service" (CPS) as the key objective of culture building in the subsequent five years – the first time the government had explicitly referred to this concept. Public service programs makes up part of the CPS project. Chapter 8 provides a detailed examination of China's cultural public service and public service broadcasting policies and its expansion in local contexts.

Domestic law

In China, there was no single standalone broadcasting law. The laws on broadcasting in China come from five sources: (1) The Chinese Constitution. China enacted four constitutions. The present one is the 1982 Constitution. According to its Article 64, amendments to the Constitution are to be proposed by the Standing Committee of the NPC or by more than one-fifth of the deputies of the NPC and adopted by a vote of more than two-thirds of all the deputies of the NPC; (2) Laws [*falv*] (legal rules promulgated by the NPC or its Standing Committee). They are usually national laws and govern the whole nation[3]; (3) Administrative regulations promulgated by the State Council[4]; (4) Department rules enacted by administrative departments of the State Council; (5) local regulations[5] (Luo, 2003) and local department rules.[6]

Constitution

In each of the four constitutions since the state was established the PRC has attached importance to the protection of citizens' freedom (Constitution of the PRC, 1954, 1975, 1978; Lin, 1990; Reed, 2000).

Many scholars have hailed the 1982 Constitution as the most advanced Constitution since the founding of the PRC. While it is the pre-eminent document within the legal hierarchy, it plays a limited role in litigation to protect individual rights (Peerenboom, 2009). Article 35 of the Constitution specifies "citizens enjoy the rights to freedom of speech and freedom of the press" (Constitution of the PRC, 1982).[7] Article 41 states that citizens may exercise oversight to ensure that state organs and functionaries (in theory, the people's servants) discharge their duties correctly and serve the public interest. This clause provides for the constitutional right of citizens to participate in the administration of state affairs (Constitution of the PRC, 1982). Moreover, the freedom to engage in scientific research, literary and artistic creation and other cultural pursuits provided for in Article 47 is important for citizens to pursue self-realization and also to express their political views and aspirations in the form of literary and artistic works (Constitution of the PRC, 1982). In accordance with the principle that lower laws shall not contravene higher laws, freedom of expression, as established and guaranteed by the Constitution, should become the basis for the enactment of laws, administrative rules and departmental regulations and for legislation and law enforcement by governments at all levels, especially by the administrative organs that deal with the media (Law on Legislation, 2000).

However, the Constitution, despite its supremacy in the legal hierarchy, has no actual value in judicial practice and remains a framework document. There is no constitutional court in China and the judicial courts have no right to interpret the Constitution. The constitutional right of freedom of expression is not protected in specific civil or criminal laws, and Chinese courts do not accept litigation on the grounds of infringement of the right to free speech as such litigation

50 Broadcasting authority in China

falls outside their jurisdiction. The power to interpret the Chinese Constitution rests upon the Standing Committee of the National People's Congress (Law on Legislation, 2000), so the courts do not have the power to strike down any legislation because of its unconstitutionality. Neither does any law expressly define who has the authority to conduct constitutional reviews of primary laws passed by the National People's Congress and its Standing Committee (Law on Legislation, 2000). In judicial practice, constitutional law is rarely invoked as a direct source for adjudication. Constitutional rights ought to be protected and resolved through laws, administrative regulations and other rules under the Constitution, but invariably the pertinent laws do not exist. These factors combine to relegate the fundamental rights provided by the Constitution into a resolution free position (Chin, 2014; Tong, 2001). This situation is inconsistent with the public's understanding and heightened expectation of individual rights and their implementation as the national economy continues to grow.

In 2014, the Chinese Communist Party announced the *Decision Concerning Some Major Questions in Comprehensively Promoting Governing the Country According to Law* (The Decision 2014). The policy document called for the advancement of the implementation and supervision of the Constitution in China. It placed the Constitution at the heart of the rule according to law, and claims that to rule according to law first means to rule according to the Constitution. Chapter 4 provides a detailed examination of governing the country according to law reform in China.

Law

The most fundamental basis of all administrative processes is the ordinary law. Broadcasting related laws involve civil, criminal, economic and administrative law.

China does not have a specific media law, although the *Administrative Licensing Law* (NPC, 2003) has been used like a legal principle when dealing with the industrial market entrance. According to Article 12 of the

Table 3.1 Broadcasting related laws in China

Civil law	Economic law	Administrative law	Criminal law
General Principle of Civil Law; Tort Law; Educational Law; Higher Education Law; Civil Procedure Law	Advertising Law; Consumer Law; Price Law; Copyrights Law	Administrative Penalty Law; Administrative Licensing Law; Administrative Review Law; Administrative Procedure Law; National Security Law; Public Order Penalty Law	Article 124, 217, 152, 181, 222, 246, 288 of Criminal Law; Criminal Procedure Law

Administrative Licensing Law, the procedure for administrative licenses may be instituted for matters such as those relating to:

1   the special activities that directly involve State security, macro-economic control and protection of the ecological environment and that have a direct bearing on human health and the safety of people's lives and property, which are subject to approval in accordance with the statutory requirements;
2   the professions and trades that provide services to the public and that have a direct bearing on public interests, the qualifications and competence to be possessed by which, such as the special credibility, conditions and skills, need to be affirmed.

For the following matters in Article 12 of the Law, administrative licenses are not required for matters:

1   on which citizens, legal persons and other organizations can make decisions themselves;
2   which can effectively be regulated by the competitive mechanism of the market; matters which the organizations of trades or intermediary bodies can manage through self-discipline; and
3   which administrative departments can solve by other administrative means such as post-supervision.

Media activities, like the online audio-visual program service, online cultural business, online audio-visual news service, online television drama production, overseas satellite television channel landing and the operation of pay television channels have all requested administrative licenses. For instance, a company must obtain an Internet audio-visual program license established by *Administrative Measures for the Broadcast of Audiovisual Programs via the Internet or Other Information Networks* before entering the online audio-visual media market. The Measures also introduce an inspection system that the regulator would cancel licenses issued if the relevant company was discovered not to be qualified for the licenses.

Administrative regulation

Administrative legislation includes two major categories in accordance with their respective order within the legislative hierarchy: administrative regulations (*xingzheng fagui,* 行政法规) promulgated by the State Council, whose legal status is only second to law; department rules *(xingzheng guizhang,* 行政规章), enacted by the State Council's broadcasting department, i.e., SARFT or SAPPRFT. China's Constitution states that both administrative statutes and department rules have legal status.

52 *Broadcasting authority in China*

By 2014, China had nine media administrative regulations. They were:

1 *Measures for Control over Imported Films* (*Guo Han Zi* No. 156 [1981], 1981);
2 *Provisional Administrative Measures on Cable Television* (Decree No. 2 of the MRFT, 1990);
3 *Administrative Measures on Reception of Satellite Broadcast Programs via Ground Facilities* (Decree No. 129 of the State Council, 1993);
4 *Administrative Regulations on Radio and Television* (Decree No. 228 of the State Council, 1997);
5 *Regulations on Protection of Radio and Television Facilities* (Decree No. 285 of the State Council, 2000);
6 *Administrative Measures on Internet Information Services* (Decree No. 292 of the State Council, 2000);
7 *Film Administrative Regulations* (Decree No. 342 of the State Council, 2001);
8 *Regulation on the Protection of the Right to Network Dissemination of Information* (Decree No. 468 of the State Council, 2006);
9 *Interim Measures for the Payment of Remunerations for the Broadcast of Sound Recordings by Radio and Television Stations* (Decree No. 566 of the State Council, 2009).[8]

Department rules

The SAPPRFT receives guidance from the State Council, and adjusts their regulatory policy accordingly. In accordance with the law, the State Council promulgated department rules, administrative legislations, decisions and orders. They were implemented within its departmental jurisdictions. By 2014, there were 41 effective departmental rules promulgated by the SARFT or SAPPRFT.

Department rules are mainly drafted by the SAPPRFT's Department of Law and Regulation. Although the whole rule-making process is not open to public engagement, it involves negotiations and coordination between the different State Council departments that are affected. A new department rule must also be submitted to the State Council's legislative department to be recorded. Important department rules include:

1 *Administrative Provisions for the Internet Audio-Video Program Service* (Decree No. 56 of the SARFT and the Ministry of Information Industry, 2007);
2 *Administrative Measures for the Broadcast of Audiovisual Programs via the Internet and Other Information Networks* (Decree No. 39 of the SARFT, 2004);
3 *Measures for the Administration of Radio and Television Advertising* (Decree No. 61 of the SARFT, 2009);

4 *Interim Provisions on the Qualifications for a Film Enterprise's Access to Commencement of Operation* (Decree No. 43 of SARFT and the Ministry of Commerce, 2004);
5 *Administrative Measures for the Examination and Approval of Radio Stations and Television Stations* (Decree No. 37 of the SARFT, 2004);
6 *Provisions on Internal Audition of Broadcasting and Film Organizations* (Decree No. 46 of the SARFT, 2004);
7 *Administrative Measures for the Broadcast of Audiovisual Programs via Such Information Networks as the Internet* (Decree No. 39 of the SARFT, 2004);
8 *Provisions on legislative procedures of Radio, Television and Film* (Decree No. 23 of the SARFT, 2004);
9 *Administrative Measures on Audio-visual Service* (Decree No. 23 of the SARFT, 2004);
10 *Measures for the Administration of the Landing of Overseas Satellite Television Channels* (Decree No. 27 of the SARFT, 2004);
11 *Interim Administrative Measures for Qualifications of Broadcasting Editors, Journalists and Anchors* (Decree No. 26 of the SARFT, 2004);
12 *Measures for Radio, Film and Television Administrative Reconsideration* (Decree No. 5 of the SARFT, 2001);
13 *Interim Provisions on Administrative Penalty of Radio, Television and Film* (Decree No. 20 of the Ministry of Film and Television, 1996);
14 *Interim Provisions on the Administration of Operation Services of Cable Broadcast Television* (Decree No. 67 of the SARFT, 2011).[9]

Normative documents and written comments

On top of administration legislation and department rules, because most terrestrial television stations[10] in China are under the direct administration of SAPPRFT or its local bureaus, the department usually governs them via normative documents (*guifanxing wenjian*, 规范性文件) including decisions, orders and directives issued either by the State Council's departments or SARFT. For instance, sometimes the general office of SAPPRFT would issue normative documents to adjust broadcasting and new media policy and to avoid possible deviations of ideology.

These normative documents do not need to be recorded by the State Council, but are only applicable to stations subjected to SAPPRFT's administration. They may not have legal status, and it is up to the court to decide their status.[11] The document-making process is also closed to the outside. Negotiations are between SAPPRFT, its local bureau and television stations through varied channels, such as the annual national working conference, internal reports and surveys. The use of normative documents was intense, both in content and for a period of time: from 2000 to mid-2014 the SAPPRFT issued at least 438 normative documents.[12] They were issued randomly and without firm standards, despite this, these documents significantly shaped today's Chinese media landscape. For

54 *Broadcasting authority in China*

instance, many normative documents were issued by SARFT to shape online audio-visual enterprises, and these decisions were angrily received by critics, although the media industry would conform to them eventually.

There has been an important practice in China of using party leaders and senior government officials' speeches and written comments to shape the development of Chinese television. These speeches, written comments and internal documents have a more profound impact than statutes, rules and normative documents. This is simply because the Party's power is greater than that of the State government in China. The Party's decisions shape the principles and directions of Chinese media policies. However, the Party's decision-making process is much more complicated as it involves negotiation between all interest groups. These include not only the State Council at the central level but also local governments and party officials, and not only domestic media operators and advertising companies but global ones as well.

From a command to a consensus mechanism

A consensus mechanism refers to a form of self-regulation involving various forms of co-operative partnership between state and non-state actors in seeking to regulate social behavior. The growth of social media applications such as social networks and audio- and video-sharing during the past few years has been phenomenal in China. Social media – characterized by participation, openness, conversation, community and connectedness – is presenting novel regulatory issues (Drucker and Gumpert, 2010; Evans *et al.,* 2010; Kluver, 2005; Liu, 2011; Mayfield, 2008; Mueller, 2004; Mustonen, 2009; Pitta, 2010; Price *et al.,* 2013; Zhang LL, 2006). The development of social media has put pressure on the state's regulation of communication and information technology in several distinct ways: distributing control; facilitating a quantum jump in the scale of communication; growing new institutions and changing the polity. In other words, the advent of social media has decentralized authority over networking, and national government not only faces the challenge of the vast volume of communication flows, but also the increasing shift of decision-making authority over social media applications' standards from government into the hands of private companies. These companies constitute a new locus of authority for key decision-making (Mueller, 2010: 4–5). In China, the proliferation and uptake of social media has also been accompanied by increasing regulatory issues. New policies towards and new rules for governing social media have appeared. For instance, the government has brought in a legal requirement for users to provide real names and identification information when registering a micro-blog account, ostensibly to curb the dissemination of rumors and false information (Xinhua News, 2011). However legal regulation through existing laws and state regulation by government agencies have been either poorly enforced or lacking in accountability; this raises questions about the existing model of social media regulation. Self-regulation and collaboration between state organizations, non-state organizations and industry in governing social media have been called for by government officials and academics (see Chin, 2013; Chen Yingfeng, 2012; Nie Juan, 2011). Moreover, since several commercial companies dominate the social media landscape, private censorship of the Internet by these companies arguably has a greater impact than state regulation. In China, *Sina Weibo*, the country's most popular social network site, has also developed its own mechanisms for checking false information and clarifying rumors, and imposes sanctions, such as disabling a user's posting function or deleting a user's *Weibo* ID. Concomitant with the establishment of Internet self-regulatory organizations, like the Beijing Internet Association (BIA), and the devolution of regulatory functions to private companies by the state, (for instance, the 2012 *Decision to Strengthen the Network Information Protection*), Internet Service Providers (ISPs) are requested to remove illegal information disseminated by social networking site (SNS) users and report them to government agencies. The more conventional legal and state regulations are being supplemented by appeals to an extra-legal framework, and to possible collaboration with private actors including the social media industry and civil society organizations to support public policy objectives.

In fact, governance in China is incrementally changing from government control (管制, *guanzhi*) to public management (管理, *guanli*) and to network governance (治理, *zhili*). This indicates a changing relationship between the state and society in which social problems are solved through multisectional collaboration between the state and private actors and states increasingly rely on the cooperation of stakeholders to mobilize fragmented resources to realize favorable outcomes (Blockson and Buren, 1999: 64; Kenis and Schneider, 1991). This type of network governance or its Chinese equivalent, *wangluo zhili* (网络治理), has been applied in various Chinese public policy research spheres, including the reform of taxation, banking, housing and estates management, education, public health insurance reform, provincial legislatures and civil society engagement (Chan, 2011; Fulda *et al.*, 2012; Levy and Meyer, 2012; Ren, 2005; Tang, 2004; Xia, 2008; Zhang and Lou, 2007; Zheng *et al.*, 2010; Zhu, 2008). It is argued that network governance has great potential for Chinese governance as the development of civil society and interest groups will be strengthened, following various cases of both government failure and market failure in China (Chan, 2011; Ren, 2005), and the "incremental change from government control (*guanzhi*) to public management (*guanli*) and to network governance (*zhili*)" in China (Fulda *et al.*, 2012: 675). The delegation of some governance functions to non-state or civil society organizations has emerged as a pattern, in a structural response to the ineffectiveness and lack of accountability of state regulation. The practices of companies such as *Sina Weibo* or social organizations like the BIA could be conceptualized as a kind of network governance.

The BIA (formerly the Beijing Association of Online Media) was founded in 2004 as a Government recognized social organization. It was the first local Internet social organization with the aim of establishing a self-regulatory system and of connecting the Internet companies with government departments. Its business is under the guidance of the Beijing Municipal Party Committee's Propaganda Department and the Beijing Civil Affairs Bureau. Members of the BIA include China's major social media companies and it has formed close links with both the social media industry and the government. It has four functional committees concerned with steering social media, including the Online News and Information Council – Beijing *Wangluo Xinwenxinxi Pingyihui* (北京网络新闻信息评议会), which monitors online news information, journalistic ethics and media infringement cases in Beijing. The Council is made up of representatives from government, online media, academics and Internet users (netizens). Each year, the Council publishes several reports, reviewing the operation of online platforms and providing suggestions for further actions. Moreover, different projects have been set up by the BIA and its governmental and industrial collaborators to govern the Internet. One of the projects is the Anti-Online Rumor Website *py.qianlong.com* (Beijing District Joint Anti-Online Rumor Platform, 北京地区网站联合辟谣平台). It was set up by six major web portal sites to combat rumors spreading on social media platforms, and is under the supervision of the BIA and Beijing Internet Information Office (BIIO). These projects have been launched to steer online media with inputs from both state and private actors. Through bilateral or multilateral interactions and agreements, those agencies can sometimes establish their own rules about how to discipline members, construct responses to unacceptable behavior, and so on.

On the other hand, as the role of the CCP is still dominant in media policy-making and regulation, the participation of multiple actors (or stakeholder groups) in a governance network does not by itself determine how power is distributed or how much weight or authority they are given in decision-making processes, or how conflicts over the distribution of benefits and costs will be resolved. The CCP is highly resourced and has a range of powers with which to retain influence over state and private agencies. Nevertheless, the emergence of network governance acknowledges a new tendency in governance, based on interdependence, negotiation and trust in China, especially in non-politically sensitive areas.

Summary

The broadcasting authority in China, since the start, has been an integrated part of the country's political system. The Party and state government exerted its control over the broadcasting authority through both administrative measures and *nomenklatura* system of appointments. As a result of lacking independence, the authority's structure, function and mission has been deeply and frequently affected not only by the political climate and struggles in the country but also by the national and local government's administrative reforms. This lack raises the question of stability and coherence of the regulatory structure and policy of the broadcasting authority. Traditionally, the broadcasting authority supervises the media through a command mechanism. The growth of social media applications and poor enforcement or lacking in accountability of legal rules and state regulations have promoted an increasingly shift to a mixed regulatory mechanism which combines state regulation with self-regulation and collaboration between state organizations, non-state organizations and industry. This indicates a changing relationship between the state and society in which media related problems are solved through multisectional collaboration between the state and private actors, and states increasingly rely on the cooperation of media companies and industry associations to mobilize fragmented resources to realize its policies and regulations.

Notes

1 Xu was the head of the SARFT from June 2000 to December 2004.
2 According to a personal interview with a senior official at SARFT's Department of Law and Regulations in Beijing on 18 September 2003.
3 This category of laws can also be entitled *tiaoli* (provision), *banfa* (measures), *jueyi* (resolution), *jueding* (decision), *fangan* (measures), *jieshi* (interpretation), and *guiding* (provisions). Legal documents in the form of resolutions, decision, plans or provisions usually tend to be temporary measures, to supplement existing laws, or to deal with issues that no law can be applied to. There is no difference between *fa* and *tiaoli*.
4 The State Council is the highest authority in the country's administration. It is empowered under Article 89 of the 1982 Constitution to "adopt administrative measures, enact administrative rules and regulations, and issue decision and orders in accordance with the constitution and statues." After the enactment of the PRC's Legislative Law in 2000, the State Council only formulated administrative regulations in order to implement laws and to deal with matters related to the administrative powers of authority of the State Council. The legal validity of administrative regulations are ranked immediately below laws enacted by the Standing Committees of the NPC. They are normally promulgated under the titles of *shishi xize* (detail implementation rules), *tiaoli* (regulations), *guiding* (provisions), *banfa* (measures), and *jueding* (decisions). The State Council often publishes *tongzhi* (circulars) and *yijian* (opinion) to supplement its administrative regulation. The status of these document is still an unsettled issue. Most Chinese jurists treat them as *afgui xing wenjiang* (administrative regulating documents).
5 In the hierarchy of Chinese law, local regulations are next to administrative regulations promulgated by the State Council. All local laws and administrative regulations are to be reported to the NPC or the State Council for record keeping and review.
6 Article 90 of the 1982 Constitution authorizes ministries and commissions under the State Council to issue orders, directives, and rules within the jurisdiction of their respective department in accordance with laws and administrative regulations, decisions, and orders. Article 71 of the Legislative law provides: "matters regulated by department rules shall belong to the realm of implementing laws and the administrative regulation, decision, or orders of the State Council." In the legal hierarchy, department rules are at the same level as local regulations.
7 This book uses the term "freedom of expression" as an umbrella term to encompass both of these rights. Also, by the term's adoption, this book uses the same standard to discuss the various rights and freedoms recognized and protected by Article 35 of the Constitution.
8 All Administrative Regulations are available at: www.sarft.gov.cn/col/col1602/index.html (accessed 8 December 2014).
9 All Department Rules are available at: www.sarft.gov.cn/col/col1583/index.html (accessed 8 December 2014).

58 *Broadcasting authority in China*

10 There are exceptions, such as educational terrestrial TV stations, operated by the State Council's Ministry of Education. Many cable TV stations are also operated by state-owned enterprises or other government units.
11 Personal interview with a senior official at the SARFT's Department of Law and Regulation in Beijing on 18 September 2003.
12 This figure was gathered from the SAPPRF.

4 State legitimacy and administration according to law for broadcasting

Introduction

The chapter explores the question of political legitimacy, which links the state and society, and shows how changes in political legitimacy affect the function of law in China, shaping the discourse of the "rule of law" in general and the country's broadcasting regulatory strategies and structures in particular. As communist ideology, economic performance and official virtue have all begun to decline, the Chinese state has moved to expand its legitimacy in a number of ways, including a mixture of improved performance and legal-rational justifications. This notion of improving the rule of law has become one of the most frequently mentioned government strategies in maintaining legitimacy, and governing according to the law is perceived as important for the long-term stability of the country. The Party-State also appeals to the rule of law in order to rationalize and legitimize its broadcasting media governance. The chapter will discuss this in detail, illustrating its implications and limits. It argues that such "administration according to law" was primarily driven by a concern for legal legitimacy, which was seen as "the most important, probably the last line of defense" for preventing institutional conflict as the reform of broadcasting deepened. However, the legal-rational legitimation efforts have primarily centered on the procedural rule of law: that is, enacting new broadcasting laws and laws with higher legal status to replace arbitrarily issued normative documents; strengthening the enforcement of laws, and placing checks on the government's administrative power. The advantages of a procedural concept of the rule of law are that it promises some degree of predictability, some limitations on arbitrariness and some protection of individual rights and freedoms. However, in the absence of democracy and with the marginalization of public participation in the law-making process, the state and broadcasting authority can also enact illiberal laws that restrict individual rights.

The question of political legitimacy

The issue of political legitimacy is very important in the discussion of the relationship between the state and society. State-society relations can be understood

60 *Legitimacy and broadcasting administration*

from three impure but non-reducible dimensions: the nature of state, the nature of society, and linkages between the state and society. Seymour Martin Lipset (1981) said that the stability of any given democracy depends on economic development, and the effectiveness and legitimacy of its political system. The nature of a regime (democratic, authoritarian or totalitarian) links the state and society politically, yet the state and society are also related through economic and psychological aspects, i.e., the legitimacy of state power as perceived by citizens and by the state elites themselves (Zhao, 2001). Seymour Martin Lipset (1981: 64) defined legitimacy as "the capacity of the system to engender and maintain the belief that the existing political institutions are the most appropriate ones for the society." Juan J Linz (1988: 65) defined legitimacy as "the belief that in spite of shortcomings and failures, the political institutions are better than others that might be established and therefore can demand obedience." Zhao Dinxing (2001) agrees that state legitimacy depends on a certain form of social structure (e.g., a strong civil society) and often correlates with a certain form of state legitimacy (e.g., legal-electoral legitimacy). However, Zhao (2001) argues that state legitimacy also confines the behavior of state elites, dominant classes, social activities, and so on. Therefore, legitimation is not only a mediating factor but also an independent factor.

The term "legitimation" refers to the process of seeking to acquire authority or legitimacy (Holmes, 1993). Legitimation can be sought in various forms depending on the source and means of acquiring legitimacy (Kwon, 2005). Max Weber (in Bendix, 1962) defines habit, affection and rational calculation as three bases of human compliance i.e., submission of this will to the authority. He proposes three types of legitimacy authority relations: traditional, charismatic and legal rationality. Leslie Holmes' (1997) classification of legitimation suggests that seven domestic dominant modes of legitimation were observed in various communist and post-communist societies. They are old traditional, charismatic, legal-rational, goal-rational (teleological), eudaemonic, official nationalist and new traditional modes. The first three modes of legitimation represent Max Weber's three models on which authority is based. In the traditional model, "a leader claims the right to rule on the basis of a long-established or widely accepted tradition." In the charismatic mode, "legitimacy is based on the charisma of a leader." Weber considers that the ultimate mode of legitimation in the modern state is the legal-rational form of legitimation. The political order is legitimated in terms of rules and laws that are binding on everyone, thus impersonal norms and a legal order give those in authority the right to rule. Regular, free and competitive elections manifest under the legal-rational mode of legitimation. It constitutes the dominant form of legitimation in the post-communist societies. The term goal-rational (teleological) legitimation describes the dominant form of legitimation in many socialist states, in which the leaders seek legitimacy in terms of their ability to steer a given country to the distant end goal of communism. The new traditional form is taken by the communist leaders who attempt to enhance their own authority by reference to an earlier phase of the communist era. Deng Xiaoping often made reference to the early phase of Mao

Zedong's leadership of communist China, which can be seen as an example of the new traditional mode. The eudaemonic mode of legitimation refers to attempts by political leaders to legitimate their rule in terms of the political order's performance, especially in the economic sphere. Under the eudaemonic mode, leaders appeal to the support of the masses on the basis of impressive growth rates, better quality and more widely available consumer goods, and stability. This may explain how China's economic success contributed to the continuation of the socialist system and dominance of the communist Party. The eudaemonic form of legitimation is closely related to economic performance, thus it becomes problematic when economic reforms fail to produce tangible results. The official nationalist form of legitimacy relies on nationalism. Communist leaderships who believed that they were failing to legitimate their rule by other modes resorted to official nationalism (Kwon, 2005). Legitimacy problems arise when the dominant legitimation mode fails to have a desirable effect. A legitimation crisis is generally induced by different factors, depending on the dominant mode of legitimation pursued. For instance, economic decline and economic reform failure impose a crisis on the eudaemonic form of legitimation.

A legitimation crisis leads to a system collapse if the leaders fail to overcome legitimacy problems. However, shifting dominant legitimation modes once the problematic nature of a given form of legitimation is recognized can prevent system collapse. When a legitimation crisis occurs because ruling elites lose confidence in the capacity of a particular dominant legitimation mode, this type of crisis can be managed as long as they believe they can enhance legitimacy by switching to another dominant mode. Holmes (1997) considers that an act of switching to another mode of legitimation provides a regime with some "breathing space." The process, therefore, can divert the attention of the masses from problems of the existing legitimation mode, and renew people's faith in the system.

In China, before the late 1980s, the state still claimed its legitimacy in a goal-rational model, i.e., the ideological terms of the "Four Cardinal Principles" – adherence to the socialist road, proletarian dictatorship, the leadership of the CCP, and Marxism-Leninism-Mao Zedong Thought – written into the preamble of the Chinese Constitution. The crackdown of the 1989 student movement significantly undermined this model of legitimacy of the Party-State. After the Deng Xiaoping's southern talk in 1992, the economic reform of state economy to market economy, economic and moral performance and territorial defense-capability to maintain political stability was the dominant dimension of the state's legitimacy. The Fifteenth National Congress of the CCP in 1997 committed to a mixed economy with the dominance of the non-state-owned sector. The state economy was declared to no longer occupy the dominant position in China's economic system. Increasing income inequality and unemployment accompanied the massive industry restructuring and the downsizing of state owned enterprises to improve efficiency and profitability. The State Statistic Bureau's figures show that from 1997 to 2001 the state sector cut more than 34 million jobs or 30.8 percent of its total employment (Yang, 2002). This resulted

62 *Legitimacy and broadcasting administration*

in a substantial increase in social tension. Meanwhile, serious corruption and the rent seeking behaviors of local government officials, combined with the widespread materialism nurtured by economic reform, sapped the CCP's political legitimacy as the defender of China's social revolution. Thus, there was a need to look for an alternative form of legitimacy.

As communist ideology, economic performance and official virtue declined, the rule of law and legal-rational legitimacy could fill the growing vacuum of belief, despite the absence of a strong rights-based tradition in Chinese history. The Chinese state moved to expand its legitimacy to include a mixture of performance and legal-rational. A study of 125 Chinese articles concerning political legitimacy in China, published between 2008 and 2012, identifies a fundamental shift in the discourse of Chinese intellectuals, including party intellectuals, on political legitimacy: goal-rational and eudaemonic legitimacy have been replaced by socio-economic inequality, corruption and the failure of the bureaucratic system. The improvement of bureaucracy, propaganda, the rule of law and promotion of equality became the most frequently mentioned strategies in maintaining legitimacy (Zeng, 2014).

Ideological adaptation remains a leading strategy. Party leaders have shown increasing concerns about the Party's declining ideological legitimacy and the Party has made efforts towards ideological adaptation. Many modern values have been absorbed so as to make the adaptation successful. Democracy and rule of law had been considered as the only solid ground for Weber's rational-legal legitimacy. It is claimed that whether or not China should become more democratic is no longer the question; the focus is on which forms of democracy China should embrace (Zeng, 2014: 634). In order to restrict state and official power, and to improve the Party-State's governance, a law to protect mass media was asked for so that the Chinese mass media could investigate corruption without government intervention (Chen, 2008).

The development of the rule of law in China

The concept of the "rule of law" takes various forms of expression in China. In Chinese, there are *fazhizhuyi* (doctrine of rule of law, 法治主义), *yifazhiguo* (governing the country by law, 依法治国) and *fazhtianxia* (the law-governed world, 法治天下). The term "rule of law" first appeared in contemporary China in 1979 in a party Central Committee document *The Instruction of the CCP's Central Committee on Strong Guarantee of Criminal Law and Criminal Litigation Law's Effect Implementation.* This document states that "whether [criminal or criminal litigation] law can be strictly enforced is an important index to evaluate the practice of socialist rule of law in our country" (Cui, 2011). Two conflicting principles have been bound together at the core of party policy since legal reform began: the law must serve the Party-State; but at the same time, China must be governed by the law and aim to attain the rule of law. In February 1996 the then Chinese leader, Jiang Zemin, spoke at the third legal system workshop entitled *Issues of Theory and Practice with Regard to the Administration of the Country according to the Law, and Establishing a Socialist Legal System in China* which was organized by the Party Central Committee. Jiang said that to govern the country according to the law is important for the long-term stability of the country and for the sustainability of the country's continuous economic growth and social advancement. Governing according to the law or the rule of law was referred to as gradually the law would govern all governmental affairs, and the country's political, economic and social life. State affairs, and economic and cultural affairs would be run according to the Constitution and law under the Communist Party's leadership, and the legalization and institutionalization of a socialist democracy would gradually be realized (Xiao, 2007). One month later, "to govern the country according to law and establish a socialist legal system country (*shehuizhuyi fazhi guoja*, 社会主义法治国家)" was introduced as a basic principle in the *Ninth Five-Year National Economic and Social Development Plan and Outline of 2010 Visions* at the Fourth Plenum of the Eighth National People's Congress. In 1997 the principle was included in the Fifteenth Chinese Communist Party Congress' report. In 1999 the principle was enshrined into the amendment of the Chinese Constitution. During the leadership of Hu Jingtao as the Party Secretary, Hu repeated the call for "the organic unity of rule according to law, the rule of people, and CCP's leadership," as well as "the continuous reform and perfection of the Party's leadership style and governing method, continuous advance the Party's governing competence and leadership quality" (Xiao, 2007). He was keen to establish the consciousness and authority of the Constitution, and to guarantee the Constitution's implementation, so that it could serve the coordinated development of socialist material, political and spiritual civilizations. In 2006 he further elaborated that to rule according to the law is to "lead the legislation of law, obey the law, and protect the execution of the law," and "enhance the leadership of the Party in legislation, and promote the scientific and democratic legislation, ensure the Party's policies are implemented and executed through the legal system and the law." In the CCP's Eighteenth National Congress in 2012, Hu Jingtao (2012) set out major aspects of political structure reform in his report (the Eighteenth CCP Report) including measures such as:

1   Promote the law-based governance of the country: government administration in accordance with the law, law enforcement conducted in a strict, fair and civilized way, according to due procedures, leading officials guided by the law in both thinking and action. The Party must act within the scope prescribed by the Constitution and laws. No organization or individual has the privilege of overstepping the Constitution and laws, and no one in a position of power is allowed in any way to take one's own words as the law, place one's own authority above the law or abuse the law.

2   Improve the mechanism for conducting checks and oversight over the exercise of power. Decision-making, executive and oversight powers check each other; government bodies exercise their powers in accordance with statutory mandates and procedures.

64 *Legitimacy and broadcasting administration*

In 2012, during Xi Jinping's presidency, the rule of law became one of the core concerns of the Party. On 23 October 2014, the Fourth Plenum of the Eighteenth Central Committee of the CCP promulgated the *CCP Central Committee Decision Concerning Some Major Questions in Comprehensively Promoting Governing the Country According to Law* (abbreviated as the Decision 2014 hereafter) (The Decision 2014). This was the first time a Central Committee plenary session addressed the topic of the rule of law (Xi, 2014). The Plenum laid out several general principles to guide the process of governing the country by law, including:

1   The leadership of the Party: the Party governs the country according to the Constitution and the laws; the Party governs the Party according to intra-Party regulations; the Party leads legislation, guarantees law enforcement, supports the judiciary and takes the lead in respecting the law; makes the Party's standpoints become the national will through statutory procedures, ensures the candidates recommended by Party organizations become leaders in State political bodies through statutory procedures.
2   The dominant position of the people: guaranteeing that the people enjoy broad rights and freedoms according to the law; guaranteeing that the people, under the leadership of the Party, and according to the provisions of the law, manage State affairs, manage economic and cultural undertakings, and manage social affairs; strengthen legal consciousness in the entire society.
3   Equality before the law: any organization or individual must respect the authority of the Constitution and the laws, and must act within the scope of the Constitution and the laws, they must all exercise their powers and rights, and carry out their duties and responsibilities according to the law, none may have privileges outside the Constitution and the laws.

While the emphasis on the "rule of law" has been part of the political rhetoric of the Party during the past 40 years, both the Eighteenth CCP Report and the Decision 2014 discuss the rule of law in close association with the term "constitution." By demanding that any organization and individual must act within the scope of the Constitution and laws both suggest the need to use the law (the Constitution) to constrain the way in which the authorities rule over people – as opposed to the use of the law as an instrument used by the authorities to rule over citizens. This is an important rhetorical development, since, in the past, previous government authorities have invoked the phrase the "rule of law" as an umbrella term for the expansion of their influence and extra-constitutional activities (Wang, 2014).

Nevertheless, compared to the 2012 Party report, the Decision 2014 expressly confirms the status quo of the Party's leadership. This includes its role in leading and coordinating the legislation and law enforcement processes, and the implementation of a two-track system of governance that the Party governs the country according to the Constitution and laws, while it governs the Party itself

Legitimacy and broadcasting administration   65

through intra-party regulations. Despite its emphasis on the equality before the laws, the Decision does not answer the vital questions of which system will prevail when the Party's intra-regulations contradict the Constitution, and who will have oversight of and check on the Party's power and its self-disciplinary system. Unlike the majority of constitutional democracies in the world, whose government powers are separated on the *trias politica* basis (executive, legislative and judicial) (Ackerman, 2000), the Chinese constitutional order is based on a principal of separation of powers that distinguishes between an administrative power, assigned to the government, and a political authority, assigned to the CCP (Wang, 2014). A fundamental principle of Chinese constitutionalism is that the political leadership of the CCP is effected through the government and that the structures of that implementation are set out in the Constitution. The CCP's political leadership is exercised through the work of the government. However, the separation power of government and the Party has not been implemented and there is a gap between constitutional provisions and actual political practice (Wang, 2014). As the President Xi Jinping confessed:

> although we celebrate the achievements, we shall not forget our weaknesses. For example: institutional deficiencies and poor oversight of the practice of the Constitution. Other issues concerning people's core interests are quite severe. Abuse of law, lax enforcement of laws and malpractice, commonly exist among local law enforcement departments, which severely harm the integrity of China's legal authority. Moreover, some civilians, including certain cadres need to improve their respect for the Constitution. For these problems, we need to concentrate and find practical solutions.
>
> (Xi, 2012)

Some commentators (Peerenboom, 2014) suggested that the socialist rule of law is an "oxymoron" as it entails the incoherent notion of the Three Supremes: the supremacy of the Party, the supremacy of the interests of the people, and the supremacy of the Constitution and laws. The Three Supremes and the emphasis on the two-track system of governance undermined the legal supremacy of the Constitution (Minzner, 2013). As such, the relationship between the Party and the rule of law will continue to be governed mainly by convention, the Party will decide such issues as part of its leadership role (Peerenboom, 2014).

Rule according to the law in broadcasting regulation

The state and the Party appeal to the rule of law in order to rationalize and legitimize its broadcasting media governance. The Decision 2014 announced wideranging governance reforms including: the principle of administration according to the law (*yifa xingzheng*, 依法行政); increasing transparency and public participation; and strengthening the various mechanisms for reining in state actors. Administration according to the law means that administrative agencies must perform their statutory roles and cannot do what is not authorized by law. They

66 Legitimacy and broadcasting administration

cannot exercise powers outside of the law, and cannot decide to impinge on the lawful rights and interests of citizens, legal persons and other organizations without a basis in law and regulation, or to increase their duties. The Decision also aims to form mechanisms for policy-making according to the law. Public participation, expert debate, risk assessment, legality review and collective discussion and decision-making are designated as statutory procedures for major administrative policy decisions. It aims to make policy-making structurally scientific, procedurally proper, and processes open and responsibilities clear. Within administrative bodies legality review mechanisms and legal advisory systems must be installed for major policy decisions (The Decision 2014).

In fact, administrative law reform began slowly in the late 1970s. The emphasis in the early years was on the use of the law as an instrument of economic development. Economic reforms called for an expansive role for government rather than a limited one. Therefore, relatively little attention was paid to administrative law. By the end of 1988, the Supreme People's Court had established an administrative law division and more than 1,400 local courts had created administrative panels to hear administrative cases. In 1987, the drafting of an *Administrative Litigation Law* commenced. The pace of administrative law legislation picked up in 1990s. In 1990, the *Administrative Supervision Law* and the *Administrative Reconsideration Law* were passed. In 1994, the *State Compensation Law* was passed, followed by the *Administrative Penalties Law* in 1996. In 1997, the Party's Fifteenth National Congress made "ruling the country by law" a basic strategy to lead the people governing the country. Law-based administration became an important principle of government management. In 1999 and 2004, the State Council published the *Decision to Comprehensively Promote Administration According to Law*, and its *Implementation Outline*. In a speech given to *The 2004 National Television and Telephone Conference on Administration Work according to Law*, former Premier Wen Jiabao stated that the comprehensive promotion of administration according to law and building a government ruled by law are the fundamental ways to strengthen the government's competence of administrative management; are core requirements for protecting the people's interests; are urgent needs for perfecting the socialist market economic system. Therefore, ruling the country by law and administration according to law is a fundamental change in governing style, and a fundamental strategy to ensure the country's lasting stability, peace and prosperity. Tian Congming (2006), the former deputy head of the SARFT, once commented that administration according to law is necessary to strengthen the Party's leadership and governance so that the Party can adapt to a new situation. Tong Gang (2014), the deputy head of the SAPPRT also reminded his colleague that "accompanying the deepening of broadcasting reform, many institutional problems would finally translate into institutional conflict and legal clashes, legal institutions would become the most important, and probably the last line of defense for risk prevention."

As an administrative department under the State Council, SAPPRT and its predecessors follow the policies and strategies of the Party, State Council and

Ministry of Propaganda. Its ideological role, of publicizing Party and government policy and guiding the correct public opinion has not changed, but its social functions and instrumental measures of administration have evolved over time. In the mid-1980s, amid a nationwide movement for legislation of governance, the then government department, the Ministry of Radio, Film and Television (MRFT)[1] started to practice "rule by law" in China's television sector (Guo, 2003). On 11 August 1997, the State Council promulgated the *Administrative Regulations on Radio and Television* following the appeal to "rule the country by law, and build a socialist country under the rule of law" made in the CCP's Fifteenth Party National Congress (Wang and Fu, 2002: 2).

However, there is no a single standalone broadcasting law (*falv, 法律*) for the whole nation which is promulgated by the NPC or its Standing Committee. The SAPPRFT and its predecessors regulates the country's broadcasting in three ways: administrative legislation, which includes two major categories in accordance with their respective order within the legislative hierarchy: administrative regulations (*xingzheng fagui, 行政法规*) promulgated by the State Council, whose legislative status is only second to law, and department rules (*xingzheng guizhang, 行政规章*) enacted by the State Council's broadcasting department, i.e., SAPPRFT or SARFT (Yang, 2002). China's Constitution states that both administrative statutes and department rules have legal status. Compared to administrative regulations, the process of the promulgation of department rules is rather less complicated, as it is mainly drafted by the SAPPRFT or SARFT's Department of Law and Regulation. Although the whole rule-making process is not open to public engagement, it involves negotiations and coordination between the different State Council departments affected. The new department rules must also be submitted to the State Council's legislative department to be recorded. On top of administration legislation, because SARFT or its local bureau operated most television stations[2] in China, which are also under their direct administration, the department usually governs them via normative documents (*guifanxing wenjian, 规范性文件*) including decisions, orders and directives issued either by the State Council or SARFT. Normative documents are administrative orders issued by administrative departments in accordance with the law, administrative regulations or department rules to control citizens, legal persons and other organizations' behaviors. They are not administrative legislations but are legally authorized with the force of law and they are binding and enforceable. In administrative litigation plaintiffs can use them as proof of whether a specific administrative act is legitimate, after a legal review in the People's Court, then the court can maintain or revoke the specific administrative act. The document-making procedures are relatively simply – negotiations are between the regulator, its local bureau and television stations through various channels, such as the annual national working conference, internal reports and surveys and, sometimes, they are made in the interests of the related administrative authorities (Zhang LL, 2006). The Department of Law and Regulation of SARFT states that these normative documents do not need to be recorded by the State Council, but are only applicable to stations subjected to SARFT's administration.[3]

68 *Legitimacy and broadcasting administration*

As all television stations in the country are owned by the State, there has been a practice in China of using both party leaders and senior government officials' speeches and written comments, as well as documents issued by the Ministry for the Central Propaganda, to shape Chinese television's development (Pei and Sun in Yan, 1998; Qian, 2002). These speeches, written comments and documents have a more profound impact than statutes, rules and normative documents. This is simply because the Party's power is superior to that of the State government in China. The Party's decisions determine the principles and directions for Chinese television policies. However, the Party's decision-making process is much more complicated than state governments. It involves negotiation between all interest groups. These include not only the State Council at the central level but also local governments, and not only domestic television operators and advertising companies but also global ones. This type of regulatory pattern has given the State and Party great power to exert direct political and administrative interference over television stations, resulting in the market and industry instability. The lack of stability, predications and transparency of the decision-making at the top of the political and regulatory system are criticized for leading to the "ad hoc, informal, and reactive [...]" of China's media policies (Hu and Du, 2002: 175–176). Many regulatory policies are disapproved of by broadcasters, professionals and academics because of their imprecision, self-contradiction, lack of deliberation, coherence, and vision (Hu and Du, 2002; Keane, 2001).

Zhu Hong (2004a), the former Director of the Law and Regulation Office at the SARFT, agreed that the slow development of administration according to law at the department was "due to the special features and marketization level of the Chinese broadcasting sector." Since the Chinese media is regarded as the mouthpiece of the Party and government and as part of the state's propaganda machine, its highest priority is to guarantee correct public opinion guidance, "propaganda work targets at constantly changed domestic and international situations and public opinions, [it] needs to follow the Party's unified deployment, and rapidly, timely, flexibly, and appropriately manage the propaganda work." The Chinese media's propaganda work has to "be policy-oriented, random and flexible" and the regulator thus needs to publish a large amount easy-to-modify, flexible and timely policies. The low level industrialization and marketization of the Chinese media also affect the development of the rule of law. Media organizations are institutional units of the government, and they are under the government's administrative management and relatively closed. They rely on the government's policies and departmental protection, and have lacked the motivation and urgent need to push forward the rule of law of its regulator (Zhu, 2004a). Also, following the media and economic reforms that have enabled self-interested media organizations and the decentralization of SAPPRFT's regulatory structure, SAPPRFT has faced a struggle to find a balance between maintaining effective governance and inviting legal forces into its governance, which could lead to a reduction of its power.

Following the publication of the State Council 2004 *Implementation Outline*, four broadcasting regulatory areas were identified for rule of law improvement:

(1) market regulation: legal regulation is required to protect media organizations' rights and responsibilities, to maintain fair competition, and to protect citizens' cultural rights; (2) constraining government's power and transforming government's functions: the regulator should shift its function from micro-management to macro-management, from running the media to regulating the media; (3) regulation and policy adjustment as a result of technology advancement: regulation and policy have to be more open and visionary, and to optimize channel resources; new rules and standards are required to govern the applications of new technologies; (4) regulation's integration with international standards and protection of national culture alongside the internationalization of the Chinese media (Zhu, 2004a). In 2010, SARFT (2010a) issued the *Notice on Work Plan of Strengthening Rule of Law Government* following State Council's *Opinion on Construction of Rule of Law Government*. The work plan aims to raise the legal consciousness of administrators, improve the democratic and scientific administrative decision-making, make law implementation more just and civil and administrative oversight and the accountability system better so that social conflict can be effectively prevented and resolved. It requests an improvement in legislation quality, with legislation adhering to democratic and scientific processes, and strictly complying with the statutory limits and procedures. Public participation, expert reasoning, risk evaluation, legality checking, collective discussion and decision-making are essential procedures for important policy-making. The open consultation system must be gradually installed in the important legislation-making process, taking solicited opinions, including those of experts, into account, improving legislative transparency and carrying out cost and benefit analyses and risk and feedback evaluations. Two principle stressed in the work plan are worth special mention: rule according to law needs to "uphold the Party's leadership, to translate the Party and government's effective policies and guidelines into laws"; rule according to law needs to "adhere to people-orientation," "maintain equality and justice," "protect people's basic cultural rights and fulfill people's cultural and spiritual needs."

In practice the administration according to law at SARFT and SAPPRFT focused primarily on three areas: the making of new legislation and public consultations, implementation of the *Administrative License Law*, and regulatory enforcement. Relying on lower rank department rules and normative documents in its past administration was considered as problematic and the regulator wanted to accelerate the law-making process on major projects to improve its legal regulatory power (SAPPRFT, 2015a). In 2003 SARFT began to draft two new laws (*falv*): the *Law on Protection of the Broadcasting and Film Program Transmission* and *the Film Promotion Law*. After many drafts and public consultation (*The Film Promotion Law* was open for public consultation in 2011), the proposed *Film Promotion Law* laws will be submitted to the NPC's standing committee for approval in 2016. On the other hand, between 2010 and 2016, SARFT and SAPPRFT drafted a total of 18 department rules for public consultations and promulgated four department rules. In the earlier period, the department rule-making was not open to public participations. For instance in 2007, SARFT and

70 *Legitimacy and broadcasting administration*

the Ministry of Information Industry of China jointly promulgated an Internet related department rule: *the Administrative Provisions on Internet Audio-Visual Program Service* (SARFT and MII, 2007). This regulation stipulates that Internet audio-visual program service providers must take measures to protect copyrights, and movies, television plays or documentaries that are distributed over the Internet must have been granted licenses by the SARFT. The legislation is instructed by and under the close leadership of the Party. The Party's Central Committee said that new media and information services, including network broadcasting, mobile visual programs and IPTV, are cultural and ideological services, and they requested that their operation have authority's approval and licenses. The SARFT started to draft the proposal in 2005 following the Party senior leaders' instruction and the release of the Party's 2004 document *Opinion Regarding Further Strengthening Internet Administration Work* (CCP, 2004). In 2006, the SARFT submitted the proposal to the Ministry of Central Propaganda for approval, the Ministry supervised the proposal's amendment and decided to upgrade the proposal from a normative document to a department rule, which would be jointly promulgated by the SARFT and the Ministry of Information Industry (Zhao, 2006).

In 2011, the public consultation system of SARFT/SAPPRFT's administration regulation and department rule has been set up at the national level. The consultation is operated through State Council Legislative Office's *Chinese Government Legislative Information Network – Public Consultation System*[4]. Since 2011, 18 SARPPFT's department rules (draft) and 4 related administrative regulations (draft) were published for public consultation via the system. The consultation period usually lasts for one month, public can submit their comments online and respond to the content of the bill point by point. For instance, the proposal of department rule *Administrative Provisions on Online Publishing Service* drafted jointly by SARPPFT and MIIT in 2016 was first published for public consultation in 2012, while other departments at the State Council and local broadcasting departments were also consulted. The SARPPFT received tens of thousands words' comments. The sources of comments came from a wide range of actors including government departments, Internet companies, oversea organizations, lawyers and individual citizens. The regulator claims that it "carefully organized and studied [those comments], strictly followed [...] the principle of promoting standardized management and orderly development, [...] and absorbed many of them" (Xinhuanet, 2016b). However, the regulator did not provide any details about such study, reasoning and deliberation processes. For normative document direct affecting citizen, legal person and organization's rights and duties, the *Work Plan 2010* demands that it has to go through stages of public consultation, judicial legality check, and collective approval by SAPPRFT's leaders. Without passing those procedures, normative document cannot be promulgated.

The *Administrative License Law* does not allow the establishment of administrative licenses in department rules or normative documents. The Law was adopted in 2003 and implemented in 2004 – it was intended to narrow the scope

Legitimacy and broadcasting administration 71

of activities for which a license or approval was required, and in the cases where a license was required, the law was in favor of self-regulation, and the imposition of fees for licenses or application documents was prohibited unless regulation expressly provided otherwise. The law aimed to curb the monetary incentive to impose a license, the tendency towards corruption, and reduce the unreasonable procedural delays and non-meritorious rejections of applications (Ross, 2004). To implement the law, the SARFT (2001) enacted *Provisional Provisions on Supervision of Administrative License Implementation* in 2004, together with *Provisions on Radio, TV and Film Legislative Procedures* and *Measures on Radio, Film and Television Administrative Reconsideration.* These three department rules standardized the SARFT's licensing activities and expressly regulated the establishment of administrative licenses, and its enforcement and grievance procedures (Zhao, 2004). Meanwhile, regulatory documents that went against or conflicted with a higher rank law were required to be revised or revoked (SARFT, 2010a). Since 2003, the SARFT has continuously cleared up its department rules and normative documents and amended 27 department rules relating to administrative licensing establishments. By 2005, seven administrative regulations, 42 department rules and a large number of normative documents were in effect, while SARFT revoked 172 normative documents and 18 department rules (Zhao, 2006). By 2010, effective legislations included nine administrative regulations, 39 department rules and 301 normative documents, while SARFT (2010b) further revoked 154 normative documents and three department rules. By 2014 SARFT or SARPPFT had revoked, devoted or amended 14 administrative licenses (Wei, 2014).

In addition, SAPPRFT was expected to act as a broadcasting lawmaker as well as to oversee the effective enforcement of regulations. Yan Xiaohong, the deputy head of the SAPPRFT, said that it has attempted to gradually change its regulatory mechanism from prior approval to ex-post regulation. He revealed:

> while there are less administrative licenses and prior approvals, there are heavier ex-post supervision responsibilities. In recent years, the number of administrative reconsideration cases received has increased year by year, which indicates the strengthening of the administrative counterpart's right consciousness, but also reflects that there are still problems at grassroots level law enforcement and administration. Therefore, strengthening enforcement supervision should be a main line of work for media and publication (copyright) legal institutions, especially at the grassroots level.

Administrative approval, administrative supervisory and enforcement supervisory authorities are expected to gradually separate. Law enforcement agencies and administrative departments must strictly implement the responsibility system for administrative law-enforcement and protect procedural justice. They must establish administrative discretion reference systems, refine and quantify administrative discretion, and refine law enforcement procedures to guarantee procedural fairness, and safeguard the legitimate rights and interests of administrative

72 *Legitimacy and broadcasting administration*

counterparts. Enforcement supervisory power is said to belong to legal institutions. Administrative supervisory power is said to belong to the NPC and its committees, the Chinese People's Political Consultative Conference, the People's Courts, public opinion supervision, intra-departmental supervision, and the National Audit Office and Ministry of Supervision.

Administration according to law and its limits

The administration according to law of broadcasting must be understood in the context of China's rule of law development. The state and the Party have appealed to the rule of law in order to rationalize its governance and legitimize its political power through legal-rational legitimation. The legitimacy of the Chinese state was based on a concrete promise (performance or ideology legitimacy) but not on a procedure (legal-rational) legitimacy, so if anything went wrong, the government had to take all of the blame for the faults arising from its policy. Thus, the whole Chinese communist regime and political system could subsequently lose its legitimacy. In a democratic country the media attack the government but not the system. The government can be changed through a democratic procedure but the legitimacy of the political system will not be questioned or challenged. In China, because of the lack of this procedural legitimacy, the communist regime's legitimacy can be seriously undermined or challenged if the media attack or criticize the wrongdoing of the government (Zhao, 2001). Thus, shifting from economic performance legitimacy to the rule of law may ease the pressure on the Party and government.

Theoretically, the rule of law is a contested concept, differences exist in the applicability of rule of law theory to contemporary China. The basic standards, or the thin version of the rule of law, include values such as imposing meaningful limits on state actors; that the law should actually guide people; that the law should be stable; that the law should be the supreme legal authority; that the law must be transparent; that laws must be prospective than retroactive; that the law must be fairly applied; and that laws must be generally applicable (Lubman, 1999; Peerenboom, 2001). The thin theory of the rule of law has a more limited understanding, emphasizing its formal or instrumental aspects – those features that any legal system allegedly must possess to function effectively as a system of laws, regardless of whether the legal system is part of a democratic or non-democratic society. The thick theory of the rule of law encompasses all elements of the thin theory and in addition means that the rule of law must be associated with capitalism, democratic government, and liberal concepts of human rights (Peerenboom, 2001).

A genuine CCP commitment to establish the rule of law would require clear separation between the relative roles of policy and law. Policy must be transformed into laws and regulations made by the law making authority to be legally binding, and Party organs and individual Party members must abide by the law (Lubman, 1999). Given that previous government authorities have invoked the phrase "rule of law" as an umbrella term for the expansion of their influence and

Legitimacy and broadcasting administration   73

extra-constitutional activities, genuine rule of law needs to use law and the Constitution to constrain the way in which the authorities rule over people as opposed to the use of the law as an instrument by the authorities to rule over citizens.

Administration according to law at the SARFT and SAPPRFT was primarily driven by a concern for legal legitimacy which was seen as "the most important, probably the last line of defense" for preventing institutional conflict and risk as broadcasting reform deepened. However, their legal-rational legitimation efforts were primarily at the procedural level of the rule of law: allow public consultation in ruling-making; enact new laws and higher ranked laws to replace the arbitrarily issued normative documents; strengthen the enforcement of laws; and check on the government's administrative power.

Despite the improved democratization of law making to enhance its credibility and legitimacy by including public and expert consultations in decision-making, the roles of the public and experts are still marginal and the fairness of procedure is still weak and the actual legislation process was under the close leadership of the Party because the predominant principle of administration according to law is to uphold the Party's leadership and to translate the Party and government's policies and guidelines into laws. The consultation process of *Administrative Provisions on Online Publishing Service* proposal shows that it neglected the reason-giving component: proposal did not provide any detailed explanation of the content of the department rule; the input of public did not get responses from the regulator; the consultation conclusion and deliberation details of decision were not published. Thus, although the public consultation was conducted, the regulatory decision-making is still not transparent and accountable to the public.

In a democratic society the governing legitimacy is already granted through democratic procedures, i.e., elections, therefore, government policy is legitimate by default and expected to be enforced by agencies through law. The governance of the Chinese Communist Party and Chinese government lacks electoral legitimacy, it chooses to rest its legitimacy claims on the thin theory of the rule of law: generality, stability, predictability, and restricted administrative power based on law and constitution – rules and laws that are binding on everyone. Thus, impersonal norms and a legal order give those in authority the right to rule, while downplaying the democratic and substantive aspects of the rule of law, such as rights and freedoms guaranteed by the Chinese Constitution. At present, the Party and the administrative department dominate the policy discourse and decision-making as the Party has not been willing to lose its control over the legislation process while role of the public and experts are marginalized. However, relying solely on legality cannot resolve the deep rooted problems of lack of due process and democratic decision-making. In recent years, SAPPRFT's regulation of media content has continually sparked debates (Coonan, 2015; Lin, 2015; SAPPRFT, 2015b, 2015c). Zhang (2008) argues that "such administrative measures do not comply with the development trend of administrative law, and they also inhibit the formation of pluralistic forces in

74 Legitimacy and broadcasting administration

television program regulation." Only the combination of pluralist forces together – government management, social supervision and self-discipline – can achieve the effective regulation of television programs (Zhang LP, 2008: 99).

Meanwhile, existing legal supervision, such as administrative litigations and administrative reconsideration, are still ineffective as remedies. For instance, in 2008, two Chinese lawyers filed an administrative action against the SARFT in the Beijing First Intermediate People's Court on the basis that the administrator failed in their duty by issuing a film screen license to the movie "Lust, Caution." The content had caused huge emotional damage to them, and they were seeking a court order to revoke the license and for compensation. The court refused to accept the case, citing that the reason for "the complaint [emotional damage] does not belong to the scope of administrative proceedings." A legal researcher affirmed the legality of the court's decision based on the existing provisions of China's *Administrative Litigation Law* while also arguing that many cases involving public interests were deemed beyond the narrow scope of case acceptance and thus dismissed by courts. Citizens who challenged administrative decisions had suffered many defeats (Shi, 2008). For instance, Article 12 of the *Administrative Litigation Law* stipulates that:

> the people's courts shall not accept actions initiated by citizens, legal persons or other organizations concerning any of the following matters: [...] (2). administrative rules and regulations, or decisions and orders with general binding force formulated and promulgated by administrative organs.
> (*Administrative Litigation Law*, 1989)

To seek remedies for rights infringed by administrative rules and regulations, parties have to appeal to the *Administrative Reconsideration Law* that is enforced by the relevant higher ranked administrative department. In SAPPRFT's case, the appeal against its administrative rules, regulations and normative documents will first be reconsidered by SAPPRFT itself. Only when refusing to accept a decision made through administrative reconsideration, may the applicant bring an administrative lawsuit before a People's Court, or apply to the State Council for arbitration (NPC, 1999). Given that the SAPPRFT exercises its administrative power mostly through department rules or normative documents, remedies can only be sought through administrative reconsideration. In other words, it is a de facto self-disciplinary system, and it is neither effective nor justifiable. As the Chinese legal scholar Wang Xixin (王锡锌) suggests restrictions of administrative power cannot be expected to rely on self-discipline given the unbalanced distribution of power between the regulator and regulated, or that media organizations are not in a position to confront the SARFT or SAPPRFT (Yang ZY, 2008). The establishment of an effective institutional mechanism to restrict the administrator's power is a must. Institutional reform is the precondition for successful administration according to law. Without effective external checks, departmental interests could drive the administrative agent to use its law-making power to satisfy its own end, and the law also risks becoming a tool for

Legitimacy and broadcasting administration 75

controlling people thus validating the spirit of the rule of law. For instance without going through any legal procedures, in 2008 the SARFT issued a document to ban all Chinese television, film and advertisements featuring the Chinese actress Tang Wei following her appearance in the 2007 espionage erotic thriller film "Lust, Caution" in order to reduce Tang's bad influence over the young generation, i.e., to gain fame through erotic performance (Yang ZY, 2008). One way to improve China's administrative supervision system would be to relax the scope of case acceptance under the *Administrative Litigation Law*. Besides, civil right empowerment – to empower the public's rights of expression, information, participation and supervision – is more important in establishing effective and fair constraint on administrative power than simply relaxing the scope of case acceptance under the *Administrative Litigation Law* (Yang ZY, 2008).

It has been suggested that the rule of law in China is adopted to justify the Party's policy through procedural legitimacy. To focus on the procedural aspects of a thin rule of law could avoid the dilemma of applying the thick concept of the rule of law, which requires a complete moral and political philosophy that is always subject to dispute and contest. The thick concept of the rule of law is part of a broader social and political philosophy therefore it decreases the likelihood that a consensus on its meaning will emerge (Peerenboom, 2001: 12). However, the advantages of a thin concept of the rule of law are that some degree of predictability, some limitation on arbitrariness and some protection of individual rights and freedoms are likely. Also, historically China favored substantive justice over procedural justice, it has been to favor particular justice at the expense of generality and rationality (Peerenboom, 2001: 10). Therefore, stressing the more procedural aspects of a thin rule of law is an important step forward for China's rule of law.

It is expected that the Party will continue to control the ideological sphere and it will also continue to oversee and coordinate reforms and determine the overall direction for China. It will propose constitutional amendments and review major legislation by the NPC, and ensure that the Party's major policy decisions are enacted as laws and regulations (Peerenboom, 2001: 10). In the absence of democracy and marginalization of public participation in the law-making process, the ruling power can enact illiberal laws that restrict individual rights. Thus, the rule of law requires "good laws" that should at least entail justice, peace, order and freedom (Dong, 1998). For administration according to the law, the core values must include: government abiding by the law, the law being just and good, and the law being universally adhered to and recognized in society (Yang ZY, 2008).

The fate of press law in China: good law or bad law?

To restrict state and official power and improve governance, there need to be laws to protect the mass media so that the Chinese mass media can investigate corruption without government intervention and build channels to communicate with the public about important policies.

76 *Legitimacy and broadcasting administration*

Chinese Constitutions have attached importance to the protection of citizens' freedom of expression (Constitution of the PRC, 1954, 1975, 1978; Lin, 1990; Reed, 2000). The 1982 Constitution specifies, in Article 35, that citizens enjoy the rights to the freedoms of "speech" and of "publication/the press" (Constitution of the PRC, 1982).[5] In accordance with the principle that a lower law shall not contravene a higher law, freedom of expression recognized and established by the Constitution should become the basis for the enactment of laws, administrative rules and departmental regulations and the basis for legislation and law enforcement by the PRC's government, at all levels, but especially by administrative bodies that deal with the media (Law on Legislation, 2000). However, the Constitution, despite its supremacy in the legal hierarchy, has no actual value in judicial practice and remains a framework document. There is no constitutional court in the PRC and the judicial courts have no right to interpret the Constitution. The constitutional right of freedom of expression is not protected in specific civil or criminal laws, and Chinese courts do not accept litigation on the grounds of infringement of the right to free speech as such litigation falls outside their jurisdiction. The power to interpret the Chinese Constitution rests upon the Standing Committee of the National People's Congress (*Law on Legislation*, 2000), so the courts do not have the power to strike down any legislation because of its unconstitutionality. Neither does any law expressly define who has the authority to conduct constitutional reviews of primary laws passed by the National People's Congress and its Standing Committee (Shen, 2003). In judicial practice, the constitutional law is rarely invoked as a direct source for adjudication. These factors combine to relegate the fundamental right of freedom of expression provided by the Constitution into a position without a remedy (Tong, 2001; Zhang, 2010).

Against this background, in 2015, it was announced at the Twelfth NPC in Beijing that the NPC was to consider introducing the country's first press law. Liu Binjie (柳斌杰), the Director of the NPC's Committee of Education, Science, Culture and Health and former Head of the press watchdog formerly known as the General Administration of Press and Publication (GAPP), suggests that the law would regulate all media outlets, including online news services (Coonan, 2015), and it could help end unbalanced development and regulations between relatively more independent new media outlets and strictly regulated traditional media outlets.

The making of press law in China first appeared on the political agenda in the early 1980s. After the Cultural Revolution intellectuals and journalists realized the importance of having a press law to protect citizen's freedom of expression and their right to publish, which was enshrined in China's Constitution. In the early 1980s, members of the NPC continually urged for the legislation of a press law. In 1984, the proposal of introducing a press law to protect the media's freedom was addressed by the NPC, and the Press Law Research Office, which included members of both the NPC's committee of education, science, culture and health and the journalism research institute of the Chinese Academy of Social Science, was set up to draft the law. In 1987, GAPP replaced the Press

Law Research Office to draft the press law. Three draft press laws were released: the *Press Law of the PRC* introduced by the Press Law Research Office; Shanghai's Several Regulations on Media Work introduced by the Shanghai Press Law Drafting Group; and the *Press Law of the PRC* drafted by the GAPP. The GAPP submitted the *Press Law of the PRC* to the State Council for review. After 1989, press law making was suspended because of conflicts and disagreements between the Press Law Research Office and CCP's senior leader, secretary of the CCP's secretariat, Hu Qiaomu (胡乔木). Their main disagreements were:

1 The Press Law Research Office (the Office) aimed for the law to protect media freedom; the CCP aimed to use the law to enhance the Party's leadership over the media.
2 For the Office, the law is binding to all citizens. For the CCP, it should stress the self-discipline of the journalists and media workers, and strengthen the Party's leadership.
3 The Office was against media censorship, the CCP insisted that any important media coverage needed to be subject to prior censorship by CCP's party committee.
4 The Office emphasized supervision by public opinion; the CCP emphasized supervising public opinion (Shen, 2013).

In 2002, Liu Binjie (柳斌杰) still denied the possibility of a press law (Shen, 2015). The announcement of press law legislation in 2015 was endorsed by some leading media scholars, like Zhan Jiang and Sun Xupei, who believe the press law cannot be a bad law (Wan, Ding and Nan, 2015). Others, like Wen Yongzheng (2015), challenge the necessity of a press law, worrying that it may further restrict the freedom of the new media. Legal scholars, Li Danling (2015) and Peng Guibing (2015), urged that the new press law must operationalize Articles 35 and 41 of the Chinese Constitution to protect the media and the public's freedom and rights.

Summary

The state and the Party appeal to the rule of law in order to rationalize and legitimize its broadcasting media regulation. The administration according to law in the broadcasting sector focused primarily on three procedural aspects of thin version rule of law: new legislation-making and public consultation, implementation of the *Administrative License Law* to restrict regulator's licensing power, and improving regulatory enforcement. By doing so, the regulator, SAPPRFT, wanted to change the past administration mode which heavily relied on few department rules and a large number of ambiguous and arbitrarily issued normative documents to a more formal and authoritative regulatory mode featured by stability, predictability, higher level legal authority.

Genuine rule of law needs to use law and the Constitution to constrain the way in which the authorities rule over people as opposed to the use of the law as

78 *Legitimacy and broadcasting administration*

an instrument by the authorities to rule over citizens. Despite the limited installation of procedural legality in the administration according to law of broadcasting regulation, at present, the Party and the administrative department dominate the policy discourse and decision-making while role of the public and experts are marginalized. However, relying solely on procedural legality cannot resolve the deep rooted problems of lacking both democratic process and substantive and rights-oriented values in regulatory decision-making. In other words, such excise of regulatory power by the state's administrative agency, i.e., SAPPRFT is not justifiable.

Under such circumstances, whether a standalone press law promulgated by the country's highest legislative body – the National People's Congress – should be made, is a controversy topic. In the absence of democracy, it is a concern that such a press law may be illiberal and further restrict the freedom of the new media. However, the introduction of China's press law may also provide an opportunity to operationalize Article 35 and 41 of the Chinese Constitution and to protect both the media and the public's freedom of rights.

Notes

1 It was renamed the State Administration of Radio, Film and Television (SARFT) in 1998.
2 There are exceptions, such as educational terrestrial TV stations, operated by the State Council's Ministry of Education. Many cable TV stations are also operated by state-owned enterprises or other government units.
3 Personal interview with a senior official at the SARFT's Department of Law and Regulation in Beijing on 18 September, 2003.
4 http://zqyj.chinalaw.gov.cn/index
5 This chapter uses the term "freedom of expression" as an umbrella term to encompass both of these rights. Also, by the term's adoption, this chapter uses the same standard to discuss the various rights and freedoms recognized and protected by Article 35 of the Constitution.

5 China's television in the 1990s

This chapter summarizes the structure and characteristics of China's television industry in the mid-1990s and shows the correlation between the configuration of the Chinese television system and China's economic-political structure. It serves as the reference base for understanding the transformation of Chinese television after 1996.

China's television by 1996: a four-tier interlocking structure

Ever since its birth, China's television industry has been structured as an integrated part of the State's political system. All television stations are owned by the State and controlled by the Party. Their regulatory system mirrors the State's political structure (Pan and Chan, 2000; Wei, 2000). In 1983, the Central Committee of the Chinese Communist Party (CCP) divided the country's TV network into four tiers: national; provincial, municipal or autonomous region; city and county. Each has its own TV station to serve audiences within its administrative boundary. At the center is the national broadcaster, the Central Government's China Central Television (CCTV) (Guo, 2003; Pan and Chan, 2000). Two interlocking systems: the ideological system of the Party's propaganda department and the administrative system of the government bureau of Radio, Film and Television constitute the regulatory structure.

The Party's propaganda department at each level exercises ideological control over the corresponding TV station, while the broadcasting bureau controls the station's personal, finance, acquisition and technological expansion. Both systems work from the top down to the bottom. At the top are the central authorities – the State Council's State Administration of Radio, Film and Television (SARFT) and the CCP's Ministry of Central Propaganda. They are the sources of all power and make all of the important decisions and policies. All of the province, municipality and autonomous regions' broadcasting bureau are subjected to SARFT's control while they also have power over their lower level bureaus (Ai and Liu in Qian, 2002; Pan and Chan, 2000). This centralized top-down TV system empowers the center's conspicuous control over the local while the local has little influence on the center (Hong in Yan, 2000).

80   *China's television in the 1990s*

The features of China's television from the 1980s to mid-1990s

China's television history began with the establishment of the Beijing Television Station on 1 May 1958.[1] Rather than pursuing economic returns, from the very beginning, television in China was considered to be a tool for glorifying socialist ideals, promoting government policy and helping to create "socialist moral standards based on Marxism, Leninism and Maoism" (Wei, 2000: 330). In 1996, these political and ideological needs were at the heart of China's television service.

By 1996, China had about 300 million TV sets, 943 free-to-air territorial television stations with 1,005 channels and 1,285 state approved cable TV stations with 200 million subscribers or 50 million households. Television coverage reached 86.2 percent of the total population (*China Radio and Television Yearbook*, 1997). On average, Chinese households could receive eight TV channels. In some large cities the number of channels available for a typical household was more than 20 (Pan and Chan, 2000). Television also became the most popular leisure activity for Chinese people, who spent 2.2 hours per day watching TV (Luo *et al.*, in Pan and Chan, 2000).

Table 5.1 TV broadcasting in China (1981–1996)

Year	TV station	TV set (10,000)	TV set/100 households	Population coverage (%)	Audience (million)
1981	42	1,562	1.6	49.5	270
1982	47	2,761	2.7	57.3	340
1983	52	3,611	3.5	59.9	400
1984	93	4,763	4.6	64.7	470
1985	202	6,965	6.6	68.4	540
1986	292	9,214	8.7	71.4	580
1987	366	11,601	10.7	73.0	590
1988	422	14,344	13.2	75.4	760
1989	469	16,593	14.7	78.0	826
1990	509	18,546	16.2	79.4	866
1991	543	20,671	17.8	80.5	908
1992	586	22,843	19.5	71.3	942
1993	684	22,563	21.0	82.3	975
1994	766	27,487	23.0	83.4	999
1995	837	28,600	24.0	84.5	1,023
1996	943	29,000	n/a	86.2	1,055

Sources: 1. Education, Science, Culture: Basic Statistics on Broadcasting and Television Stations. In: China Statistical Yearbook (中国统计年鉴) 1981–1997. Compiled by National Bureau of Statistics of China. Published by China Statistics Press; 2. China Radio & TV Yearbook (中国广播电视年鉴) 1994–1998. Published by China Radio and TV Press; 3. China Central Television Yearbook (中国中央电视台年鉴) 1995 and 1998. Published by China Radio and TV Press.

Marketization of China's television

The term "marketization" is used to describe the trend in China's socio-economic transformation during the 1980s and 1990s. In the media sector it refers to the transition from the state-planned economy to the embracing of market forces in allocating the material resources of mass communication. "Marketisation has reduced the institutional dependency of the media on the state, mainly through the commercialisation of the media's interests, behaviours and finally, their structural change" (Wu, 2000: 57).

The marketization of China's television started with the re-emergence of television advertising in the late 1970s. Previously, under the state-owned and centrally planned economic model, television stations in China were totally funded by the government. In 1979, however, the government started to request that the television industry balanced its budget and reduced its financial dependence on the government. Shanghai Television broadcast the first television advertisement in March 1979.

In 1992, amid the transformation from a planned economy to a "socialist market economy with Chinese characteristics", the Party and State Council legitimized the role of advertising in the media. The cultural institution was defined as part of the "third industry of services" and TV stations could operate within a market environment, seeking funding from the market and being responsible for their financial self-sufficiency (Huang and Green, 2000).

Table 5.2 Growth of advertising revenue in China (1981–1996)

Year	TV Advertising (RMB million[2])	Total Advertising (RMB million)
1981	n/a	118
1982	10	150
1983	16.2	234
1984	34.0	365
1985	68.7	605
1986	115.1	844
1987	169.3	1,112
1988	271.8	1,492
1989	392	1,999
1990	561	2,501
1991	1,001	3,509
1992	2,055	6,786
1993	2,944	13,408
1994	4,480	20,026
1995	6,600	27,327
1996	9,079	36,600

Sources: 1. China Statistical Yearbook (中国统计年鉴) 1981–1997. Compiled by National Bureau of Statistics of China. Published by China Statistics Press; 2. China Radio and TV Yearbook (中国广播电视年鉴) 1994–1998. Published by China Radio and TV Press.

Note
The exchange rate is about US$1= RMB 8.

82 *China's television in the 1990s*

As government funding declined to a very low level or even stopped in many cities, television stations were increasingly dependent on advertising as an essential financial resource.

The introduction of a market-oriented mechanism and advertising funded system led to the commercialization of television, subsequently creating a dual-identity for television stations. On the one hand, they must serve the Party's political goals and on the other, they needed to satisfy audiences' tastes to attract advertisers. This co-existence of the Party's political discipline with the TV stations' pursuit of entrepreneurial practices has continually caused conflicts between the State and television (Huang and Green, 2000; Pan and Chan, 2000; Wei, 2000; Wu, 2000).

The commercialization of television weakened the Party's ideological control, increased the television stations' operational autonomies and bargaining power with the Party-State and stimulated competition (Ma, 2000). However, contrary to the romantic view of market forces driving the democratization of the media, television commercialization is more a process articulating power, money and the media. Since in China's media scene, "neither the state nor the market is external to each other" (Ma, 2000: 27), but market forces are absorbed by the State. In other words, the State is both a player in the market and the regulator of the market. For instance, a television station manager is simultaneously playing the roles of party member, journalist and entrepreneur, thus, the government can exercise control over the station both by political power and the rule of the market.

More importantly, despite China's TV stations being granted more autonomy in their daily operations and management due to commercial pressure in the 1990s, the Party still adhered to the policy that the media were ideological apparatuses and maintained tight political control. In the Party's words, the four major responsibilities of the media were: "to arm Chinese people with scientific theories; to guide Chinese people with correct public opinion; to develop Chinese people with noble spirit; and to encourage Chinese people with outstanding product." The core values of media propaganda were "unity," "stability," "encouragement" and "positive publicity" (Li, 1995a: 252). The extended media space was restricted to apolitical and entertainment content (Ma, 2000). In other words, "[the] mission of TV service is more or less the same as a party mouthpiece and a government propaganda institution dancing to the tune of the party line" (Wei, 2000: 335).

Decentralized television sector and chaotic television market

The 1983 decentralization of China's television system into four tiers led to the structural diversity of the sector. This happened alongside the redistribution of economic power from the center to the different local stations and television was localized and used to promote local interests (Wu, 2000). This change made the center's monitoring of local stations difficult, and political supervision was particularly loose at the municipal and county levels.

In addition, the rapid growth of local territorial and cable TV stations has threatened the domination of CCTV (Huang and Green, 2000; Zhao, 1998a). As the only national television broadcaster, not only are CCTV's programs, particularly the evening newscast, a "must-carry" for local stations, but also the central authority – SARFT and its predecessor, the Ministry of Radio, Film and Television (MRFT) – help to secure CCTV's national monopoly by repressing the attempts of provincial TV stations to expand beyond their administrative boundaries with the aim of becoming regional TV broadcasters. This is understood as the underlying reason for the small increase in new TV stations at the provincial or national level (Wei, 2000) (see Table 5.3). Despite this policy protection, replacing CCTV's channels with local or imported programs was common practice among municipal and county stations, driven by local interests (Zhao, 1998a).

Moreover, the growth of unregulated cable TV outlets, which attempted to make a quick fortune in the advertising market, also caused disorder in the television market in China (Huang and Green, 2000; Zhao, 1998a). Cable television first emerged in large state-owned enterprises (*danwei*) between the 1960s and 1970s as alternative entertainment for their employees (Wu in Wei, 2000). Unlike territorial television, cable television was entirely self-financed; it was not attached to the government's administrative structure, was operated on market-oriented principles and driven by market forces. Consequently, it was more flexible in catering for the audiences' tastes, especially in their demands for entertainment programs (Wei, 2000). By 1996, the total number of cable television networks reached 1,285 with 51 million cable households, sharing 22.6 percent of the total audience market. However, because of the scarcity of self-made productions, many local cable networks filled their channels with foreign

Table 5.3 Growth of Chinese television stations (1983–1996)

Year	Total	National	Provincial	Municipal	Counties
1983	52	1	29	n/a	n/a
1984	93	1	29	n/a	n/a
1985	202	1	29	112	60
1986	292	1	29	147	115
1987	366	1	29	181	135
1988	422	1	31	207	183
1989	469	1	31	231	206
1990	509	1	31	250	227
1991	543	1	32	265	245
1992	586	1	32	275	278
1993	684	1	35	288	360
1994	766	1	34	289	442
1995	837	1	35	308	493
1996	880	1	32	n/a	n/a

Source: 1. China Radio and TV Yearbook (中国广播电视年鉴) 1986–1996. Published by China Radio and TV Press.

84 *China's television in the 1990s*

programs, particularly those from Hong Kong and Taiwan,[2] which are considered by the Chinese government as "ideological instruments of a 'peaceful evolution' to capitalism" (Huang in Zhao, 1998a: 169).

Where national meets transnational: trans-border satellite flows in China

In the early 1990s, given the restrictions applied to foreign investment and ownership in the media, foreign media companies usually accessed China's television market in three ways: program sales, satellite broadcasting and co-production with domestic television stations and production houses (Weber, 2003; Zhao, 1998a). Among these, the advent of trans-border satellite broadcasting was a key dynamic in propelling the transformation of television in China.

The 1993 State Statistic Bureau's figure showed that about 11 million[3] Chinese households owning up to a million satellite dishes could access trans-border satellite television. Meanwhile, more than 100 foreign satellite TV channels, including entertainment and news channels, like the Japanese cable channel (NHK2), the US Cable News Network (CNN) and the British Broadcasting Corporation (BBC), spilled over into China, and most were unencrypted and could be easily accessed by individuals with the proper equipment (Cao *et al.*, 1997).

China's satellite broadcasting started in the mid-1980s and was initially used to improve the quality and coverage of television signals in the country's rural and mountainous areas. By 1994, China had 73,000 satellite receiving stations and provided 20 domestic satellite TV channels received by audiences either through the direct-to-home (DTH) platform or via a cable-operator. However, contrary to the government's initial motivation, most satellite dishes were owned by individuals who lived in urban cities and towns and wished to use these dishes to receive trans-border satellite television channels because their programs were more entertaining. The central authorities in Beijing regarded trans-border satellite broadcasting as an invasion and accused their news programs of distorting China and attacking China's domestic and foreign policies. This undermined the Chinese State's communication sovereignty and eroded its national culture and therefore it was considered that the State should resist on the grounds of protecting the nation and the dignity and purity of Chinese national culture (Yan, 1998; Zhao, 1998a).

State's regulation and local's commercial concern

As early as 1990, the MRFT restricted access to foreign satellite channels to particular institutions, hotels and apartments with special permission from the government. In 1991, it prohibited cable operators from transmitting trans-border satellite channels. Two years later, the State Council (1993) further banned unauthorized production, sales, installation and use of satellite dishes.

Despite the State's ban, local cable operators and individuals still illegally transmitted and received foreign satellite TV. Besides the empirical dilemmas, such as the massive administrative task and practical difficulty of removing illegally installed satellite dishes, the ineffectiveness of the regulation was believed to be precisely due to the conflicts between the central and local authorities regarding their separate interests and concerns on this issue (Cao *et al.*, 1997).

In contrast to the Central Government's official tone, the local authorities were rather reluctant to operate the restriction and ban. They tended to protect the commercial interests of local cable operators and satellite equipment manufactures because the former relied on transmitting foreign satellite programs to increase subscription and advertising revenues, while the latter made a large amount of profit by producing and selling satellite dishes and decoders. This reluctance was particularly pronounced in the coastal regions (Cao *et al.*, 1997). Local government continued to push Central Government to lift the total ban on foreign satellite programs (Yan, 1998) and they challenged the ban by claiming that, "watching foreign satellite television programmes can increase [citizens'] abilities to resist [foreign cultural erosion]" (Cao *et al.*, 1997: 140).

It is therefore suggested that the Chinese state faces challenges from both inside and outside, and international and local interests are linked through "technological configuration: foreign satellite television broadcasting/local cable network transmission combination" (Zhao, 1998a: 174).

Despite the seeming setback of Central Government, it did not let the foreign and local stations feel triumphant in the tug-of-war. Rather, the center took a further hardline position.

From 1995, the center ordered all decoders of foreign encrypted satellite television to be centrally imported through the China International Television Corporation (CITVC), a subsidiary of China Central Television (CCTV) and distributed through organizations authorized by provincial broadcasting bureau (MRFT, 1995). More profoundly, the state started to think of using the cable network to manage and filter satellite channels. Since 1993, the central authority had planned to integrate local cable television networks into a single system so that it could better exert control over programs and filter out any unwanted foreign content. A Deputy Minister at the MRFT revealed that "in future, [we] can consider following overseas practices to centrally monitor the cable television network to classify and retransmit satellite TV programmes according to different circumstances" (Wang, 1993:8).

In 1996, for the first time, Central government permitted foreign satellite channels to be carried on China's cable television system. Although the landing right is restricted within Guangdong province, it has been widely interpreted as a symbolic movement towards the foreseeable deregulation of the television market for foreign engagement.

Summary

This chapter has reviewed the structure, regulatory regime and major features of China's television sector in the 1980s and mid-1990s. It has found the beginnings of a substantial restructuring of China's television since 1997.

86 *China's television in the 1990s*

First, until 1996, all television stations in China were state-owned and party-controlled. A top-down four-tier interlocking industrial and administrative structure was developed to empower the center's authority over local television media. Second, the most prominent features of China's television from the 1980s until the mid-1990s were marketization, decentralization and the advent of trans-border satellite broadcasting. Marketization led to the commercialization of television stations and reduced their institutional dependency on the State; the co-existence of the Party's political demands on television stations and the television stations' pursuit of entrepreneurial practices have continually caused conflict between the State and television. The decentralization of the television structure made the center's monitoring of the local stations difficult and the rapid growth of local territorial and cable television stations, partially due to structural diversification, has threatened the position of CCTV as the sole national television broadcaster.

The advent of more than 100 foreign satellite television channels also caused controversies between the central authorities and local TV stations in China because of their different concerns and interests. The central authorities regarded these satellite channels as invasive and accused them of undermining China's communication sovereignty and eroding China's national culture. Reception of these channels was restricted and the installation of satellite dishes banned. Local authorities prioritized their local commercial interests over the nation-state's political concern, and, as a result, had a rather reluctant attitude towards the ban and restriction. This tendency may indicate the convergence of international and local power in challenging the Chinese nation-state.

Notes

1 It was renamed China Central Television Station (CCTV) in 1978.
2 Despite Hong Kong and Macao having been politically a part of China since 1997 and 1999 respectively, as a result of the "one country, two system" policy, both Special Administrative Regions have their own economic, political and media systems that are significantly different from Mainland China. The Central Government in Beijing also adopts special economic, political and media policies towards the two regions and refers to their media, as well as those of Taiwan, as outside-border media. For the convenience of discussion, here, I refer to all media based outside Mainland China as foreign media.
3 For the direct-to-home (DTH) platform, each household did not install a satellite dish. Instead, the satellite signal was collected by a satellite dish installed in the compound of a unit or a building, then distributed via a master access television system (SMTV) to each individual household (Yan, 1998).

6 China's television policy between 1996 and 2003

> The core [of the observed situation] is that China's media has been seeking to "marketize" itself as much as possible within an allowed space.
> (A senior manager at the China International Television Corporation)[1]

Introduction

This chapter studies the four-phase development of China's national television policies and industrial structure between 1996 and 2003, and spells out the initial implications observed in the process of the changes in relation to domestic political and economic interest groups, and external factors including the General Agreement on Trade Services negotiations, China's World Trade Organization accession and the international ideological conflicts. The restructuring carried out since 1996 is particularly crucial for Chinese television as, not only does it involve an institutional, structural and regulatory transformation, but it also signifies an ideological shift from a hardline position towards the global media to a more flexible attitude from the Chinese state. During this period, the Chinese television sector was transformed from a planned economic system with sole state-ownership, to a quasi-market system co-existing with public service and commercial broadcasters. Significant industrial reforms included the recentralization of the television network, the concentration of media resources, and digitalization. A "reaching out" project was launched to assist the international expansion of China's television channels in order to increase the political influences of the Chinese state in international society through the power of the media. The initial implications of the restructuring upon China's television industry are the prominence of the economic function of the broadcasters and the increase in cross-regional competition. The development of China's national television policies and industry structure are conditioned by, as well as reflecting, the transformation of the country's internal and external socio-economic-political order.

The Party-State's television policy since 1996

Christopher Ham and Michael Hill point out that it is difficult to clearly and specifically define the concept of policy because there is little agreement on what

88 Television policy between 1996 and 2003

policy generally is. In this book, WI Jenkins' definition is followed. It conceptualizes policy as "a set of interrelated decisions [...] concerning the selection of goals and the means of achieving them within a specified situation [...]" (Jenkins in Ham and Hill, 1993: 11). Besides this, because of the characteristics of China's regulatory regime and policy-making process, China's television policies also include decisions and orientations revealed in speeches and written comments made by senior government and Party figures.

Between May 1994 and February 1995, following CCP's instruction, the State Council's Ministry of Radio, Film and Television (MRFT) produced a comprehensive analysis, i.e., the *Report to Further Strengthen and Improve Radio, Film and TV Work*, on China's broadcasting, designing the "guiding notions, objectives, tasks, strategies and important areas" of China's television development in the next five years. In this report, MRFT brought forward 30 opinions that were "accepted in principle" by the CCP in February 1995. The report suggests that the guiding notion is to follow Deng Xiaoping's theory on "socialism with Chinese characteristics"; its four major objectives are to retain correct opinion guidance, improve program quality, enhance the government's administration and to propel the television industry's technological development.

The speech of Li Tieying, a member of CCP's Central Committee, at a national broadcasting and film working conference in 1995, reveals important motives in the Party's policy-making.

Economically, from 1996, China entered the *Ninth Five-Year Development Plan*, starting to build up a market economic system. The Party anticipated that social tension would increase due to the advent of new social problems caused by inflation and reforms in social protection and housing systems. While the media in China have traditionally been used by the state and Party to exercise political and ideological influence over the public, to unite the nation, to maintain social order and to present a favored image to the world, "to lead people with correct public opinion became especially important" when social unrest is anticipated. Therefore, for the state and party, to provide a "good opinion environment for reform, development and stability" and "let the whole party and entire people of the country recognize the socialist market economic system and understand its basic elements" were the "top priority" for China's TV broadcaster. The Party believed that the deeper the reform became, the stronger publicity is required (Li, 1995a: 254 and 259).

Second, it aimed to improve the quality of China's radio and TV programs and double their volume by the end of the twentieth century. Media products were requested to "promote the main melody and advocate diversity" which, it is said, are the concrete representation of the "serving the people, serving socialism and allowing a hundred flowers to bloom, a hundred schools of thought to contend" (Li, 1995a: 255). The main social melody, according to China's then President, Jiang Zemin, was "patriotism, socialism and collectivism." In the cultural sphere, the main melody was to "reflect the spirits of the era and nation, unite people's hearts, encourage progress and propel social development and advancement." Diversity meant that "under correct ideological guidance," the topics and presentation of cultural and art products could be "richer," more "colorful" and "creative" (Li, 1995a: 255) so that they could attract more ordinary people and increase their economic and social effects.

Third, MRFT's roles, as both the government's broadcasting regulatory institution and its news and publicity institution, were reinforced in the report. As the regulator, MRFT was instructed to focus on macro management; as a news institution, it must be responsible for daily publicity control. Li Tieying emphasized that to strengthen MRFT's administration over broadcasting via macro-control and the rule of law was "a long term important job" for the broadcasting regulator (Li, 1995a: 257).

Finally, regarding industrial development, modernization via technological advancement, for example, digitalization and multi-media technologies, was perceived as the dominant need. It is believed that "science and technology are the foundation for the survival and development of broadcasting", so, China must "gradually reduce the technological gap with developed and newly industrialised countries" and "achieve the advancement through technology" (Sun,[2] 1995: 277).

Nevertheless, the report did pinpoint a significant conflict emerging alongside "the establishment of the socialist market economy system and the expansion of broadcasting's functions [...]." In Sun Jazheng (1995: 273–274), the then Minister of MRFT's words: "how to correctly manage the relations between television and radio's multi-functions and their publicity main function, and how to effectively deploy macro-control, while avoiding and defeating the commercialization of spiritual products" is a critical question for MRFT and the Party.

The principle strategy of the country's foreign media policy was to maintain China's opening up while also effectively resisting the erosion of a decayed ideology and culture (Sun, 1995). To increase the mutual understanding between China and the world was perceived as a pressing demand in light of the Party-State's commitment to continuous reform and liberalization. In order to let China understand the world, the Party encouraged domestic television stations to import "beautiful, good, progressive, civilised and scientific" cultural products (Li, 1995b: 262). However, the Party warned that:

> to expect the West to realistically promote China's excellent traditional culture to the world is difficult, [to expect the West] to introduce the new conditions of [China's] reform and liberalisation and new environment is more difficult. Therefore, China ought to push forward this work through our own efforts. CCTV and local TV stations must clearly know what to introduce to the world and what to let the world understand.
>
> (Li, 1995b: 263)

1996–1997: the traditional phase of the national television policy

In the mid-1990s, inspired by the country's press and radio reform,[3] the concept of *Chan Ye Hua* (*commercialization*, 产业化) was proposed by Huang Shengmin, an often quoted Chinese media expert, as the "guiding theoretical principle

90 *Television policy between 1996 and 2003*

for broader and more advanced media development" (Guo, 2004). Huang and Ding (1997) define the media's *Chan Ye Hua (commercialization)* as a process that transforms the ideological media into the businesslike media that undermines the traditional control of the ruling powers and promotes the media's nature as an economic interest seeking organization. In his words:

> first, the media are directed by economic interest; secondly, the political administration of the media is weakened to allow them to emerge as relatively independent businesses; and their *"shi ye xing zhi"* (nature of non-business, not-for-profit institution, 事业性质) is (also) weakened.
>
> (Huang and Ding, 1997 in Guo, 2004: 9)

His conceptualization of the media's nature expresses the desire of media elites, who occupy senior positions in media organizations, to change the main goal of the media from ideological work to the pursuit of economic self-interests, and from a non-economic driven operation to an economy driven one. It also expresses the demands of some media elites and intellectuals for further political autonomy as well as their ambitions to accumulate wealth for themselves (Guo, 2004).

Not surprisingly, this urge for political autonomy and commercial operation caused controversy in the field. Just before the publication of Huang's book, the MRFT (1996) submitted a report *Several Important Problems and Opinions about Our Country's Present Broadcasting Development*[4] to the CCP's CC and the State Council.

In the report the MRFT was explicitly against the notion of *Chan Ye Hua* and the financial independence of television stations. It argued that in China most television and radio stations actually had insufficient funding. Second, advertising revenue is supposed to be used to fill the gap between government funding and the media's operational costs, but not for the purpose of making profits. Third, the MRFT emphasized that "TV and radio stations are the Party and government's publicity apparatus and a public opinion battlefield, [they] are public interest serving institutions and must be completely held in the hands of the Party and government [...]". This sector must be monopolized and cannot be deregulated. Elsewhere, the report warned that:

> if pushing the electronic media into the market and society, on the one side, in order to survive, it will inevitably push TV and Radio stations to pursue economic interest to the utmost, violating their nature as the Party and government's "mouthpiece" and diverting them away from correct public opinion guidance, either by will or by nature. On the other side, [it] must lead to the participation of the entire society [in the sector], [...] and the inevitable emergence of foreign ownership, joint ownership, collective ownership and private ownership of stations and the changing nature of radio and television.
>
> (MRFT, 1996: 23–24 in *Guidebook for Decision Making*)

In addition, it is argued that television and radio stations in economically under-developed regions are the most vulnerable to commercial competition and will be harmed most severely. The MRFT thus suggested maintaining the government's role as the major funding channel for electronic media, and encouraging the media to improve program quality to increase advertising income and provide special support to remote and underdeveloped regions.

On 11 August 1997, the State Council promulgated the first broadcasting administrative regulation the *Regulations Governing the Administration of Radio and Television* following the appeal to "rule the country by law, and building a socialist country under the rule of law" made in the CCP's Fifteenth Party National Congress in 1997 (Wang and Fu, 2002: 2). It legitimates the role of TV and radio broadcaster as being "to serve the people, to serve socialism and insist on correct public opinion guidance" (State Council Decree No. 228, 1997). The regulation did not define the concrete criteria "to serve the people and serve socialism." At a later news conference, officials of the MRFT elaborated that it was essential for the mass media to "meet the spiritual and cultural needs of ordinary people" and to "enhance socialist material and spiritual civilization" (MRFT, 1997: 6–7). Despite this explanation, it is still obscure. For instance, what are the qualities of ordinary people's spiritual and cultural needs? Which institution or organization can decide on these qualities, and through what channel?

The regulation also upholds "the socialism with Chinese characteristics" broadcasting management system. In this system the State Council's broadcasting department simultaneously performs three functions – publicity and propaganda, industrial development, and regulation. It supports the legitimacy of censorship: the MRFT censors imported television programs, and television and radio stations censor their own programs. The regulation also explicitly requests that TV and radio stations must be set up by national or local broadcasting administrative departments who represent the State and government. It prohibits private, non-broadcasting systems and foreign ownership and bans foreign joint venture and joint-force TV and radio stations (State Council Decree No. 228, 1997).

Until 1997, the official attitudes of the Party-State towards the TV media did not shift significantly from their traditional positions: the political and social roles of television, such as those of mouthpiece, public opinion guidance and spiritual civilization, dominate the mainstream discourse in the Party-State's broadcasting policy-making.

1998–2000: the transitional phase of the national television policy

From 1998 to 1999, institutional reform was launched in China to slim down the bureaucratic structure of both central and local governments. With others, the MRFT was downgraded from a constitutional Ministry of the State Council to the State Administration of Radio, Film and Television (SARFT), a state bureau

92 *Television policy between 1996 and 2003*

directly subordinated to the State Council. In 1998, a new chief, Tian Congming, replaced Sun Jiazheng to lead the bureau.

This was a period characterized by institutional and structural adjustments not only within the MRFT but also throughout the entire government. The transition was moving towards "simpler administration," "consolidation," "convergence," "concentration" and "improvement of quality" but was no longer concerned with its economic viability.[5] Reflected in the national television policy, it was the continuous slimming down of the four-tier television networks into two-tier networks, the removal of unapproved television outlets and a call for quality improvement instead of growth in television channels (Sun 1998; Xu, 1998). Meanwhile, the MCP also released an internal document, *MCP (98) No. 1*, instructing the start of planning for broadcasting conglomeration in China (*SARFT [1998] No. 585*, 1998). Accordingly, the drafting of CCP's influential *No. 17 document* was started in 1998, and the document eventually came into force in 2001. Its main theme was to accelerate the commercialization, concentration and conglomeration of the electronic media.[6]

After its 1997 Fifteenth National Congress, the Party pledged to accelerate socialism with Chinese characteristics development to full-scale, and instructed that it should "push forward radio and television reform, step by step" (Xu, 1998: 261). Xu Guangchun, then Vice-Minister of the MCP, stated that the reform principles are "four no changes" and "all others can be changed"; "no change in [radio and television's] nature as the Party, Government and people's mouthpiece and the Party's important public opinion apparatus and battlefield"; "no change in [radio and television's] glorious duty of serving the Party's national work", "no change in [radio and television's] responsibilities of persisting on correct public opinion guidance, creating a good public sphere and providing strong public support for reform, liberalization, economic and social development"; "no change in the leadership of the Party over broadcasting." "Except for these, all other areas, like the content and format of publicity, program structure, internal systems, working mechanisms, liberalization to the outside and so on, can be reformed" (Xu, 1998: 262).

SARFT's position towards *Chan Ye Hua* was also softened. In an internal meeting its new Chief, Tian Congming, asked provincial TV stations not to talk about television *Chan Ye Hua* "in general," "because some [sectors] cannot practice it, at least the news reporting and news program cannot [practice] *Chan Ye Hua*. Their political and public service natures determine [they] can only be run by the state broadcasting institution." He also urged no discussion about "integration with international practices in general, because some [practices] can be integrated, some cannot, some are feasible in the longer term or in theory, but they cannot be done at the present due to the immature conditions" (Tian, 1998: 245).

He acknowledged that to increase the profits of the stations are the "problem that concerns all [TV stations]" and attempted to convince the leaders of the stations that "to insist on correct public opinion guidance and improve program quality" are key for increasing profits. He stressed that the criteria for quality programs are based on "whether the public is satisfied, happy and agree."

However, 70 percent of audience letters and phone calls received by SARFT criticized radio and TV programs (Tian, 1998: 249).

In 1999, after the Party's endorsement of the reform principles, the "establishment of an administrative system and operation mechanism which is compatible with socialist market economic system, which is compatible with the requirement of new century and fits into its development logic" was set as the major task of reform (Tian, 1998: 254). The priorities of reform were given to business and technology models rather than propaganda functions; to entertainment, art and cultural content rather than news; to local levels rather than the central institution (Tian, 1998: 247).

Television stations should sever a multifunctional role, providing public opinion guidance, service and entertainment, as well as pursuing industrial development. They need to "serve reform and liberalization; provide people and society with rich and speedy information and educational services; provide affecting, tasteful and multi-layer cultural and entertainment services." They "possess industrial functions," "[...] must put social effect in the first place but also must consider cost and economic interests" (Tian, 1998: 247).

In June 2000, the former Vice-Minister of the Ministry of Central Propaganda (MCP), Xu Guangchun, followed Tian Congming as Chief at SARFT. Compared to Tian, Xu held rather conservative views on news media reform, partly due to his MCP background: the MCP had been considered to be one of the most conservative departments in the country.

In a speech given at the National TV and Radio Propaganda Working Conference in January 2000, Xu openly criticized the appeal for news media *Chan Ye Hua* (commercialization) and *Qi Ye Hua* (enterprise-like) and the superiority of the people's needs over the Party's.

In the Chinese context, *Chan Ye Hua* is concerned with macro-issues, for instance the prominence of the business nature of the media over its ideological function. The concept *Qi Ye Hua* is more associated with the micro level transformation of the media's operational and management model. It refers to a transformation from the non-business, not-for-profit government institution to a modern enterprise. The former's important business activities are determined by government and its personnel and wage systems are affiliated to the government's bureaucratic hierarchy. For the latter, it puts making profits, if not as more important, at least as of the same importance as its political function, and it has more autonomy in making decisions on personnel, wages, business and investment strategies according to market mechanisms and economic logic.

Xu suspected the *Chan Ye Hua* of the media sector and the *Qi Ye Hua* of the media institution would inevitably lead to a change in the nature of the news media as the Party's mouthpiece, and the sacrifice of the news media's public guidance and educational functions. He criticized this, saying that to divide the people's needs from the Party's needs was to "divide Party from people and divide Party's will from the people's wish." In addition, Xu represented the MCP, ordering strict control over non-broadcasting capital investment in the electronic media, despite the Ministry agreeing that those investors "may not

94 *Television policy between 1996 and 2003*

want to control our news media and practice 'westernization' and 'disintegration'," but there was a worry that they "might undermine [the Party's] leadership of the news media" (Xu, 2000a: 447–448). In 2000, the dominant television policy was to strengthen ideological control and program censorship, and to enhance the media's publicity function. The MCP responded to reforming voices by allowing television stations to restructure their internal organizational structures and personnel and wage systems (Xu, 2000a).

However, the apparent slowdown of the pace of reform was partly influenced by the domestic and international political-economic environment at the time. Domestically, the crackdown on the "*Falun Gong*" movement in late 1999 continued to affect the CCP's policy-making and became a crucial motive for the Party's reinforcement of its ideological and political work in 2000. Economically, reform of the domestic medical, housing and social protection systems were accelerated with the government's increasing withdrawal of its subsidiaries in these social services. Internationally, the Party was concerned with the implications of the political transitions in the USA, Russia and Taiwan[7] upon China, the growing demand for independence in Taiwan and the possible victory of the pro-independence Democratic Progressive Party (DPP), as this could cause serious conflicts across the Strait. In the meantime the Chinese government was fighting for its WTO membership. For the Party in 2000, it was overwhelmingly important to maintain social stability.

Despite the temporary setback, the directional tendency towards a more capital friendly and operationally liberalized environment in China's TV sector was irreversible.

This was evident in Xu's speech given seven months later at a National Broadcasting Bureau meeting. In the speech, Xu outlined the next Five-Year Broadcasting Development Plan. The plan targets to build "top standard, top teamed, top equipped and top managed broadcasting and film aircraft carriers [i.e., big broadcasting media conglomerates]," to "become stronger and bigger" and to expand the country's influence on the world and enhance the country's voice in the international public sphere.

In order to achieve this, "three innovations" were urged by Xu and the Party. The first was the theoretical innovation to "liberalize mind," "refresh concept" and "form new understanding." The second was institutional innovation so that a future institutional system "must match the request for production force development, if not, it must be reformed and innovated." Finally, it was technological innovation, which will profoundly influence television and radio and effectively resolve problems caused by the present institutional, administrative and operational arrangements (Xu, 2000b: 469 and 471). Xu warned that without reform and innovations there would be no future for China's broadcasting.

2001: a quasi-market and dual system phase

Several months later, in January 2001, the then Minister of the MCP, Ding Guangen, at a National Propaganda Ministers' Conference, advocated that the

Chinese media should accelerate its pace of reform to cope with the market economy, the country's increasing liberalization and the advancement of media technology (Ding, 2001).

The Party requested that the broadcasting sector transform itself from a planned economic system to a quasi-market economic system, to increase its competitiveness and strength. It first aimed to establish a control mechanism that could both uphold the Party's leadership and improve the government's macro-management of the media. Second, it demanded reformed media organizations, which could function as the mouthpiece of the Party on the one hand, and operate like a modern enterprise on the other. Third, it needed a regulatory regime, which could reflect the propaganda and cultural nature of the media within the frame of the rule of law. Finally, it wanted a pattern of liberalization that could help the industry to absorb advanced technology and the culture of foreign countries, while keeping "decadent culture" outside the border.

Soon after Ding's speech, the crucial *Document No. 17* (2001) jointly promulgated by the Party, SARFT and State General Agency of Press and Publications (SGAPP) came into force in 2001 after three years of drafting. The document set out the basic layout and overall requirements of mass media reform. The five major reforming areas were macro-management, micro-operation, the regulatory system, market structure and the pattern of liberalization. Reform measures included conglomeration, enterprise-like management, digitalization, cable network distribution and channel specialization. These measures showed a visible tendency towards broadcasting *Chan Ye Hua* (Zhao, 2001).

In 2001, Huang Shengmin modified his definition of *Chan Ye Hua* in his new book and stated that the term *Chan Ye Hua* now refers to "a phenomenon where media institutions that used to be purely cultural, spiritual undertakings are being transformed into profitable corporations along the track of rational business" (Huang and Ding in Guo, 2003: 10). Compared to the previous one, the new conceptualization strengthened the economic trait but reduced its political edge. Meanwhile, the international factor was also brought into this discussion when Huang urged consideration of the Chinese situation against a wider background (Guo, 2003).

In the same year, a "reaching out" project was launched by SARFT as a result of Jiang Zemin's instruction to "let China's voice broadcast to the world" (*People's Daily Online*, 2001; Xu, 2001: 537). The goals of this "reaching out" project are: first, in five years' time, to launch China's television and radio channels overseas, making an international impact especially in countries in North America and Western Europe; second, in ten years, China's television and radio channels could provide multi-language, regionalized broadcasting and coverage. "Any place that has CNN, BBC and other Western big media's voices and images, must have [China's] voice and image".

The strategies proposed include broadcasting the CCTV-4 and CCTV-9 channels and other programs in important regions; encouraging central and important local television and radio stations to expand overseas, and to carry out international cooperation; establishing strong overseas marketing and distribution

96 *Television policy between 1996 and 2003*

teams and agencies; and improving research on foreign countries' laws, regulations and policies, their culture and audience tastes, their politics, history, economy etc., to help with the government's policy-making (Xu, 2001).

In 2002, because of China's successful accession to the WTO in 2001, the Party and government's confidence in domestic economic reform was reinforced and consequently created a more liberal atmosphere for the transformation of domestic broadcasting. In Xu's words: "the situation [of China] is very good though there are many problems, we must be fully confident. [...] We must also be fully confident of our broadcasting" (Xu, 2002a: 7). Within this kind of optimistic and liberal climate, "becoming bigger and stronger through conglomeration" was the most popular slogan, and "development," "structural transition," "empowerment," and "strengthening competitive power" were the dominant objectives to achieve in the TV industry. The government also advocated the idea that development is the source of power and only by becoming richer and stronger can China win respect and influence in international society (Zhu H, 2002: 24).

Xu Guangchun, even at a National Working Conference, blamed senior broadcasting officials for not having "business sense," and demanded that they be visionary, occupying markets with economic potential, such as the interactive TV and Video-On-Demand (VOD) businesses. He told them:

> [The] broadcasting and film industry is a piece of fat meat, in foreigner's words China's broadcasting sector is the last steak they want to eat. But we are lacking this kind of energy, [...] all foreign media's businesses in China are losing money. Why? Because they want to occupy the market. AOL-Time Warner's CETV, News Corporation's Xing Kong Satellite Channel lost several thousand million (RMB). Are they so stupid? Don't forget, they are [doing this] for the purpose of making money back later.
>
> (Xu, 2002a: 5)

The Sixteenth CCP Party Congress on 8 November 2002, officially accepted the "cultural industry" nature of broadcasting, approved the institutional reform of the country's cultural industries which include TV, radio and film, and pledged to open up the service sector to the world step by step (CCTV, 2003b; Jiang, 2002). Institutional reform aimed to build up three systems in the cultural sector – a socialist market economy system, a socialist ideological system, a legal system and developed advanced culture characterized by "modern," "global," "forward," "national," "scientific" and "mass" (Jiang, 2002). In the same month, Jiang Zemin said at a public meeting that the *Chan Ye Hua* of China's broadcasting had been developing continuously (Liang in Guo, 2003). This speech was widely interpreted as official legitimatization of the concept *Chan Ye Hua* and related discourses. After that, the State and Party's senior leaders reiterated the business nature of media on various occasions, emphasizing its profit-making characteristics. Since then the business practice of the media has been endorsed and encouraged from the top of the political order (Guo, 2003).

Subsequently, the pursuit of economic welfare was defined as the general nature of Chinese broadcasters while the mouthpiece function and fulfillment of ideological work became their peculiar nature. The Party encouraged Chinese broadcasters to gain experience from both the country's market economic reform and foreign media's practices, but warned them not to copy them totally. It again upheld the Party's decisive roles in important decision-making, asset allocation, program censorship and senior management employment.

> No matter what the situation, the [media's] nature of the Party and the people's mouthpiece cannot be changed, Party control of media cannot be changed, the Party's leadership over officials cannot be changed, insistence on correct public opinion cannot be changed.
>
> (Zhu H, 2002: 25)

In the National Broadcasting and Film Working Conference held in January 2003, the separation of the institutional and enterprise natures of broadcasting was brought forwards. In late 2003, the *Opinions on Experimental Works of the Cultural System's Institutional Reform*, formulated by the Party, clearly divided the cultural sector into two parts – cultural institutions serving the "public good" and cultural industries pursuing commercial interests. In terms of the television sector, the institutional part includes information collection, production and editing of news publicity programs, censoring and broadcasting of public welfare programs. The industrial part includes the production and editing of non-news content, buying and sales of programs, transmission and covering of various programs, the operational business of pay programs, developing and operating post and derivative products, as well as the production and sales of video programs (Ding, 2004: 37). The focuses and breakthroughs of the reform include three groups based on the division of the institutional and industrial attributes of media: the separation of the institution and enterprise, separation of ownership and managerial authority, and the separation of production and broadcasting. The separation of the institutional and enterprise aspects of broadcasting does not mean to simply cut off the corporate part from the institution, but to establish two operational systems under one institutional entity. For the separation of ownership and managerial authority, the precondition was that the channel resources must remain under the control of the state, as must the asset ownership, the controlling stake, the final adjudication of programs, and the power of appointment and removal of senior management. Under this precondition, certain channels could implement the separation of ownership and managerial authority, and establish sole proprietorship or majority shareholding companies. The third group was the separation of production and broadcasting: only certain television series, animations, sports and music channels or programs were allowed to implement the separation of production and broadcasting. Programs or channels with news or political content were strictly prohibited from industrial operation, including the separation of production and broadcasting, or becoming listed companies (Zhao, 2004).

98   Television policy between 1996 and 2003

The *Opinions* requested the establishment of a market and public service system. The Party chose some cities and TV stations to test the model so that it could learn from the trial (Xu, 2003a). It was requested that the TV and radio stations' business-oriented units split from their main bodies and converted into enterprise-like companies constituting the market system. The goal of these companies was to achieve commercialization through strategies like resource concentration, management modernization and market-oriented operation. Non-business units were categorized as the public service system and were continuously managed by the government, functioning as both the Party's mouthpiece and as propaganda tools. Their nature as government institutions was retained, but internal reforms on wages, personal and financial systems were essential. The "Four No Changes" principle was applied to the "public service" elements of television and radio. (Xu, 2003a: 7).

A government monitoring system was also put into place to secure organized transformation. Under this system, the government's central and local broadcasting authorities no longer ran television or radio stations, but functioned as administrators and regulators, performing social, administrative, policy and legislative regulatory functions. They employed both legislative measures, such as the law and rules, and administrative means, for instance, instructions and notices, to guide operations, penalize violations and so on (Xu, 2003a).

At the end of 2003, SARFT released *Opinions on Improving Broadcasting and Film Industry Development.* This was the Party-State's biggest step towards deregulation of television channel's production and the liberalization of the domestic television market. First, it reshaped the ownership structure of China's television media from a state monopoly to a mixed ownership system, provided that the majority stake is owned by the state. This mixed ownership restructuring was said to help business-oriented television to "fully absorb and use social resources to development [...], and establish a fair, open and organized market to propel the prosperity of the market and growth of industry" (SARFT, 2003a). Second, the market mechanism was prominent in resource allocation. The consumer orientation of broadcasters was promoted while the public was spontaneously equalized as consumers. The document stated that "everything must consider whether the public, i.e., consumers will accept and be satisfied or not" (SARFT, 2003a). Nevertheless, the document appealed for reconciliation of the social and economic effects but without details of how to achieve this. So it was under these circumstances that SARFT determined 2004 to be the year of the industrial development of radio, film and television (Xu, 2004a: 13). For the market issue, Xu Guangchun, the former head of SARFT, stated that having awareness of the market was the first step. The second step was to shape "the main market players," but a government institution cannot be the principle part of the market. Just as government institutions can regulate the market, thus they should not be the major component of the market (Xu, 2004c: 5). He explains further, using CCTV Children's Channel as an example, saying that the channel belongs to a public institution, thus only when a separate production company is established could it enter the market and become the "main market player." The

Television policy between 1996 and 2003 99

third step is to run the separate production company with enterprise-like management instead of in an institutional manner. Zhu Hong, the former Director of the Law and Regulation Office at the SARFT, said in 2004 that the emphasis of the future reform of television broadcasting was to greatly develop its market attributes (Zhu, 2004b). Zhu Hong put forward "three transformations" as the step-by-step commercialization procedures: the first was to transform from state-owned institutions to state-owned enterprises; the second was to transform from general state-owned enterprises to corporate enterprises, and the third step was to transform from corporate enterprises to listed companies (Zhu, 2004b). As a result, non-broadcasting departments and all other non-news production units would split from their TV stations, and convert into "modern enterprises" with managerial authority and financial independence. They could be listed on domestic or overseas stock markets in the future. Qualified foreign companies were able to take a minority stake in these enterprises. With the Chinese government reserving state ownership of news channels and continuing to exercise censorship for all program types, most TV and radio channels, including sports, movies, general entertainment, music, lifestyles, financial, science and education could be transformed into shareholding companies controlled by stations, having minor domestic private investment and able to sell shares inside or outside China (SARFT, 2003a; Zhu, 2004a).

Re-centralization, conglomeration, de-regulation and digitalization after 1996

Alongside the development of the Party-State's national TV policies, the Chinese TV industry has undergone structural recentralization, resource concentration and deregulation of production processes since the late 1990s.

Structural reorganization began with the promulgation of the CCP and State Council's 1996 notice on *Strengthening the Governance of Press, Publication and Broadcasting* (*CCP [1996] No. 37*, 1996). Consequently, MRFT[8] launched a campaign to re-centralize the "chaotic" and "disordered" four-tier TV network by administrative means.

In 1996, it first ordered the elimination of unapproved TV outlets in the country. Second, it consolidated the television structure by merging county level cable, terrestrial, educational television and radio stations (*CCP [1996] No. 37*, 1996) and city and provincial cable and terrestrial TV stations (*State Council [1999] No. 82*, 1999). Third, it tightened control over program sources, requesting county TV stations to allocate most of their airtime to transmitting central and provincial TV stations' programs, and integrating the cable networks into various state-owned enterprises (*danwei*) and district cable networks (*CCP [1996] No. 37*, 1996; Guo, 2003). After three years of recentralization, in April 1999, SARFT announced that the total number of television organizations in China had dropped by 68 percent (*SARFT [1999] No. 174*, 1999). The number of TV stations fell from 880 in 1996 to 357 in 2001, ironically, the number of TV channels dramatically rose, from 983 to 2,194 during the same period, under

100   *Television policy between 1996 and 2003*

the banner of channel specification (CCTV Yearbook, 1997; Huang and Wang, 2003). This meant that, on average, every television station in China had six free to air channels broadcasting 9.5 million hours of programming annually. Given that the total domestic production capacity was two million hours per year, it is not surprising to learn that the program repeat ratio is very high. The 2003 *China TV Report*, states that about 40–50 percent of programs on 190 stations were recycled (Huang and Wang, 2003).

The process of concentrating media resources started with the construction of China's first media conglomerate, the Wuxi Broadcasting Group, in 1998, which pooled radio, television and cable resources in four cities – Wuxi, Yixin, Jiangyin and Xishan (Media, 2001). Because of the state-owned nature of the media, conglomeration was inevitably State and Party driven and was implemented via administrative instruction rather than market forces.

In September 1999, the State Council's *Document No. 82* (*State Council [1999] No. 82*, 1999) for the first time explicitly requested the establishment of broadcasting conglomerates at the provinces, autonomous regions and municipalities level. In 2000, SARFT released guiding principles for conglomeration at the national and provincial levels. It defined a conglomerate as, by its nature, a state-owned institution but running as an enterprise (*SARFT [2000] No. 841*, 2000).

One year later, in December 2001, *Document No. 17* (*CCP [2001] No. 17*) and the following *Implantation Rules* (*SARFT [2001] No. 1452*; *SARFT [2001] No. 1485*) broke former geographic and platform boundaries by allowing cross-regional and cross-media ownership of media conglomerates through acquisition, merger and joint-venture in the audio-visual, print media and publication sectors.

By 2002, 20 media conglomerates had been approved in Hunan, Shanghai, Beijing, Shandong, Jiangsu, Zhejiang and other provinces or municipalities (SARFT, 2003a). The biggest "aircraft carrier" – the China Radio, Film and Television Group, which combines China Central Television Station (CCTV), China National Radio, and other national broadcasting and film production and distribution companies – launched in December 2001 (Guo, 2003). In 2003, the government suspended new conglomerations on the grounds of reassessing their effects and considering the solutions of the existing problems (Xu, 2003a).

To enable the entry of collective and private capital has been the major negotiating problem since restructuring began in 1996 (Hu, 2003). The restructuring of Chinese television eventually led to liberalization of the ownership of television channel's production units.

After the opening of the Sixteenth CCP's National Congress on 8 November 2002, a more market friendly cultural policy was committed to by the Party. *Opinions on Improving Broadcasting and Film Industry Development* was released by SARFT at the end of 2003 and permitted non-broadcasting departments and all other non-news production units to split off from their TV stations, converting them into "modern enterprises" with managerial authority and financial independence. They could be listed on domestic or overseas stock markets

Television policy between 1996 and 2003 101

in the future. Qualified foreign companies were able to take minority stake in these enterprises (SARFT, 2003a).

Most importantly, the government for the first time permitted change in the ownership of television and radio channels' production units. It announced that by guaranteeing state-ownership of the channel spectrum, the programming production units of most television and radio channels, including sports, movies, general entertainment, music, lifestyle, financial, science and education, could be transformed into shareholding companies controlled by stations, having minor domestic private investment and able to sell shares inside or outside China (SARFT, 2003a; Zhu, 2004a). The Chinese government reserved state ownership and content production of news channels and continued to exercise censorship for all program types.

In an interview given to the *Wall Street Journal*, Zhu Hong, a spokesman for SARFT, asserted that deregulation was granted "in light of the principle of separating [the state's] ownership from operation," and the decision to exempt the news programming operation, production and ownership from deregulation was to "serve public interests," to "deliver the Party and State's voices to Chinese households" and to "convey China's voices to the world" (Zhu, 2004a).

Technologically, SARFT was actively pushing the digitalization of broadcasting in order to deliver new services such as direct broadcasting satellite (DBS), pay-per-view and other interactive services. In 2000, SARFT proposed a "three-step" digitalization plan for China's 320 million TV households who owned 370 million analogue TV sets. The first step of the plan was to switch 100 million cable TV users[9] to the digital platform from 2003 by installing decoders on top of their television sets. Second, the plan expected the direct broadcasting satellite (DBS) service to start with a 120 channel capacity in 2005 following the launch of China's own broadcasting satellite. After 2008, the broadcasting industry was to focus on the development of digital high definition TV (HDTV) and the digitalization of terrestrial channels. The deadline for the analogue switch-over was between 2010 and 2015 (Zhang, 2003).

Under the push to digitalization, a pay TV service emerged in China. Zhang Haitao, the Deputy Chief of SARFT, expected China's Pay TV to operate in a commercial environment and be run by enterprise-like companies. Its development was to use non-state resources, "depend on the market and establish an open and competitive pattern." A guarding, moderating and coordinating role was to be played by SARFT to "formulate regulations" and "maintain a fair, competitive and healthy playing field." It would "not be involved in or intervene with" the daily operations of the Pay TV service but leave it to the individual operator (SARFT, 2003b).

On 9 August 2004, with the opening of the 2004 Olympic Games, six national pay TV channels provided by two companies, CCTV Fengyun Broadcasting Ltd and China DTV Media Inc. Ltd (CDM), were launched. Their monthly subscription fee was RMB58[10] (China Cable TV, 2004; Hong Kong News Yahoo, 2004).

102 *Television policy between 1996 and 2003*

Domestic political economy and international communication order

The transformation of China's TV policy and structure from 1996 to 2003 was influenced by the socio-economic transition of the country and international communication order, and driven by the economic and political welfare pursuit of various interest groups.

The change was linked to China's economic transition as examined in Chapter 2. As a result of the transformation from a state-owned centrally planned economy to a quasi-market economy with mixed ownership, in 2001 the non-state sector, including enterprises privately and collectively owned, contributed 43 percent of the country's Gross Domestic Product (GDP) growth (Lian, 2002). "Is China still a socialist country?" An official at CCTV questioned.[11]

Accompanying this transition was a proliferation of consumerism in both society and the media. For today's television organizations and broadcasting policymakers, serving the Chinese people's needs is almost equivalent to "fulfil[ing] the demands of consumers and provid[ing] quality products and services to them" (SARFT, 2003a).

Second, different interest groups, including domestic private capitalists, local media elites and transnational media companies, enthusiastically promoted transformation in order to increase their own benefits, to increase economies of scale and to serve the market expansion of their respective organizations.[12] The pursuit of economic welfare, which was the driver of commercialization in the 1990s and media concentration in the new century, has been the most stable dynamic in the shaping of China's television institutions.

On the other hand, as the legitimacy and stability of the central powers were built upon the resources that they provided and the support that they obtained from the local governments and their elites, reciprocity is therefore a necessity (Tang *et al.*, 2000). As happened with the reform of state-owned enterprises (SOEs), the economic ambitions of the local media elites meant the State and Party could no longer dismiss their commercial demands. This subsequently resulted in the deregulation of non-news channels' content production to domestic private capital following the Sixteenth National Party Congress in November 2002. If in the 1990s, market forces were absorbed by the Chinese Party-State through ownership monopoly, through which the government was "flexible enough to contain strong commercial development within political control" (Ma, 2000: 28), then in the new century, alongside increasing liberalization, economic welfare has been prominent, and market forces have been strengthened and, may, finally, reveal an unpleasant face. Having said that, this should not undermine another important reason for the triggering of television transformation, particularly, the separation of non-news units from TV stations. This institutional conversion from a government institution to an enterprise-like company is, to a certain degree, to accommodate the media's demands for more operational autonomy. All terrestrial TV stations in China are affiliated to the government's administrative structure, under which they have little flexibility to choose their talent or decide on wages. Thus, transferring from being a state institution to being a "modern corporate system," with clear industrial attributes, enables TV organizations to adopt more flexible personnel and wage systems for the recruitment of employees and to reward those who work well.

Third, the restructuring is articulated to the domestic political imperatives of the Party in a transitional society. Compared to economic interests, for the Party and Central Government, political and social "stability outweighs everything else" (*wending yadao yiqie*，稳定压倒一切) (Zhu, 2003: 37).

Re-centralization and conglomeration could reshape the former four-tier industry into a pyramidal structure that would help consolidate the central governance that had been undermined by the decentralization of the TV industry in the 1980s and 1990s. The government only needed to keep a close eye on those conglomerates that were responsible for the supervision of enormous local stations and newspapers.

As the Party understood the significance of the ongoing media reform for the political stability of the Party-State's ruling, and the social stability of the country, the "Four No Changes" principle was persistently retained throughout the transformation (Xu, 2003a: 7; Zhu, 2004b).

Despite institutional conversion and ownership deregulation, the Party and government could still filter media content by censorship. In an interview a senior manager at the China International TV Corporation (CITVC) stressed that:

> private capital is allowed to enter [channel operation], but the gate is kept in the hands of the government. Senior management [of media organizations] are delegated by the government, censorship is controlled by the government. [...] [Compulsory censorship has been imposed so that] all programmes must be censored before and after broadcasting [...]. Money is the second thing. If the programmes produced do not meet [the government's] requirement, the CEO, without any doubt, will be fired and the official who censored this program will also be fired. It ends up with self-censorship and program producers are even more cautious and strict [than the government].[13]

It was anticipated that the Party would be tightening its control over news materials in spite of the relaxation of operations. A senior journalist at CCTV News Channel commented that

> the prerequisite [of all changes] is the state's [political] interest and the position cannot be changed. Although the pattern [of operation] and format [of progams] has changed, the requirements and principles do not change. Therefore, this is nothing really special.[14]

If in the 1990s, the core of the struggle in China's TV sector was with the ideological imperative of the Party and the market needs of the media, then the late development of Chinese television demonstrated that future contestation will

104 *Television policy between 1996 and 2003*

center on the interplay between ideology, the market and the economic powers of different interest groups where the Party will "actively employ economic, regulatory and administrative means to strengthen macro-management" (SARFT, 2003a), e.g., by manipulating the advertising market to influence the funding of the media.[15]

The Party-State was seemingly learning from a "state corporatism" model, as demonstrated in Taiwan's martial law period, by adopting "a policy of incorporation marked by a simultaneous and intermittent interplay of repression and cooption" (Lee, 2000: 125) in a state-engineered oligopolistic media market. By so doing, the Party-State could control its major "mouthpieces" and politically sensitive content while allowing "limited pluralism" in nonpolitical areas. The Party-State could also keep privately owned media, or those contested by the existing power structure, either politically or economically subordinated to it. Under an authoritarian political regime, "business people will not be willing to take political risk because of economic profits" as a Chinese media scholar admitted.[16]

In respect of the global context, the Chinese state's desire to be actively involved in, and benefit from, the process of media globalization has reinforced the pro-market policy. Partial liberalization of the Chinese TV sector were voluntary results from the very beginning of GATS (*General Agreement on Trade in Services*) negotiations i.e., the Uruguay Round, 1993, when the audio-visual sector[17] was exempted from free trade rules due to member states' opposition on the basis of protection of national cultural identity.

The Seattle ministerial conference of January 2000 featured tens of thousands of anti-corporate protesters, demonstrating their opposition to transnational corporation (TNCs) led globalization and liberalization. Again, the ministerial meeting in Cancun in September 2003, failed because of anger from developing countries towards demands made by the developed world (*The Guardian*, 2003).

By 2003, only two of 143 WTO member states – the USA and the Central African Republic – committed to all of the sub-categories of the audio-visual sectors, and seven members had made commitments to "radio and television services" but none of the EU countries had made any commitment.

This unwillingness to make commitments was precisely because few countries have more offensive (i.e., liberalizing) interests than defensive (i.e., protectionist) interests. It is predicated that, given the domination of the US in the international audio-visual market, the only winner from liberalization in economic terms, would be the US. Thus, most WTO members were adopting a rather "defensive" approach and were not prepared to discuss this issue. In the light of the service export interests of China, it is apparent that China was not strong and had little economic interest to gain (see Table 6.1). In the short or mid-term, the GATS negotiations will not be the source of pressure, which will lead to the inevitable liberalization of China's audio-visual market.

Returning to China's own WTO access agreement, the Chinese government did not commit to liberalizing its broadcasting on the grounds of protecting national culture and state security from outside erosion, though it agreed to open

Table 6.1 China's service export and share of the world total (1985–2001) (million US dollars)

Year	Service export	Share in the world total (%)
1985	2,925	0.77
1990	5,748	0.73
1995	18,430	1.55
1998	23,879	1.79
1999	26,165	1.90
2000	30,146	2.06
2001	32,903	2.26

Source: 1. World Trade Organization, International Trade Statistics, 2001, 2002. In report issued by World Trade Organization, Council for Trade in Services Special Session, 19 December 2002. Available at: https://goo.gl/gYTvjJ (accessed 23 February 2016).

up certain sectors[18] of the audio-visual market to encourage cultural interaction, as Xu Guangchun, Chief of SARFT claimed (WTO, 2001; Xu, 2002b).

Despite this, the notion of "China's media under siege" still gained a prominent voice in China's academic writings and was a popular slogan with Chinese political and media elites. Rather than appeal to protectionism, as it did in the early 1990s, a pragmatic position combining both liberalization and resistance has dominated the Chinese political and media elites' policy and strategy making in an attempt to achieve a mutually beneficial principle and to facilitate the international expansion of Chinese television.

The two groups endorsed the opinion of the inevitability of the future liberalization of the domestic broadcasting market to foreign capital, and asserted that what will be negotiated is not whether the market will be opened or not, but rather about how quickly, to what extent, and in what way (CCTV, 2002; Yu, 2002). A senior manager at a foreign media company echoed this speculation.[19] Local broadcasters were therefore warned that they would have to face challenges and competition from global media moguls sooner or later, and

> in order to [...] fulfill the increasing cultural needs of the public, defend against invasion" and penetration by Western media, [China] needs to study the development experiences of international media, adapt them to local conditions and accelerate the pace of broadcasting and film conglomeration.
>
> (SARFT [2000] No. 986, 2000)

They have interpreted WTO entry and possible liberalization as an opportunity for China's TV industry. First, it could lead to the intensification of local-global interactions, bringing successful management models and advanced technologies. Second, it is believed that liberalization would inevitably involve rationalization of the Party-State's policy-making and regulatory process and lead to possible communication democratization in China. In addition, they tended to subscribe to the notion that market forces and competition, particularly

106 *Television policy between 1996 and 2003*

those from global conglomerates, could help improve program quality and bring development and prosperity to the local TV industry. In short, from the domestic elites' point of view, market liberalization is a win-win case, through which the Chinese media could accelerate its development while foreign media could make money by investing in China (Yu, 2002; Zhu, 2003; Zhu JF, 2002).

Last, but not least, as a Chinese media scholar pointed out "[the aim of the government's reform policy] is 'reaching out' (*zou chuqu*) to become influential in the world. The drive [of the policy] is to become modern, strong and to be taken seriously in international society". Her words, however, point us to another important factor that has profoundly influenced the Chinese-state's national television policy-making.

As Zhang Yongjin (2003) argues in his study of China's economic transformation, if the integration of the Chinese economy and the country into the dominant global ideology of neo-liberalism, capitalism and the world order is "voluntary and enthusiastically embraced," then it should be recognized that, to a certain extent, China's "convergence" and "conformity" with the global economy are also "externally enforced." In Robert Cox's words:

> the ideological and political power of global hegemony restricted the forms of state that were tolerated within this world order. A combination of rewards and penalties – access to credit for compatible and political destabilization of incompatible national regimes – enforced conformity.
>
> (Cox, 1987: 266)

A senior official at SARFT blamed the extremely unequal and unjust international communication order as one major obstacle to China's liberalization. He considers that, after the collapse of the Eastern European block, the West has ideologically suppressed China while alleging that China's sky is not opening up enough. The Chinese government has had to adopt a defensive policy and conduct gradual reform to retain social stability and state security. He stressed that to understand China's situation, this international context must be taken into consideration.[20]

Nevertheless, this defensive policy was adjusted slightly following China's WTO accession in 2001. It was believed that WTO entry would make the country more interdependent with the world economy, broaden the issues that the Chinese state considers as its national interests and subsequently increase China's need for political power (Perritt and Clarke, 1998: 395). Like its counterpart in America, the mass media, particularly the broadcasting media, has been considered by the Party and the State as a powerful weapon for political publicity, both within and outside China. In the Party's words, it aims to "let China's voice broadcast to the world" (Xu, 2001: 537).

Given this historical background, it is not difficult to understand why the Chinese state was so eagerly utilizing both private and state capital, and inviting successful business models, managerial experience, advanced technologies and equipment to strengthen its own TV industry and build up its own "world class" "modern" media conglomerates, thus entering the global market.

Summary

Since 1996, China's national television policy has been through four-phases of transition in which the formerly state-owned and centrally planned television system has transformed to a quasi-market system with both state and private ownership. Television organizations are divided into business-oriented and politically oriented, belonging to the commercial and "public service" sectors respectively. The two sectors have different autonomies, institutional arrangements, ownership structures and funding sources.

The "public service" sector merely consists of news channels. It has been continuously owned by the State and operated by the government, functioning as the Party's mouthpiece and the government's publicity arm. The commercial sector includes production units and business-oriented, non-news channels. The objective of this commercial sector is to pursue economic profit and achieve industrialization through the modernization of its business strategies, management and operations.

Meanwhile, the economic function of television has become prominent in national broadcasting policy. The pursuit of economic welfare is defined as the general nature of the television media, while the mouthpiece function and the fulfillment of their ideological work has become their peculiar nature. Technological advancement, for instance, the television broadcasting digitalization plan, was forced forward to facilitate the exploration of new economic interest areas such as the Pay TV service.

Internationally, a "reaching out" project was launched to assist the international expansion and multi-language coverage of China's television channels. It aimed to increase the political influences of the Chinese state in the international society through the power of the media to protect its broadening economic interests as a result of the country's growing interdependence with the world.

In conjunction with this national policy development, the Chinese television industry has consequently undergone a restructuring process since the late 1990s. First, the older decentralized four-tier TV network was re-centralized by removing unapproved TV outlets and merging local cable and terrestrial TV stations. Second, the former market and media boundaries were abolished. Print and electronic media sources were concentrated in the hands of national or local cross-media conglomerates. Third, non-news channels' production unit were split off from stations and converted to enterprise-like companies. The state's ownership monopoly of these entities was deregulated and private and foreign capital investment was allowed. Moreover, the digitalization plan and Pay TV channels were launched to capitalize on the new economic opportunities provided by technological advancement.

The underlying reasons for the changes were both economic and political. First, the economic transformation of China from a state-owned, centrally planned system to a quasi-market mixed ownership economy had provided the essential condition in the change of its broadcasting sector. Second, the pursuit

108 *Television policy between 1996 and 2003*

of the economic welfare of different interest groups, including private capitalists and local and transnational media organizations, dynamically propelled transformation. Third, the institutional conversion of TV channels also accommodated the TV media's demands for further operational autonomies so that they can run the channels in a rational and commercial way.

Moreover, the restructuring of the broadcasting sector is also linked to the Party-State's political imperatives. As the Party has attempted to employ not only the regulatory and administrative means but also economic measures to strengthen its control over the media, recentralization and conglomeration could help to consolidate its central governance in both political and economic terms. The separation of news channels from the transformation maximally secures the Party's monopoly of mainstream political voices.

Internationally, the GATS negotiations and China's WTO accession were not sources of pressure leading to the liberalization of China's broadcasting market. However, the ideological and political tensions between China and the West, and the country's increasing need for international political power as a result of its growing interdependence with the world, more or less influences the Party's adoption of a more expansive and liberal TV policy.

Notes

1 Personal interview with a senior executive at the China International TV Corporation (CITVC) on 18 September 2003.
2 Sun Jiazheng was the then Minister of the MRFT. The text is extracted from his report, given at the 1995 National Broadcasting and Film Working Conference.
3 Huang found that the Guangzhou Radio Station had an enterprise-like internal management and had been commercially oriented (Guo, 2004).
4 The report is published in the *Guidebook for Decision Making*. The guidebook is an internal journal published by the General Office of the then MRFT, later SARFT. It collects important policies, regulations, decisions and speeches made by officials of MRFT and SARFT.
5 According to a personal interview with a senior official at SARFT's Department of Law and Regulations in Beijing on 18 September 2003.
6 According to a personal interview with a senior official at SARFT's Department of Laws and Regulations in Beijing, 18 September 2003.
7 All three countries had presidential elections in 2000.
8 Renamed the State Administration of Radio, Film and Television (SARFT) in 1998.
9 Residents in rural and remote areas depend on wireless broadcasting.
10 About US$7.
11 A personal interview conducted at the CCTV on 9 September 2003.
12 Extract from my interview data. Hu (2003) and Zhao (2003) have also done detailed analysis on this.
13 Personal interview with a senior executive at the CITVC on 18 September 2003.
14 Interview conducted in Beijing on 20 September 2003.
15 Personal Interview conducted at CCTV on 9 September 2003.
16 Personal interview with a media scholar in Beijing on 8 September 2003.
17 The WTO defines audio-visual services as a sub-sector of communication services (along with postal, courier and telecommunication services) which is then divided into a further six categories: motion picture and videotape production and distribution

service; motion picture projection services; radio and television services; radio and television transmission services; sound recording; other audio-visual services (Freedman, 2002).

18 China agreed to increase the annual import of foreign films to 20 and allows less than 50 percent foreign ownership of cinemas; foreign investors were permitted to join ventures with Chinese partners to distribute audio-visual products such as audiocassettes, VCD, DVD, and to run advertising enterprises. In the telecommunication sector, foreign companies can invest in its value-added services including ISP (Internet Service Provider) and ICP (Internet Content Provider) related businesses.

19 Interview conducted with a former Vice President of New Corporation's Beijing Representative office in Beijing on 20 September 2003.

20 An interview conducted with an official at the SARFT's department of laws and regulations in Beijing on 18 September 2003.

7 China's television policy between 2004 and 2015

Since 2004, with advancement of digital broadcasting and mobile broadband technologies, the convergence of the Internet, telecommunication and broadcasting networks became the focus of China's media and communication policy-making.

Digitalization

China's broadcasting digitalization begun in 2000. In 2000, SARFT proposed a "three-step" digitalization plan for China's 320 million TV households which own 370 million analog television sets. The deadline for the analog switchover was set to be between 2010 and 2015 at that time (Zhang, 2003). Later in May 2003, SARFT issued *The Timetable of Digitalization of Domestic Cable TV*, in which it clearly stipulated that the digitalization of domestic cable TV would follow four stages: 2005, 2008, 2010 and 2015 within three areas: the East, Middle and West part of China. The "three-step" digitalization plan was also modified first, to comprehensively promote cable digital TV in 2003; second, to develop the digital direct broadcasting satellite service (DBS) and start the experiments with terrestrial digital TV, with a target of 30 million digital cable TV users by 2005, and third, to comprehensively promote the digitalization of terrestrial channels and digital high definition TV (HDTV) in 2008, especially in terms of the re-broadcasting of the 2008 Beijing Olympics on HDTV. Eventually, all analog TV broadcasting would cease by 2015 (Zhu, 2004c: 10). In 2008, the General Office of the State Council (2008) clarified the goals of broadcast TV digitalization: (1) to speed up the popularization of digital TV broadcasting, and strengthen the convergence of three networks: the broadband communication network, the digital TV network, and the next-generation Internet, as well as to form a complete industry chain of digital TV; (2) to speed up the integral transformation of cable TV from analog to digital: by the year 2015, most of the analog TV programs were to be stopped from broadcasting; (3) to realize the strategic transformation of the nation's TV industry from analog to digital – by the year 2015, to try to become the largest development and manufacturing base of digital TV sets and their key components worldwide. In 2009, 100 cities were implementing the integral transformation and the two-way reconstruction

Television policy between 2004 and 2015 111

projects of cable TV digitalization and more than 30 cities had already finished the transformation and reconstruction task by that time (Delegation of China Broadcast Television, 2009).

Back to 2004, one-third of the 320 million households received TV programs through the wired mode, others received their TV programs through wireless launcher or "village-to-village" (村村通; *Cuncun Tong*) satellite transmission. Although most of the broadcasting stations had achieved the digitalization of gathering, making and broadcasting programs, and satellite and fiber optic trunk cable had also achieved digital transmission, many user receivers were still analog. Therefore, a major task of broadcasting digitalization in and after 2004 was to realize the transformation from analog to digital in the process of receiving. Also, the transformation should cover the entire system, that is, all of the cable TV network should be transformed into a digital system. The reason for this was that if the analog and digital signals co-exist for a long time in the cable TV network, the limited channel resources would not be able to satisfy the development of various new businesses associated with digital TV (Science and Technology Division of SARFT, 2004). Also, if the analog and digital signals co-existed in one cable, the best frequency band would be occupied by the analog signal (Zhang, 2004a).

The way adopted by SARFT to implement the integral transformation of cable TV from analog to digital was mainly by promoting the use of the Set Top Box (STB), because STB can transfer the signal from analog to digital as the final process of the user receiving. There are three types of STB: the basic type, the enhanced type and the advanced type. The basic type of STB can fulfill the functions of improving the quality of the television signal, providing the guide service of electronic programs and managing each STB including each program and service based on the requirement of users. The enhanced type has the extra function of Near-Video-on-Demand (NVOD), and the advanced type has the additional functions of interaction and value added service (Science and Technology Division of SARFT, 2004). The method adopted by Qingdao, as the first trial city of television digitalization in China, was to distribute free STBs to households by increasing programs and services, while at the same raising the maintenance charge from 12 yuan to 22 yuan per month (Zhang, 2004b). This method proved to be successful as 83.5 percent of Qingdao's citizens agreed to pay the 22 yuan per month maintenance charge in order to get a free STB (Xu, 2004b). Thus SARFT encouraged other cities to follow Qingdao's method (Zhang, 2004b).

This was different to the way adopted by most Western developed countries, which promoted digitalization through pay TV. Broadcasters in Western developed countries are mostly run by business entities, and the governments have few restrictions on program content, thus pay TV can broadcast adult programs and gambling shows to attract the audiences. Moreover, income levels are relatively high in developed countries, therefore, it is relatively easy for households to afford pay TV (Zhang, 2004b). For example, Sky TV in UK invested £900 million to distribute free STBs to its residents in 1998, and the transformation from analog to digital television was fully completed by 2001 and Sky TV has profited from pay TV even with the £900 million investment. In China the average charge for cable television in 2003 was 70 yuan per year per household, which was too low to provide free STBs. Moreover, SARFT does not allow adult programs or gambling shows to be broadcast, even on pay TV, claiming that "broadcast and TV in China is the key position for the construction of the socialist spiritual civilization" (Zhang, 2004a: 5).

Thus, pay TV is one of the businesses based on digitalization instead of the approach to realize digitalization (Zhang, 2004b). The right to participate in pay TV was open to the following: first, the inner system of radio, film and television. Thus, apart from the central and provincial broadcast institutions, the film institutions of provincial capitals and municipalities with independent planning status could also set up pay TV channels, for instance, the China Film Group. Second, pay TV was open to the external system of radio, film and television, including the central units and the state-owned institutions with program resources, like the National Meteorological Center, and the health system units. Third, pay TV was open to both private capital and social capital. Thus any state-owned or privately operated organization established in accordance with the law, with registered funds over 15 million yuan and net assets over 30 million yuan, could participate in cooperating with pay TV channels. Fourth, pay TV was open to foreign investment, allowing the influential overseas film and TV production companies, as well as the joint venture companies controlled by the Chinese parties to join in with developing pay TV channels. Since 2001, SARFT has allowed six overseas satellite TV channels to operate in Guangdong Province: China Entertainment Television (CETV), Star TV, Phoenix TV Chinese Channel, Asia TV Home Channel, China International TV and MTV. By 2004, the number of foreign TV channels in China with limited operating rights was 31 (Zhu, 2004b). In 2007, digitalization moved into a new stage of all-around promotion (Zhang, 2007a). From then on digitalization did not only refer to the digitalization of cable TV, but also to HDTV, territorial wireless TV, and TV stations' production and broadcasting (Zhang, 2007b).

Convergence of three networks in China

"Three networks convergence (三网融合, *Sanwang Ronghe*), namely, the integration of telecommunications, broadcasting and the Internet, is a state policy of China for promoting network convergence" (Richard and Grace, 2012). Three networks convergence is not just a physical combination of the infrastructures of the three networks, but more importantly a convergence of business models (Wei, 2010). It is not only a technical problem, but also involves interaction among multiple interest groups, which influenced the implementation of the policy (Yuan *et al.*, 2011). In the mid-1990s, the broadcasting and telecommunications sectors in China both tried to develop cross-sector businesses, but without commercial success. In 1994, after the commercial success of the Internet, they found a way to integrate the different networks. With the development of broadband Internet Protocol (IP) technology, the broadband IP network became the point where the three networks converge.

SAPPRFT and MIIT

Network convergence involves three communications sectors – telecommunications, broadcasting and the Internet – as well as different national networks – the cable, the fixed line telephone and mobile network, and the Internet network. The Ministry of Industry and Information Technology (MIIT) supervises the telecommunications and Internet networks while SAPPRFT regulates the broadcasting network. The divisions of supervisory labor are outlined in Figure 7.1.

The different ideological roles affected the two ministries' perceptions of convergence from the very beginning. As shown in Figure 7.2, MIIT is directly under the State Council while SAPPRFT is simultaneously under the State Council and the Propaganda Department of the Chinese Communist Party (Feng et al., 2009). By 2013, China's broadcasting sector consisted of 2,207 television and radio stations, 166 television stations and 153 radio stations. The total income of the broadcasting sector was 373.4 billion yuan (All-China Journalists Association, 2014). In comparison, China's Telecommunication sector had only three national operators, i.e., China Mobile, China Telecom and China Unicom after the restructuring in 2008. They provided fixed line telephone, mobile phone and Internet access services. The total income of the telecommunication sector in 2013 was 1,168.9 billion yuan. The assets of the telecommunication operators were state-owned and regulated by the State-owned Assets Supervision and Administration Commission (SASAC), which aimed to protect and increase the value of state-owned assets (National Bureau of Statistics of China, 2014). Their market operations were regulated by MIIT with the aim of "utilizing the market's decisive function in allocating resources" and "accelerating the convergence of information and industry; the convergence of telecommunication,

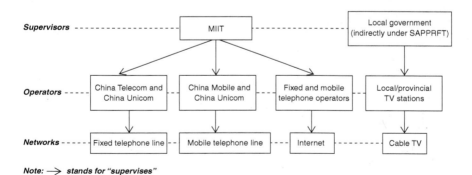

Note: ⟶ stands for "supervises"

Figure 7.1 China's national networks distribution (source: 1. Adapted from Wu and Leung [2012: 956]. Wu RWS and Leung GLK [2012]: A new institutional analysis. *Telecommunications Policy* 36 [10–11]: 955–965).

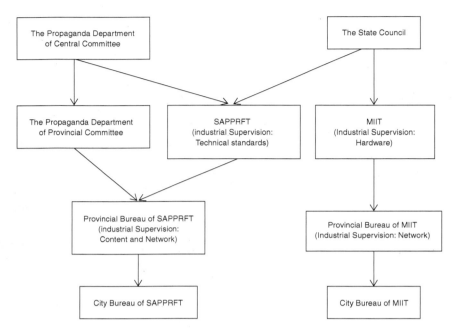

Figure 7.2 Division of labor between SAPPRFT and MIIT (source: 1. Adapted from Wu and Leung [2012: 958]. Wu RWS and Leung GLK [2012]: A new institutional analysis. *Telecommunications Policy* 36 [10–11]: 955–965).

broadcasters and the computer network; promoting the industry to grow stronger" (State Commission for Public Sector Reform, 2015). China's broadcasters were state-owned institutions, their operations regulated by the State Council's broadcasting administrative departments at national and local levels. The national and local party's Propaganda Departments were responsible for controlling media personnel and the content of the media and the Propaganda department's state-owned assert supervision and administration office was responsible for monitoring broadcasters' assets on behalf of the government (Central Propaganda Department, 2009). The propaganda departments also controlled SAPPRFT and its local bureaus through the *nomenklatura* system of appointments (Esarey, 2006). Therefore, China's broadcasters have dual responsibilities – to protect and increase the value of state assets and to lead public opinion and carry out ideological work.

Three network convergence required collaboration and restructuring of the two systems, apart from interconnection and mutual access to networks. However, neither department was willing to concede to the other. The advantage of the SAPPRFT and its predecessor SARFT was that it had a higher political status than the MIIT because of its political function. However, in terms of infrastructure, policy enforcement power and economic power, the SAPPRFT was in a weaker position. First, the broadcasting sector's four-level coverage policy had produced a fragmented broadcasting network and supervisory structure in China. As local broadcasting networks are constructed and owned by local governments, the national regulator SAPPRFT cannot compel local governments to join the convergence bandwagon because different provinces have different developmental priorities and network integration may not be their top priority in comparison with other economic initiatives. Moreover, network convergence at the local level is dependent on the resources available to provincial governments, the visions of their leaders and political pressure from the Central Government (Wu and Leung, 2012). Meanwhile, some of the unsatisfactory progress lies in the lack of upgrading of infrastructure. At the county level, there were about 3,000 networks (Chen, 2011 in Wu and Leung, 2012), but, in many provinces, a large portion of cable networks were not digitalized, were disconnected or had a narrow bandwidth. It was difficult to provide multi-media services with such scattered and low-capacity networks, particularly compared to the nationwide telecommunications network (Wu and Leung, 2012). In comparison, MIIT enjoyed superior economic power as it had a higher earning power and was in a better position to implement network integration. Structurally speaking, there were only three operators in the telecommunications market. This made coordination easier for MIIT, which also had relatively unified control over provincial bureaus of industry and information technology. The sector was also more competitive, with the construction of a national interactive telecommunication network in the 1990s (Wu and Leung, 2012).

The cooperation required for three network convergence were rational choices based on mutual interests and on sharing an optimistic projection of the network convergence project. However, the uneven economic developments of the two systems, coupled with the unequal political status of the two regulators, made full collaboration difficult in reality (Wu and Leung, 2012). It was difficult to resolve issues like which regulator should have control over the convergence project (Economist Intelligence Unit, 2011); how network convergence should proceed, and which sector would take more profit from network convergence. Neither department was willing to concede to the other on these issues (Zhao, 2011).

Development of three network convergence policy

In March 1998, the Ministry of Post and Telecommunications (MPT) and the Ministry of the Electronics Industry were merged to create the Ministry of the Information Industry (MII) and the Ministry of Radio Film and Television was renamed the State Administration of Radio Film and Television (SARFT). Accompanying these changes, the State Council issued the notice *Provision on SARFT's Functions, Internal Organs and Staffing* (State Council, 1998b) ordering a reallocation of "the functions of planning, industry management and the design of the radio and television transmission (including terrestrial and

116 *Television policy between 2004 and 2015*

cable) network's technical standards" from SARFT to MII. For a variety of reasons this reallocation was not carried out, but it nonetheless indicates the State Council's original plan to devote the regulatory power of the telecommunication, information and broadcasting infrastructural network to the single department, i.e., the MII, and it also reveals the long-standing conflicts between the SARFT and MII. Although the three network convergence became a national development strategy in 1998, the actual process took nearly ten years. In 1999, the State Council issued an important No. 82 policy document, instructing that "telecommunication operators shall not run radio or television businesses and radio and television stations shall not operate telecommunication businesses. Both parties must resolutely implement [this policy]" (Wei, 2010). The document also explicitly stated, "broadcasting and its transmission network has become an important component of the national information technology." The State Council's policy to distinguish the telecommunication operation from that of broadcasting, while simultaneously recognizing the information technology nature of the broadcasting network shows that, rather than a pure technical convergence, the network convergence in China involved continuous battles between two economic interests groups, MII and SARFT. The progress of convergence stagnated over the next ten years, from 1999 to 2009.

During this period, the telecommunication sector experienced major restructuring and technological advancement. Between 1973 and 1998, MPT provided China's telecommunication and post service under the name of the China P&T Directorate General of Telecommunication (China Telecom) and Directorate General of Post, P&T China (China Post), which were state-owned companies. In 1994, in order to break the market monopoly held by China Telecom, China United Network Communications Ltd (China Unicom) was set up. However, market competition did not occur because of the lack of competitiveness of China Unicom whose assets and turnover were tiny compared to China Telecom's in 1998. In the same year, the MPT and the Ministry of the Electronics Industry were merged and then split into two parts, the Ministry of Post and the Ministry of the Information Industry, and its post and telecommunication services were also separated. In 1999, the State Council approved the reform plan of the China P&T Directorate General of Telecommunication, and its mobile, fixed line telephone and satellite businesses were separated to form China Mobile Communications Corporation (CMCC), China Telecommunication Group Corporation (fixed line service), and China Satellite Communications Corporation (China Satellite) in 2000, all three being state-own enterprises. Other smaller telecommunication operators were also set up by various government departments or organizations, such as China Network Communications Ltd operating a broadband Internet business, the first Sino-foreign joint-venture, Shanghai Symphony Telecommunications Co. Ltd (SST) and Railway Telecommunications and Information Ltd, running a fixed line telephone service. China Mobile Limited (China Mobile), CMCC's subsidiary, is listed on both the New York and Hong Kong stock exchanges since it was renamed from China Telecommunication (HK) Ltd in 2000. China Telecommunication (HK) Ltd was listed on the Hong Kong and New York Stock Exchanges in 1997, and the state-owned China P&T Directorate General of Telecommunication originally owned it. China Telecom, a subsidiary of the China Telecommunication Group Corporation, was listed on the New York and Hong Kong stock exchanges in 2002. In 2001, the State Council General Office issued the *Telecommunication Reform Plan* to restructure the telecommunications sector. Following the plan, in 2002, China Telecommunication Group's businesses in ten provinces were merged with China Network Communications Ltd to form China Network Communications Group Corporation (China Netcom) (Xu XY, 2008). From 2002 to 2008, China's telecommunication sector had six service providers, China Mobile, China Telecom, China Netcom, China Unicom, China Satellite and China Railway Telecom. In 2007, China had the world's largest mobile and fixed line telephone market with nearly one billion subscribers (including half a billion mobile users) and a turnover of 728 billion yuan. During this period, while there was a slow increase in the number of fixed line telephone subscribers, the number of mobile users increased rapidly, and, as a result, market competition became unbalanced between fixed line and mobile operators (Xue and Jiang, 2010).

In 2008, the Ministry of Information Industry was renamed as the Ministry of Industry and Information Technology (MIIT). Its main responsibilities include: to design industrial planning, policies and standards; to supervise the daily operation of industrial branches; to promote the development of major technological equipment and innovation concerning the communication sector; to guide the construction of information system; and to safeguard China's information security (State Council, 2014[1]). In the same year, the MIIT, the National Development and Reform Commission and the Ministry of Finance jointly issued the *Notice on Deepening Telecommunication Reform* in order to form "relatively balanced competitive telecommunication market, enhance independent innovation capability, increase the competitiveness of telecommunications enterprises, and promote the healthy coordinated development of industry". The policy wants to "develop the third-generation mobile communications (3G), rationally allocate the existing telecommunications network resources [...], to form a moderate, healthy market competition, both to prevent monopoly, but also to avoid excessive competition and duplication". The reform aims to "issue three 3G licenses, and support to form three telecommunication operators which have national network resources, relatively closed strength and size, full business capacity and strong market competitiveness" (Feng and Zhang, 2008). Following the reform plan, China Telecom acquired China Unicom's CDMA (Code Division Multiple Access) network and China Satellite's telecommunication business, while China Unicom and China Netcom merged, and China Railway Telecom merged with China Mobile. Since the restructuring, China's telecommunication sector has maintained three operators, i.e., China Telecom, China Mobile and China Unicom. The three operators were granted 3G licenses in 2009 and 4G licenses in 2013 (China Mobile, 2015; Lin, 2014). Apart from increasing the speed of communication, because it has the necessary bandwidth, the 3G technology enables provision of various value added services like video calling, live

118 *Television policy between 2004 and 2015*

streaming, mobile Internet and mobile online game access, IPTV and online shopping on the mobile phones. The introduction of 3G led to the adoption of the term "mobile broadband," as users can use the Internet whilst on the move, for example on a train or as a passenger in a car (All about 3G, 2009).

With the advent of this new technology, the three network convergence again gained primacy on the State Council's policy agenda. In 2009, the State Council held a standing committee meeting to accelerate the three network convergence. Under the coordination of the State Council's general office, the MIIT and SARFT formed the drafting group, embarked on the drafting of the overall convergence plan and arrived at a consensus on some major issues. In May 2009, the State Council approved and issued a notice from the National Development and Reform Commission (NDRC) named *Opinions On the Work of Deepening the Economic Reform in 2009* (关于2009年深化经济体制改革工作意见). This document requests "to implement national policy, achieve the two-way access by telecommunication and broadcasting enterprises, promote the substantive progress of the three network convergence" (State Council, 2009). In January 2010, the Premier Wen Jiabao held a State Council standing committee meeting to speed up the progress, made three network convergence a priority policy and the meeting approved the *Overall Plan for Promoting Three Network Convergence* (State Council, 2010a). The State Council and the Party made the three network convergence in its strategic plan conducive to the rapid increase of national informatization and to promote innovation and the application of information technology to meet the people's increasingly diverse demands. The country's participation in the global information technology competition also helps to ensure China's network information security. The construction and upgrading of communication and broadcast transmission networks were included in the range of national critical information infrastructure construction, and they were granted more policy support to achieve interoperability, resource sharing, improve network utilization and avoid duplication. The policy aims to gradually and incrementally implement the convergence programs to ensure substantive progress. The plan organizes the convergence in two stages. From 2010 to 2012, pilot convergence programs on two-way access of telecommunication and broadcasting networks were to be carried out to explore possible industrial policy and institutional mechanisms, to upgrade telecommunication and broadcasting networks and establish a national cable television network company (中国广播电视网络有限公司). From 2013 to 2015, the pilot programs were to be evaluated, the network convergence fully rolled out, and institutional mechanisms and an effective and efficient new regulation system were to be established.

The conditions of two-way access include two parts. Eligible broadcasting companies can operate value-added telecommunications services, basic telecommunications services being managed like value-added telecommunications services, Internet access services via cable network, Internet data transmission value-added services, and domestic IP telephone service. Eligible state-owned telecommunication enterprises may engage in the production of non-current affairs television programs, transmission of Internet audio-visual programs, the retransmission of current affairs and news programs, the IPTV transmission services, except those operated in the form of television and radio stations and the mobile television distribution service (MIIT and SARFT, 2010).

The regulatory responsibilities are divided between SARFT and MIIT, which will supervise broadcasting content and telecommunication businesses respectively. They must adhere to the principles of transparency, fairness and impartiality, and non-discrimination. The SARFT regulates the broadcasting companies' business planning, business access, operations supervision, content security, broadcast, broadcast safety, quality of service, public service, network equipment and network interconnections. It is also in charge of the integration broadcast control of the IPTV and mobile TV, and, most importantly, for issuing permits for audio-video programs transmitted through the information network. No entity or individual is allowed to provide services related to Internet audio-video programs without such a permit. The Propaganda Department provides guidance to SARFT. The MIIT is responsible for the administration of the telecommunication companies' network interconnections, service quality, universal service, network equipment, network information security and for issuing the permits for telecommunication business operation.

In addition, the *Administrative Provision for the Internet Audio-Video Program Service*, jointly promulgated by SARFT and MIIT in 2007, states that: (1) for the provision of radio or television station services, or current political news audio-video services, an entity also needs to hold a permit for radio and television broadcasting organizations or a permit for Internet news information services; (2) for the provision of hosting, interviewing and reporting audio-video services, an entity must have a permit for broadcasting program production and a permit for Internet news information services; (3) for the provision of self-produced Internet series (films) related services, an entity needs to hold a permit for broadcasting programs production.

An entity that has obtained a permit for audio-video programs transmitted through the information network must also apply for the permits for telecommunication business operation. Only current affairs and political news produced and broadcast by radio or television stations at or above prefectural level, or published on a central news media unit's website, can be broadcast online. Internet audio-video program service providers cannot allow individuals to upload current political news audio-video programs. An Internet audio-video program service provider shall immediately delete the audio-video programs violating laws and regulations, keep relevant records, perform reporting obligations, and implement the administrative requirements of the relevant authority. The major investors and operators of Internet audio-video program service providers shall be liable for the contents of the audio-video programs broadcast and uploaded.

In June 2010, after long negotiations and five revisions to resolve their disputes, the MIIT and SARFT finally reached agreement on *the Working Plan for Pilot Sites of Three Network Convergence* (sixth version). The plan was

120 *Television policy between 2004 and 2015*

approved and promulgated by the State Council for implementation. In July 2010, 12 Chinese cities including Beijing, Shanghai, Shenzhen, and Hangzhou were chosen to pilot the program. In 2011, 41 more cities joined the second phase of the pilot study. The duty head of the three network convergence team, Zou Jiangxing, commented that the cultural backgrounds of the MIIT and SARFT were clearly different, they did not work well together in the past, and thus faced big challenges [to work together now] since they are in direct competition with each other under the three network convergence strategy (Lin, 2010).

The State Council set up the Three Network Convergence Coordination Group Office that issued the *Notice on Issues concerning the Pilot Program for Convergence of Three Networks* (State Council, 2010b). The policy document requests Party committees and governments of the pilot areas to mobilize propaganda, telecommunications, radio and television and public security departments to form a provincial three network convergence work coordination team to organize and implement the three network convergence pilot program. The provincial coordination office must communicate with the central office under the State Council. Under the team's leadership, broadcasting institutions are responsible for formulating the plan for building the IPTV platform and for mobile television integrated broadcasting and control. Also under the team's leadership the telecom enterprises are responsible for IPTV transmission, mobile television transmissions, and public Internet audio and video program services in forms other than those covered in the radio and television stations implementation plan. Cable television network enterprises are responsible for local areas value-added telecom services, Internet access based on the cable television network, Internet data transmission value-added services, and for the domestic IP phone services plan. The local Party committee and governments are responsible for formulating the specific objectives and tasks; for development plans, supporting policies, organization and guarantees.

The converging broadcasting and telecommunication industry in China has not adopted the same communication regulating strategy as in other convergent industries, such as Ofcom in the UK, which regulates the entire TV and radio sectors, fixed line telecoms, mobiles, postal services, plus the airwaves over which wireless devices operate; or the Office of the Communications Authority (Ofca) in Hong Kong, which regulates both telecommunication and broadcasting industries. Instead, broadcasting and telecommunication regulation is a sector and geography-based administration with the aims of strengthening safety regulation, maintaining industrial administrative order, supervising the pilot enterprises and organizations to perform their security responsibilities, and guaranteeing the coordinated and orderly progress of the pilot businesses. The sector and geography-based principle in China is largely due to the diversities of China's localities, the historical legacy of the multi-level administrative and industry structure of the broadcasting sector, and, more importantly, the struggle for protecting departmental interests between the SARFT and MIIT.

The deputy head of the SARFT, Tian Jing, asserted that the three network convergence policy needs to maintain Chinese characteristics, which include leading correct public opinion guidance, paying attention to social benefits, and broadcasting institutions being in charge of the IPTV broadcast platform and mobile television. Also, the policy must ensure cultural and information security, and social stability, and it needs to accept differences and formulate different regulations for different areas. To perform well, the SARFT should work on four areas: strengthening law-making to promote policies, restricting monopoly in order to create fair competition, recognizing differences by implementing sector-based regulation, and progressively conducting the work step by step (Tian, 2011).

The head of the SARFT's technology department, Wang Xiaojie, outlined the picture of network convergence in China:

> Three network convergence is the transformation of telecommunications, broadcasting and Internet network to the broadband communication network, digital television network and next generation Internet. The three networks' technical function and business model converge, infrastructures connect and resources share, they can provide voice, data and radio-video multiple services.

The convergence:

> is not the merging of three networks, nor do they replace each other, but each network can provide multiple services. Users can access the telephone and broadband Internet service on the broadcasting network; and they can also watch television on the telecommunication network.

Wang added that "due to historical reasons and competition needs, the co-existence of three basic networks will last for a long time, convergence is a gradual process" (Chen *et al.*, 2010).

Key stage of three network convergence policy

Since 2010, 54 cities have been approved to join the convergence pilot scheme, but the fragmented schemes did not provide an effective model for implementing network convergence and many cities did not make any real progress. In 2012 the State Council (2012) approved the establishment of the China Broadcasting Network Ltd (CBN), which was launched in May 2014. A charter jointly promulgated by the SAPPRFT and Ministry of Finance (2014) states that CBN is a state-owned cultural enterprise and the Ministry of Finance injected 4.5 billion yuan as its start-up capital. The SAPPRFT was responsible for setting up and hosting the CBN, which will build a national cable network interconnection platform and operational support system. It will integrate the countrywide broadcasting cable networks and upgrade the existing national backbone network and cable networks to enable the two-way and interactive transmission so that the cable networks can interconnect with each other. The CBN's business includes

122 *Television policy between 2004 and 2015*

carrying out convergence related services, the planning, construction, operation and maintenance of the cable television network, national cable network interconnection services, radio and television transmission, distribution services, radio and television program production and transmission services (China Broadcasting Network Ltd, 2014).

In 2015, the State Council issued the *Three Network Convergence Promotion Plan*, to comprehensively push forwards the three network convergence nationwide (State Council, 2015). Based on the experience of the pilot program, the plan provides detailed instructions on technical standards and implementation requirements (MIIT and SARFT, 2015) and it sets up four major tasks: (1) to promote a two-way access nationwide broadcasting and telecommunications business; (2) to accelerate the transformation and construction of the broadband network; (3) to strengthen the network, information security and cultural security supervision; (4) to effectively promote the development of related industries.

The Chinese government introduced various preferential policies to speed up and deepen the convergence of the three networks, but the actual process is not attractive to potential customers. The growth rate of IPTV users in China is far below the world average level. As Dong Jun (2013) pointed out: "The fragmented pilot of 54 cities in China failed to provide an effective model for other cities to implement network convergence; moreover, a lot more cities did start the reform but got nowhere." The poor implementation is mainly due to the lack of detailed rules and regulations regarding the integration of the three networks, and most importantly, due to the absence of a unified regulator and the limited legal powers of both SAPPRFT and MIIT. Currently, there are telecommunication regulations and broadcasting regulations issued by the telecommunication and broadcasting departments respectively, as well as various policies issued by Central Government, but no specified law with higher legal authority, therefore both departments tend to enact and interpret the regulations and documents from their own perspective and try to protect their own interests. So, not only detailed rules and regulations, but also a unified independent regulator and law above both the SAPPRFT and MIIT are needed to guarantee the implementation of the three networks convergence (Fang, 2015).

Summary

China's broadcasting, telecommunication and Internet network convergence became a national development strategy in 1998, the actual process took nearly 10 years. Departmental protections, fragmental infrastructure and market have hindered the progress and restricted the potential benefits of technology advancement. The sector and geographical based regulatory structure is neither effective nor compatible to the convergence principle but as a product of intergovernmental contests, and it not only resulted in preferable reading and implementation of policy and regulation, but also created extra bureaucratic burdens such as different operation licenses for network operators. The question of how to combat departmental protectionism and build up a compatible regulatory structure with clear overarching principles and implementation procedures is crucial to the success of China's three-network convergence project.

Note

1 State Council (2014).

8 Public service broadcasting

Introduction

The "cultural public service" policy introduced by the Chinese government in the middle 2000s has prompted renewed discussions on the public service functions of broadcasters in China. After emerging first in Britain during the 1920s, public service broadcasting (PSB) has taken root in societies characterized by democratic institutions and pluralistic values. This pattern is beginning to change. Despite significant differences in its political conditions and policies, since 2006 the Central Government of the People's Republic of China has undertaken the construction of a PSB system of its own. The result, as described in this chapter, is a new form of a top-down public communications network with similarities to both Chinese and European precedents. Coinciding with the new emphasis placed by the Chinese state on public cultural service (PCS), a vigorous academic debate has also emerged about how basic cultural rights, such as equal access to state-owned media in both urban and rural locations, should be guaranteed and protected. Academic researchers and state officials seem to agree that China's PSB system plays an important role in achieving such aims, and advocate the establishment and expansion of a system according to China's social conditions (see Chin, 2012; Chin and Johnson, 2012). These developments come at a time when public service media (PSM) around the world face serious economic challenges that have been exacerbated by global recession. In contrast, the Chinese state is beginning to take initiatives in major urban areas to extend PSB and other public information services (e.g., digital information resources, museums and libraries) to citizens, and that PSB will be likely to continue to expand there as a result.

These developments raise interesting questions concerning the origins and role of PSB within an ostensibly authoritarian society, and the extent to which the media's public service functions can co-exist with a state-owned broadcasting sector. Meanwhile, the contentiousness and ambiguity of the public service concept and the lack of coherent models of PSB poses hard questions regarding the aims and principles of PSB policy in the Chinese social and political context. Answering them is essential to framing a meaningful critique that may help us understand the role of PSB in China and its implications for the lives of Chinese citizens and for the limitation of state power.

In this chapter I approach these questions from two perspectives, the normative and the historical. First the Chinese normative concept of PSB is compared with one typical of a liberal democracy, and both their differences and commonalities are unpacked. Second, I ask which values and functions of PSB are privileged or neglected in the Chinese discussion by those who hold power. Normative conceptualization is essential, as the destiny of social organizations is determined by the character of the dominant discourse, which prefers norms and values differentially (Hall, 1993; Sparks, 1998; Tracey, 1998). The comparison to liberal democracy as benchmark is justified by the broad agreement in political theory on the basic principles of liberalism (Buckler, 2010). Questions of fundamental importance are addressed: which functions of PSB are given precedence at the expense of others? To what ends are these functions intended?

Next, a historical perspective will be taken up to inquire into the origins and actual evolution of Chinese PSB policy, posing the fundamental questions: why did PSB in China evolve into its current form? How well does this form match the normative justifications for it proffered to the public? The historical approach is particularly pertinent given the self-reinforcing and evolutionary features of public policy-making in China (Chin, 2011).

The chapter concludes with an examination of PSB expansion in the local context to add an empirical perspective on the state's normative rhetoric. Throughout the chapter I consider the degree to which PSB is sustainable in China, and argue that the answer is wholly dependent on how one defines "public" within an authoritarian context, and whether institutional and fiscal support for this new concept will continue in the period of China's next Five-Year Plan and beyond. As it demonstrates, although the initiative for the development of PSB has been predominantly generated by the state, opening this door has allowed a range of actors to enter into debates concerning the legitimacy of individual cultural, political, and civil rights – all under the rubric of public service. This, in turn, gives rise to the possibility that, although PSB in China remains state-controlled, its function and content are not solely determined by the Central Government.

Public service frameworks in Europe and China

Public service (公共服务, *gonggong fuwu*) is a relatively new concept in China, and reflects a turn toward egalitarian public policies intended to smooth over inequalities created or exacerbated by post-Mao economic reforms. The historical emergence of PSB and its role in achieving public policy goals has depended on conditions that vary. In this section previous arguments concerning factors that have given rise to PSB quite generally are summarized. Frequently emphasis is placed on political culture and state support as key factors affecting the formation of PSB institutions, and finance and governance are considered to be the two variables on which a sustainable and independent PSB system depends. The major difference between the two frameworks – European and Chinese – can be understood in terms of the ideal degrees of separation between

126 Public service broadcasting

state and society. Perhaps unsurprisingly, a relatively high degree of separation is posited in the liberal notion of "public," but remains comparatively absent within China's authoritarian political system – despite the emergence of rhetoric about public service.

Where PSB in Europe is concerned, most researchers agree that certain programming and institutional conditions must be met to secure an independent status and sufficient separation from both the state and the market to guarantee a public service orientation. These conditions include:

1   Universal service obligations which guarantee that the majority of the population must have access to PSB programming regardless of geographic and financial constraints (Born and Prosser, 2001).
2   The ability to produce news and current affairs programming that informs and enlightens the citizenry, and contributes to content diversity (Harrison and Woods, 2001).
3   The ability to produce and provide mass audience programming which confers a shared sense of community and cohesion (Harrison and Woods, 2001).
4   Inclusion or integration of marginalized or socially excluded groups (Curran and Seaton, 2003; Harrison and Woods, 2001).
5   A commitment to quality service and output based on standards that reflect the public interest rather than consumer demand (Born and Prosser, 2001).
6   The absence of undue influence by any single power group (Murdock, 2000).

Generally speaking, there are two primary methods for institutionalizing PSB provision: either provision by multiple bodies or by one specifically designated broadcaster. A third formulation has been discussed of late, establishing a public service publisher (PSP) (Humphreys, 2010).

For PSB to be legitimate as an institution, its creation must be justified by an existing and identifiable social need, examples of which might include education of the citizenry, incorporation of diverse groups into the social and political order, or prevention of revolt from below (Scannell, 2000). In each case, the creation of PSB requires state support. One cause of the erosion of PSB functions in Britain has been the deterioration in the relationship between the state and the institution (Curran and Seaton, 2003). The political culture of a given state – referring to the written and unwritten rules, norms, and practices that govern the routine exercise of political power within a society and, with respect to its media sector, the prevailing political attitudes or ideologies which confer legitimacy on PSB norms and functions – together determine the degrees of broadcaster freedom within society (Hallin and Mancini, 2004; Sparks, 1998; Tracey, 1998). Internally, the PSB system depends on a stable financial base to facilitate programming decisions that contribute to the public interest (Sparks, 1998). From a governance perspective, additional regulations, such as those creating an independent and rational-legal regulatory agency that operates according to

Public service broadcasting 127

transparent, coherent guidelines (e.g., laws and fixed procedures), may also be required to ensure the public broadcaster's compliance with PSB obligations (Hallin and Mancini, 2004; Sparks, 1995).

In China, the mandate to develop nationwide public service broadcasting originated with the state. In September 2006, the State Council published its *Outline of Cultural Development for the Eleventh Five-Year Plan.* This important policy document championed "cultural public service" (CPS) as the key objective of culture building in the subsequent five years – the first time the government had explicitly referred to this concept. Public service broadcasting (PSB) makes up part of the CPS project.

Although the Chinese academic literature on PSB goes back to 1980 (Guo, 1998; Hu, 1980; Hu *et al.*, 2008; Xia, 1988; Zhang, 1992; Zhao, 1998a), the surge in publications on the subject did not happen until 2007, after the official announcement of the CPS policy (Hu *et al.*, 2008). This literature falls into two primary categories: (1) reviews of the evolution of PSB in foreign countries, and (2) articles purporting to define "public interest" and "public service," and to construct a PSB concept compatible with the Chinese social and political context. This latter aspect is extremely important given that PSB in China is in its infancy.

The substantive normative reasoning justifying the functions of PSB relies on its relation to the "public interest" (PI), a presupposed common welfare of the community or "common good" over and above the interests of particular individuals (Feintuch and Varney, 2006; Van Cuilenburg and McQuail, 1998). The substance of PI remains highly contested and subject to capture and reinterpretation, inasmuch as the values in question are inseparable from those involved in democracy and the good society (Dahlgren, 2000; Freedman, 2008; Hargrave and Shaw, 2009; McQuail, 1992). Interpretations of PI range from skepticism about its very existence, through equating it to the national interest in certain circumstances, to the common good "assessed in context" (Hargrave and Shaw, 2009: 44). The contested nature of PI has vividly transpired most recently in the Chinese context.

Defining the public interest: principle, substance and procedure

European legal and media-studies theories tend to identify citizenship in liberal-democratic theory as the fundamental basis for discovering the normative principle of the public interest in such societies. Marshall (2009: 150) considers that: "Citizenship is a status bestowed on those who are full members of a community. All who possess the status are equal with respect to the rights and duties with which the status is endowed." Citizenship is closely intertwined with human rights, as historically they shared roots in liberal individualism (Nash, 2009). "Civil" citizenship includes "the rights necessary for individual freedom"; "political" citizenship implies "the right to participate in the exercise of political power"; "social" citizenship ranges "from the right to a modicum of economic

128 *Public service broadcasting*

welfare and security to the right to share ... in the social heritage and to live the life of a civilized being according to [prevailing] standards" (Marshall, 2009: 148). "Cultural" citizenship enables one to "take part in cultural life; enjoy the benefits of scientific progress and its applications" (Article 15, ICESCR). Striking a balance between citizens' individual rights and self-interest, and their social responsibilities and civic virtues, such as participation in the political process, tolerance of differences, and a sense of justice, is also stressed as essential to citizenship, for its contribution to the health and stability of democratic regimes (Born and Prosser, 2001; Kymlicka and Norman, 1994: 353). Citizenship is key to discovering the principles of PI, first, because it features both the common good and shared identity, and equal individual rights and obligations; and second, because it unifies the public domain, and its formal legal status provides a starting point for debates over exactly which rights and obligations are to be given recognition and therefore political existence (Born and Prosser, 2001; Dahlgren, 2000; Feintuch and Varney, 2006: 108; Morgan and Yeung, 2007; Murdock, 2000; Ranson and Stewart, 1989).

The Chinese academic debate on PI has achieved little consensus, either on principle or in spirit, regardless of the approach taken. Xiao (2009) identified ten different viewpoints in theorizing the concept, concluding that none of them are "better" or "more persuasive" than the others. Xiao and other like-minded academics have suggested concentrating on inventing legitimate procedures for involving all interested parties and opinions in deciding collectively the substance of PI – procedures such as public hearings – rather than attempting to finalize a comprehensive definition a priori. The latter would contribute little to resolving practical problems. This reliance on deliberation and dialogue is supported by academics in both China and Europe (Morgan and Yeung, 2007: 36–37).

Citizenship, however, is not deployed in China to serve as the basis for the normative conceptualization of PI, as the word is contested in the Chinese political context. First, both Chinese officials and academics tend to prefer words like "the People" or "individual" instead of "citizen." "The People" is a politically restrictive and exclusive category in China, its membership is not fixed but changeable according to the interpretations of politicians (Keane, 2001), unlike "citizen," a legal concept that establishes the equality of all Chinese nationals before the law (Article 33, Chinese Constitution, 1982). The Constitution also provides that "all power in the People's Republic of China (PRC) belongs to the People" (Article 2, Chinese Constitution, 1982). Peng Zhen, the Vice-Chairman of the 1982 Constitutional Revision Commission, in his report to the National People's Congress (NPC), the national legislature, stressed that:

> freedoms and rights in an absolute sense subject to no restrictions whatsoever have never existed in the world. [...] Only when the democratic rights and fundamental interests of the majority of people are ensured and extended will it be possible for the freedoms and rights of individual citizens to be effectively ensured and fully realized.
>
> (Peng, 1982)

Even liberalism accepts that individual freedoms and rights are not absolute, and may be limited to prevent harm to others and to protect the general welfare; however, its principle is respect for the equality and autonomy of all citizens, and "general welfare" is a universal value shared by all, not just some individuals (Swift, 2004). By conceptualizing persons in competing guises – "the People" and "citizens" – Chinese law and policy actually militate against the constitutional protection of equal individual rights from violation by the "majority," even in the spirit of socialism.

Historically, the individualizing concept of citizenship has been spurned in the PRC as "antithetical to the socialist goal of mass mobilization, class struggle, and collectivism" (Keane, 2001). Article 51 of the Chinese Constitution of 1982 states, "The exercise by citizens of the PRC of their freedoms and rights may not infringe upon the interests of the state, of society and of the collective, or upon the lawful freedoms and rights of other citizens." This clause justifies subordinating the individual citizen's liberty, autonomy and rights to the tyranny of the majority at best, and at worst, to Party-state dictatorship when the latter monopolies the interpretation of majoritarian interests. One consequence of this collectivist bias is that the official deployment of the word "citizen" has been confined to the campaign to improve the "civic virtue" of the people so as to meet the needs of the market economy (Nathan, 1989). In recent years, the concept of citizenship has attracted growing attention in Chinese academic and public debates alongside the renewed call for political reform at the top and public participation in politics at the bottom (Yang G, 2008).

The Constitution of the PRC indeed speaks the language of the public interest, and the term regularly appears in legal provisions without definition, even though nearly every law enacted by the NPC and its Standing Committee has utilized it (Han, 2005). There have been no juridical interpretations of "public interest," either. This ambiguity gives discretionary power to the authorities to interpret "public interest" in ways that invade and deprive individuals of their rights (Ren and Ji, 2005). It is unsurprising then, that so few studies have been done on the relation between broadcasting and the public interest in China.

Three approaches to the public interest current in public forums will now be identified and summarized. The ruling Chinese Communist Party (CCP), with its one-party authoritarian mode of governance, assert the identity of the interests of the Party-State, of society and of the people, whence Party and governmental policies necessarily reflect the public interest.[1] Peng Zhen in the above-mentioned report to the NPC claimed that "as ours is a socialist country, the interests of the State and society are in basic accord with the citizens' personal interests" (Peng, 1982). This statement subsumes individual, public and State interests under one comprehensive doctrine. However, both Europe's and China's own recent histories prove that such a claim is untenable, and it has also been contested by many Chinese academics (He, 2007; Xiao, 2009; Xiong and Zhu, 2005). In 2004, the CCP's role as representative of the fundamental interests of the broad majority of citizens was inscribed in the Chinese Constitution as the result of an amendment to its Preamble incorporating the "important thought" of the "Three Represents."

130   *Public service broadcasting*

The public interest, as defined by the Party-State, assigns to the Chinese cultural sector the duty to "protect, realize and develop the basic cultural rights of ordinary people"; to "develop the nation's moral, intellectual, scientific and cultural standards"; and to "build up a wealthy and strong, democratic and harmonious modern Socialist country"; aims which "reflect the public desire and the superiority of China's socialist system" (CCP, 2007). Some Chinese intellectuals concede the key role of the State in protecting the public from harm caused by private interest groups. In their view, the major weaknesses of US-style commercial broadcasting are its de-politicization, corruption by public relations firms and their amoral methods, subservience to advertisers, and close working relationship with private interest groups (Li, 2008; Wang, 2008). In general, both Western European public broadcasting and US commercial broadcasting are seen as pervaded by the rhetoric of "liberal" values, yet increasingly dominated by profit- and rent-seeking motives at odds with their claims to serve the public interest (Xu F, 2008). The Chinese people, academics argue, require instead a fair government protecting all members of society equally (Pan, 2008).

Indeed, all Chinese constitutions since 1954 have stressed the role of the state as the safeguard and realization of the public interest (Han, 2005). This proposition differs little from the general expectation in democratic societies for the state to pursue the public interest on behalf of its citizens by providing necessary regulatory frameworks and material resources to enable its members to pursue a better life and to safeguard the common good (Buckler, 2010; Gearty, 2007; Swift, 2004). Instead, the Party has historically considered its socialist ideology to place it above and beyond the Constitution, and it is this that has justified the Party-State's intervention into every area of life.

Other Chinese academics are concerned with the pragmatic questions of PI: how to apply it, in what context, and for what purpose. From their perspective, a substantive definition is less important than developing procedures for its articulation, its representation in public policy, and for identifying who ought to participate in making policy in the public interest. They suggest that PI in the media sector can be constructed only through rational public discussion, under public scrutiny. These scholars concede the legitimacy of governmental coordination of social activities and public order, but doubt governmental discretion and unaccountability in interpreting PI. Neither government nor media are "owners" or "arbiters" of the public interest; but the public may confer on them rights of implementation (Luo and Liu, 2006; Xia, 2005). The formation of the public interest depends on the formation of a modern public: citizens who can discuss and act upon issues and events affecting their interests (Xia, 2005).

These strictures resonate, given that the Head of State is not popularly elected, that the CCP is a political power superior to State authority, and is intolerant of dissenting voices (Esarey, 2006). The Party ideologically controls the government's media policy-making (Chin, 2011); thus, it is difficult to see how the government could be able or willing to defend the public interest from the Party's political interference, still pervasive in the media's day-to-day operations. The legitimacy even of the judiciary to vindicate the public interest is

Public service broadcasting   131

questionable, because of concerns over its lack of independence. One concludes that a feasible way of realizing the public interest would be to resort to a public hearing procedure involving the administration, the judiciary and the public (Xiao, 2009).

Defining PSB's normative functions: striking a balance between freedom of speech, development and social stability

As no consensus has been reached concerning who should define the public interest, so likewise no consensus currently exists regarding the normative qualities of PSB in the Chinese social context (Hu *et al.*, 2008). Chinese academics resist replicating the Western model, maintaining that China should learn from the West, but be creative in adapting and implementing their models to accord with Chinese social conditions (Shi and Zhou, 2006: 15). Chinese academics support PSB for its symbolic importance to a diverse society pursuing democracy, transparency, fairness, and minority rights (Yuan and Xiang, 2006); for contributing to a balanced media ecology amid intensified media commercialization (Guo, 2006; Zhang LP, 2008); for its facilitation of exchange and dialogue between government and society, reducing social tensions; and for its role in developing democracy, the rule of law, and the market economy (Yuan and Xiang, 2006). Discussions converge on PSB's non-profit and public interest-serving purposes, and on its social and cultural products of education, enlightenment, moral critique, quality information, defense of minorities, and national cohesion (Shi and Zhang 2007, Shi and Zhou, 2006; Yang C, 2008; Yuan and Xiang, 2006). Some go further and suggest that PSB needs to be publicly owned, independent of interest groups, universally accessible, socially responsible and impartial, and facilitative of the formation of a free, open and equal public sphere that fosters public participatory consciousness for the democratization of society (Shi and Zhang, 2007; Shi and Zhou, 2006).

Qi Yongfeng, a policy-maker on the State Council's National Development and Reform Commission (NDRC), agrees with his academic counterparts on the educational and social functions of PSB, but differs on institutional independence and the media's role in upholding citizens' civil and political rights (Qi, 2006). Qi considers that the media's degree of freedom and priority of rights and responsibilities are determined by the developmental stage of society. China's situation as a transitional society requires stricter supervision of the media as a precaution against chaotic social upheaval resulting in economic and other losses. The media need to concentrate on their social responsibilities to improve cultural, scientific and moral standards, to create channels for citizens to publicly and orderly participate in the processes of governance, and to facilitate social consensus supporting reform and institutional innovation and reconcile competing interests (Qi, 2006: 21). Qi's formula marginalizes impartiality and independence in PSB, prioritizing the values of social solidarity.

Coming from a high official, Qi's reasoning exposes the profound differences between Chinese and Western assumptions about the relationship between state

132   *Public service broadcasting*

power and individual rights and about the values that might justify political freedom for PSB. Liberal democracy recognizes media freedom as an "instrumental freedom" that promotes the values and ends of freedom of speech on behalf of everyone (Barendt, 2007: 422–424; Gibbons, 1998). While liberal states reserve the right to impose restrictions on freedom of speech for reasons of national security or to maintain public order, the formal approach is "no prior restraint". Freedom of speech is paramount for securing individual liberty, discovering truth, participating in a democratic political process, holding authority accountable, and promoting individual development and fulfillment (Emerson, 1977; Gibbons, 1998; Greenawalt, 1980; Perry, 1984). The justification for an independent means of discovering truth rests on three principles: a refusal to accept the infallibility of authority; the utility of exposing accepted facts and received opinions to criticism; and a conviction that rational discussion yields better judgments (Emerson, 1977: 740–741).

Chinese philosophy, by contrast, has traditionally been elitist and paternalistic, holding that rulers and elites are best situated to discern the common good, and are entitled to rule by their superior moral wisdom or technical knowledge. The Chinese government has traditionally pursued a substantive moral agenda defined by the normative vision of the ruling class (Nathan, 2008; Peerenboom, 2006: 61; Shue, 2004: 31).

Liberalism preconceives the state as a neutral arbiter and presupposes a social contract whereby individuals precede the state and are entitled to choose society's normative agenda, which the state enforces, or to pursue individual normative agendas without state interference. Moreover, "governments derive their just powers from the consent of the governed" and should be accountable to the people (Greenawalt, 1980: 674; Peerenboom, 2006). Because people reasonably disagree about the common good, a procedural mechanism (namely, elections) for resolution is set up. The legitimacy of the Chinese government is rooted not in procedures and contracts, but in its capacity to preserve the peace and impose order (Shue, 2004). The dominant academic discourse since 1989, which might be styled "neo-conservatism," champions a powerful central authority guaranteeing stability during a socio-economic transition, directed by the CCP's wise politicians, "to achieve effective modernization, fair distribution, political order, and national security" (Chen, 1997; Nathan, 2008: 33). Grave doubts as to the feasibility of liberal democracy in China still heavily influence official policy (Chen, 1997; Nathan, 2008; SohuNews, 2008).

Liberalism regards freedom of speech as a deontological value intrinsic to the autonomous subject, which develops more reflective and mature individuals. To achieve self-development, the mind must first be free, even if its exercise may be inimical to the welfare of society (Barendt, 2007; Greenawalt, 1980; Perry, 1984). In contrast, the Chinese Constitution conceives of rights as granted by the state. Liberalism also prioritizes first-generation civil and political rights over second- and third-generation economic, social and cultural rights, and collective or group rights (Freeman, 2002); in China, as elsewhere in the developing world, the discourse of a collective right of development predominates. The Party-State

Public service broadcasting 133

upholds subsistence as the primary right from which all others derive (Li and Wei, 2011; Peerenboom, 2006; Potter, 2003). The 2009 *National Human Rights Action Plan of China* (2009–2010), published by the State Council, underlines that "while respecting the universal principles of human rights, the Chinese government, in light of the basic realities of China, gives priority to the protection of the people's rights to subsistence and development" (IOS, 2009).

From a liberal perspective, the media provide the most important institutional channels for exchanging information and opinion between individuals and groups; functioning as a Fourth Estate checking government's actions. The media must be independent of the state since "any restrictions on the media's ability to communicate will broadly tend to interfere with speech" (Gibbons, 1998: 21). In the Chinese context, the dominant discourses – an elitist philosophical tradition, the conception of governance as maintenance of harmony and social stability, and the privileging of the right to development – underpin an authoritarian and paternalistic media whose remit is to mold public opinion to perceive the Party-State as performing and legitimate; to "enlighten" the public in morality and virtue; and to mobilize support for the state's socio-economic reform agenda. Coercive information control and asymmetrical information dissemination are routinely deployed to these ends (Zhang, 2009).

Qi also reflects on the Party-State's inconsistent attitudes towards freedom of speech and social order. Coercive information control has become a barrier to national integration (Zhang, 2009), and "long-term structural stability" depends on the incorporation of different interests into the political system under the control of the Party (Weng Jiemin *et al.*, 1996 in Chen, 1997: 606). Freedom of speech could function as "a form of social control that strikes a balance in society between stability and movement, thereby allowing for necessary change without resort to violence, contributing to social stability" (Emerson, 1977: 742–743). The denial of any chance to present their interests may itself drive people to rise up against existing institutions. "Thus, liberty of expression, though often productive of divisiveness, may contribute to social stability" (Greenawalt, 1980: 673). It is not surprising that Qi advocated strict supervision of the media to prevent social upheaval while stressing their social responsibility to reconcile conflicts and channel citizen participation in governance, but in a "public and orderly" fashion.

Qi also emphasizes the main characteristics of China's development strategies since the 1980s, especially the privileging of economic growth and efficiency. In China economic development need not contribute to human development; suppression of individual civil and political rights is justified by the necessity to facilitate economic development and foreign investment. In contrast, a human development approach aims to enhance individuals' opportunities for education, health care, employment, and economic and political freedom (Hamm, 2001). Freedom of speech is a "cornerstone" right enabling these other rights and opportunities, and the free flow of information is key for an effective interaction between the state and society. Both are a requisite to human development (Callamard, 2006; Zhang, 2009).

134   *Public service broadcasting*

Whose interests are served by privileging social order and economic development over individual rights? Is such a state of affairs just? If unjust, it would be legitimate to challenge it (Freeman, 2002: 62). In China, the media's role is structured according to the Party-State's priorities: first and foremost, they must serve the CCP's interests, protecting its legitimacy and capacity to govern; second, they must serve the "collective or national interest" as defined by the Party-State; third, they are required to serve the marketplace to sustain economic capacity; fourth, they may serve individual cultural and social rights; finally, they are permitted to enable individual freedom of speech and facilitate political participation only insofar as this does not interfere with the higher priorities. Nevertheless, channeling the public and orderly expression of opinion is necessary to achieve the first two priorities. Like Qi, officials within the CCP's Propaganda Department do not discount the importance of public opinion for policy change; public opinion does influence policy agendas and affects the success of policy implementation (Chin, 2011). Given the failure of coercive information control to reconcile ethnic conflicts or palliate social grievances, the media is increasingly seen as an instrument of social modulation. A certain degree of freedom of information and opinion conserves social cohesion and enables a more efficient policy process.

It follows that freedom of speech in China is not protected as a fundamental right conducing to the intrinsic value of developing human beings who are more reflective and mature because their minds are free. Authoritarianism implies a preference for hierarchical relations characterized by dominance and submission; countervailing control of power requires a capacity to transcend the "law and order" mentality the powerful exploit to justify their rule, and, standing outside, to generate and apply an independent morality. The rise of the autonomous self and the decline of conformity serve such ends (Lane, 1979: 72–73). The Party-State, however, perceives individual Chinese not as citizens who take part in democratic governance informed by a free press, but as obedient receivers of messages (Lee, 2005: 122). Indeed, Chinese law forbids radio and television stations to be set up except by the State's broadcasting administrative departments (Article 10, Broadcasting Administrative Regulation). Public opinion and the flow of information must be managed to ensure that criticism of the Party does not impair its capacity to govern effectively. Historically, democracy and press freedom in China have not been valued as ends in themselves, but as a means to national modernization, even at the expense of individual autonomy or democratic citizenship (Lee, 2005).

The Chinese government has shown some willingness to relax the suppression of civil liberties (Tsang, 2009; Yang G, 2008). The Constitution was amended in 2004 to provide that the "state respects and protects human rights." Such protection thus becomes an obligation incumbent upon the State (Li and Wei, 2011: 18). In 2007, the government revised the country's development strategy away from economic development alone toward the Harmonious Society, and "efficient, human-oriented, comprehensive, coordinated and sustainable scientific development" (CCP, 2007). In 2009, it announced the

National Human Rights Action Plan, "the coordinated development of economic, social and cultural rights as well as civil and political rights, and the balanced development of individual and collective rights" (CCPLRO, 2008; IOS, 2009; Li and Wei, 2011: 18). The plan pledges to develop the civil and political rights to: (1) be informed of government affairs; (2) participate in an orderly way in political affairs at all levels and sectors; (3) be heard (through the development of the press and publication industries and protection of journalists' rights); and (4) to oversee (through improving mechanisms of restraint and supervision) (IOS, 2009). It is unclear how far the Action Plan will be implemented or what mechanisms will be instituted to realize them.

At the international level, the NPC's ratification in 2001 of the *International Covenant on Economic, Social and Cultural Rights* (ICESCR), binds the PRC legally to the obligations enshrined therein. In 2005 the UN Committee on Economic, Social and Cultural Rights (CESCR) published its concluding observations on China's implementation of ICESCR (E/C.12/1/Add.107, 13 May 2005), highlighting its concerns over income inequalities between rich and poor and urban and rural areas, and over adequate standards of living. It urged the Chinese government to allow freedom of information, that all Chinese may take part in cultural life and enjoy the benefits and applications of scientific progress (E/C.12/1/Add.107, 13 May 2005).

The emergence of the CPS and PSB policies are embedded in China's social, political and legal context in the last decade. The following sections examine these policies and their historical origins, and inquire how far PSB policy has responded to the broader issues, discussed above, of the relationship between state power, development and individual rights.

Public service policy: equalization, universal coverage and protection of cultural rights

The development of PSB is integrated with the nationwide construction of a cultural public service system. The notion of CPS first appeared in the CCP's 2005 recommendation document submitted to the State Council (CCP, 2005a), and was officially adopted by the State Council in its 2006 *Outline of Cultural Development during the Eleventh Five-Year Plan* (CCP and State Council, 2006).

Cultural public service is intended by the Party to "enrich the people's spiritual [and] cultural life and establish a harmonious society." Launched to ease the inter-regional and urban–rural socio-economic development gaps, the social welfare system crisis, the lack of the rule of law, the deterioration of morality and trust, and corruption, the Harmonious Society aspires to "human-based individual comprehensive development," "social justice," "sharing of the fruits of reform by all people," "formation of the rule of law and democracy," and "the correct management of the relationship between development and stability in order to maintain social unity" (CCP, 2005a; CCP, 2006). The national construction of CPS is thus informed by the policy goals of social equalization – universal coverage and equal access – through public funding provision, and

136 *Public service broadcasting*

protection of the basic cultural rights and needs of the Chinese people, in particular low-income and other vulnerable groups (CCP, 2006; CCP, 2007; Wen, 2007). The Party-State defines cultural rights as rights to education, science and culture; and rights to enjoy the benefits of cultural life, take part in cultural activities, and carry on cultural creation (CCP Theoretical Bureau, 2008: 172). Basic cultural rights are rights of access to TV, radio, books and newspapers (CCP and State Council, 2006). Measures prioritizing cultural resource allocation to minority groups and rural areas and enhancing the "production and provision of public cultural products" have been introduced. Cultural public service is planned and funded by the government, and provided through public cultural institutions such as libraries, museums, and television and radio stations (CCP, 2007; CCP and State Council, 2006).

On the other hand, PSB policy rhetoric reveals little indication that the Chinese government is preparing to establish a PSB provider that is separate from the existing state-controlled media sector. Instead, PSB is viewed as a kind of separate media function whose performance can be demanded from existing broadcasters – a new range of service obligations mandated by the state. For example, broadcasters can be required to carry certain levels of news and current affairs programming intended to enlighten the citizenry, which can be represented as fulfillment of democratic imperatives within the media sector. Unlike museums and libraries, for which ownership can reside "among the people" (民间, *Minjian*, privately), all news and current affairs-focused media, including Party newspapers and magazines, news agencies, radio and television stations, and important online news websites, are defined as important ideological "battlefields" and remain entirely state-owned. They are requested to enhance positive reporting on, and dissemination of CCP and state policies, and to report accurately on public opinion. The overarching view is of the media as a tool for mediating and correcting public opinion, and as a mouthpiece for the CCP and the people (CCP, 2007; CCP and State Council, 2005, 2006). Thus, despite the new PCS rhetoric, the government's primary expectation vis-à-vis the media is that it will continue to support ideological "services" and to propagate news supporting a pro-security, pro-stability national agenda through its non-commercial information programs. For these reasons, news media independence cannot be truly realized or protected in the People's Republic of China. Given the ongoing political dependency of the news media, and the separation of cultural content production from the public service system, what core public service the broadcast media in China will provide is an open question. The subordination of media independence to support entrenched political actors and their policy initiatives does not mean, however, that the notion of a "public" media is meaningless in contemporary China. One important goal of PSB planning is to enlarge the media system to provide guarantees of access for rural and ethnic minority citizens, to ensure improved basic access and content for all citizens, and to make permanent a state-created, state-funded PSB system which balances the ongoing urbanization of the media with greater equality for all, using infrastructure expansion as a base.

Public service broadcasting 137

Government policy documents refer to PSB predominately as "universal coverage" and "equal access." Yang Mingpin, Deputy Director of Development and Research at the then SARFT, the State Council's department for broadcast policy and regulation, who participated in the drafting of these documents, considers that PSB will address the urban–rural development gap by focusing first on universalizing the basic broadcasting service in rural areas, while enhancing programming and service quality in urban areas. Broadcasting services are divided into two types: basic and non-basic, and implemented separately in towns and the countryside. Terrestrial broadcasting is a basic public service; its infrastructure is state-funded and free to the whole nation. Cable television is non-basic, and available in urban and some rural areas. Satellite broadcasting is a restricted public service, provided free to rural villages with electricity (Yang B, 2009; Yang M, 2009).

To reach rural areas state spending on universal coverage and equal access has focused overwhelmingly on the Connected Village Project (CVP). Between 1998 and 2009 central and local governments spent a total of ten billion yuan on the CVP, bringing access to approximately 100 million rural inhabitants; nevertheless, as of 2009, 11.61 percent of the rural population (some 40 million) had no access of any kind (Yang B, 2009: 127). Despite the successes, problems of infrastructure, funding and corruption have reduced the CVP's effectiveness.

At the same time, however, television content producers and distributors, as well as key news media departments (e.g., advertising, distribution, printing, information, Internet services and sales) are excluded from this growing public service sector. The state instead defines these as cultural industries in order to accelerate their transition to "market entity" status – a designation denoting those companies who have become economically efficient and able to compete locally, nationally, and even globally. The aim of such policies is not to improve programming quality or social inclusiveness, but rather to increase the competitiveness of existing media institutions and introduce mixed ownership of cultural industries (CCP and State Council, 2006). Market entities in the media sector are managed by television stations and news media organizations in order to promote competitive business practices (CCP and State Council, 2005). Projected plans for cultural industry's generation of PSB content for the public service sector thus relies on government payments, or subsidies, for the production of quality, inexpensive programming by transferring resources to this increasingly commercialized media sector (CCP, 2007).

In fact, no television broadcaster in China is supported purely by public funds (see Table 8.1). At the provincial level government subsidies amount to 10 percent of broadcaster revenue; at the city and township level 11 percent; and at the national level 22.3 percent (Yang M, 2009: 129).

Currently commercial revenues through internal cross-subsidies finance the not-for-profit production of broadcasters. This is prey to two weaknesses: (1) the implementation of public service responsibilities is endangered, as investment depends on the attitudes of the broadcasters making the decisions; and (2) equalization of access is endangered, as broadcasters differ in economic power and

138 *Public service broadcasting*

Table 8.1 Income of Chinese broadcasters in 2009 (billions, yuan, %)

	Income	*% of total income*
Total income	185.3	100.0
Government funds	24.5	13.2
Advertising	78.2	42.29
Internet service	41.9	22.6
Others	40.7	22.0

Source: 1. Development and Research Centre, SARFT, 2010. Report on development of China's radio, film and television (2010年中国广播电视发展报告). Beijing: Xinhua Press.

investment ability (Yang B, 2009; Zhang ZF, 2008: 127). Data from 2008 shows that entertainment content dominated provincial networks, while programming dedicated to rural areas, children, minorities and women represented a very low percentage. Yang concluded that "although China's broadcasters are defined as public service, the public service features of their contents are not visible" (Yang B, 2009: 128). Yet the 2008 SARFT policy placed special emphasis on establishing a PSB regulatory framework defining and mandating its objectives, service standards, infrastructure and assessment (SARFT, 2008a).

The funding of public service programming is also an area of dispute. Broadcasters believe that funding should come from the government, despite some of them making substantial profits in monopolized local markets; they also complain that the CCP already requires central and provincial level broadcasting networks to produce propaganda and informational programming, cutting into profit margins and leaving little incentive for additional public service programming (Zhang ZF, 2008). National policymakers reply that both government and broadcasters ought to contribute to funding. The proposal of using state funding to hire or subsidize private production companies to provide public service content is an uneasy option: its implementation would pose huge challenges to government administrators, broadcasters and the production industry, all of whom manifestly lack transparency and accountability. In 2009, the Vice Director of SARFT, Zhang Haitao, revealed that China's Ministry of Finance is researching a "cultural public service system financial protection mechanism," a solution that would be both compatible with Chinese reality and comprehensive and sustainable.

Antecedents of public service: commercialization and socialist spiritual civilization

While the terms "public service" and "public broadcasting" did not typically appear in conjunction with the State-owned media prior to 2005, the early years of China's broadcasting history nevertheless did create a foundation for contemporary CPS initiatives. The Party-State's own definition of propaganda (*xuanchuan*) imbued the media with social, political and educational functions, represented by educational television stations and the science and educational channels of the Chinese national broadcaster, CCTV (Yuan and Xiang, 2006).

Public service broadcasting 139

The shift from state funding to finance by commercial advertising began in 1979, and became ubiquitous after 1992 (Mao, 2009). This led to the commercialization of content and a dramatic decline in its social and educational value. Another consequence was the neglect of the rural broadcasting system (Zhou, 2006). In response, the Party launched a large-scale Spiritual Civilization project during three successive Five-Year Plans for Economic and Social Development (1991–2005), which endeavored to uplift civic virtue (CCP, 1996b). The civilizing of rural areas was among several important policy goals (CCP, 1998); a 2002 State Council policy circular decried an "impoverished" cultural life, widespread "decadent ideas" and "pornography, gambling and drugs," and illegal religious activities that undermined local authorities in the countryside. Grassroots cultivation became important for policy dissemination, the connection of the Party-State with the populace, and public virtue (State Council, 2002, No. 7). Remedies included increasing investment in impoverished areas, constructing infrastructure, expanding national and provincial broadcasting channel coverage, and enlisting the cultural industry to reinvest some of its commercial profits in State ideological programs and other cultural activities (CCP, 1996b; State Council, 1991, No. 31). The government also announced a rise in national and local public funding for cultural institutions, tax incentives and economic support for culture production, and encouragement of social investments (State Council, 1996, No. 37; Ministry of Finance, 1996, No. 469; Zhu, 2001).

The pre-2005 Spiritual Civilization building project focused on broadcasting coverage and specifically on coverage of the countryside (Zhou, 2006: 46). Two projects were conceived: CVP, which targeted rural regions and was launched in 1998; and the Tibet-Xinjiang Project (TXP), targeted at sub-national regions with high concentrations of national ethnic minorities, launched in 2000. Although different in name and regional focus, the CVP and TXP shared several key similarities. First, television broadcasts consisted of existing China Central Television (CCTV) content and provincial or regional programming. Second, the projects focused almost entirely on the creation and maintenance of new infrastructure, not of new channels. Coverage, not content, was the goal. The basic model can be summarized as follows:

1 Leadership and regulation provided by local governments;
2 Funding drawn from state sources, primarily central or provincial budgets;
3 Administration required the integration of cultural construction into existing fiscal, government, and poverty relief structures (Zhou, 2006: 47).

In the 2006–2010 Outline, state spending on spiritual civilization construction was replaced by spending on PSB. Continuity between the two policies, however, can be seen in the emphasis both place on infrastructure construction and coverage expansion (CCP, 2005b). The CVP and TXP were simply reframed as steps toward the establishment of a broader PSB system with the goals of "strongly advancing the penetration of broadcast television into villages and households." Since 2005, ensuing PCS initiatives began to shift from a

140 *Public service broadcasting*

normative rhetoric of spiritual civilization, aimed at countervailing commercialization, to one of public service and interest, emphasizing urban–rural equalization and the protection of "basic" rights (State Council, 2006). Despite such changes, this is largely a continuation of initiatives begun almost 20 years ago.

Nevertheless, the Spiritual Civilization to public service re-conceptualization reflected a considerable revision of the official ideology on the roles of the media and individuals. The media are no longer conceived merely as instruments of the Party-State, but also as serving a "public interest," despite the fact that the Party still monopolizes its interpretation. This shift may indicate the beginning of a new relationship between political authority and the individual, who as citizens are to be empowered at the Party-State's expense.

Implementation of PSB policy: infrastructure, funding, and governance

PSB policy implementation has proceeded along two main lines. First, the construction of infrastructure for increasing broadcast access throughout the general population, especially for rural communities. Second, through the funding of additional broadcast stations and content, to enhance governance in the form of supervision by CCP and government committees.

A closer look at several case studies, published in 2009 under the auspices of an official think tank (the Chinese Academy of Social Sciences), demonstrates that while public service media initiatives in China have undeniably resulted in expansion of infrastructure and access, local funding and independent content creation remain severely challenged. They are challenged by fiscal and regulatory shortfalls at the sub-national level, and lack of station and state support for the creation of independent, public service-oriented content, which diverges from existing propaganda or commercialized models.

Infrastructure expansion

The intended benefactors of PSB initiatives and accompanying "equalization" (*jundenghua*) of broadcast television access have been targeted to rural regions and regions with large populations of non-Han ethnic minorities. State investment, rather than market forces, has resulted in the construction of CVP- and TXP-style broadcast television public service systems by city, township, and county governments (Yang B, 2009). By 2005, a total of 3.44 billion yuan had already been spent on CVP and TXP initiatives using central and local public funds. On 9 June 2008 a new satellite network, Central Satellite Number Nine, was launched to cover mountainous regions and other areas whose terrain and local economies make terrestrial broadcast and cable infrastructure impractical. As of 2009, 11.61 percent of the rural population, or approximately 700,000 villages, remained without access to terrestrial broadcasting of any kind (Yang B, 2009: 127).

Indeed, broadcasting infrastructure construction has proved a challenge for local governments. First, human and financial capital in marginal regions

Public service broadcasting 141

remained scarce. Local governments often lacked a permanent workforce dedicated to the task. Second, the requirement of some local governments for households to bear part of the financial burden, such as a 300 yuan installation fee and 12 yuan monthly service fee, made expansion more difficult (Zhou, 2006: 47). Moreover, even in comparatively wealthy provinces, substantial differences exist between urban and rural regions. Public service broadcasting policies include separate goals for urban and rural communities, with urban households receiving a minimum of 40-plus television channels and households in villages and smaller towns receiving a minimum of eight channels (Zhang G, 2008: 120; Zhang ZF, 2008). The situation is exacerbated because rural regions are typically unable to support (through household usage-based fees or county and village government public funds) the conversion to cable services that is a prerequisite for access to a wider range of channels and networks. Even within urban centers, such as Beijing, the presence of a large rural-to-urban "floating" population (approximately 4.18 million individuals, or 25 percent of the total population) are without regular access to broadcast television (Zhang Z, 2008).

In short, recent PSB initiatives have not substantially altered infrastructural disparities between urban and non-urban, coast and hinterland, or rich and poor, although it is important to note that they have improved levels of coverage considerably in rural and ethnic minority regions. Infrastructure, available funding and local levels of consumption (including the ability of households to pay for services), vary considerably by geographical location and population segment (Zhang ZF, 2008).

Funding public media

Along with China's recent economic development, the national government has promoted "service-style government construction" and "letting the masses enjoy the sunshine of public finance." Television broadcasting, though accounting for a small proportion of this spending, is nonetheless tied to the overarching agendas of administrative reform and resource redistribution. However, state spending on the cultural system, including PSB services, accounts for approximately 0.3 percent to 0.5 percent of total expenditure (Zhang, Mao and Zhang, 2009), and this ratio has not changed appreciably since the launch of China's First Five-Year Plan in 1953 (Xu, 2009). In addition, state spending on rural PSB infrastructure has produced mixed results (Xu, 2009: 23). Misappropriation of central funds by local governments remains an area of significant concern, and monitoring this misuse of funding remains a challenge to regulators (Yang B, 2009).

The practice of using commercial revenue to support state-funded projects, or "using culture to supplement culture" (*yi wen bu wen*), first emerged in 1987 (Chen and Hu, 2009: 54). This model of investment was adopted on a wider basis in the Outline, which included policy goals that "cities and towns support villages," and "industry supports agriculture" as keys to raising rural living standards (Yang B, 2009: 179). Through taxes on the local cable network

142 *Public service broadcasting*

company, local broadcasting bureaus, such as Sichuan province's Shehong town, had raised enough money that, when paired with central allocations, made possible the construction of a unified fiber optic cable system shared by nearby towns and villages, and which provided free cable television and Internet services to recipients. This arrangement soon became a model of PSB implementation at the county level and below.

As Shehong's reforms demonstrated, sustainably financing the expansion of broadcasting public service at the local level depended in practice on several sources: (1) funding from central and provincial governments, (2) fees and other revenue derived from broadcasters, and (3) financial support from local (e.g., county, town, village) governments. In addition, the Shehong model included management of the CVP system by the county cable network company on a contractual basis, and supervision of the project at the county, town and village levels in order to prevent misallocation or redirection of funds (Yang B, 2009: 182). While taxes on county cable networks represent one potential source of revenue, as in Shehong, not all localities are endowed with similar alternatives. The result is that while investment in public service broadcasting remains high, services are better in cities than the countryside (Yang M, 2009: 126), with local networks further weakened by the expansion of central and provincial broadcasting resources. To date, there appears to be little spending in rural areas on public cultural products called for by the State Council's 2007 documents (CCP, 2007).

Governance and regulation

In addition to financing infrastructural expansion, the functional separation of government cultural institutions from existing administrative departments, as well as strengthening the role of government as a regulatory entity, represents another key aspect of the PSB system creation. This oversight role primarily consists of the state making decisions concerning standard setting for PSB content, and supervising the implementation of these directives. Since 2006 implementation of PSB policies has been integrated into the CCP and government's everyday work, national economic planning institutions, public budget and poverty relief programs, and the examination system for state administrators and managers.

Despite the creation of these mechanisms, the decentralization of China's administrative and broadcasting system, along with the concomitant creation of different interest groups at different institutional levels (Chin, 2011), provides enormous challenges to the implementation of PSB policy at the broadcasting level. Direction and policy guidance from central and provincial governments is ubiquitous, yet conflicts between regulatory strata are not infrequent. In Beijing, researchers have observed clashes between the Municipal Broadcasting Bureau, endowed with a supervision and advisory role vis-à-vis local (district and county) broadcasters, and broadcasting personnel appointed by these local governments (Zhang Z, 2008: 127). Political orders from above are difficult to enforce. Given the rural focus of most PSB expansion work, the most important supervisory and regulatory government institution should typically be the county-level broadcasting bureau, whose functions include the enforcement of technological standards in broadcast work, and lawful registration or confiscation of private satellite technology (Yang, 2009: 184). Although the local district and county government cultural committee had been granted a regulatory role vis-à-vis television broadcasting, it lacks programming production functions, as well as the financial and human resources – and economic motivation – to devote its efforts to sustained PCS and PSB construction.

On the production side, as of 2008 the Beijing Television Station (BJTV) and its municipal public service channel, BJTV-9, represented the sole means by which programming was disseminated to municipal audiences (a population scattered across 14 districts and counties). Like the sub-municipal broadcasters beneath it, however, BJTV's response to PSB directives from higher authorities has been to argue that it should not be made responsible for producing additional, non-commercial programming, and that its BJTV-9 channel is already being operated at a loss, to the detriment of the station as a whole. In China, almost no television channels exist which are purely supported by public funds. State spending accounts for only 13.3 percent of the income received by television broadcasters, while 86.7 percent comes through the market. Thus, lack of motivation to produce PSB programming stems from profit-minded concerns; the station accords little priority to programming with no clear revenue-generating potential. For programming that meets PCS and PSB standards and does show commercial potential, the station is unwilling to provide this for public access because doing so would force it to share proprietary content with lower-level broadcasters. These local broadcasters, which rely primarily on government funding and self-generated revenue, likewise claim that they lack the capacity to produce new PSB content on their own, and are similarly unmotivated to support and maintain public media initiatives that demonstrate no promise of financial returns.

Summary

From the normative perspective, the basic principles underpinning PSB in Western liberal democracies entail serving the "public interest," for instance enhancing and developing political, civil, social and cultural citizenship. In the Chinese context the substance of the public interest is subject to arbitrary interpretation by the Party-State, apt to be contested by rival camps of academics, and tends to be narrowed down by commercialized, government-controlled broadcasters. The lack of consensus undermines any meaningful political construction of PSB in China, and a fair and legitimate procedure of deliberation is urged by Chinese academics as a pressing need in determining what the public interest is.

By asserting that the interests of the Party-State, society and the individual are identical, the CCP at present claims entitlement to privilege its own version of the public interest, which prioritizes the values of national wealth creation,

144   *Public service broadcasting*

national strength and social harmony; the propagation of the Party's own moral, intellectual and scientific standards; and the promotion of a narrowly defined basic cultural right. Individual political and civil rights, such as freedom of speech and participation in political affairs, are not regarded as making any part of the public interest. Such depoliticization of PI is exacerbated by the de-emphasis of individual equality, and the subordination of individual liberty to collective and state interests in the Chinese Constitution, as well as by the government's practice of implementing collective rights to subsistence and development ahead of civil and political rights.

Nevertheless, the revision of China's development strategy from economic growth to human development, and the Party-State's willingness to concede some civil liberties, partly in response to the pressures of its legal obligations to the international human rights treaties it has committed itself to, may help bring about improved protection of individual rights, even if economic, social and cultural rights continue to have priority. It is within this fluid context, between maintaining an old order and developing a new social relationship, between political authority and the individual citizen, that the discourse of cultural rights and public service first appeared in official policy documents. In consequence, growing academic and public interest is being given to the functions of PSB and its possible future in China.

Actual PSB policy continues to be motivated predominantly by a narrowly defined basic cultural right and an emphasis on social equalization between urban and rural access to broadcasting networks. Other values of PSB, including high-quality programming, universal accessibility to content, independence and impartiality, are still marginalized, if not ignored.

Despite the importance accorded to the creation of an independent provider by some analysts, no such institution has yet been created. Rather, the distinction between "commercial" and "public" occurs primarily at the level of content. Public service channels and programming are provided by state-owned broadcasters and funded by a combination of government and private investment, and some of the profits from commercial channels. Whether oversight of PSB will be transferred to China's People's Congress remains to be seen. At present, China's PSB policy emphasizes the right to access for all citizens; this does not necessarily mark any momentous shift from a political culture that has emphasized the continued importance of socialist spiritual construction under CCP guidance. However, it does indicate an effort by the government to push back against the uninhibited commercialization of the media sector. The principle challenges to this effort include a paucity of local funding, coupled with the inability of many households to afford additional services that would make infrastructure expansion more productive, and production of programming more self-supporting without central and provincial government aid. The key for the further progress of PSB initiatives lies in the support of the Central Government for public service media initiatives beyond those focused on infrastructure and access. Change will also depend on the creation of new forces for content production and content regulation.

The Chinese state is beginning to take initiatives in major urban areas to extend PSB and other public information services (e.g., digital information resources, museums, and libraries) to citizens, and that is likely to continue to expand. Whether this growth will be sustainable without again giving way to commercialization in the process remains an open question. For the moment, however, government funding of national and local PSB infrastructure is the most significant form of systemic expansion. Given China's current political and economic structure, it is inevitable that in the short term PSB will continue to be characterized by high levels of state involvement. However, insofar as the public service sector is, by definition, a state legislative and institutional creation, this fact alone does not distinguish China from other countries. Rather, differences continue to exist concerning the degree to which China's national government feels comfortable entrusting state actors to speak for the public interest, and the ability of that government to provide reliable media access and a participatory voice to its citizenry.

On the other hand, the conceptual changes of PSB policy from Socialist Spiritual Civilization to "cultural public service" may be justified by its somewhat enlarged purpose; what is still in question is why the substance and scope of the policy remain basically unchanged after 20 years? We are obliged to raise the question of how far the Chinese Party-state genuinely supports the popular demand for public service broadcasting.

The development path of the Chinese cultural public service and its embedded PSB is reminiscent of the early history of the first PSB, the British Broadcasting Corporation (BBC), created in the divided British society of the 1920s. History shows remarkable similarities but also differences. The notion of cultural public service in Britain was first inspired by a sense of moral purpose and social duty in meeting the educational and cultural needs of the working classes, but also by the pragmatic and instrumental political purpose of "civilizing the masses" as "a means of alleviating the strain and hostility between classes in a deeply divided society," and "a means of incorporating the working classes within the existing social and political order, and thus preventing the threat of revolt from below" (Scannell, 2000: 55–56). The ideals of the BBC as a public service included serving the public interest, social unity and national pride. The role of the BBC as a public forum independent of the state developed slowly and in tandem with the long battle for a fully democratic representational system and the introduction of limited competition in the broadcasting sector (Scannell, 2000). The politicization of the public interest concept was crucial to this process. In the Chinese context, the broadly similar project is motivated more by the purely pragmatic end of social stability and cohesion than by moral or humane concerns for the development of citizens, as the lack of investment in high-quality public service programming has demonstrated. Indeed, the marginalization of individual self-development and autonomy, and the continued support amongst political and intellectual elites for an authoritarian Party-state, cast serious doubt on the future possibilities of realizing a genuine PSB in China, serving the needs of democracy, culture and social inclusion.

146 *Public service broadcasting*

Certainly the long-term implications of the Chinese public service project and policy depends on the legitimization of the discourse of individual rights and equality, and on recognition of the broadcast media's role in serving the public and common good, and the State's obligation to respect individuals as citizens having equal and unalienable rights. As with all Chinese public policy-making, the development of PSB and relevant governmental policy will be a long, incremental process. The future of Chinese PSB is uncertain, but at least the wind of individual rights and equality is blowing.

Note

1 Personal interviews with a Chinese official and an academic in Beijing, February 2010.

9 Shanghai television

From state institution to enterprise

Shanghai has a prominent status because of its political and economic importance as well as its role in China's international integration. Shanghai's broadcasters, like other media in China, were traditionally owned by the State and controlled by the Chinese Communist Party. Since the early 2000s, amid the transformation of China's national television policy and the subsequent relaxation of cross-regional operation, media organization's ownership and rapidly internationalized of Chinese economy, Shanghai's broadcasting media not only has gone through a significant structural, operational and institutional change, but also become a test zone for the further reform of the Chinese media. This chapter studies the historical development of Shanghai's broadcasting media from the 1990s to 2015, aiming to illustrate the progress, strategies and principles of China's national broadcasting policy over the last two decades. It shows that the "three separations" reform – the separation of the institution and enterprise, the separation of ownership and managerial authority, and the separation of production and broadcasting in Shanghai ultimately transferred the Shanghai Media Group from a state-owned institution to an independent state-owned enterprise with private investment and international expansion in the future. At the same time, the state-owned television channel and spectrum resources were relocated to lie under the direct supervision of the propaganda department of the Communist Party. The legal and capital links between the channels and programming productions no longer exist. Furthermore, the role of the Propaganda Department of the CCP moved from the background to the foreground. The political and economic consequences of such separation remains to be explored, but the implications for Chinese broadcasting system is certainly significant.

The role of Shanghai

Shanghai, one of four municipalities[1] in China, has traditionally had a very prominent political status in China, has been an alternative to Beijing and a major economic contributor to the country. Its position was particularly advanced after Jiang Zemin became General Secretary of CCP in 1989 (Bao, 2004; Li, 1998).

148 *Shanghai television*

Demographically, Shanghai is one of China's biggest cities with a total population of over 23 million in 2010. It is a global city, having influence in commerce, culture, finance, media, fashion, technology and transport. It is a major financial center and the busiest container port in the world (Guo *et al.*, 2015). As early as the 1930s, Shanghai was already the largest international trade and financial center in Asia, having the most highly developed urban amenities in Asia besides Tokyo. After 1949, although it was the single largest contributor to the country's national revenue, Shanghai was neglected but still under tight Central Government control. In the 1980s, Central Government focused on the development of Guangdong and Fujian while granting Shanghai little in the way of preferential policies for its development (Wu, 1999: 208; Han, 2000). This was partly due to Central Government's concern with the city's social and economic stability, as it was the country's main industrial and economic center, so the Beijing Central Government was reluctant to conduct any drastic experiments (Han, 2000: 2006).

The significant change in Shanghai's less favorable status happened with the opening of the Pudong New Area in April 1990, a new district to the east of the city and the Huangpu River. Ten preferential policies were awarded to Pudong to develop it into the country's largest special economic zone (SZE). The CCP's Fourteenth Congress Report, convened in October 1992, pledged to "build Shanghai into one of the international economic, financial and trade centers in order to stimulate a new economic leap forward in the Yangtze River Delta and the Yangtze River valley" (cited in Han, 2000: 2096). Rather than becoming another labor intensive manufacturing center, like Guangdong Province, Pudong SZE targeted a higher-level economic configuration, such as the capital and technology intensive sectors. Internationalization was used as a development strategy for Shanghai, aiming to develop it as China's world-class modern metropolis and international financial and trading center, facilitating interaction between China and the world (Han, 2000; Wu, 1999).

More than simply wanting foreign investment, leadership in Shanghai saw the opening up of Pudong as a catalyst for Shanghai's integration with international economic and business norms. In the words of Wu Bangguo, then Shanghai's Party Secretary:

> To open and develop Pudong would inevitably break ground for the all-round opening of Shanghai. We have to utilize fully the high degree of openness of Pudong ... to bridge Shanghai to the international economy in the areas of finance, commerce, industry and management. [...] [We need] to establish multinational corporations of our own, so as to enhance the capability of Shanghai in international economic participation.
>
> (Statistical Yearbook of Shanghai, as cited in Li, 1998: 253)

This goal of internationalization was also used as an instrument for the Shanghai municipal government to bargain with Central Government for more resources and autonomy (Li, 1998).

After Deng Xiaoping's Southern Tour in early 1992, the pace of Shanghai's economic development was accelerated (Li, 1998). Nowadays, Shanghai is China's leading city, not only measured by local Gross Domestic Product (GDP), but also by its fiscal income, foreign investment and international trading.

Politically, China's political landscape is two-fold. The first consists of three major formal institutions: central institutions, provincial units and the military. The second consists of informal factional groups, for instance, the Chinese Communist Youth League (CCYL) Group, Qinghua Clique, Shanghai Gang and the Princelings (Bao, 2004). It is well known that "Chinese politics has long been perceived as the politics of political factions." The Shanghai Gang, which "refers to politicians who have used Shanghai as a springboard to launch their political careers" was ranked as the third powerful faction group. Prominent members of the Shanghai Gang at the central institutions include the former General Secretary of the CCP, Jiang Zemin, who has deep roots in Shanghai and was its mayor from 1985 to 1989, three former standing members of the Politburo of CCP's Central Committee – Wu Bangguo, Zeng Qinghong and Huang Ju, and five former State Council Ministers, including Xu Guangchun, the former Head of the State Administration of Radio, Film and Television (SARFT)[2] (Bao, 2004).

Since the 1990s, with its economic and political empowerments, Shanghai has restored its status as China's most important city besides Beijing. Internationalization has been actively employed by local government as a development strategy to build up Shanghai as a leading international city and a bargaining instrument for better resources and more autonomy from the Central Government.

Shanghai's television before 1996: the "controlled competition" model

Unlike many other TV stations in China, which are supervised by a relatively overpowering Broadcasting Bureau, the municipal government has tightly controlled Shanghai's television for two major reasons.

First, Shanghai's municipal status enables it to have a simpler but integrated and empowered political structure.[3] The political tensions and struggles within a municipality, such as Shanghai, are less intricate and intensive compared to a fragmented province. Second, China's politics have a long tendency towards personal rule over institutionalized rule (Saich, 2001). A powerful political figure could greatly influence, or even decide, the development of an institution. Gong Xueping played such a role in Shanghai's television system. Gong graduated from Shanghai Fundan University's Journalism Department and since the early 1980s he has headed the Shanghai TV Station, Shanghai Broadcasting Bureau, Shanghai's Propaganda Department and Shanghai's Party Committee. Because of his deep involvement in broadcasting organizations, the municipal government and the Party, he has been able to exercise his influence across

150 *Shanghai television*

Table 9.1 The important stages of Shanghai's television development before 1996

Date	Important event	Finance
1958	Started to establish Shanghai Television Station in March 1958 and officially launched in October 1958	Fully subsidized by government
1973	Establishment of Shanghai Broadcasting Bureau. Both the Shanghai TV Station and Radio Station were work units of the Bureau; Transition from black-and-white television to color television starting from 1 August 1973	Programming productions, finance, human and infrastructure resources were centrally controlled by the Shanghai Broadcasting Bureau
1979	First TV station to restore TV advertisements	Gained 0.6 million yuan advertising revenue; Started to have self-raised funds
1987	Introduction of internal competition among TV and radio stations, practicing the "one bureau, five stations and three centers" operational pattern	Generated 23.88 million yuan commercial revenue
1992	Establishment of Shanghai Oriental Pear Ltd on 8 August 1992 and listed on China's stock market; Launched Shanghai Cable TV on 26 December 1992	Absorbed 204 million yuan capital from stock market
1993	Launched Shanghai Oriental TV Station on 18 January 1993 and competed with Shanghai TV station in the Shanghai's market	The annual commercial revenue was 477 million yuan
1995	Merged the film and broadcasting bureau, forming Shanghai Radio, Film and Television Bureau in August 1995	Commercial revenue was about 800 million yuan, equivalent to 97% of the industry's total expense

Sources: 1. Official Website of Shanghai Local Chronicles Office (上海市地方志办公室). Available at: www.shtong.gov.cn/node2/node2245/node4510/node11505/node11512/node63816/userobject1ai 12553.html (accessed 23 February 2016); 2. Official website of SMG. Available at: www.smg.cn/ review/201409/0163891.shtml (accessed 23 February 2016).

boundaries and draw on different administrative resources and political powers to shape Shanghai's television development. Amid this strong governance, the most distinguishing feature of Shanghai's television system in the 1990s was the introduction of the "controlled competition" mechanism (Lu, 1998; Weber, 2002).

In 1983, the Ministry of Radio, Film and Television's (MRFT) four-tier mixed coverage policy was criticized for leading to a fragmented TV system in China under which the administrative boundary becomes the boundary of the market (Lu, 2002). Neither cross-regional competition or competition within the same administrative region actually existed[4] (Lu, 1998). Each province was, for instance, only allowed to have one provincial TV station, whose coverage was

Shanghai television 151

bounded by the provincial border. Local government saw television stations as their mouthpieces as well as moneymaking machines, employing a rage of measures to protect their monopolies in the local markets. In Shanghai's case, before 1993, Shanghai TV Station (STV) was the only TV broadcaster in the municipality, and it monopolized the country's largest local TV market for three decades (Huang *et al.*, 1996; Lu, 1998).[5]

In January 1993, alongside the development of the Pudong SZE and the call for further market reform by the then CCP leader, Deng Xiaoping, the Shanghai Broadcasting Bureau set up the second municipality TV station, Shanghai Oriental TV Station (OTV), in Pudong. Shanghai was thus the first city to break the "one city, one station" monopoly policy. In December of the same year, Shanghai Cable TV was also launched[6] (Lu, 1998).

In an interview in 2003, the former President of OTV recalled that the early 1990s was an era during which the country was actively seeking the "liberal mind," to "learn how to compete in the market" and "prescribe how to develop through competition," so, the establishment of OTV became possible. The Shanghai government expected that the existence of the second TV station would "bring in a competition mechanism [to Shanghai's TV system]" (Ye, 2003: 2).

Nevertheless, the reform was a top-down process. It was not self-driven, initiated by the immediate needs of the TV station, but was driven by local government and the Shanghai Broadcasting Bureau to fulfill the desire for development. As Shanghai media scholar Lu Ye observed: "every reform of Shanghai's broadcasting is not because 'change is inevitable', but [it is because] the leadership hope to 'reform for betterment'" (Lu, 1998: 9).

Second, instead of following the free market principle in full, Shanghai's television competition was under the macro-control of the Shanghai Broadcasting Bureau and was described as "moderate" or "appropriate" competition. Ye Zhikang, Head of the Shanghai Broadcasting Bureau, considered that it meant new stations were set up to enhance the competition and the bureau's control [over the media] was reinforced in order to "reduce the negative effects caused by disordered competition" (Shen, 1998: 11[7]).

The degree of appropriateness was reflected in two major aspects: competition would not affect the media's propaganda function; and competition would not damage the economic welfare of the Shanghai TV industry as a whole. From the Bureau's point of view, the long term goal of reform was not only to improve program quality via competition, but more importantly, it was about strengthening the local TV industry through "coordinated development" (Lu, 1998: 8).

In fact, the notion of "unified leadership" or "centralized control" has dominated throughout Shanghai Broadcasting Bureau's policy. In the 1990s, although competition was introduced into Shanghai's television, the pattern of competition was "friendly competition" (Weber, 2002: 65) or "appropriate competition" (Lu, 1998: 8) under the control of the Shanghai Broadcasting Bureau.

In Zhao Kai, the Bureau's Party Secretary's words, "over almost 20 years' practices [...], we [the Shanghai Broadcasting Bureau] have gradually developed

152 *Shanghai television*

a working philosophy, which is compatible to Shanghai's reality, and Shanghai's broadcasting and film industry realities." The Bureau sought to develop the local TV industry towards a socialist, marketized and professional model on the basis of the "five unification" principle: "unification of development strategies and plans, unification of propaganda management, unification of technological management, unification of finance, and unification of infrastructure construction" (Zhao, 1998a: 4).

Shanghai's television after 1996: conglomeration and channel specialization

After the CCP's Fifteenth Congress in 1997, the Shanghai Radio, Film and TV Bureau[8] began to prepare for media conglomeration to "fully develop the potential of the third industry function of broadcasting and film sectors," while the prerequisites for the conglomeration were "the assurance of [the media's] mouthpiece function and the [media's] correct guidance of public opinions" (Zhao, 1998a: 6).[9]

The bureau justified its conglomeration plan primarily for economic reasons. First, as the media had been accepted as an industry since June 1992,[10] it should follow "the logic of industrial development." Conglomeration has resulted in a leap in the scale and scope of the foreign media and, in order to compete with them, China's media needed to use "every effective and feasible means to strengthen our industry" (Zhao, 1998a: 7). Second, the Bureau criticized the co-existence of several thousand TV stations in China "validated the development logic of broadcasting industry" and suggested developing five TV networks in China including one national and four regional ones (Zhao, 1998b). Shanghai, as an international city, aimed to be one of the regional leaders and to have a "first class culture" and a "first class media" (Zhao, 1998a).

The TV media's pursuit of an industrial objective would not undermine its mouthpiece function. The Bureau would "control tightly media's propaganda function and give the media managerial freedom" (Zhao, 1998a: 8). It further proposed "four separations" to assist the conglomeration process. First, to separate the regulatory role of the Shanghai Radio, Film and TV bureau from its production and broadcasting functions. Second, to separate television's propaganda function from its business function, so that the Party could still control its mouthpiece while the business entity could develop according to market logic. Third, to separate news programs from other content, so that the latter's production could be outsourced. Finally, to separate non-business-oriented State assets from business-oriented state assets so that the value of the former can "be safe" and "be kept," while the value of the latter were expected to grow (Zhao, 1998a: 6).

From 1997, a series of preparations were carried out before the formal launch of the media conglomerate in 2001. In April 2000, the Shanghai Radio, Film and TV Bureau was merged with the Shanghai Culture Bureau, forming the Shanghai Culture, Radio, Film and TV Administrative Bureau. The immediate result of this merger was that, except for the print media, the new Bureau controlled almost all of Shanghai's media and cultural institutions (see Table 9.2). The

Shanghai television 153

Table 9.2 The major institutions under the Shanghai Culture, Radio, Film and TV Bureau in 2000

Broadcasters
Shanghai TV Station, Shanghai Oriental TV Station, Shanghai Cable TV Station, Shanghai Radio Station, Shanghai East Radio Station

Magazines
Shanghai Radio and TV Weekly

Film
Shanghai Film Group, Shanghai Paradise Film Group, Shanghai Film Archives

Technology
Technology Centre, Service Centre, Programming Centre, Shanghai Oriental Pearl (Group) Co. Ltd.

Arts
Shanghai Grand Theatre Group, Shanghai Art Museum, Shanghai Children's Library, Shanghai Special Events Office

Sources: 1. Official website of Shanghai Culture, Radio, Film and TV Bureau. Available at: http:// wgj.sh.gov.cn/wg/node1439/index.html (accessed 31 October 2004); 2. Official website of Shanghai Media & Entertainment Group (SMEG). Available at: www.smeg.com.cn/ (accessed 31 October 2004).

merger aimed to break down barriers between two systems and help municipal government to restructure resources and create new economic growth areas. This merger would also help the government's macro control over the two sectors (*The establishment of*, 2000).

Merger of OTV, STV cable TV and conglomeration since 2001

On 19 April 2001, the Shanghai Media & Entertainment Group (SMEG) was founded. The purpose of the conglomeration was to uphold the leadership of the Party over broadcasting, to strengthen the power and competitiveness of broadcasters, to establish an administrative and management system which is compatible with the quasi market economy. The SMEG was expected to "establish a new management system to enable the socialist ideological work's character to be maintained and be compatible with the development of the socialist market economy," to "establish a cross-sector, cross-regional, cross-country, new business structure," to "widen financing channels and improve core competitive power through institutional innovation" and to "push forwards technological advancement [...]." It aimed to develop the SMEG as "one of the most influential cultural and broadcasting organizations in the Western Pacific coastal region and one of the world class news and cultural groups" (Ye,[11] 2002a).

Meanwhile, the administrative tie between the Shanghai Culture, Radio, Film and TV Bureau and the SMEG was abolished when the administrative control of the SMEG was officially handed over to the Party's organ in Shanghai. The status of the SMEG was defined as an institution under the Propaganda Department of the Shanghai Party Committee. It was managed as an enterprise, but

154 *Shanghai television*

enjoyed the same administrative rank as the Shanghai Culture, Radio, Film and TV Bureau. A party committee at the SMEG acted as the highest power source. The Bureau still remained as the department of the Shanghai municipal government, regulating Shanghai's culture, broadcasting and film sectors and managing the non-business but social service oriented cultural institution (*The reply to*, 2001).

The ownership of the SMEG included the traditional media, such as TV, radio and press, new media, for instance broadband, and interactive TV and cultural organizations. It also controlled production and distribution companies. The group claimed to be "one of the largest media conglomerates in China" with its 17,000 thousand employees and more than US$1.8 billion in assets (Wang Y, 2003). This cross-ownership of the SMEG was well demonstrated through the structure of the Shanghai Media Group (SMG), the most important constitutional component of the SMEG (see Table 9.3). In fact, the SMG brought almost Shanghai's entire electronic media and cultural resources under its umbrella.

In the process of conglomeration, two terrestrial TV stations, the STV and OTV, were kept. The Shanghai Cable TV (SCT), which operated six channels,[12] was merged with the STV in July 2001. Soon after its launch, the SMG's senior management began to consolidate STV and OTV's advertising and program operations, and set up two centers in August 2001 to centrally control the

Table 9.3 The major entities of the Shanghai Media Group (SMG) in 2002

Broadcasters, Newspapers and New Media	Radio Shanghai; Eastern Radio Shanghai; Shanghai Television Station (STV); Shanghai Oriental Television Station (OTV); Shanghai Radio & TV Weekly; www.eastday.com; Shanghai Interactive Television Co. Ltd.
Network Companies	Orient Network Ltd.
Production Companies	Shanghai Broadcasting and Television Production Co. Ltd., Eastern Shanghai International Culture Film and Television Co. Ltd.
Investment Companies	Shanghai International Conference Center Co. Ltd.; Oriental Pearl CLS.
Cultural Performance Organizations	Shanghai Dramatic Arts Center; Shanghai Symphony Orchestra; Shanghai Pingtan Troupe; Shanghai Oriental Youth Troupe; Shanghai Kun Opera Troupe; Shanghai Peking Opera Theatre; Shanghai Song & Dance Ensemble; Shanghai National Music Orchestra; Shanghai Circus School; Shanghai Acrobatic Troupe; Shanghai HuaiJu Troupe; Shanghai Light Music Ensemble; Shanghai Farce Troupe; Shanghai Opera House.
Sport Clubs	Shanghai STV Women's Football Club; Shanghai Oriental Basketball Club; Shanghai Oriental Volleyball Club.

Source: 1. Official website of Shanghai Media Group. Available at: https://web.archive.org/web/20080916114203/www.smg.cn/Index/Index.aspx (accessed 23 February 2016).

advertising sales and program purchases of all of the channels (*SMG's 2001 Year*, 2002; Ye, 2002b). In other words, Shanghai's TV advertising and programming markets were almost entirely in the hands of SMG's two centers.

In response to concern over monopolization, the Director of SMG's Advertising Centre, Shen Mingchang (2002) denied that the center had the ability to monopolize the market and defended the strategy by adding that the SMG had faced mounting competition from various sources including provincial satellite channels, print media, foreign media and outdoor advertising companies. China's TV advertising industry in particular has had a difficult time since 1999 because of the Asian Financial Crisis and a sharp increase in the number of TV outlets. Mergers and concentration of ownership to enlarge the scale of business is "a trend and necessity" to eliminate price competition, to standardize the advertising and programming markets, to avoid unhealthy competition[13] and, in Shanghai's case, it was about to move from internal competition to internal unity in order to defeat outsiders. Otherwise, Shen warned, intensive local competition could cause "the loss of the State's media resources" and an "unnecessary waste of human resources" (Shen, 2002: 52).

In 2001, SMG generated 1.9 billion yuan of advertising income, which was a 56.7 percent share of Shanghai's total advertising revenue (Shen, 2002). The group aimed to save 20 percent of program purchasing costs in 2002 (Zhu YL, 2002) through lowering the price paid to domestic production companies. Although some independent production companies criticized SMG's anti-competition behavior as a setback for the industry, the group retained its strong stand (Media, 2001). Zhu Yonglei, then President of SMG explained, "after 1997, people increasingly realized that the disadvantages brought by internal competition outweighed the advantages it offered, and [we] need to be united." Second, he emphasized that, compared to other regions, the control of the Shanghai's party and government over local TV stations has traditionally been the strongest in China. From his point of view, the concentration of Shanghai's media resources was not a change that happened suddenly but was rather the natural outcome of self-development, having "a clear historical and empirical logic" (Zhu YL, 2002: 16). Having said this, Zhu also revealed that the group recognized the importance of competition and sought to stimulate it through encouraging internal competition between its channels. Zhu said that SMG would assess each channel's performance by various indices, such as "channel ratings, advertising revenue and management responsibilities." The assessment result would affect the resources allocated to the channel (Zhu YL, 2002: 17).

Channel specialization

Before conglomeration, Shanghai's three TV stations STV, OTV and SCT, together had 11 channels (see Table 9.5) and dominated the local audience market. After conglomeration, SMG revamped these 11 channels and re-launched them as specialist channels in January 2002, on the grounds of better utilization of channel resources (see Table 9.6) (SMG's 2001 Year Report, 2002).

156　*Shanghai television*

Table 9.4 Shanghai TV market in 2000

Population	Household	% of TV household	TV audience	Average TV watching time/day	Advertising revenue (million yuan)
14.83 million	5.29 million	98	14.54 million	2.52 hours	STV 71.48 OTV 66.49 SCT 40.07

Sources; 1. Shanghai 2000 Population Census Assembly. Available at: http://chinadataonline.org/member/census2000/# (accessed 23 February 2016); 2. Zhang Y (2001) Analyzing 2000 Shanghai TV Rating. Shanghai Broadcasting Studies. 03/04:31–33; 3. Zhang ZL (2002) Behind the Figures: the case study of STV's Sports Channel. Shanghai Broadcasting Studies. 03/04:55–59.

Table 9.5 TV channels in Shanghai, 2000 (before conglomeration)

STV (3)	News and General Channel; Business Channel; Shanghai Broadcasting Network (satellite channel)
OTV (2)	News & General Channel; Children, Technology and Sports channel
SCT (6)	Entertainment Channel; News Channel; Sports Channel; Music Channel; Classic Operas Channel; Finance Channel
Educational TV Station	Educational Channel
Others	10 provincial satellite Channels; 4 CCTV Channels

Source: 1. Official website of Shanghai Media & Entertainment Group (SMEG). Available at: https://web.archive.org/web/20051124145144/www.smeg.com.cn/intro1/tv.asp (accessed 23 February 2016).

Table 9.6 TV Channels in Shanghai in January 2002 (after conglomeration)

STV (7)	News Channel; Channel Young; Business Channel; TV Drama Channel; Shanghai Broadcasting Network (satellite channel); Sports Channel; Documentary Channel
OTV (4)	News & Entertainment Channel; Music Channel; Folk Opera Channel; Arts & Entertainment Channel
Educational TV Station	Educational Channel
Others	10 provincial satellite Channels; 4 CCTV Channels

Sources: 1. Official website of Shanghai Media & Entertainment Group (SMEG). Available at: https://web.archive.org/web/20080916153721/www.smeg.com.cn/group/group-overview1.asp (accessed 23 February 2016); 2. Official website of Shanghai Culture, Radio, Film and TV Bureau. Available at: https://web.archive.org/web/20070104213129/http://wgj.sh.gov.cn/wg/node1439/node1463/node1464/userobject1ai16543.html (accessed 23 February 2016).

Interestingly, a speech delivered by Zhu Yonglei in February 2002, disclosed that Xu Guangchun, then Head of SARFT, admitted at a national TV conference, that inadequate domestic production capacity stretched by the strong growth of specialist channels had caused the penetration of foreign media through program co-production. The enhancement of production capacity was perceived as the core issue in China's TV development and was regarded as a political battle for the control of public opinion (Zhu YL, 2002). Why did the SMG still maintain 11 specialist channels? One reason was related to the status of SMG. As a state institution, to lay-off a large number of employees was a sensitive and difficult action. Second, in China, the channel spectrum was an important resource for a TV station because of the degree of difficulty in having the local and national broadcasting bureaus' approval for a new channel. The SMG was also willing to keep these channels. Moreover, the President of SMEG, Ye Zhikang, openly urged fostering new economic growth through developing pay-TV. In July 2001, Shanghai launched its own pay-TV service (Ye, 2002b). The aim of these free-to-air specialist channels was to occupy Shanghai's niche markets to serve future pay-TV business.

Channel Young: from an institution to a quasi-company

Since 2002 SMEG has also sought to reform its management and personnel systems to facilitate the organization's pursuit of the "organic unification of social effect and economic interest" (SMEG 2002 job summary, 2003: 2–4). In other words, it needs a new institutional arrangement so that not only is the TV organization managed like an enterprise, but it is also conceptualized as an enterprise.

First, SMG started to assign fiscal quotas to its senior management and requested that "all channel and program managers need to also act as financial managers, no matter whether the program is an existing one or a new one, [managers] need to consider profitability, input and output and need to control costs" (Lu SG, 2003: 1).

Second, in June 2003, SMG took a further big step, setting up a company to operate its urban affluent-audience-targeted life style channel, Channel Young. The company, Shanghai Fashion and Culture Media Co (*Shanghai Shishang Wenhua Chuanmei Gongsi*, 上海时尚文化传媒公司) is wholly owned by SMG and is run by Channel Young. The company is responsible for Channel Young's daily management, program production and advertisement sales, while the channel is also the company's core business. In other words, although company and channel are separated by name, they are actually integrated into one entity and run by the same team. The Channel's then Director, Jiang Weimin, was also the company's General Manager.

The company's management structure simulated a commercial corporation. At the top was the General Manager, Jiang Weimin and there was a four-member Executive Committee, comprised of representatives from the company's different departments. Below these, four different departments: production, business,

158   *Shanghai television*

publicity and finance, were responsible for in-house production and program purchase, program and advertisement sales, marketing and finance, respectively. However, the legal representative of the company is the President of SMG, which reflects the company's ownership.

Jiang saw the company as equivalent to a TV station[14] but also different to a traditional TV station because it was given unprecedented autonomy to organize its personnel, fiscal and business models to cater for the transformation from an institution to a quasi-company. Financially, the company was no longer attached to the fiscal budget system,[15] instead, SMG only provided the company's start-up capital. The company then had to be financially self-dependent[16] and, in line with this, the channel's advertising was no longer managed by SMG, but by the company itself. Regarding concern about a possible financial deficit, Jiang replied frankly, "I don't know. We are not allowed to lose money. I have not thought about this question."[17]

In terms of its employment system, the channel's labor force was no longer allocated only by SMG, instead the company could recruit talent from the market, provided that the decision was approved by SMG's personnel department.

For Jiang, the most important implication of this company reform and channel specification was the introduction of market consciousness into the TV channel. Before transformation, the propaganda and publicity function was at the heart of the TV channel's concern. To secure "broadcasting safeties," i.e., political correctness and technical safety, was the top priority. As a department leader at a state institution, besides executing her senior's instructions and to ensure that her staff made no mistakes, it was not essential for her to have a long-term vision of the department's development. After converting to a quasi-company, although the broadcasting safeties were still required, the channel still needed to cater to the government and Party's propaganda and publicity work. More importantly, the company had to make a profit. In Jiang's opinion, this was a significant change: "In future, the business nature [of the media] will be further stressed, particularly for those non-news media."

On the other hand, she criticized the incompleteness of the ongoing reform and demanded ownership relaxation and further autonomy in the personnel and wages systems. She admitted that she was not the most suitable person to manage the company because she was trained as a journalist and had no managerial experience at all, but from the Party's point of view, she was politically reliable, hence their choice. She also revealed that the company planned to list on the stock market in order to absorb non-state capital and to diversify its ownership structure. In 2009, the Shanghai Fashion and Culture Media Co. was renamed the Channel Young Media Co., Ltd (星尚传媒有限公司), and it was wholly owned by Shanghai *Dongfang Chuanmei Jituan Youxiangongsi.* Soon after Channel Young's conversion, another company, Shanghai CBN Ltd (*Shanghai Diyicaijing Chuanmei Youxiangongsi*), was also launched on a similar model to operate SMG's CBN channel, then the national satellite channel Dragon TV channel also followed the same step since 2003. Companies manage these three channels and they are not only content production departments, but also market players, and possess the right to negotiate external cooperations and industrial development rights. Under the SMG's management, they have certain rights and autonomy to hire personnel, and distribution rights (*An interview with Yang Xingnong*, 2006). The Vice President of SMG, Yang Xingnong, said that there were three reasons why the three channels were chosen to implement the entrepreneurial reform. First, they were small channels and thus their reform would not affect the SMG's total advertising; second, the three channels had market potential; and third, they also had teams who could operate the entrepreneurialization, Yang said that the entrepreneurial reform was to increase their competitiveness through system and institutional innovations that established a rights and responsibility unified market system and mechanism. Yang endorsed the growing contributions of the channels, i.e., advertising revenues, to the SMG after the reform (See Figure 9.1) (*An interview with Yang Xingnong*, 2006)

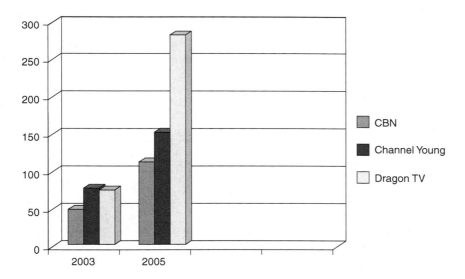

million RMB	2003	2005
CBN	46	110
Channel Young	75	150
Dragon TV	73	280

Figure 9.1 Three channels' revenue in 2003 and 2005 (in million yuan).

Separation of broadcasting and production – SMG

Jiang's urge for further reform on the structure and ownership of the SMG was gradually realized during the next decade. Since 2003, a series of policies and documents have been issued to promote the separation of broadcasting and the production of broadcasting TV. The general office of the State Council's 2003 No. 105 document encouraged and supported social capital to invest in private and joint-stock cultural enterprises, and SARFT's 2005 department rule *Regulation on Production and Management of Radio and Television Programs* (SARFT, 2004a) and the State Council's *Several Regulations on Non-public Capital's Entrance into the Cultural Industry* (State Council, 2005) regulated that domestic private capital could invest in music, technology, sports and entertainment program production, providing the company had state ownership of at least 51 percent. (Liu and Xiao, 2010). The SARFT policy document of 2004 *Opinions on Promoting the Development of Radio, Film and Television Industry* (SARFT, 2004b) proposed to expand investment and financing channels, expand market access and allow qualified program production enterprises to seek financing by listing on the stock market. By 2015, 32 media companies, under the category R of culture, sports and the entertainment industry, had listed on the Chinese stock market (China Security Regulatory Commission, 2015). In 2009 SARFT issued the documents of the *Reform on Promoting "Separation of Broadcasting and Production" of Broadcasters* and *The Opinions on Earnestly Implementing the Separation of Broadcasting and Production* to local radio and TV bureaus (Du and Chen, 2009). The documents encouraged broadcasters to "actively cultivate new market players, and promote the transformation of broadcasters' program production units and departments to enterprises." A production company owned by a broadcaster can absorb social capital, but broadcasters must ensure that they have a controlling stake, have control over asset allocation, decision-making power on major issues and the power to appoint or dismiss senior staff. Production companies were allowed to be publicly financed, and to achieve economies of scale and cross-regional development through mergers and reorganizations (SARFT, 2015e). As a result, the old SMG (Shanghai *Wenguang Xinwen Chuanmei Jituan,* 上海文广新闻传媒集团) was restructured into an institution RTS (上海广播电视台) and a new enterprise SMG (Shanghai *Dongfang Chuanmei Jituan Youxiangongsi,* 上海东方传媒集团有限公司) to run broadcasting and production separately.

Back in 2004, the then President of the SMG, Li Ruigang, announced that the SMG aimed to achieve two "transformations": transformation from producing programs for broadcast to producing programs for the market; transformation from a local broadcaster to a content provider, distributor and service provider for the national and international Chinese culture market (Zong, 2006a) and the strategies of "specialized division of labor, brand building, industrial expansion, the entrepreneurialization of the operation" were also endorsed by leaders at Shanghai's propaganda department and the Central propaganda department in Beijing (Zong, 2006b).

Shanghai television 161

In October 2009, the SARFT approved the reform scheme of the SMG, which was initially called Shanghai *Wenguang Xinwen Chuanmei Jituan* (上海文广新闻传媒集团), meaning to deepen the reform of the "separation of broadcasting and production." The SMG was restructured into two parts: Radio and Television Shanghai (RTS, Shanghia *Guangbo Dianshitai* 上海广播电视台) and Shanghai Oriental Media Group Ltd (*Shanghai Dongfang Chuanmei Jituan Youxiangongsi*, 上海东方传媒集团有限公司) i.e., the new SMG.

The new SMG was transformed to an enterprise owned, administered and controlled by RTS; while RTS maintained its public institution structure and was directly led by the propaganda department of the CCP Shanghai Municipal Committee (Fan, 2015). Since RTS still belonged to the public institution, it was responsible for the broadcasting of all programs, program planning, evaluations, examinations and acquisitions, as well as the production of news programs. The new SMG, on the other hand, was a media enterprise responsible for the production management of TV programs, new media and media-related business operation services and was funded and controlled by RTS. The aim was to list the new SMG on the stock market in the near future, so that the media industry could enter the capital market, and the industrial capital and financial capital could be integrated. This move was regarded as "ice-breaking" in broadcasting reform, because the previous separation of broadcasting and production was mostly limited to certain programs or columns, while the reform of SMG was the complete separation of the TV station from the production organization. Policies also encouraged the alliances and mergers of different program production companies. The new SMG was expected to become a multi-service, large-scale and cross-regional media group and content provider for the overseas Chinese culture market (Du and Chen, 2009). The SMG's reform was regarded not only as an internal management mechanism change, but also a watershed for broadcasting system reform that other media stations and conglomerates, such as the China Central Television Station and the Hunan Media Group, would follow (Liu and Xiao, 2010).

However, such separation is just separation at the operational level; at the ownership level, the SMG still belonged to and was owned by RTS. The ultimate aim of the separation was to transform the production units of broadcasting stations to independent legal bodies with corporate governance structures, and to diversify the investment bodies, accelerate the shareholding ownership reform and absorb social capital. The original equipment, capital and technology assets of the production units were converted into shares in the production companies. The relationship between a television station and a production company was a shareholding relationship, relying on the capital ties connecting each other to achieve the separation of ownership and management rights, and make the production company a real market player with its own decision-making. The separation of broadcasting and production was expected to lead to the advent of cross-region, cross-media platforms, cross-industry, cross-ownership multimedia conglomerates that would target regional, national and international markets (Liu and Xiao, 2010).

162 *Shanghai television*

Five years later in March 2014, Shanghai Media & Entertainment Group (SMEG) undertook another historic change: the organizational system of SMEG as a public institution was revoked. This meant that, except for the Shanghai Film Group Corporation (上海电影（集团）有限公司) and eastday.com (东方网), which would operate independently, other enterprise units under SMEG were all restructured to establish the new solely state-owned Shanghai Media & Entertainment Group Inc. (Shanghai *Wenghua Guangbo Yinshi Jituan Youxian Gongsi,* 上海文化广播影视集团有限公司). Moreover, the new SMG (Shanghai *Dongfang Chuanmei Jituan Youxiangongsi,* 上海东方传媒集团有限公司) was integrated with the newly established Shanghai Media & Entertainment Group Inc. through a transfer of state-owned equity (Fan, 2015). Non-enterprise units under SMEG, the Shanghai International Film Festival Center and the Shanghai Film Archive, were to be administered by the Shanghai Municipal Culture, Radio Broadcasting, Film and Television Administration. Other public institutions will be transferred to be under the administration of RTS (TMT, 2014).

In summary, SMEG officially transformed itself from a state institution to a corporation, and merged with one of its wholly owned subsidiary, i.e., the new SMG, to become a new media and entertainment conglomerate – the Shanghai Media & Entertainment Group Inc. (SMEG Inc.) (Huang, 2014). The Shanghai State-owned Assets Supervision and Administration Commission (SASAC) wholly owned the new SMEG Inc. (Fan, 2015). The SASAC was set up based on the State Council Institutional Reform Scheme approved at the First Session of the Tenth National People's Congress of PRC. Based on the principle of separating government administration from enterprise management, and separating ownership from management power, SASAC undertook the responsibility of the investor on behalf of the state; supervised and managed the state-owned assets of enterprises according to law; and guided and pushed forward the reform and restructuring of state owned enterprises (SOEs). The SASAC was responsible for appointing and dismissing the top executives of the enterprises under the supervision of the Central Government, evaluating their performance, and granting them rewards or punishments. The SASAC also directed and supervised the management work of local state-owned assets (Li, 2003). Unlike the Shanghai Media & Entertainment Group Inc., which is invested in and owned by the SASAC, Radio and Television Shanghai (RTS, 上海广播电视台), as a state institution, is led by the Propaganda Department of the CCP Shanghai Municipal Committee. Ling Gang, the President of BesTV New Media, the Internet TV service operator under the Shanghai Media & Entertainment Group Inc., said in an interview:

> After the integration, media's public resources, its functions enacted by laws or regulations will be undertaken by the television station institutions (i.e., RTS, 上海广播电视台) and controlled by the state; while the entity of enterprise (i.e., the Shanghai Media & Entertainment Group Inc.) will be wholly held by the SASAC. The legal relation between institutional RTS

and entrepreneurial Shanghai Media & Entertainment Group Inc. is separated instead of being superior and subordinate, nor the capital-linked relation. They are in collaborative operation with each other.

(Fan, 2015)

Li Ruigang, the then chairman of SMEG Inc. hoped that marketization could force the reform of the broadcaster's internal system and mechanism. "The power of capital can never be overlooked," Li said (Yuan, 2014). Several months after the formation of the Shanghai Media & Entertainment Group Inc., in November 2014, its BesTV New Media and Shanghai Oriental Pearl Group were merged to create a new Internet and TV company called *Shanghai Oriental Pearl New Media Co.*, with the Shanghai Media & Entertainment Group Inc. having a 45.07 percent stake in the merged company. The merged company will be the sole capital and business platform for Shanghai Media & Entertainment Group Inc., and the largest Chinese online media conglomerate. The move to form a giant company was recognized as chiming with President Xi Jinping's plans to rationalize the state-owned media sector into a few large, powerful conglomerates. Li Ruigang also revealed that after the restructuring, the company would invest more in digital channels, including PC and mobile Internet, and focus on both content production and channel-building (Coonan, 2014).

The merger process will also involve the absorption of a handful of unlisted SMEG Inc. subsidiaries, including SMEG Pictures, Oriental CJ Home-shopping, Wings Media and Shanghai Interactive TV (Frater, 2014). Up to the time of integration, the stock market listed company owned 70 percent of SMEG Inc.'s business assets, income and profits. Thus, Shanghai Oriental Pearl New Media Co., to some extent undertakes the responsibility of the SMEG Inc.'s initial public offering (IPO) in the future (Fan, 2015). Meanwhile, Li Ruiguang, the Party head of the Communist Party of China Committee, Chairman and President of SMEG Inc., resigned the president position at the end of 2014 and Wang Jianjun, the Deputy Party Chief and Executive Vice President of SMG, was appointed as the new President. However, Li continued to be Party head of the Committee and Chairman of SMEG Inc. (Frater, 2015). This change of personnel was interpreted as a move that allowed Li Ruigang to focus more on a state-backed investment fund for media and culture – China Media Capital (Shanghai Daily, 2015).

By July 2015, SMEG Inc. had 13 functional departments, eight business units, 16 first-level enterprises (including one listed company, the Shanghai Oriental Pearl New Media Co.) and nine secondary enterprises, as well as over 17,200 staff (SMG, 2015). The SAPPRFT stated that the broadcasters at national and provincial levels were the focus of the separation of broadcasting and production reform, and analysts believe that the transformation and merger of the two state-owned Shanghai media groups set an example for the future market reform of China's media system (Li, 2014).

164 *Shanghai television*

Internationalization

If, in the 1990s, the main feature of Shanghai's television was to develop through controlled competition in the local market, since 2000, along with the relaxation of the government's restrictions on cross-regional operation and ownership, local leadership has forcefully reshaped the goals and structures of Shanghai's broadcaster.

The decentralization of resources and internal competition was no longer the guiding principle of development; instead, the "consolidation" of resources, "unity" and "competition with outsiders" were encouraged (*SMEG 2002 job summary*, 2003: 1). SMG's ambition was no longer confined to the Shanghai market, and was seeking to become one of the most influential Chinese broadcasters in the world (Zhu YL, 2002).

In October 2002, 35-year-old Li Ruigang replaced Zhu Yonglei, becoming the youngest President of the SMG. An interview conducted by the Chinese newspaper, *Economic Observer*, states that soon after Li took over the leadership he undertook a short visit to the General Electrics (GE) company in the U.S and studied its internal management. He admitted that this visit impressed him very much. On his return, he outlined a 2003 development plan. One of three main strategies he proposed for SMG's future development was to be involved in external collaboration[18] (*Economic Observer*, 2003b).

In April 2003, SMG established a strategic partnership with CNBC Asia Pacific, a business and financial news broadcaster owned by the Dow Jones and Company and NBC.[19] The two companies agreed to collaborate in the areas of business and financial program co-production and broadcasting. The collaboration was in two parts. First, CNBC committed to broadcast China's financial and business news updates live from Shanghai throughout its Asian, European and American networks, twice a day from 14 April 2003. This three to five minute English language morning briefing and afternoon update was co-produced by SMG's Shanghai Business Channel and CNBC and hosted by SMG's reporters. The logo of the Shanghai Business Channel could also be seen on-screen during the program.

Second, it was agreed that a special edition of CNBC's program *Managing Asia* be broadcast on the Shanghai Business Channel. The 20-minute in-depth one-to-one interview program was produced by CNBC, but repackaged by the SMG (*Economic Observer*, 2003a).

CNBC commented that this collaboration gave its viewers "an unprecedented daily look into China's latest business news" and it recognized that "China is the world's fastest growing economy," and Shanghai is emerging as "one of the world's financial capitals" (CNBC Asia, 2003). However, as foreign TV channels are still not allowed to broadcast to China's households[20] and there are still many policy restrictions on foreign capital investment and ownership, as well as industrial and cultural barriers concerning domestic ideology, custom and language, in order to expand in China transnational media corporations tend to form partnerships with local media organizations (Shen, 2004).

Shanghai television 165

SMG also presented the collaboration as an important step for Shanghai media's "reaching out" project.[21] Leaders of SMG praised the appearance of Chinese media and its programming on Western major media as "an important breakthrough in China's publicity work" (*Economic Observer*, 2003a) and announced "this is a win-win partnership: it will not only benefit viewers of CNBC and the Shanghai Media Group, but will also explore ways for cooperation between international and Chinese media companies" (CNBC Asia, 2003).

Despite this, Shen Li, the then head of SMG's Research and Development (R&D) Department admitted that the glue that kept the two parties, local and foreign media, together was their common interests in developing China's national and regional TV markets. For the foreign media, such as CNBC, local partners were needed to overcome or circumvent industry barriers and strict investment and ownership policy restrictions. For the local media, like SMG, they expected to gain business and management experience, program resources and international investment through international collaboration. Amongst these, local media tended to "put the successful business mode in first place, then [using] the capital, program resources and management experience to carry out the mode" (Shen, 2004: 6). The permission for cross-regional expansion also reinforced the local media's desire to control geo-regional, national and regional through teaming up with larger and more influential foreign media. Therefore, for SMG, the predominant aim of its international collaboration is "to create a new competitive business mode targeting at the national or regional market" (Shen, 2004: 5).[22] In addition, having an international partnership could also help SMG develop towards the Mexican Televisa or Brazilian Globo models of a geo-regional media conglomerate in the long term (Shen, 2004).

On 10 April 2003, SMG and CNBC Asia Pacific formally signed up to the partnership. Li Ruigang announced that "[this collaboration with CNBC] is only beginning, we will later have bigger actions," and "we are open to any possible cooperation as long as it is allowed by the government's policy" (*Economic Observer*, 2003a). In fact, not only SMG, but also domestic TV media in general tended to see foreign media as competitors as well as collaborators. In other words, through collaboration with, and competition against, foreign media, domestic television sought to gain creativity while realizing substantial development.

After the announcement of the partnership with CNBC in July 2003, SMG revamped the Shanghai Business Channel and the Oriental Financial Radio Channel into a new specialist network, the China Business Network (CBN). The network is set to "root in the Yangzi River triangle region, to serve the country and enter the world," aiming to become a famous brand amongst business news media (*CBN officially launched*, 2003). CBN has strived to dilute its local character while stressing the national and international features of its business and financial information. It set up studios, journalists and editorial teams in Shanghai, Beijing and Shenzhen and sought cooperation with different local media in order to enter their local networks (CBN, 2003).

Shen admitted that both the channel's foreign collaboration and re-positioning have inevitably influenced the channel's programs. In order to create a successful

166 *Shanghai television*

business model, the principle of management has been transformed from catering to public benefit to meeting financial needs. Accordingly, its programming principle has also been changed from general economic news covering the domestic economy, life, consumers and the stock market to investor-oriented professional business information.

International collaboration has enabled two of the changes that SMG was aiming for: the first change was to produce programs for market; the second was to alter its position as a local broadcasting station to a national and international content provider and distributor. The partnership with CNBC Asia Pacific, established in April 2003, was an example of a pioneer program with a broadcast on an overseas TV network followed by a series of other cooperations.

In April 2009, the first private equity fund in China's cultural industry, China Media Capital (CMC) with a fund of 5 billion yuan, was launched after gaining the approval of the National Development and Reform Commission. Li Ruigang, the then President of the SMG and Director of RTS at that time also acted as the chairmen of CMC. One-third of the fund was sponsored by the Shanghai Oriental Huijin Culture Industry Investment Co. Ltd (上海东方惠金文化产业投资有限公司) led by the SMEG; another third was sponsored by CDB Capital under the China Development Bank, one of China's largest financial institutions; and the remaining funds were raised by Li Ruigang from the market including sponsors like China Merchants China Direct Investments Limited (CMCDI), *Wenhui-Xinmin* United Press Group and so on (Yang, 2014). The SMEG is one of the Limited Partners of CMC (Zheng, 2013). Although the major sponsors of CMC are all state-owned enterprises, CMC is a completely market-oriented entity while SMEG still belongs to a state-owned enterprise (Liu, 2015). Thus CMC plays an essential role in pushing forward SMEG's internationalization and access to capital markets.

In 2010, CMC launched its first investment since establishment – the acquisition and control of Star China, formerly News Corporation's China assets which included three TV channels: Star (星空, *Xing Kong*), Star International, Channel V China, and the Fortune Star Chinese movie library (Business Wire, 2014). The SMG used to cooperate in program production with Star TV (Zheng, 2013). The direct acquisition of Star China by CMC could help Chinese programs to become established outside Mainland China in the name of Star TV, and also strengthen the market-oriented identity of Chinese media in foreign negotiations as Star TV originally belonged to the News Corporation owned by Rupert Murdoch (China Entrepreneur, 2013). Indeed according to Li Ruigang, "over the past three years, the company has achieved outstanding performance," and in January 2014, CMC and 21st Century Fox announced that they have signed an agreement under which Star China's management team together with CMC will further acquire 21st Century Fox's 47 percent stake in Star China (Business Wire, 2014).

Besides the acquisition of Star China, DreamWorks Animation SKG, Inc. (DreamWorks) agreed to form a joint venture with CMC, SMG and SAIL (Shanghai Alliance Investment Ltd) in 2012, and the new entity is called Oriental

DreamWorks. DreamWorks holds approximately 45 percent of the stake in the venture while its Chinese partners including CMC, SMEG and SAIL hold the remaining majority stake of approximately 55 percent (Deadline Hollywood, 2012), among which SMEG accounts for 30 percent (Zheng, 2013). Oriental DreamWorks's headquarters are located in Shanghai, and it is dedicated in creating high-quality entertainment content for audience, including Computer Graphics (CG) animation and film, as well as television programs. Its aim is to establish a leading China-focused family entertainment brand, and meanwhile promote the content on a global scale (Oriental DreamWorks, 2015). Li Ruigang, Chairman of CMC and President of SMEG pointed out that the new Oriental DreamWorks can combine and lever "the expertise of CMC in investment and operation, SMG in media and entertainment management, SAIL in high-tech R&D, as well as DreamWorks Animation in creative processes, innovative technology and global network capabilities" to provide creative high-quality content for China and international markets (Oriental DreamWorks, 2012).

In 2014, SMEG expanded its strategic relationship with the Walt Disney Company, to include television content development, movie co-production, content distribution, and cooperation on marketing. The multi-faceted alliance with Disney is expected to "serve as the cornerstone of actualizing SMG's vision in applying world-class creative process; contribute towards the success of local content creation for international markets and create new business models across both digital media and traditional spaces" (The Walt Disney Company, 2014). Also in 2014, SMEG and CMC joined forces with Warner Bros. Entertainment, RatPac Entertainment and WPP to create a global content investment fund called the "CMC Creative Fund" (跨国文化创意投资基金). The fund is dedicated to investing in Chinese and international entertainment content opportunities covering film, TV and live entertainment. By virtue of this new platform, CMC and SMEG will be able to adopt the expertise of their partners Warner Bros, RatPac and WPP in production and distribution. This move again shows SMG's ambition to become an innovative media and entertainment conglomerate with global influence.

Wang Jianjun, the President of SMG, said:

> Content has been one of the main driving forces underpinning SMEG's development. [SMEG is] keen on participating in the international content market on a broader and deeper basis through this strategic partnership, which is expected to enhance our capabilities in content creation and thus help us meet the increasing demand for cultural products and the challenges of promoting China's creative industry and international exposure

and "this platform will enable SMEG to explore the industrialization and internationalization of our content creation, further help with consolidating and enhancing SMEG and our new public listed company's content competitive edge, and accelerate our new media transformation" (Warner Bros., 2014). The most recent cooperation between SMEG and foreign TV companies were the

168 *Shanghai television*

five projects co-produced by DocuChina (真实传媒有限公司), the SMEG funded first TV channel in China dedicated only to documentaries, and media organizations overseas. The five documentaries were: *Coast China*, produced in collaboration with BBC Worldwide; *Celebrities vs. Wild*, with Discovery Channel; *Super Asia* with KBS TV from South Korea; *Desire for Food*, with MBC, a TV company from South Korea; and *China by Your Side* with A+E Networks of the United States. *Celebrities vs. Wild* (also named *Survivor Games*, in Chinese: 跟着贝尔去冒险) was the first to go on air in October 2015 on Dragon TV, a SMG satellite channel. However, no matter how much marketization and internationalization SMEG strives for, it is still characterized to serve political end like all other state-owned media organizations in China (Ollig, 2007).

Summary

In this chapter we have looked at the structural, operational and strategic transformation of Shanghai's television since 1996. We found that the most profound reason underlying the transformation is the local television stations' desire for audience market expansion nationally and internationally. This is made possible by the government's abolition of geographic restriction on the coverage and operation of local TV stations in its national television policy.

Structurally, since the late 1990s ownership concentration of both media and cultural resources through conglomeration, to increase economies of scale and secure maximization of profits, has replaced the "development through controlled competition" principle practiced in the early 1990s. The local media elite has tended to identify concentration as a natural need and logical outcome of local's media self-development.

Operationally, channel specialization has been established as a common strategy for the newly established Shanghai Media Group (SMG) to facilitate the occupation of niche audience markets. the SMG has split off its business-oriented channels and has converted them into quasi-companies with unprecedented autonomy on personnel, finance and operations providing that the Party holds the delegation of politically reliable senior managers tightly.

The separation of broadcasting and production ultimately transferred the SMG from a state institution to an enterprise the Shanghai Media & Entertainment Group Inc., owned, administered and controlled by the Shanghai State-owned Assets Supervision and Administration Commission (SASAC). At the same time it also keeps the state-ownership and state institutional nature of television channel and spectrum resources and news production activities. They are also under the direct leadership of the propaganda department of the CCP Shanghai Municipal Committee. The legal and capital links between the institutional RTS and the entrepreneurial Shanghai Media & Entertainment Group Inc. no longer exist.

The change from institution to enterprise is partly about the autonomy of the broadcasting media and partly about capitalization of political power to personal

Shanghai television 169

welfare as CMC's case demonstrates. The appearance of mixed-owned and state-owned commercial media enterprises do not guarantee plurality of voices, given the control of broadcasting channels by the Party.

Notes

1 Which are under the direct administration of Beijing's Central Government.
2 Xu Guagnchun was replaced as the head of SARFT in January 2005. Wu Bangguo was the No. 2 person in the Standing Committee of the Poliburo and Chairman of the Standing Committee of the National People's congress; Huang Ju was the No. 6 person in the Standing Committee and Vice-Premier and worked in Shanghai for 40 years.
3 The main body of a municipality is usually a city that has both political and regional significance. Within a municipality's jurisdiction, only a small number of local governments exist. In Shanghai's case, it has one city and a few borough governments, amongst which only the former has a comprehensive governmental function. In contrast, the political hierarchy of a province is more complicated, because it involves more layers of local governments including those at provincial, capital city, city and county levels. Not only the provincial government, but also several lower governments have comprehensive functions and can operate independently (Yang, 2002).
4 China Central Television is the exception. Its footprint is allowed to reach the entire country. Besides, beginning in the 1990s, in some cities, the second TV stations, usually called Economic TV stations, appeared.
5 Shanghai has about 4.5 million TV households. In 1997, the city of Chongqing was designated as the fourth municipality with provincial status. It is now considered the largest city in China measured by metropolitan population (Wu, 1999).
6 In early 1998, Shanghai already had 2.2 million cable households.
7 This article is about an interview with Ye Zhikang, Chief of the Shanghai Radio, Film and TV Bureau.
8 In August 1995, the Shanghai Broadcasting Bureau merged with the Shanghai Film Bureau, forming Shanghai Radio, Film and TV Bureau (Lu, 1998).
9 Zhao Kai was the Party Secretary of the Shanghai Radio, Film and TV Bureau.
10 The State Council has recognized that the media sector belonged to the Third Industry since June 1992. The Third Industry refers to the service industry, differing from the agricultural and manufacturing industries.
11 Ye Zhikang was the President of the SMEG.
12 They were the Entertainment, News and Finance, Sports, Music, Classic Operas and Life Channels.
13 For Shanghai's senior media management, unhealthy competition mainly refers to price wars caused by the three TV stations competing for advertisers and for TV programs (See Zhu YL, 2002).
14 Personal interview with the Director of Channel Young, Jiang Weimin, 22 October 2003, in Shanghai.
15 Within the system, the channel's financial resources are centrally allocated by SMG.
16 The interview was conducted in October 2003, only four months after the company was established. Therefore, the company was still in a transitional period, its financial arrangement still being formed. It has not had complete fiscal autonomy and SMG had delegated a finance controller to manage the company's money.
17 She revealed that SMG assigned the senior management of the company to achieve a financial quota, if they failed to fulfil the quota, they would lose 8 to 12 percent of their yearly bonus.
18 The other two include resource concentration and structure adjustment.

170 *Shanghai television*

19 Dow Jones & Company, the publisher of *The Wall Street Journal* and its international and online editions, is a provider of vital world business and financial information; NBC, a leading television network in the USA, is a division of the General Electric Company (CNBC Asia, 2003).

20 Except for three-star hotels and certain institutions.

21 Personal interview with Li in Shanghai, June 2002.

22 According to Shen Li's answer to the audience's questioning during the Transnational Media Corporations and National Media Systems: China after entry into the World Trade Organisation Conference, 17–21 May 2004, The Bellagio Study and Conference Centre, Rockefeller Foundation, Italy.

10 Guangdong

The role of local in China's media policy-making process

Introduction

Since its inception China's television system has been structured as an integrated part of the state's political system (Pan and Chan, 2000; Wei, 2000). The 1983 multi-tier mixed coverage decentralization policy[1] led to the structural diversity of Chinese television within the Party-State system, while the recentralization of the television network from four tiers to two tiers, and the subsequent conglomeration since 1996, consolidated the power of broadcasters at the provincial level. Nevertheless, the hierarchical nature of the Chinese television system created a close bond among local television stations, broadcasting authorities and government at the same administrative level. Television stations depend on the local government and broadcasting authority's policy protections to monopolize the market; local government and the broadcasting authority count on television stations to advance their political influence and generate financial income. Since the early 1990s, the funding allocated to the broadcasting authority by local governments could only support their daily operations; therefore, capital required for development relied on financial contributions from the media, especially television stations (Wang, 1998). Broadcasting authorities are de facto economically "affiliated" to television stations at different levels and are used to protect local interests (Chin, 2006).

The fragmented nature of the governance structure of the Chinese television system raises interesting questions about the balance of power between the Central Government and localities, in general, and in media policy-making, in particular. Recent studies of media policy processes suggest that either the national policy-making process is closed or that the influence of localities in national media policy are confined to loosely interpreting and implementing policy (Kean, 2001; Lau *et al.*, 2008).

This chapter expands the second argument further, and suggests that (1) the state is selectively effective and the local authorities are selectively compliant depending on the nature of the policy; therefore, the historical and socio-political contexts are an essential and indispensable background to understanding why certain policies are important and strictly implemented while others are not; (2) the analysis of the interaction between policy formulation, implementation

172   *Guangdong: the role of local*

and evaluation is particularly important in understanding the complexity of Chinese policy processes and policy behavior.

Incorporating the concept of social learning, which sees policy development as a process of social learning by actors at or near to the center of policy-making (Pierson, 1993), this chapter examines the roles of provincial media and officials in China's Guangdong province in the national policy process of the entry of overseas television channels (OTvC) into China, and their patterns in articulating policy influence through policy implementation and learning. Key issues are (1) the role of the Province in policy formulation, implementation and learning (2) the mechanism through which the provincial media can influence national policy makers, and (3) the function of policy learning in the overseas television channels policy process. The analysis has found that: (1) despite there being little space for the provincial media to participate in national policy formulation, they have practiced great discretion in policy implementation, and (2) policy input is primarily through the policy learning process. The policy learning process in Guangdong, China not only functioned as a response mechanism to the legacies of previous policies, but also provided a legitimate platform for the provincial media to negotiate with Central Government for both policy change and policy incentives.

This chapter is in six sections: section one and two conceptualize policy-making as an aggregated process and introduce the concept of policy learning; section three discusses the links between the concept of policy learning and the common characteristics of China's policy-making process; section four reviews policy decisions on the entry of OTvC; section five looks at the implementation of the incentive policy on advertising insertion, and provincial discretion in the OTvC's supervision; section six examines policy learning both at the top (i.e., responses of the Party and state to the consequences of the advertising policy) and from below (i.e., provincial media's deliberate efforts to pursue OTvC policy reform).

China's media policy process conceptualization

The media policy process in China, when compared with other social policies, is a controversial topic on which there has been little research (Chin, 2007; Feng *et al.*, 2009; Keane, 2001; Lang, 2002; Zhou, 2007). The term "policy process" refers to the process of public policy-making, including problem conceptualization, solution formulation, implementation, evaluation and revision (Sabatier, 2007: 3). The conventional research approach focuses on a single phase of the process, typically either the formulation or implementation of the solution stage. Analysis of the former tends to contrast the "closed" and "clandestinely consulted" Chinese process with the "pluralist" USA model, in which Congress, the courts, regulated industries and citizens' groups are policy "determiners" (Lau *et al.*, 2008: 21). Researchers on the implementation stage argue that political participation in China is different from that of the West, as local officials, cultural producers and intellectuals do not play substantive roles in policy formulation;

however, they do have the capacity to influence policy interpretation and implementation (Keane, 2001).

There are, however, two weaknesses in the conventional approach. First, dividing a complex policy process into discrete stages and confining the research scope to a single stage, without reference to other stages, could result in the inability to identify a set of actors that drive the entire policy process (Sabatier, 2007: 7). For instance, different actors could perform different roles for diverse aims at different stages of the policy process. Second, focusing solely upon formulating and implementing policy neglects the interaction of the implementation and evaluation of the pieces of policy documents or legislation. Research shows that the evaluation or "learning" process of existing policy produces feedback, which could result in policy reform (Daugbjerg, 2003; Pierson, 1993).

These two weaknesses become especially prominent when attempting to precisely analyze China's media policy process due to its experimental nature. Like other social policies, China's media policy-making is confined to experimental and incremental approaches; consequently media policy is gradually adjusted according to empirical experiments and past experiences (Lang, 2002; Zhou, 2007). Policy-making is not a static but an ongoing and continual process, and is subjected to the influences of the consequence of policy implementation and evaluation or learning (Chin, 2007). Therefore, sub-national actors could perform multifaceted roles, and have the potential to influence national government's policy-making through policy implementation and learning.

This chapter has conceptualized policy-making as an aggregated process, and examined provincial policy actors across major policy phases. The research has especially focused on the policy learning stage, which is still an unexplored area in Chinese media literature. This neglect has resulted in a lack of understanding of media policy-making in both substantive (i.e., the effects of a policy document and its change), and procedural terms (i.e., the diverse roles of sub-national actors in the policy process).

This chapter aims to address this gap through a systematic and in-depth analysis of the formulation, implementation and learning processes of the national media policy of entry of overseas television channels (OTvC) into China. As we shall see later, the three processes are intricately interconnected to each other.

The concept of policy learning (PL) is central to this analysis for four reasons: primarily, PL provides a theoretical means for establishing linkages between formulating, implementing and learning from policies. Learning is a response to the consequences of either or both of the phases of formulating and implementing a policy. Therefore, to understand the learning process, encompassing "what," by "whom" and "how," we need initially to understand the processes of policy formulation and implementation. Besides, the function of the learning process is to adjust to either or both of the goals and techniques of an existing policy, or, indeed, to make wholesale policy changes. Second, PL analyses provide rewarding insights into the roles of both state and societal actors in influencing public policies through the learning process (Bennett and Howlett, 1992; Hall, 1993;

174 *Guangdong: the role of local*

Pierson, 1993). Third, the Chinese government has a distinct preference for including PL in policy-making (Beland and Yu, 2004: 270). Fourth, PL has functioned as a major vehicle for sub-national actors to influence national policy in other social policy areas in China (Moore and Yang, 2001).

This chapter examines the entry of OTvC into China, from 2000 to 2008, which provides an excellent case on which to test the arguments of the Party-State and societal actors' roles in media policy-making, since the power of the former should be at its maximum in a highly sensitive policy area like the entry of overseas television channels.

The concept of policy learning

The relevance of the concept of PL to the discussion of the provincial media's role in policy processes has two aspects. First, it conceptualizes policy, not only as an output of, but also an important input to, policy processes, since policy-making is an ongoing process. Second, different formulations of PL have provided fruitful insights into the roles of both state and societal actors in influencing public policies through learning processes (Bennett and Howlett, 1992; Hall, 1993; Heclo, 1974; Pierson, 1993).

Bennett and Howlett (1992) identify three types of PL: government learning, lesson-drawing and social learning. Although all tend to support pre-existing public policies and their consequences significantly influence policy-makers' designs and the enactment of new legislation, they vary considerably on three critical components of the learning process: who learns, what is learned, and their effects on resulting policies. This chapter focuses on one aspect of PL, i.e., social learning. Hall (1993) developed the concept of "social learning" in a study on macroeconomic policy-making in 1970–1989, in Britain, in relation to the debate on the state's autonomy in policy-making processes. Instead of emphasizing the importance of either the state or society, he identifies that the predominant agents of learning are the state and societal actors and distinguishes their roles in the light of the magnitude of the policy changes involved. Hall's approach is pertinent to China because of the patterns of state and social actors' policy participation observed in China.

Hall (1993: 278) defines social learning as "a deliberate attempt to adjust the goals or techniques of policy in response to past experience and new information. Learning is indicated when policy changes as the result of such a process." He articulates three levels of learning according to the magnitude of the changes involved: (1) policy goals and instruments remain unaffected but the settings of instruments are adjusted; (2) policy goals remain unaffected but new policy instruments are introduced; (3) the actual policy goals or paradigms are the focus of change. He concludes that PL at the first two levels is the autonomous state's responses to past policy and its consequences. The civil service drives policy innovation, and the learning process takes place within state institutions. The learning process involves rational policy analysis, serving the object of better goal attainment.

However, PL can also be a spontaneous and "contingent" response to imperatives emitted in societies as a consequence of pre-existing policies (Heclo, 1974: 316). Thus, the significant actors are not state officials but rather the societal actors who create the external policy conditions to which state actors must respond (Bennett and Howlett, 1992). As Dye (2008: 55) observes in the American context, most PL is impressionistic and unsystematic, and came in the form of interest group complaints about the inadequacies of laws; media exposure of mismanagement; legislative hearings, and citizens' complaints to the authorities. This learning process often succeeds in stimulating policy changes designed to remedy perceived inadequacies and mistakes.

Hall stresses that any changes of policy goals and paradigm are responses to "evolving societal debate" which is represented by mechanisms of the media, the financial markets, research institutes and the political arena (1993: 288). The learning process spilled beyond the boundaries of the state bureaucracy, and involved a much broader participation in which politicians and the media played the pre-eminent roles.

Ideas play a central role in the PL process because policy makers usually work within a policy paradigm, a key characteristic of policy discourse, with a set framework of ideas, parameters and standards. The key actors in the policy-making process – politicians, officials, organized interest groups and policy experts – work within the terms of political discourse, which generally have a specific configuration conferring privilege on some lines of policy over others. The actors not only exert power, but they also acquire power in influencing the political discourse "To the degree they are able to do so, they may have a major impact on policy without necessarily acquiring the formal trappings of influence" (Hall, 1993: 290).

In general, a policy paradigm is an interpretative framework that operates in the policy-making process; specifically, it refers to the ideas and standards that specify the goals, instruments and the very nature of the policy problems to be addressed (Hall, 1993). In this chapter, the media policy paradigm refers to a set of ideas about fundamental principles, overachieving policy goals (standards and strategies) and policy instruments. The fundamental principles "guide the overall communication and journalism activities, it is highly general but more stable" (Wang *et al.*, 2008). The principles are relatively stable and consistently applied across a very long time span and rarely changed. In the Chinese case, they typically include that the news media must be in line with the CCP's Central Committee's tone and that the news must correctly guide public opinion. While policy goals or policy directions are usually designed for a particular period and are usually reflected in the National People's Congress report, the CCP's national assembly report, and speeches made by party and government leaders (Wang *et al.*, 2008). Policy instruments are detailed measures to realize basic media policy goals, and they usually need to be flexible, operational and substantive. Policy instruments are usually found in documents of the Ministry of Central Propaganda, SARFT and other government departments.

176 *Guangdong: the role of local*

Policy learning and the Chinese policy-making process

The policy-making process usually involves time spans of a decade or more, as that is the minimum duration of most policy cycle, from emergence of a problem through sufficient experience with implementation to render a reasonably fair evaluation of a program's impact.

(Kirst and Jung, 1982; Sabatier and Jenkins-Smith, 1993 in Sabatier, 2007)

However, the usual period of a media policy cycle varies, some policies can be completed in less than two years after implementation, due to a lack of success and the absence of strict procedures for public deliberation and legislative procedures, and the arbitrary nature of policy formulation and termination.

The characteristics of China's policy-making process correspond fairly closely to the concept of PL. First, the common Chinese practice of launching "pilot projects" demonstrates the government's preference for including learning in its policy-making, which sequentially impacts on the decision-making process. This feature is known as "crossing the river by feeling the stones" (Beland and Yu, 2004: 270; Saich, 2001).

The general policy formulation procedure loosely practiced by the SARFT demonstrates the consideration of the impact and consequence of previous policies. After a policy question or problem is identified, the policy formulation begins with research on industrial practices. This can take various forms, including physically visit media organizations both inside or outside China; studying existing research reports and documents; and having meetings or discussion groups with industry actors and experts. Their experience, including both successful and unsuccessful activities, is analyzed and policy proposals are drafted between the SARFT and its affiliated think tanks, such as the Centre for Development and Research. The proposals are then studied and modified by senior policy-makers and their research teams in different SARFT's departments, and external experts may also be invited to give opinions. The Party Committee, the most powerful group in the SARFT, whose members usually consisted of the chief of the SARFT, the heads of the three national broadcasters and the head of the Party Commission for Inspecting Discipline, then vote to make a final decision.[2] Zhao Suifu, the former head of the SARFT's Policy and Regulation department once elaborated the model of decision-making in his department:

> policy itself is a dynamic process. Old policy gradually ceased, new policy gradually evolved, it repeatedly occurred and formed the policy cycle. A policy cycle usually goes through four stages: formulation; implementation; reaction; and termination. For existing policies, we need to consider their implementation, their interrelations; constraints on implementation and enforcement measures.

(Zhao, 1992 in Lu, 1999: 152–153)

The interaction between the policy makers and the industrial actors, and between policy formulation and evaluation, is vividly exemplified in a study of China's digital television policy (Zhou, 2007). Zhou's study suggests, horizontally, a reciprocal relation between the policy-makers and a limited number of industrial actors, and vertically, interdependence between media policy-making, policy implementation and evaluation. The constraints of the feasibility of implementation on policy formulation, the reciprocity between the policy-makers and a number of social and governmental actors, and the interaction between policy formulation and evaluation, creates space for scholars to conduct further investigations into the dynamics of the Chinese media policy process.

Meanwhile, despite the increasing policy space for individuals, organizations and provincial state agencies, the influence of lower-level participants comes in effect primarily as the policy is implemented, and through their feedback about the policy impact (Lampton, 2001). As Moore and Yang (2001) put it: "subnational actors typically have greater input into policy feedback than into policy formulation." This policy feedback, in turn, shapes the agenda of the central decision-makers.

Nevertheless, the relationship between the state, the Party and China's authoritarian society differs from the USA and UK contexts. This difference raises interesting issues concerning the role of the state and societal forces in the PL process, and the function of PL.

First, the power of the CCP is still superior to the state's, and the most senior Party leaders have had decisive roles in establishing broad national strategies and agendas, and in crisis management (Lampton, 2001).

Second, the decentralization of governance and the multi-level and fragmented governance structure produce two by-products: (1) any major policy initiative needs the support of one or more "unit" leaders in order to overcome bureaucratic impasses at lower levels (Lieberthal and Oksenberg, 1988: 23); (2) the hierarchical nature creates a close bond between provincial television stations, the broadcasting authority and government at the same administrative level.

Moreover, China's authoritarian political system has not provided transparent procedures for different interest groups to contribute to the policy process. The role that the provincial Chinese broadcasting media could play in the PL process and the function of the process currently remains unanswered. The rest of this article aims to provide some insights into these issues.

China's foreign TV policies

One of the significant developments of China's national TV policy-making towards the foreign media since the late 1990s is an ideological departure away from the core concern of how to resist foreign media flows, towards an attempt to maintain both the openness and the effective resistance of the television industry. Broadcasting policies were strategically adjusted, from the protectionism of the early 1990s to a pattern combining resistance with limited liberalization, to facilitate mutually beneficial principles, and to combine defensive measures to strengthen domestic champions vis-à-vis the foreigners with a more offensive and expansive approach to increase the country's international influences.

178 *Guangdong: the role of local*

Several factors have contributed to those changes. With its accession to the WTO in 2001, and its hosting of the 2008 Olympic Games, China has become more integrated and interdependent on the global community. This increasing interdependence will broaden the issues that the Chinese state considers to be in its national interest. Subsequently, the Party has to take the country's international political influence more seriously, precisely because it is directly linked to the country's economic welfare, which is no longer nationally confined (Perritt and Clarke, 1998).

The media in China have long been used by the Party to exercise ideological influence over the public, to unite the nation, and to present a favored image of the country to the world. The Party also has a long tradition of being, if not hostile, at least cautious towards foreign media, casting a large doubt on its impartiality when reporting on China.

Following Jiang Zemin's instruction to "let China's voice broadcast to the world," a "reaching out" project was launched by the SARFT, the national broadcast and film regulator (Xu, 2001: 537). The ultimate goal of this project is to present China's voice in all of the places that the BBC and other big Western media have reached. One of the strategies proposed is to expand China's television and radio channels into important overseas markets, such as Western Europe and North America, in order to have an international impact (Xu, 2001). To assist this, the state decided to liberalize local cable networks in the Pearl River Delta region of Guangdong province to foreign satellite channels in exchange for access of the China Central Television Station (CCTV) to international markets.

Guangdong province and its TV market landscape

Located on China's southern coast and adjacent to Hong Kong and Macau, Guangdong was one of the first provinces in China to open up to foreigners in the late 1970s. Its capital city, Guangzhou, is China's third largest city. Although Mandarin (Putonghua) is the official language, over half of its population speaks Cantonese, a local dialect that is also widely used by people in Hong Kong and Macau. As Guangdong is located at the southern corner of China, it is remote from the political and cultural center in the north and, as a result, its culture and languages have been less influenced by the mainstream. Local officials have also protected the Cantonese dialect from being replaced by Mandarin in the mass media for both cultural and economic reasons (Fang, Que and Tan,[3] 1996: 17).

In China, Guangdong is recognized as China's "experimental field" for reform and liberalization (Cai and Yang, 2004: 223). Due to geographic and cultural proximities, as well as kinship ties with people in Hong Kong, Macau and overseas, as early as 1979, the province was opened up to international investment and started to introduce market economy reform[4] (Liang, 2002). In 1984, the Pearl River Delta[5] "economic open region" was formed (Li, 2000). With this backing, not only did Guangdong establish itself as one of the pioneer provinces of China's reform progress, it also successfully expanded its autonomy in local financial and planning management (Li, 1998).

Overseas satellite television policy formulation: the decisive role of the Party

In 2001, for the first time, SARFT, permitted China's domestic cable television networks to carry OTvC including the AOL Time Warner owned China Entertainment Television channel (CETV) and News Corporation's Starry Sky Satellite Television (Starry Sky). The chosen networks were in the Pearl River Delta region of Guangdong province. CCP leaders, instead of SARFT, decisively shaped this policy (AOL Time Warner, 2001; STAR, 2001).

Individual Party leaders' interests and/or foreign economic demand can determine whether a particular policy initiative will be decided by top-ranking CCP leaders, rather than by the State Council bureaucratic units in China (Lieberthal and Oksenberg, 1988). In the case under discussion, the convergent interests of the top CCP leaders and foreign media companies during a transitional period of China's international integration determined its place on the Party's policy agenda. The negotiations were conducted at the CCP's most senior level, who made the decision to "tailor" China's OTvC policy to meet the needs of reciprocal access to overseas markets by the Chinese media, and the winning of the major Western media's support in reporting China (People's Daily, 2001; AOL Time Warner, 2001). Guangdong was chosen as the experimental site for liberalization because of the common perception that after two decades of reform, audiences in the province were more mature and sensible about foreign information, compared to China's other regions.[6] Therefore, there was little room left for provincial media and officials to negotiate at the decision-making stage. Despite the claim that the national regulator, SARFT, had consulted the Radio, Film and Television Administration of Guangdong (Guangdong Broadcasting Bureau, GBB) prior to approving the entry decision,[7] an interview with senior management at the Guangdong Cable TV Network revealed "[...] Guangdong is only responsible for implementation. As for the media's concern, of course, they were not happy because if one more [media] enters, their market will be seized. But this is not up to the media [to decide]."[8]

Grindel and Thomas (1989) suggest that resistance to policy will rise when the costs are borne by an organization or locality. Policy makers, therefore, need to consider how to mobilize resources, such as high-level support, consensus and behavioral incentives to sustain this policy. SARFT's consideration of the feasibility of incentives is evident in permitting the Guangdong broadcasters and cable operators' insertion of advertisements into the OTvCs. This policy has generated substantial financial benefit and considerable controversy for the operators. The entry agreements of the CETV and Starry Sky were made on conditions to secure three equal access rights for both sides. One condition allows each cable operator to insert advertisements into the channel they carry: three minutes per hour but two minutes during prime time.[9] Advertising insertion, driven by the potential of high profits, into OTvCs in Guangdong can be traced back to the 1990s when many cable television stations in Guangdong started to carry Hong Kong's four spill-over channels. Although neither the national

180 *Guangdong: the role of local*

regulator nor channel companies authorized this activity, no regulatory sanctions were applied. The provision of equal rights to insert advertisements in these two carriage agreements legitimized the practice and set the precedent for other media companies to follow. Similar conditions were also introduced in five other OTvCs' entry agreements (Nanfang Daily, 2008: A09).

Policy implementation: regulatory enforcement and discretion in supervision

Since 1997, SARFT or its predecessor, the MRFT, have issued more than ten documents regulating television advertising including the content, scheduling, length and presentation. The general provision is that advertising should be broadcast within the principle of keeping the programming integrity. Prohibitions include arbitrary adverting breaks during the programs, the insertion of their own advertising by relay organizations, such as cable network operators, or arbitrarily replacing original advertisements (MRFT [1997] No. 76; SARFT [1999] No. 117; SARFT [2002] No. 355; SARFT Decree No. 17, 2003; SARFT [2007] No. 74; SARFT, 2008b).

However, the measures of central authority control over the provinces in policy monitoring and enforcement are quite weak. If the central authorities want to monitor the implementation of a particular policy in the provinces they must either rely on information from provincial CCP officials, and public complaints, or pay significant transaction costs for inspection teams (Tanner and Green, 2007). The ineffectiveness of SARFT's enforcement and sanction failed to support the policies on television advertising (Song, 1999; Yu, 2006). Problematic television advertisements proliferate nationwide, not just in Guangdong. Local Guangdong television stations and cable operators not only arbitrarily forced the insertion of their advertisements and programs on to OTvCs, but they also covered some channels' off-peak programming with their medicinal products (Nanfang Daily, 2008: A09). In 2007, SARFT admitted to receiving 1,680 public complaints related to advertisement insertions, and identified it as an urgent problem (D&R SARFT, 2008; Tian, 2007). The Deputy Director of SARFT said that there was no shortage of advertising rules, but the keys for effective regulation are learning, comprehension and complying with them. He pledged to improve the monitoring system and strengthen sanctions, by requesting provincial broadcasting bureaus to firmly and fairly implement the rule and apply the penalties (Tian, 2007).

Consequent to the media and economic reforms that have promoted self-interested media organizations, and the decentralization of its regulatory structure, SARFT faces a struggle to find a balance between maintaining an authoritarian but effective governance, and inviting societal forces to participate in that governance, which could lead to the reduction of its power. In 2008, SARFT created a new national radio and television monitoring system to record advertisements broadcast on 1,372 television programs. The State Administration of Radio and Television considered that the old manual system did not effectively catch the problematic advertisements, and, as a result, it could not launch investigations (Sina News, 2008). Comments from the public on news. sina.com.cn (2008) questioned SARFT's claim to a lack of evidence as well as the effectiveness of the new system when it does not involve the public participation.

The role of provincial media and broadcasting bureaus is further complicated by the nationwide administrative and legal reforms to rationalize and improve governance. The government not only has to withdraw from direct intervention in the economy so as to create room for the market place, but it also has to strengthen its regulatory authority to support orderly market-oriented economic reform (Ngok and Zhu, 2007, Peerenboom, 2001). The core issue facing the Party and SARFT is how to provide provincial authorities with sufficient flexibility to administer the media in their jurisdictions and to respond to provincial circumstances, while preventing abuse of discretion. In 2003, the National People's Congress passed the Administrative Licensing Law. The implication of this law upon the broadcasting administration agency, SARFT, lay in the demand for a law-based administration. SARFT interpreted the impact more widely, and said that in order to implement the law it needed to both streamline its administration and delegate control (Xu, 2004d). In the context of OTvC licensing and regulation, SARFT issued Decree No. 22 (2003) and No. 27 (2004). Their purpose was to clarify the responsibilities of different agencies and broadcasting bureaus.[10] The decrees officially devolved the supervision of the OTvCs to the designated agencies, in Guangdong's case, the GBB. They require that:

> The designated institution shall take necessary prevention and treatment measures to assist the administrative department of Radio, and television to supervise the relevant acts and the contents by the foreign satellite television channel for which it acts as an agent, cooperate with SARFT in the relevant handing, and report in good time for any problems that have been found out.

Decree No. 27 gave the provincial authority the discretionary powers in deciding which content of the satellite channels broadcast violated the existing rules, and to cease transmissions. More importantly, it did not provide any remedies for resolving disputes. A provincial senior official[11] said that disputes would be referred to China's Council for the Promotion of International Trade (CCPIT) for resolution. However, in reality, as the Vice President of one OTvC explained: "we ... rarely violate policies ... If a problem occurs, we will inform the GBB ... [we] can only rely on the GBB."[12]

In 2006, despite the promulgation of the provincial rule *Provisional Provisions of Guangdong Province on Administration of Overseas Satellite Television Channels* (The Yearbook of Guangdong, 2007), on 5,000 occasions the GBB blocked OTvC programs involving four types of content: (1) political news related to sensitive topics; (2) news related to social unrest; (3) promoting religious freedom; (4) demonstrations by Falun Gong and Tibet Independent

182 *Guangdong: the role of local*

movements (STS, 2007). The frequency and breadth of this provincial censorship, the lack of procedures on checking the provincial authority's power, and the costs and technical difficulties for the national authority to monitor the provincial's daily administration all raise concerns about the justification of such supervision. This discretion on supervision becomes more problematic when the provincial media and authorities showed strong concerns not only over OTvCs' political materials but also the content of their entertainment, dramas and cartoon programs. The provincial Southern Television Station (STS), which is involved in OTvC supervision, complained about the decline in taste and quality and the increasing indecency, violence and pornography in OTvCs at a national industrial meeting. The Southern Television Station urged that "although these materials do not meet the standards of filtering, [we] cannot neglect their long term impact" (STS, 2007).

When asked what the government should do to improve their governance, the same Vice President responded: "it is best that SARFT does not delegate power [...]. The lower level agency even does not implement our agreement with its superior authority, so OTvC operators do not know what to follow and whom we should talk to." His response illustrates the dilemma between the decentralization of power and the enhancement of the function of national government in such a vast and segmented country with large number of provincial broadcasting authorities. A resolution is required to build up a functional and effective media regulatory institution whose power is institutionalized and constrained, and which also needs to abide by the law.

Social learning: the roles of the Party, provincial media and officials

The identity of the learning agent is an interesting issue when discussing the PL process. The CCP, rather than the state bureaucracy, has a vital role, not only in initiating major policy change, but also in adjusting the regulatory style. The choices of regulatory style can vary between an informal path of education and negotiation and a more formal and interventionist enforcement of standards, and also between being reactive and proactive (Baldwin and McCrudden, 1987). The State Administration of Radio and Television and its predecessor, MRFT, were aware, through a range of audit processes, including in-house surveys, public phone calls and letters, and online forums, of the public's discontent concerning television advertisements, broadcasting and insertion. However, a stiffer and more proactive enforcement of advertising codes towards television advertisement broadcasting was only introduced when the issue was brought to the attention of the senior CCP leaders. These included Hu Jintao, the Party's secretary and Wu Guangzheng, the Secretary of the Party's Central Commission for Inspecting Discipline. Both of them stressed, at the Central Commission's general meeting in 2007, that the Commissions' major task for constructing a harmonious society was to stop infringing on ordinary people's interests (Wu, 2007: 2). They requested the Commission at different levels to "supervise and

Guangdong: the role of local 183

collaborate with" other state departments to vigorously tackle the problems of most concern to the public, e.g., the proliferation of untruthful and illegal advertisements for medicine and food (Wu, 2007). China's *Advertising Law* states that the examination and identification of illegal advertisements is within the jurisdiction of the State Administration for Industry and Commerce, Ministry of Health, the State Food and Drug Administration and other state departments. However, none of them has sufficient influence to launch a cross departmental action; instead the CCP's committees and designated agencies have the authority to coordinate the activities of state administrative units within their geographic jurisdiction (Saich, 2001). This was the case when the CCP's Ministry of Central Propaganda coordinated a joint action by 12 Ministries to eliminate illegal sexual medical advertising from all types of media platforms in 2007 (SAIC [2007] No. 266). The State Administration of Radio and Television also held a national conference, in 2007, to organize "thoroughly cleaning up and rectifying" unhealthy television and radio advertising. Measures SARFT proposed to introduce include "to impose severe sanctions; to accept the People's Congress and social groups' supervision on advertising regulation; to properly deal with public complains and criticisms, and strengthen societal supervision on illegal advertisements" (Tian, 2007). In 2008, SARFT created the national radio and television monitoring system.

At the provincial level, Guangdong's television broadcasters and provincial officials have persistently complained of the inadequacy of the existing regulations on OTvC services, and systematically campaigned for a policy change. In order for their voices to reach the national policy makers, multifaceted measures have been used: (1) undertaking research and writing reports, and attending industry meetings and workshops; (2) personal connections with senior party officials, the industry regulator and influential people at the national level; and (3) mobilizing academic discussion and media coverage to promote policy achievements in return for national government's policy rewards. Their efforts not only targeted policy instruments and settings, e.g., the regulatory mechanism and sanction level, but also at creating a favorable ideological climate for Guangdong.

The SARFT's *Provisional Measures for the Administration of Examination and Approval of the Landing of Overseas Satellite TV Channels* issued in December 2001 set out the conditions of entry and the penalty for violations. Specifically, if violations occur three times in a year, the qualification for landing shall be revoked (SARFT Decree No. 8, 2001). In 2003, Wang Keman and Liu Hongbin, who were Vice Directors of the GBB, published articles in the journal *South China Television and Radio Research.* Liu advocates a media policy, which gives provincial industry more protection in order to gain the time to become more robust. Liu argues this is a policy commonly adopted by different countries around the world (Liu, 2003). Liu also pressed SARFT to establish comprehensive rules to regulate OTvC broadcasters and media flows, which should include at the least:

184 *Guangdong: the role of local*

1 transparent and justified market entry and assessment standards adhering to international practices;
2 content regulation; and
3 restrictions over the proportion of foreign and personal investment and ownership (Liu, 2003).

Wand and Liu criticized SARFT's current regulation for undermining provincial broadcasters and forcing them to compete unfairly with OTvCs (Liu, 2003; Wang K, 2003). The SARFT, for the convenience of the Party-State's administrative interface, often uses normative documents to govern domestic broadcasters. OTvC companies do not have any obligation to comply with those normative documents. They are only used by SARFT to govern broadcasters within its departmental jurisdiction. This difference gives OTvCs more autonomy in discussing sensitive topics, such as sex. The Vice President of a provincial broadcaster complained "we should regulate those foreign signals according to China's laws. But there is no proper law available."[13]

The SARFT's department rule Decree No. 27 *Measures for the Administration of the Landing of Foreign Satellite Television Channels*, promulgated in 2004, partially responded to their requests. First, it clarifies the regulated body by explicitly defining that terrestrial OTvCs from Hong Kong and Macau also fall into the regulatory scope of new rule. Second, it removes the requirement of ranking amongst the top three national channels as the condition for granting the entry license while adding two more reasonable new conditions concerning (1) home nation legal entity status and (2) entrusting the designated Chinese institution to act as its agent in China. Meanwhile, the new rule imposes seven comprehensive prohibitions on the content of OTvCs, and increases the level of penalty by removing the condition of two prior violations before SARFT can revoke a channel's entry right.

The research and development (R&D) department of STS also conducted its own research on the impact of OTvC upon the ecology of Guangdong television broadcasters. The research, according to the authors, "[...] possesses important reference value for the national and provincial broadcasting regulators' policy decision-making" (Ou *et al.*, 2006: 4). The research provides comprehensive policy recommendations on regulating OTvCs in the five broad areas: (1) regulatory style; (2) content regulation; (3) enforcement; (4) strengthening domestic media's competitiveness, and (5) specific regulations for Hong Kong and Macau's channels because of the differences in political, legal and media systems under the "one country and two systems" structure (Ou *et al.*, 2006).

The Southern Television Station presented these policy recommendations at the National Forum of Presidents of Television Stations organized by SARFT in 2007 (STS, 2007). This important forum, like others organized by provincial Guangdong broadcasters, e.g., the Chinese Television South Forum and the Chinese Television Theoretical Forum, attracts hundreds of delegates. The forums are important public platforms for media professionals, academics, and, increasingly, policy-makers, to discuss, debate and express their concerns on topical issues with the intent of impacting on national policy.

Provincial broadcasters also mobilized media and academic support to promote their policy achievements in order to create a favorable ideology for them to bargain with national government for policy rewards. "Politics is a battle for minds [...]. Hence policies have not only to work, but also to be seen to work" (Walker and Duncan, 2007: 169). The notion of policy success, or failure, is however more complex than anything achievable in objective terms, being subject to wider influences such as media reaction and public opinions (Walker and Duncan, 2007). Since 2005, the Southern Media Group has started to conceptualize a Southern Model drawing on its experiences of reform and foreign competition. The R&D departments at both the Group and STS have organized the publications of more than ten books to introduce their concept of institutional reform and accomplishment in overtaking the OTvCs' dominance in the Guangdong audience market. Wang Keman, the President of the Southern Media Group, and Ninyi Feng, the Deputy Director of the R&D department explain their accomplishment in their book:

> after five years' dancing with the wolves [OTvCs], through arduous exploration, Guangdong broadcasters made great efforts to strengthen themselves. It finally shattered the more than 20 years' market monopoly of overseas television in Guangzhou, ended their domination in the Guangdong audience market, and changed the competition structure.
>
> (Wang and Feng, 2008: 464)

The Southern Media Group's R&D department also organized two symposiums – "Guangdong broadcasting reform and the Southern Model" (2005), and "the Southern Model of China broadcasting reform" (2006). Academics from leading Chinese universities were invited to participate. The symposiums are said to have significantly accelerated the theorization of the Southern Model. The Group also signed 16 academics and experts as contracted research fellows. China's most influential television channel, CCTV-1, reported on 7 January 2007 on Guangdong and Southern Media Group's triumph in the competition with OTvCs and the Southern Model in its Seven O'Clock National Newscast. China's national news agency, Xinhua News, carried a similar report (Wang and Feng, 2008).

One of the effects of this mobilization effort was gaining the open support from the senior CCP member, Li Changchun (李长春), who was Guangdong's Party Secretary before his promotion to national level. During Li's visit to the China Radio, Film and Television International Exposition in August 2006, he openly endorsed Guangdong's accomplishment in competing with OTvCs in front of the leaders of the Ministry of Central Propaganda and SARFT. Li also said "they [the Southern Media Group] have made the biggest step in institutional reform in the broadcasting system, [therefore we need] to study its effects. The direction of [the reform] was decided by me when I was in Guangdong" (Newscast of GDTV, 24 August 2006). Two months later instructions from a senior party member sent a national research team, led by Yuan Tongnan, the Deputy Director of SARFT's General Office, to Guangdong (SARFT, 2007).

186 *Guangdong: the role of local*

The national research tours are usually organized by either the Party or SARFT to allow officials at national level to visit localities for either research or inspection. The provincial organizations use the national policy learning research as part of the political process aiding them to advocate issues and persuade national policy makers to act in their interest through influencing the research process. For example, in July 2005, a team of seven Party cadres visited the Guangdong and Zhejiang provinces to research provincial media. Its members include the Director of SARFT's Law and Regulation Bureau, and the leader of the Policy and Regulation Bureau at the Ministry of Culture. Prior to their visit, the team communicated with provincial broadcasting bureaus, asking them to prepare materials and assist the research. Over a two-week period, the team participated in 14 discussion forums with provincial media, and visited 40 media projects in the two provinces (CPS, 2005). When Yuan Tongnan's research team visited Guangdong a year later, the team heard reports from the GBB and the Southern Media Group, and met leaders of broadcasting bureaus and broadcasters from Guangdong's 14 other cities. The activities of both research tours demonstrated that their research processes are neither independent, nor systematic and inclusive. They depended on the support, data and information provided by the broadcasting bureau and media in the provinces, and the consultation processes were also confined to the opinions of senior personnel at those organizations (SARFT, 2007d).

Both research teams published their reports in the journal *Guidebook of Decision*, one of three journals published by SARFT for information exchanges between broadcasters, SARFT, the State Council and the Ministry of Central Propaganda. Unsurprisingly the policy recommendations offered in those two reports reflect the policy demands of Guangdong. The 2005 team's report contains three articles. The first suggests Guangdong, given its geographic, linguistic and cultural proximity to Hong Kong, Macau and South Eastern Asia, should "enlarge its development space" and become active in overseas markets with broadcasting services and programs (CPS, 2005). The second, by Gao Shuxun, a senior cultural policy-maker in the State Council, suggests the competition between Guangdong and overseas media is unfair because the former is subject to tighter regulations, which undermine Guangdong's competitiveness. Gao recommends that the national government adjust its digital television market access, financing, and tax policies to support provincial broadcasters (Gao, 2005). In the third article, another CCP official explained how the Guangdong media managed to compete with the overseas media, and concluded that the government should offer Guangdong policy support in four areas: "(1) perfecting regulation of overseas media in China; (2) enhancing overseas media's supervision and sanction; (3) creating a fair playing field; (4) providing policy incentives to strength Guangdong's media" (Liu, 2005). The General Office's report says that Guangdong's reform has enhanced its publicity function because "the provincial media by large possesses the dominant influence over the public opinion with the increase of its radio and television's ratings." It suggests that the national government "practically strengthen the administration of overseas media in Guangdong," and warns "the lack of suitable regulations and administrative measures in this area not only can easily cause problems, but also can affect the development of domestic broadcasters. [...] Therefore, to issue relevant regulations and measures is in urgent need" (SARFT, 2007d: 34–38).

The extent to which these multifaceted efforts have positively affected the reform of OTvC policy is debatable and requires more research on the subtle interactions between the provincial Guangdong policy-makers and individual policy-makers at the national level. Since 2005, no particular policy changes have been announced to directly address the concerns of Guangdong. The government and Ministry of Central Propaganda did, however, announce that in principle they would no longer permit the entry of OTvCs into Mainland China. Furthermore, the supervision over existing OTvCs would be tightened, and the necessary monitoring techniques would be adopted to prevent the invasion of harmful programs (MCP [2005] No. 15). The reason for these drastic changes in the OTvCs policy is complicated. The shift of the emphasis of China's cultural policy from friendly exchange to "improving the governance of cultural import, protecting intellectual property rights, and protecting national cultural security" is one reason (MCP [2005] No. 15). The Chinese government also adjusted the priority of its "reaching out" project from market exchange to the creation of its own Great Wall Television Platform in North and Latin America, Asia and Australia via satellite, Internet Protocol (IP) TV and cable networks (CICC, 2008).

Nevertheless, the protracted efforts of Guangdong do provide a salutary indication that there is a certain incentive for the provincial media to approach and persuade national policy-makers. Speaking during his tour of Guangdong in 2006, the Vice Director of SARFT said that the national government regarded Guangdong's institutional reform as highly important, and has therefore created a favorable environment and given support (Wang and Feng, 2008). Since 2004, only a Macau based cross-border satellite channel, the Macau Asia Satellite Television (MASTV), has gained the necessary license to enter Guangdong's cable television networks. In contrast to the CETV and Starry Sky's strategy in relying on power from the top, MASTV consulted the GBB, the Guangdong Cable Network Ltd, and the Southern Media Group, and had their support before submitting its license application. Its Vice President asserted "it is essential to communicate with all interest parties in China. Foreign television operators do not know the Chinese culture and ways of doing business, therefore it is very difficult [for them]."[14] A policy advisor at the Southern Media Group also revealed "without our agreement, SARFT will not approve its [MASTV's] entry."[15] He said "we are policy implementer, and they [SARFT] need our support." This change indicates that both the national government and the OTvC have recognized the importance of the provincial media's support and have consulted and respected their voices. Accordingly, provincial media interest could increasingly circumscribe the policy framework on the entry of OTvCs.

In terms of the national government's policy rewards, two of Guangdong's television channels are categorized as "external publicity" channels, and have been included in the "reaching out" project to expand both inside and outside

188 *Guangdong: the role of local*

China. In 2004, these two channels entered the Hong Kong and Macau cable television networks, and also the Great Wall platforms. Overseas joint-venture media outlets of Guangdong broadcasters were also established. In 2005, the Guangdong Television Station set up a joint-venture television channel in Kuala Lumpur with a Malaysian production company. In 2007, the Southern International Media Corporation, which is controlled by the Southern Media Group, joined with Hong Kong capital, setting up a Cantonese satellite television station – Dim Sum Satellite – broadcast in Hong Kong (Wang and Feng, 2008).

Summary

By incorporating the concept of PL this chapter has extended the scope of previous studies to include the policy learning process in the analysis of China's digital television policy (DTvP) process. This chapter has analyzed the roles of Guangdong province's television broadcasters and officials in applying the national government policy of the entry of overseas television channels (OTvCs) into the cable television networks in the Pearl River Delta Region of Guangdong Province. The chapter has also analyzed the mechanism whereby the television broadcasters and officials can acquire leverage to influence national policy. This analysis, through emphasizing the policy implementation and learning stages, has considerably broadened our understanding of the characteristics of China's DTvP process and also shed light on the function of the PL process.

The analysis has found that despite the small space for the provincial media to participate in national policy formulation, they have practiced great discretion in policy implementation, and policy input is primarily through the PL process. The policy decision to open the Pearl River Delta to OTvCs was taken by the CCP at the highest levels as an outcome of the convergent interests of the CCP and foreign television companies. The media representatives in provincial Guangdong were largely excluded from the policy formulation and negotiations. However, due to the three key processes: (1) decentralization of the regulatory structure; (2) the national regulator's ineffectual enforcement measures; and (3) the commercialization of the media market, provincial television stations and cable operators were able to arbitrarily implement an incentive policy on advertising insertion. Concomitant with China's national administrative reform in streamlining governance and delegating power to the provinces, Guangdong's provincial broadcasting authority was also given great discretionary powers in supervising the daily broadcast of OTvCs. The provincial broadcasting authority can decide whether OTvCs have violated any of the entry rules and, if they have, can block their signals. Despite the nationwide impact of a law-based administrative reform, the lack of effective checks on the provincial authority's power, and the contradiction between the decentralization of power and the function of an authoritarian national government raise the issue of whether there is any justification for this supervision.

Arbitrary advertising insertion by the provincial authorities has produced some important PL effects. There were a large number of public grievances, which were brought to the attention of CCP leaders and placed on their policy agenda. The grievances became an issue that needed to be addressed to preserve social harmony. As a result of these developments, the locus of authority over the advertising issue began to shift from the department tasked within SARFT, to the CCP's Ministry of Central Propaganda and the Commission for Inspecting Discipline. Stiffer and more proactive enforcement was adopted, and societal participations in advertising regulation were proposed. The role of the Party remains vital in driving this policy learning and regulatory change due to the fragmentation of authority and the departmental protection inherent in the state bureaucracy. In comparison to Hall's observation of the instrumental feature of the first and second level learning in Britain's macroeconomic policy-making, the CCP and SARFT's learning process is less instrumental, but more contingent to public discontent. This feature more or less manifests the general concern amongst academics about the function of state authority in China (Wang S, 2003).

Provincial broadcasters and officials in Guangdong have also played an active role in the PL process. The provincial media has persistently complained about the inadequacy of the OTvCs regulations and pressed for policy changes. They have used multifaceted methods to place pressure upon the national policy makers. Their ability to mobilize media coverage and academic support and competence to formulate an overarching set of ideas on OTvCs policy through self-conducted research play an important role in lending legitimacy to their policy demands. They also used national policy research tours for their political self-interest through influencing the research process. The provincial media has successfully initiated policy changes at technical levels, obtained policy incentives in overseas expansion and had their interest acknowledged by both China's national regulator and the OTvCs. The PL process in this case, therefore, not only functioned as a response mechanism to the legacies of previous policies, but also provided a legitimate platform for the provincial media to negotiate with Central Government concerning policy change and policy incentives.

However, will the intent of provincial broadcasters and officials to promote "self-interest" discredit the process of policy change as policy learning? I do not think so. To borrow Hall's words "actors in this process inside both the state and society were not simply seeking to advance their own interest. They were also seeking solution [...]" (1993: 289). Like 1970s Britain where society was dominated by the collective puzzlement and uncertainty about the economy, the contemporary Chinese society and government have also experienced similar uncertainty and puzzlement not only about the country's economy, but also about how society will be governed and how the country will relate itself to the outside world. As part of such collective uncertainty, the provincial media and GBB not only acquired power to influence the OTvCs policy but also to puzzle about the policy. This perplexity became apparent when one policy adviser at the STS sought my advice on the European experiences on OTvCs' regulation. The policy process regarding overseas television channels is a micro-example of the socio-political challenges facing China, and further research alone will clarify the success or failure of the policy learning.

190 *Guangdong: the role of local*

Notes

1 In 1983, the Central Committee of the CCP divided the country's TV network into four tiers: national, provincial or municipal or autonomous region, city and county. Each has its own TV station to serve audiences within its administrative boundary. At the center is the national broadcaster, the China Central Television (CCTV) of the Central Government. From 1996 to 1999, the central broadcasting authority ordered the recentralization of China's TV network from four tiers to two tiers.
2 Interviews with Huang Yong, the Director of the Research and Development Centre at the SARFT and Zhang Zhi, in Beijing, June 2008.
3 Fang Kan was the then Deputy Chief of Film, Radio and TV Bureau of Guangdong, Que Zhimin is the Director of the Bureau's Chief Editorial Office, Tan Feibo is Deputy Director of the office.
4 According to a report delivered by Liang Lingguang who was Governor of Guangdong Province 1983–1985 (Liang, 2002).
5 Including the cities of Guangzhou, Shenzhen, Zhuhai, Foshan, Dongguan, Zhongshan, Huizhou, Jiangmen, Zhaoqing.
6 Personal interview with a senior official at the editorial and development research offices at Guangdong TV station, 19 November 2003, Guangzhou, China.
7 Personal interview with a senior official at editor-in-chief office at GBB, 9 December 2003, Guangzhou, China.
8 Personal interview with a senior manager at Guangdong Cable TV Network, 24 November 2003, Guangzhou, China.
9 Personal interview with a senior official at editor-in-chief office at GBB, 9 December 2003, Guangzhou, China.
10 Telephone interview with a senior manager at CITVC's overseas satellite program department, 23 November 2008, Beijing, China.
11 Personal interview with a senior official at editor-in-chief office at GBB, 9 December 2003, Guangzhou, China.
12 Email interview on 28 October 2008.
13 Personal interview, 19 November 2003, Guangzhou, China.
14 Email interview on 28 October 2008.
15 Person interview, 21 July 2008, Guangzhou.

11 A reconsideration of national, local and global relationships

Nature of transformation

Until 1997, the political interests of the CCP and government still largely dominated China's television policy. Although television policy changed between 1998 and 2015, the political goal did not change. The Party's prerequisite for any policy change is the maintenance of television's mouthpiece and propaganda apparatus function so that it can protect the political interests of the Party and government (see Chapters 6 and 7).

However, with China's political and economic integration and interdependence with the world, it is increasingly difficult for the government to suppress societal unrest. For domestic political elites, all the resources and privileges they enjoy are subjected to a monopoly in political power. The Party considers "national stability," "being sustained and supported by the public" and "being trusted by the public" as three elements crucial to maintaining their political status. The public's trust and support become especially important in a situation where social stability is under threat or some unstable elements are emerging (Xian, 2002: 199). In order to maintain political stability, the government needs to respond to social demands to a certain extent, reinventing itself and reforming the existing system, with a scope and at a pace that it can control, while also trying to divert public focus to less politically sensitive areas.

Reflected in the national television policy between 1998 and 2015, the best way to achieve both goals – responding and diverting – is to deregulate apolitical content while keeping tight control over politically sensitive news and current affairs materials. This is one of the crucial reasons behind the Party's decision to separate the economic and political functions of broadcasters and separate program production and broadcasting. This has led to the division of the broadcasting system into a dual model – the co-existence of state owned media institutions, i.e., broadcast stations, controlled by the Party's Propaganda Department and state owned media enterprises, i.e., commercial content production companies, supervised by the State-owned Assets Supervision and Administration Commission (see Chapter 9).

This strategy is the continuation of the mid-1990s policy, i.e., to allow a limited consumerist democracy to satisfy social desire but retain complete

192 *A reconsideration of relationships*

political control (see Chapters 5, 6 and 8). However, the differences between the mid-1990s and 2000s are in the scope and means of political control.

From the mid-1990s to 2015 the scope of control was narrowed from wide ranging content down to the core of media content – the news and current affairs. The leading principle of restructuring was to transform the sector from a state owned model to a quasi-market economic model, featuring mixed-ownership and the co-existence of the state and commercial sectors. The focuses of the reform were about "three-separation" and "three-transformation" based on the division of the governmental and commercial attributes of the media. First, this meant the separation of governmental institution and enterprise, the separation of ownership and operational autonomy, and the separation of production and broadcasting (see Chapter 9). Second, it meant the transformation from state-owned institutions to state-owned enterprises; transformation from state-owned enterprises to corporate enterprises, and transformation from corporate enterprises to listed companies. In other words, the broadcast station was responsible for the broadcasting of all programs, program planning, evaluations, examinations and acquisitions, as well as the production of news programs. The state-owned media enterprise was responsible for the content production, new media and media-related business operation services.

By keeping the existing governmental institutional status of news and current affairs channels and maintaining the state's monopoly of ownership, operation and production, the Party aimed to maintain its control of mainstream public opinion. These news and current affairs TV channels were categorized as Chinese versions of non-profit public service programs – a term borrowed from Western Europe that has become popular in China's policy circles. The favoring of one or other of the versions of the idea of public service broadcasting was also observed in many former Eastern European countries (Sparks, 1998). In China's context the adoption of the public service policy was motivated by the pragmatic end of securing social stability and cohesion, rather than by moral or humane concerns for the development of citizens. The public service broadcasting policy still focuses predominantly on social equalization between urban and rural and universal coverage of broadcast networks. The political independence, at least in theory, of the public service media, is not a feature being considered.

In the commercial sector, the objectives of non-news and current affairs channels are to pursue economic profit and achieve the reconciliation of social and economic benefits. In other words, the policy required those commercial television channels to satisfy consumers' needs and make profits, while at the same time providing an advanced and healthy culture. The definitions of "advanced and healthy culture" are not the focus of discussion in this book, the interesting point is the mechanism employed to secure reconciliation.

First, the production units of TV channels were allowed to convert from state-owned institutions to companies, such as the case of Channel Young Media Co., Ltd, and the conversion of the government institution, Shanghai Media & Entertainment Group (SMEG), to a solely state-owned enterprise – Shanghai Media & Entertainment Group Inc. This transformation from institution to commercial enterprise could spur the production and managerial autonomy of the media. Instead of relying heavily on advertising revenue, listing on the stock market could strengthen their financial power and improve the diversity of their business models. Like most state-owned enterprise in China, the biggest boss, i.e., the Party-State, still sets the rules through employment of key personnel and the ownership pattern.

More importantly, the Shanghai case in Chapter 9 showed that with the split between government broadcasting bureaus and broadcasters, and the separation of broadcasting and production, the role of the Propaganda Department of the CCP's Shanghai Committee moved from the background to the foreground. It not only controls the ideological work, as it did before, but also directly manages Radio and Television Shanghai (RTS, 上海广播电视台). In other words, before transition, it was the government's broadcasting department functioning as an agent representing the Chinese state and Chinese people to manage the broadcaster. After transformation, the Party replaced this role, becoming the virtual agent. If Shanghai's case is propagated to other regions,[1] the long-term impact upon Chinese broadcast stations needs to be closely monitored.

In addition, the cases of Channel Young and China Media Capital (CMC) in Chapter 9 demonstrated that entrance to the commercial sector is not equally open to every player in the media field. Only certain personnel with the political approval of the ruling group are allowed to join the sector and share the interest. These personnel may either be someone who has been in the ruling elite group, and thus, the movement is about the redistribution of interest and power among elites themselves; or it could be someone who was out of the ruling group, but whom the dominant ruling elites aim to absorb into the existing structure. This is more about the expansion of the ruling base through integration, and it is a very important means through which the ruling group maintains the political stability of their power. In either case, the self-interest of these personnel is subjected to their political compliance to the dominant structure.

The change from institution to enterprise and from state-owned to mixed-ownership is partly about the autonomy of the broadcasting media and partly about capitalization of political power to personal welfare. The appearance of mixed-owned and state-owned commercial media enterprises do not guarantee plurality of voices, given the control of broadcasting channels by the Party and self-interest-oriented media. This has supported the observations of Colin Sparks (1998 and 2008) that the transformation in China is not a social revolution but is a political process: it is the transformation of the way in which the country and the media is governed, but not a fundamental change of social order and elite composition in media or the state machine. There was continuity amongst the elite personnel in the media sector and throughout the society, which demonstrates a shift from political to economic power.

The development of China's broadcasting policy and structure since the late 1990s was largely influenced and constrained by the country's economic transformation and the political adjustment of the CCP (see Table 11.1). The nature of the broadcasting sector's transformation has reflected the logic of the

Table 11.1 China's political economy and television policy from the late 1990s

Time	Political and economic change	Television policy	Industrial change
1992	The Fourteenth CCP National Congress: accepted market mechanisms as the most important force in resource allocation and defined the "socialist market economy" system.		
1993	Passed the Company Law: to cater for the reform of the SOEs to a modern enterprise system.		
1995	CCP anticipated social tension would increase as China moved into a market economy system.	Maintaining correct public opinion guidance; modernizing broadcasters via technological advancement.	
1996	Launch of the *Ninth Five-year Plan*: started to build up a market economy system.	Against: economic driven media; non-state ownership; market competition. Support: state subsidy; party and government control; state's ownership monopoly; political publicity function; serving public interests; improve program quality.	CCP [1996] no. 37 eliminated unapproved TV outlets and streamlining of TV structure: four tiers to two tiers; appealed for the marketization of the TV sector by media elites and intellectuals; first newspaper conglomerate appeared.
1997	Fifteenth CCP National Congress: committed to the dominance of the non-state-owned sector.	Uphold 1996's position.	

1998	Government's institutional reform: streamlining; efficiency; separation of government from enterprise; rule by law. Economic development was moving towards consolidation, convergence, concentration and improvement of the quality but no longer quantity.	The party instructed to "push forwards radio and television reform step by step" and announced "four no changes" and "all others can be changed" reform principles.	MRFT downgraded to SARFT. Drafting of CCP No. 17 document began, its main themes: marketization; concentration and conglomeration. SARFT started the plan to conglomerate media. First broadcasting conglomerate established.
1999	CCP's *Decision of Important Issues of the Reform and Development of SOE*: encouraged the transformation of small SOEs' into non-state owned; corporationalization of medium and large SOEs.	TV reform: to establish a socialist market economic broadcasting system; to follow development logics; business model and technology reform put before propaganda function reform, entertainment, art and culture reform put before news; local reform prior to central institution.	Merge of cable and terrestrial TV stations in city and provincial Level; establishment of broadcasting conglomerate; ban on listing on stock market of TV and cable company.
2000	The end of the *Ninth Five-Year Plan*; Falun Gong Movement; Taiwan, USA, Russia's presidential election; Jiang Zemin announced the "three represents."	Strengthen ideological control and program censorship; become stronger and bigger; improve law and regulation; advance broadcasting technology; perform institutional reform.	SARFT announces guiding principle on conglomeration.
2001	China's WTO accession. Launch of the Tenth Five-Year Plan. Jiang Zemin upheld the "three represents" and urged "let[ting]' China's voice to broadcast to the world."	WTO agreement does not commit to liberalizing domestic broadcasting sector. Five major reform areas: macro-management, micro-operation, regulatory system, market structure and liberalization pattern. Launch the "reaching out" project.	Cross-region and cross-media ownership of media conglomerates; redefining the concept of "commercialization"; landing of foreign satellite TV.

continued

Table 11.1 Continued

Time	Political and economic change	Television policy	Industrial change
2002	Sixteenth CCP National Congress: leadership transfer from Jiang Zemin to Hu Jintao; ideological and ethical correctness is the prerequisite of the cultural industry's development; deepened institutional reform; economic structure adjustment; strengthen rule of law; more interdependent with the global economy.	Officially accepted "cultural industry" nature of broadcasting; approved institutional reform; committed to opening up the service sector to the world step by step.	Upholding ban of private and foreign investment.
2003		Emphasizes profit-making, instead of non-profit characteristic of TV media; emphasizes the market mechanism; promotes the consumer-orientation of broadcasters.	Divided the state-owned TV system to dual ownership systems; opened program production sector to private and foreign capital.
2004	Equality and social harmony are the themes of Hu-Wen administration. Issued the *Provisional Regulation on the Party and Government Resignation*, which provided a legal base for the accountability system.	2004 was set to be "the year of digital and industrial development of radio, film and television" by SARFT, and pay TV was promoted on the basis of digitalization. Decree No. 27 gave the provincial authority discretionary powers in deciding which content of the satellite channels broadcast violated the existing rules, and to cease transmissions.	Promote "three separations": separation of the institution and enterprise, separation of ownership and managerial authority, and separation of production and broadcasting. Allow qualified program production enterprises to seek financing by listing on the stock market.

Year			
2005	Adopted more egalitarian and populist policies in economy. Reversed some of Deng Xiaoping's reforms by halting privatization and privileging state sectors. Launched the campaign called "maintain the advanced nature of the Party." Proposed the concept of "Harmonious Society" and "Scientific Development."	CCP's recommendation document in 2005 first proposed "cultural public service." Both cultural public service (CPS) and public service broadcasting (PSB) are part of the nation's goal to establish a harmonious society. Basic cultural rights are defined as the rights of access to TV, radio, books and newspapers.	Despite the new public cultural service (PCS) rhetoric, the government's primary expectation is that the media will continue to support ideological "services." Domestic and foreign capital could invest in music, technology, sports and entertainment program production, providing the company had state ownership of at least 51 percent.
2006	Administration reforms including the merge of ministries and commissions, and the final establishment of an accountability system. The Sixth Plenum of the Sixteenth Central Committee formally adopted "Harmonious Society" as the supreme goal of Party governance.	The State Council officially adopted the "cultural public service" proposal in *Outline of Cultural Development during the Eleventh Five-Year Plan*. The Connected Village Project and the Tibet-Xinjiang Project were re-launched in order to achieve universal coverage and equal access to the PSB.	Infrastructure and coverage expansion in the countryside gradually shifted from the discourse of Spiritual Civilization to "public service", emphasizing urban–rural equalization and the protection of "basic" rights. Preferable conditions should be created in order to transform the business-oriented institutions to enterprises.
2007	The Seventeenth CCP National Congress confirmed the Three Rural Issues, equal access to basic public services, narrow the gap in development among regions are top priorities of the Party. "Scientific Development" concept was incorporated into the Party constitution's preamble.	CCP's Ministry of Central Propaganda coordinated a joint action by 12 Ministries to eliminate illegal sexual medical advertising from all types of media platforms.	The dilemma between the decentralization of power and the enhancement of the function of national government exacerbated.

continued

Table 11.1 Continued

Time	Political and economic change	Television policy	Industrial change
2008	2008 Olympic Games was held in Beijing; China becoming more integrated with and interdependent on the global community; tighten political control; further economic and social reforms and the reform of the CCP leadership.	SARFT created a new national radio and television monitoring system to record advertisements broadcast on 1,372 television programs.	The separation of broadcasting and production of TV stations to be actively promoted.
2009	The first private equity fund in China's cultural industry, China Media Capital (CMC) with a fund of 5 billion yuan, was launched after gaining the approval of the National Development and Reform Commission.	The State Council held a standing committee meeting to accelerate the "three network convergence." SARFT approved the "separation of broadcasting and production" reform scheme of the Shanghai Media Group (SMG), the first complete separation of the TV station from the production organization.	SARFT issued series of documents to encourage broadcasters to "actively cultivate new market players, and promote the transformation of broadcasters' program production units and departments to enterprises."
2010	CMC launched its first investment since establishment – the acquisition and control of Star China.	The State Council committee meeting approved the *Overall Plan for Promoting Three Network Convergence*. Pilot convergence programs on two-way access of telecommunication and broadcasting networks were to be carried out.	CMC plays an essential role in pushing forward SMG's internationalization and access to capital markets.

2011	The government brought in a legal requirement for users to provide real names and identification information when registering a micro-blog account, ostensibly to curb the dissemination of rumors and false information.	Forty-one more cities joined the second phase of the pilot study of the "three network convergence."	SARFT's 2011 *Opinions on strengthening management of satellite channels' programs* restricts the volume of entertainment programs relayed on satellite channels.
		The Party further emphasized that strengthening the public cultural service is the major approach to realizing people's basic cultural rights.	
2012	Xi Jinping took office as the General Secretary of CCP.	State Council issued the first national plan for public service.	The establishment of the China Broadcasting Network Ltd, a two-way access of telecommunication and broadcasting networks was approved.
	Xi Jinping proposed the concept of the "Chinese Dream."	The plan sets the goal of cultural reform and development to establish a public cultural service system that covers the whole society and provide urban and rural residents with a relatively convenient public cultural service by 2015.	
	The rule of law became one of the core concerns of the Party.		New Sino-foreign joint venture Oriental DreamWorks was founded.
2013	The Third Plenum of the eighteenth CCP National Congress reconstructed the role of the government and the market: market forces should play a "decisive" role in resource allocation, and government should transfer from resource allocation to macroeconomic regulation, market supervision, public service provision, social management and environmental protection.	State Council announced the reform plan for its departmental structure and functions in order to "simplify administration and devolve power," "increase administrative efficiency" and "enhance the market economy."	The new SAPPRFT (State Administration of Press, Publication, Radio, Film and Television) was established in 2013, merging the former GAPP (General Administration of Press and Publication) and SARFT (State Administration of Radio, Film and Television).
		State Council issued a normative notice to formally announce the functions and organizational structure of the newly formed SAPPRFT.	

continued

Table 11.1 Continued

Time	Political and economic change	Television policy	Industrial change
2014	Premier Li Keqiang delivered his first Government Work Report at the Second Session of the Twelfth NPC, set reform as the top priority for the government by reducing bureaucratic red tape and shifting from a planned economy to a one based on market forces. The Fourth Plenum of the Eighteenth Central Committee addressed rule of law for the first time.	The merge of BesTV New Media and Shanghai Oriental Pearl Group into the largest Chinese online media conglomerate chimed with President Xi Jinping's plans to rationalize the state-owned media sector into a few large, powerful conglomerates.	Shanghai Media & Entertainment Group (SMEG) officially transformed itself from a state institution to a corporation, and become a new media and entertainment conglomerate. "CMC Creative Fund" was created to invest in Chinese and international entertainment content opportunities covering film, TV and live entertainment.
2015	The publication of the *Thirteenth Five-year Plan of China* set 2020 as the deadline for achieving "decisive results." Review of 2013–2015 shows the reform was economically motivated rather than politically motivated, the power of the central government was strengthened, and media regulation was increased. 22 central leading small groups have been established by 2015.	State Council issued the *Three Network Convergence Promotion Plan*, to comprehensively push forwards the "three network" convergence nationwide. Shanghai employs foreign collaboration as its strategy to expand domestically and internationally.	Some domestic media organizations strive for marketization and internationalization in order to become media conglomerate with global influence.

economic and political changes of the country. From this point of view, it is not surprising to see that the most significant changes have happened in the economic domain.

The central-local relationship

As with the phenomena of decentralization and localism observed in China's economy (see Chapter 2), a similar tendency was also found in China's television sector. Zheng Yongnian's (2006) observation of a de facto federal central-local relationship (see Chapter 1) is supported by evidence drawn from Chapters 7, 9 and 10. All three chapters convincingly show that since the late 1990s, the intensification of central-local struggles and inter-governmental competitions have significantly driven the major national broadcasting policy-making and broadcasting market restructuring in China.

The department interests of the MIIT and SAPPRFT have spurred the inter-governmental conflicts and policy gridlock that greatly obscured the progress of broadcasting-telecommunication-computing network convergence in China (see Chapter 7). The State Council's general office and the Communist Party had to act as mediators to organize, mobilize and coordinate the policy implementation and resolve departmental disputes. Contrary to having a single and coherent regulator for the converging industries, which was also the State Council's initial intention, the Chinese "three networks" convergence project finally divided the regulatory responsibilities between the SAPPRFT and MIIT, which will supervise online content/technical standards and telecommunication network/hardware respectively (see Figures 7.1 and 7.2). An Internet audio-video program service provider has to obtain several licenses from both the MIIT and SAPPRFT in order to operate in China. This sector based regulatory principle stems from the department protection of self-interest by the SAPPRFT and MIIT.

Chapter 9, the Shanghai case study, has also shown that the one of the most important factors triggering the restructuring of Shanghai's television since the late 1990s was the expansion of the audience market, which is no longer confined to the local population. Before 1997, the most distinctive feature of Shanghai's broadcasting system was developed through controlled competition in the local market, partly because the audience market of local broadcasters was restricted by the administrative boundary. From 1997 to 2003, along with the government's abolition of geographic restrictions and permission for cross-regional operation and ownership, the decentralization of resources and internal competition were no longer the guiding principle in Shanghai's television development. The establishment of a cross-region and cross-sector business structure through resource consolidation and unity became the main theme for Shanghai's TV restructuring. First, in order to strengthen its competitive power, the cross-media conglomerate, i.e., the Shanghai Media & Entertainment Group Inc. (SMEG), was funded through a concentration of Shanghai's electronic media and cultural resources, to increase the economies of scale and eliminate competition in the advertising and program markets. Second, nationally targeted

202 *A reconsideration of relationships*

television channels were launched. Third, alliances were formed between the Shanghai Media Group and foreign media so that the latter could help the Shanghai TV Media Group to explore national and global markets.

In Chapter 10 in Guangdong, from 2001 to 2003, four foreign satellite television channels were permitted to enter the Pearl River Delta Region's cable TV network by the Party and SARFT. In return, the national broadcaster, China Central Television Station (CCTV) could access overseas markets. However, the local Guangdong Broadcasting Bureau and its broadcasting media were largely excluded from the negotiation process of the carriage agreement, mainly functioning as the executor of the centrally made decisions. Local officials and media elites were frustrated about the decision. Nevertheless, despite the small space for the provincial media and broadcasting authority to participate in national policy formulation, they practiced great discretion in policy implementation. This great discretion was due to three key processes: (1) decentralization of the regulatory structure and China's national administrative reform in streamlining governance and delegating power to the provinces; (2) the national regulator's ineffectual enforcement measures as the costs and technical difficulties for the national authority to monitor the provincial's daily administration were high; and (3) the commercialization of the media market promotes the self-interested media. The lack of effective checks and transparency on the provincial broadcasting authority's power, and the contradiction between the decentralization of power and the function of an authoritarian government also exacerbated the situation. In other words, the national regulator, SAPPRFT, faced a dilemma finding a balance between maintaining an authoritarian but effective governance, and inviting societal forces to participate in that governance, which could lead to the reduction of its power. Therefore, the core issues facing the Party and national regulator are two folds: (1) how to provide provincial authorities with sufficient flexibility to administer media in their jurisdictions and to respond to provincial circumstances, while preventing abuse of discretion; (2) the dilemma between the decentralization of power and the enhancement of the function of national government in a vast and segmented country. To build up a functional media regulatory system whose power is institutionalized and constrained and abides by the law is one way to constrain the abuse of discretion and power. However, this alone is not sufficient to solve a deep-rooted accountability problem if the supervisory role of social organizations and the public is not empowered. Nevertheless, to suggest that central-local tension in the media sector will lead to a crisis in the SAPPRFT's authority is premature. Despite the existing conflict between the local Guangdong authorities and central authorities, and despite Guangdong's long tradition of bargaining with the center, the center still has decisive power over the local. This is because the nature of conflict resolution in China is not unconditional and based on a set of constitutional procedures, but rather, is through varied negotiations within the ruling bureaucracy itself, which constrains the effects and possibilities of localism to challenge the existing political order.

The modernization of the media: global capitalism and neo-conservatism in the Chinese context

Looking at China's television sector from 1996 to 2015, it may seem that neo-liberalism has triumphed: the eager acceptance of market forces, the WTO and globalization, the rule of law, transparency of governance, media autonomy and economic prosperity. However, real change in the sector is a more complex process as it involves a combination of strategies of liberalization of the production and financing of broadcasters, maintaining control over the broadcasting network and political content, selectively adopting successful international models and rules of law, and rejecting liberal values such as the primacy of individual liberty.

In terms of national television policy-making, it is an ideological departure, from the core concern of how to resist the foreign threat, to the question of how to maintain openness as well as sustaining effective resistance. The policy strategy has also shifted from the protectionism of the early 1990s to a pattern combining resistance with liberalization. This is to facilitate the mutually beneficial principle of combining defense with a more offensive and expansive internationalization approach in order to increase the country's international political influences. This ideological shift is best illustrated by the change in the core values of the officially promoted national culture from patriotism, socialism and collectivism to values like "modern," "globalism," "scientific" and "popular". This is a significant rebranding of Chinese society, from a socialist and national-centered cultural tradition to a contemporary, outward-looking and consumerist cultural model, which is found not only in most developed Western societies but also in its rich neighbors in Asia, e.g., Hong Kong.

Limited market liberalization is exemplified by:

- the opening up of the program production sector to foreign capital;
- permission for international collaboration between local and foreign media;
- the encouragement of the adoption of advanced and internationally successful technology and business models;
- the launch of the digital economy which may contingently create business opportunities for foreign programs, equipment and technological services (see Chapter 7).

The state's determination to achieve international expansion was demonstrated by the launching of the "reaching out" project. This was designed to assist the overseas growth of the Chinese media and Chinese private equity funds, such as China Media Capital, and the liberalization of the Pearl River Delta region's cable networks to enable national TV channels access to international markets (see Chapters 9 and 10).

Notwithstanding these attempts, three points are worth special mention. First, Guangdong's case shows that the impacts of foreign satellite television channels can be both controlled and manageable: their market sizes are limited within a

204 *A reconsideration of relationships*

province; their program content is restricted to non-news and is primarily entertainment; their channels are filtered by local broadcasting authorities; and their signals can be suspended if the content is seen as unsuitable.

Second, in spite of limited liberalization, appealing the national broadcasting industry to strengthen itself is the most prominent call, supported not only by political and media elites but also by a large number of intellectual publications in China. Chinese self-strengthening is characterized by a pragmatic and economic benefit driven formula that has been demonstrated as being the correct path for reaching economic success by media transnational corporations (TNCs) in other developed countries. Models such as ownership concentration, rationalization of management and wages, channel specification and digitalization also highlight this self-strengthening project.

More profoundly, in Chinese politics, the dominant discourses – an elitist philosophical tradition, the conception of governance as maintenance of harmony and social stability, and the privilege of the right to development – underpin an authoritarian and paternalistic media. This media's remit is to mold public opinion to perceive the Party-State as performing and legitimate; to "enlighten" the public in morality and virtue; and to mobilize support for the state's socioeconomic reform agenda. Coercive information control and asymmetrical information dissemination are still routinely deployed to these ends. Therefore, the media's role in China is structured according to priorities: first and foremost, they must serve the CCP's interests, protecting its legitimacy and capacity to govern; second, they must serve the "collective or national interest" as defined by the Party-State; third, they are required to serve the marketplace to sustain economic capacity and serve individual cultural and social rights; finally, they are permitted to enable individual freedom of speech and facilitate political participation only insofar as this does not interfere with the higher priorities. Channeling the public and orderly expression of opinion is necessary to achieve the first two priorities. As Chapters 8 and 9 show, no matter what the new public culture service rhetoric might be – universal coverage, equal access, protection of the basic cultural rights and needs of the Chinese people, and no matter how far the three separations go – separation of the institution and enterprise, separation of ownership and managerial authority, and separation of production and broadcasting, the Party and government will continue to maintain its ideological work through non-commercial programs, primarily news and current affairs, to secure and stabilize its governance of the country. Therefore, Chinese broadcasting policy and structural transformation has been motivated more by the pragmatic aim of securing social stability and cohesion, and strengthening media's commercial power, than by moral or humane concerns for the development of citizens. The administration according to law reform in broadcasting regulation (see Chapter 3) promises some degree of predictability, some limitation of arbitrariness and some protection of media rights. However, the State can also enact illiberal laws to restrict media freedom given the absence of democracy and the marginalization of public participation in the law-making process. The continuation of the consensus on the authoritarian political model and the prioritization of social order and collective rights over individual political and civil rights have restricted the scope of any meaningful reform in media sector. In the long-term, any fundamental breakthrough in Chinese broadcasting policy will depend on the legitimization of the discourse of individual political and civil rights, on the recognition of the broadcast media's role in independently serving the public and common good, and on the State's obligation to respect individuals as citizens having equal and unalienable rights to free expression.

Having said that, the government has attempted to relax the suppression of civil liberties. For instance, the Constitution was amended in 2004 to cover that the "state respects and protects human rights". Such protection thus becomes an obligation incumbent upon the State. In 2007, the government revised the country's development strategy away from economic development alone toward the "Harmonious Society", and "efficient, human-oriented, comprehensive, coordinated and sustainable scientific development". The establishment of an accountability system makes government officials and cadres more responsive to society demands and more accountable for poor performance. In 2009, it announced the *National Human Rights Action Plan*. It pledged to develop civil and political rights to: (1) be informed of government affairs; (2) participate in an orderly way in political affairs at all levels and sectors; (3) be heard (through the development of the press and publication industries and protection of journalists' rights); and (4) to oversee (through improving mechanisms of restraint and supervision). Given Xi Jinping's leadership clearly shows the tendency to strengthen the power of the Central Government, and the increased emphases on media regulation, in order to control the news flows and quell the spread of rumors. Thus, it is unclear how far the Action Plan will be implemented or what mechanisms will be instituted to realize them.

This evidence shows that the real ideology behind the political elites' policy-making and the media elites' operational strategy is the Chinese neo-conservative philosophy. This compromising and pragmatic strand is featured by its opposition to both national cultural essentialism and total Westernization, but calling for national self-strengthening on the one hand, and the adoption of Western bureaucratic rationality and pragmatism, based on the perception of "what works" at the expense of the pursuit of theoretical justification, on the other. It opposes liberalism but supports a strong authoritarian political system, promoting law and order at the expense of individual political rights and freedom from state control because it believes this path can facilitate China to achieve a peaceful transition to a civil society rather than a revolutionary one.

When considering economic and political conditions in China since the late 1990s, it is not difficult to understand the reasons for this non-radical, compromising and pragmatic neo-conservative movement in China's TV sector.

First, Chinese intellectual, political and economic elites endorse both the inevitability of China's global integration and the economic benefits gained through engaging in globalization. Even the self-identified nationalist intellectual Wang Xiaodong,[2] who had advocated the government to adopt a more selective and protectionist approach towards globalization, agreed that the country was

206 *A reconsideration of relationships*

benefiting from the present international order, and so domestic elites, including himself, wanted to preserve this order for pragmatic reasons (Jacques, 2005: 6). In the television sector, both China's WTO entry and international negotiation on the *General Agreement on Trade Services* (GATS) have not been the sources of sweeping pressures, leading to the inevitable liberalization of China's broadcasting market. The opening up of China's production market and the Pearl River Delta's cable TV networks was however partly supported by the domestic political elites and was conducted according to local economic and political needs, and based on a mutually beneficial principle.

Second, accompanying the country's growing interdependence with global economic markets, the state has strategically driven the international expansion of national enterprises. Its aim was to capitalize on its soaring economic power for international political influence in order to protect its broadening national interests. However, the political and ideological tensions between China and the West and between China and the region, the Chinese political elites' fundamental distrust of the West and their mounting skepticism about the impartiality of foreign media have convinced them that it is essential to have the voices of the Chinese news media heard by international society. Therefore, the Party-State has to adjust its broadcasting policy not only in accordance with domestic needs but also in terms of the global political structure. This global-national disjunction reinforced the desire for an internationally expansive broadcasting policy.

Nevertheless, China's national broadcasting policy is still primarily a defensive one, endorsing a gradual transformation to preserve social stability and state security. Both the political and media elites believe that necessary protection is a common and reasonable practice through which to secure the marketplace for local broadcasters and sustain their growth and development.

Third, neo-conservative development is a response to the crisis of the CCP's ruling legitimacy, which was seriously weakened by capitalistic market economic reform and 1989's Tiananmen Square student movement. Worrying that they might undermine the Party's leadership, the Party-State rejected Western liberal political values and prohibited the separation of the operation and ownership of news and current affairs channels and the independence of its content production. However, it opened an apolitical channel to be converted to an enterprise and to satisfy the operators' commercial and autonomy demands.

The Chinese Party-State is relatively powerful and the local political elites are sophisticated in national-global negotiations. In particular, its political, media and intellectual elites are very aware of the cultural and industrial impacts of the foreign media on local areas. There have been over 150 years of debates (see Chapter 1) on the modernization path for China and the Chinese ruling elites have not simply adopted and disseminated Western ideology. Instead, they have actively appropriated or resisted the modernization values of the West. This evidence supports both Ingrid Sarti (1981) and Anthony Giddens's (see Tomlinson, 1999) perceptions on the active engagement of the localities in the process of appropriation of Western ideologies.

Having said this, despite this consciousness, the key question is what the patterns of appropriation and resistance are. In other words, the core issues of the historical and concurring debates on the Chinese media's modernization is about two questions: first, the question of what is the dynamic driving China's appropriation and resistance; second, the question of which values are appropriated, which rejected and which ones are lost.

Regarding the first question, Sarti (1981) and Geoffrey Reeves (1993) argue that where the compatibility of ideology serves local elites and international capitalist's interests, appropriation happens. In the case of the incompatibility of interests, the local ruling classes could resist the international capitalist interests through state-action, such as the enacting of law and regulation. So, in China's television sector, what are the compatible ideologies and interests and what are the incompatible ones?

This leads to the second question. In order to answer it, the domination of Chinese neo-conservatism has to be reconsidered.

What the Chinese ruling elite classes want from the outside is a pragmatic and successful model that can make China's broadcasters bigger and stronger, powerful and wealthy. In other words, a formula approved as the correct path for the achievement of economic success by media TNCs and other countries' broadcasting industries. The guiding principle of this formula appropriated by the Chinese elites is the acceptance of market forces in media resource allocation, permission for non-state ownership, encouragement of capital accumulation and international expansion. Concrete measures include:

- embracing consumer-oriented television culture in its national broadcasting policy;
- rationalization of management to increase productivity;
- separation of television channels' broadcasting and content production, and allowing mixed-owned production enterprise companies;
- the maximization of economies of scale and scope through conglomeration;
- technological advancement to cater for convergence between broadcasting, telecommunication and computing;
- adaptation to the channel specialization and Pay TV economy;
- creation of investment fund to enter multi-media and multi-sector industries in order to diversify business models;
- international expansion through market exchange and collaboration.

International corporations could benefit from the local elites appropriation of the formula in four ways: (1) having joint-venture program production companies and a possible increase in the export of program or program formats to the local regions in the light of the booming demand for content caused by the rapid growth of specialist channels and the insufficiency of domestic production; (2) the possible increase in the export of software, hardware and technical support services caused by the technological advancement of the local regions; (3) reducing cultural discount and local industrial barriers through partnership with local

208 *A reconsideration of relationships*

television operators; (4) being able to gradually expand markets in the local regions as the return from the local's international expansion. These four benefits match surprisingly well with the targeted interests of major media corporations' internationalization projects (Prestinari, 1993).

The Chinese political elites do underplay the political independence of the broadcaster from government, a fundamental principle widely accepted in the Western broadcasting industry, at least in theory. Nicholas Garnham (1990) pinpoints the inherent contradiction in the process of the development of capitalism, due to the existing tension between nation-state and media capital, and the existing conflict between the developing and developed world on the issue of an uneven information order. In China's case, for instance, the local Chinese political elite and local and international media capitalists have found common ground in the contradiction between market liberalization and the political fear of the weakening of the Party-State's leadership. Apolitical and consumerist entertainment content has been freed from control to offset or avoid this contradiction. Even the CCP officials at the Ministry of Central Propaganda believe that foreign capitalists may not aim to practice "Westernization" and "disintegration".

The resistance pattern above supports the criticism of the anti-democratic record of international capitalists in local areas (Rosenberg in Lee, 2003) and the rather economically motivated international expansion of media companies (Tomlinson, 1999).

The appropriation pattern above, on the other hand, supports one fundamental argument of the modernization. This is the international propagation and extension of the capitalist economy and commercial broadcasting model and the diffusion of consumerism in China, though how the nature of this propagation and diffusion should be labeled is still debatable.

The modernization theorist, Daniel Lerner (1958), claims that local appropriation is essentially Westernization and it provides the most developed model and the most effective way for a developing country to become modern. The political economist, Nicholas Garnham (1990), calls this propagation and extension the consequence of the incompleteness of the development of capitalism, i.e., consciously pursuing capital accumulation on a global scale. John Tomlinson (1999) argues that this global capitalism is decentered and not necessarily affiliated to the interests of the West, but rather it inherits some elements that are universally applicable.

The mainstream ideology of the political, media and intellectual elites in China agrees with Daniel Lerner in supporting the escalation of a capitalist economy as the most developed and effective way for China's broadcasting industry to achieve modernization. Chinese media elites, as the Shanghai case has shown, on the other hand, tend to distance their broadcasting modernization projects from the Westernization discourses, and assert that the modernization model is not purely implanted from the outside, but is rather a natural outcome of the self-development of the local, having a clear historical trajectory and empirical logic. Despite the fact that the capitalist economy model originated from the West, certain of its characteristics, such as the rule of law, private ownership and belief in capital growth and expansion, have universal appeal to developing countries, particularly to a society in transition. Subscription to these values is not necessarily imposed by outside forces but could be motivated by the local's natural desire to accumulate wealth and power. It is reasonable to argue, therefore, along with Garnham, that the structural transformation of China's broadcasting sector indicates a triumph of the state-driven capitalist economy.

Conclusions

The findings of the local diversity and the dynamic central-local relationship provide another theoretical approach to an understanding of the media in China. More generally, it invites the reconsideration of the existing national-global analytical framework and theorization in media studies. In other words, more than asking how local is local in the global-local nexus, what we need to reconsider, as China's case indicates, is the more complex interactive relations between the global, national and its different locals: a local-national-global analytical approach under which the local may build up alliances with the global, as Shanghai's case showed; or an arrangement may be made between the global and national at the expanse of the local, as Guangdong broadcasting media experienced; or if common ground is found by all three parties, a mutual legitimatization of each other's interests could happen.

Scholars have called for a new framework in media studies which can link both the master narratives developed in the global context and specific narratives derived from the local, national and regional context (Lee, 2003 and 2015). This essence of the local specification is particularly significant for the study of a country like China precisely because of the diversity of its local conditions and the historical and political differences between the country and those of the Euro-American context. This differences require us to depart from solely normative approach in studying Chinese media but to include historical, sociological and anthropological perspectives in understanding the development of Chinese media and its "media culture" – a term borrowed from Nick Couldry (2012). In other words, we need to explore how the historical and social contexts and human needs shape the media landscape and how through media, people collectively make sense of the world in different societies. The best example of this national peculiarity observed in this study is the Chinese intellectual conceptualization of modernization, featuring the double critiques of Chinese cultural essentialism and Western centralism (see Chapter 1), and how the Chinese neo-conservatism influenced the Chines media policy and developmental path.

Will this ideological pursuit of the synthesis of the national and global be eventually materialized in China's society and its media industry? Or will it eventually be abandoned and replaced by a new framework? This leaves us an interesting question about the future developments of both China's intellectual discourses on local-global relationships and the Self-strengthening Movement of the country and its media industry.

Notes

1 For instance, the Party's propaganda department of the Dongguan City in Gongdong Province explicitly states that it is responsible for "supervising, coordinating and managing" the local Dong Guang city broadcast station and newspaper. Available at: www.dg.gov.cn/sofpro/otherproject/dgzzjg/zzjg_view.jsp?id=765 (accessed 19 January, 2016).
2 He is a former economics professor at the University of International Business and Economics in Beijing and former editor of *Strategy and Management*, an important literary and intellectual journal in China.

Appendix I
Laws, regulations and documents

Administrative License Law (National People's Congress, Order of the President No. 7, 1 July 2004). 中华人民共和国行政许可法. Available at: http://news.xinhuanet.com/zhengfu/2003-08/28/content_1048844.htm (accessed 10 May 2016).

Administrative Litigation Law (National People's Congress, Order of the President No. 16, 1 October 1990, 2014 Amended). 中华人民共和国行政诉讼法. Available at: www.spp.gov.cn/sscx/201502/t20150217_91466.shtml (accessed 10 May 2016).

Administrative Measures for the Broadcast of Audiovisual Programs via the Internet or Other Information Networks (SARFT, Decree No. 39, 11 October 2004). 互联网等信息网络传播视听节目管理办法. Available at: www.sarft.gov.cn/art/2004/10/11/art_1583_26295.html (accessed 10 May 2016).

Administrative Measures for the Examination and Approval of Radio Stations and Television Stations (SARFT, Decree No. 37, 20 September 2004). 广播电台电视台审批管理办法. Available at: www.sarft.gov.cn/art/2004/9/24/art_1583_26293.html (accessed 10 May 2016).

Administrative Measures on Internet Information Services (State Council, Order No. 129, 5 October 1993). 互联网信息服务管理办法. Available at: www.gov.cn/gongbao/content/2000/content_60531.htm (accessed 10 May 2016).

Administrative Measures on Reception of Satellite Broadcast Programs via Ground Facilities (State Council, Order No. 129, 5 October 1993). 卫星电视广播地面接收设施管理规定. Available at: www.gov.cn/fwxx/bw/gjgbdydszj/content_2262992.htm (accessed 10 May 2016).

Administrative Penalty Law (National People's Congress, Order of the President No. 63, 1 October 1996). 中华人民共和国行政处罚法. Available at: www.gov.cn/banshi/2005-08/21/content_25101.htm (accessed 10 May 2016).

Administrative Procedure Law (National People's Congress, Order of the President no. 16, 1 October 1990). 中华人民共和国行政诉讼法. Available at: www.gov.cn/flfg/2006-10/29/content_1499268.htm (accessed 10 May 2016).

Administrative Provisions on Internet Audio-Visual Program Service (SARFT and MIIT, Order No. 56, 20 December 2007). 互联网视听节目服务管理规定. Available at: www.sarft.gov.cn/art/2007/12/29/art_1583_26307.html (accessed 10 May 2016).

Administrative Review Law. 中华人民共和国行政复议法. National People's Congress, Order of the President No. 16. 1 October 1999). Available at: www.gov.cn/banshi/2005-08/21/content_25100.htm (accessed 10 May 2016).

Advertising Law (National People's Congress, 27 October 1994, 24 April 2015 Amended). 中华人民共和国广告法. Available at: www.gov.cn/xinwen/2015-04/25/content_2852914.htm (accessed 10 May 2016).

212 *Appendix I*

Broadcasting Administrative Regulations (State Council, Order No. 228, 1 September 1997). 广播电视管理条例. Available at: www.gov.cn/banshi/2005-08/21/content_25111.htm (accessed 10 May 2016).

China Broadcasting Television Network Limited Charter (Ministry of Finance and SAPPRFT, 23 April 2014).中国广播电视网络有限公司章程. Available at: www.cssn.cn/xwcbx/xwcbx_zxgg/201404/t20140424_1082095.shtml (accessed 10 May 2016).

Circular on the Outline of the Report on Broadcasting Work (Central Committee of CCP, Zhongfa [1983] No. 37, 26 October 1983). 关于批转广播电视部党组〈关于广播电视工作的汇报提纲〉的通知. Available at: http://xuewen.cnki.net/R2006061470006223.html (accessed 10 May 2016).

Civil Procedure Law (National People's Congress, 9 April 1994, 2007 1st Amended, 2012 2nd Amended). 中华人民共和国民事诉讼法. Available at: www.npc.gov.cn/wxzl/gongbao/2012-11/12/content_1745518.htm (accessed 10 May 2016).

Communiqué of the Third Plenum of the Eighteenth CCP Central Committee (Central Committee of CCP, 12 November 2013). 中国共产党第十八届中央委员会第三次全体会议公报. Available at: http://cpc.people.com.cn/n/2013/1112/c64094-23519137.html (accessed 10 May 2016).

Constitution of the PRC, 1982. 中华人民共和国宪法（1982年) (National People's Congress, 4 December 1982, Amended in 1988, 1993, 1999 and 2004). Available at: www.gov.cn/gongbao/content/2004/content_62714.htm (accessed 10 May 2016).

Consumer Law (National People's Congress, Order of the President No. 11, 1 January 1994). 中华人民共和国消费者权益保护法. Available at: www.gov.cn/banshi/2005-08/31/content_68770.htm (accessed 10 May 2016).

Copyrights Law (National People's Congress, 1 June 1991, Amended in 2001 and 2010). 中华人民共和国著作权法. Available at: www.gov.cn/flfg/2010-02/26/content_1544458.htm (accessed 10 May 2016).

Criminal Law (National People's Congress, 1 July 1979, Amended in 1997, Order of the President No. 83, 1 October 1997). 中华人民共和国刑法. Available at: www.npc.gov.cn/wxzl/gongbao/2000-12/17/content_5004680.htm (accessed 10 May 2016).

Decision Concerning Some Major Questions in Comprehensively Promoting Governing the Country According to Law (Central Committee of CCP, 23 October 2014). 中共中央关于全面推进依法治国若干重大问题的决定. Available at: www.gov.cn/zhengce/2014-10/28/content_2771946.htm (accessed 10 May 2016).

Decision of the First Session of the Twelfth National People's Congress on the Plan for State Council Restructuration and Function Transformation (National People's Congress, 14 March 2013). 第十二届全国人民代表大会第一次会议关于国务院机构改革和职能转变方案的决定（草案. Available at: www.gov.cn/2013lh/content_2354443.htm (accessed 10 May 2016).

Decision on Important Issues of the Reform and Development of SOEs (Central Committee of CCP, 22 September 1999). 中共中央关于国有企业改革和发展若干重大问题的决定. Available at: http://cpc.people.com.cn/GB/64162/71380/71382/71386/4837883.html (accessed 10 May 2016).

Decision on Several Major Questions about Deepening Reform (Central Committee of CCP, 12 November 2013). 中共中央关于全面深化改革若干重大问题的决定. Available at: http://news.xinhuanet.com/politics/2013-11/15/c_118164235.htm (accessed 10 May 2016).

Decision on the Establishment of Social Market Economy (Central Committee of CCP, 14 November 1993). 中共中央关于建立社会主义市场经济体制若干问题的决定. Available at: www.china.com.cn/chinese/archive/131747.htm (accessed 10 May 2016).

Decisions on the Reform of Economic Institution (Central Committee of CCP, 20 October 1984). 中共中央关于经济体制改革的决定. Available at: http://news.xinhuanet.com/ziliao/2005-02/07/content_2558000.htm (accessed 10 May 2016).

Decision to Comprehensively Promote Administration According to Law, and its Implementation Outline (State Council, Guofa [2004] No. 10, 22 March 2004). 国务院关于印发全面推进依法行政实施纲要的通知. Available at: www.gov.cn/zhengce/content/2008-03/28/content_1925.htm (accessed 10 May 2016).

Educational Law (National People's Congress, 1 May 1995). 中华人民共和国教育法. Available at: http://old.moe.gov.cn/publicfiles/business/htmlfiles/moe/moe_619/2004 07/1316.html (accessed 10 May 2016).

Explanation of the Chinese Communist Party Central Committee *Decision on Several Major Questions About Deepening Reform* (Xijinping, 15 November 2013). 习近平：关于《中共中央关于全面深化改革若干重大问题的决定》的说明. Available at: http://news.xinhuanet.com/politics/2013-11/15/c_118164294.htm (accessed 10 May 2016).

Film Administrative Regulations (State Council, Order No. 342, 12 December 2001). 电影管理条例. Available at: www.gov.cn/banshi/2005-08/21/content_25117.htm (accessed 10 May 2016).

General Principle of Civil Law (National People's Congress, Order of the President No. 37, 1 January 1987). 中华人民共和国民法通则. Available at: www.npc.gov.cn/wxzl/wxzl/2000-12/06/content_4470.htm (accessed 10 May 2016).

Guiding Opinions on Further Strengthening Grassroots Cultural Construction (State Council, Guobanfa [2002] No.7, 30 January 2002) 关于进一步加强基层文化建设指导意见的通知. Available at: www.pkulaw.cn (accessed 10 May 2016).

Higher Education Law (National People's Congress, Order of the President No. 7, 1 January 1999). 中华人民共和国高等教育法. Available at: www.moe.gov.cn/publicfiles/business/htmlfiles/moe/moe_619/200407/1311.html (accessed 10 May 2016).

Implementation Rules of Multimedia and Cross-Region Operations of Broadcasting and Film Conglomerates (SARFT, Zhongbanfa [2001] No. 17, December 2001). 国家广播电影电视总局关于广播影视集团实行多媒体兼营和跨地区经营的实施细则. Available at: www.reformdata.org/index.do?m=wap&a=show&catid=320&typeid=&id=24636 (accessed 10 May 2016).

Implementation Rules of the Financing Broadcasting and Film Conglomerates, (Tentative) (SARFT, Guangfabanzi [2001] No. 1485, 20 December 2001). 国家广播电影电视总局关于广播影视集团融资的实施细则（试行）. Available at: www.pkulaw.cn (accessed 10 May 2016).

Instruction of the CCP's Central Committee on Strong Guarantee of Criminal Law and Criminal Litigation Law's Effect Implementation (Central Committee of CCP, Zhongfa [1979] No. 64, September 1979). 中共中央关于坚决保证刑法，刑事诉讼法切实实施的指示. Available at: www.reformdata.org/index.do?m=wap&a=show&catid=427&typeid=&id=9323 (accessed 10 May 2016).

Interim Administrative Measures for Qualifications of Broadcasting Editors, Journalists and Anchors (SARFT, Order No. 26, 18 June 2004). 广播电视编辑记者、播音员主持人资格管理暂行规定. Available at: www.sarft.gov.cn/art/2004/6/22/art_1583_26283.html (accessed 10 May 2016).

Interim Measures for the Payment of Remunerations for the Broadcast of Sound Recordings by Radio and Television Stations (State Council, Decree No. 566, 1 January 2010). 广播电台电视台播放录音制品支付报酬暂行办法. Available at: www.gov.cn/zwgk/2009-11/17/content_1466687.htm (accessed 10 May 2016).

214 *Appendix I*

Interim Provisions on Administrative Penalty of Radio, Television and Film (MRFT, Order No. 20, 19 December 1996). 广播电影电视行政处罚程序暂行规定. Available at: www.sarft.gov.cn/art/1996/12/30/art_1583_26276.html (accessed 10 May 2016).

Interim Provisions on the Administration of Operation Services of Cable Broadcast Television (SARFT, Order No. 67, 2 December 2011). 有线广播电视运营服务管理暂行规定. Available at: www.sarft.gov.cn/art/2011/12/12/art_1583_26315.html (accessed 10 May 2016).

Interim Provisions on the Qualifications for a Film Enterprise's Access to Commencement of Operation (SARFT and Ministry of Commerce, Order No. 43, 10 October 2004). 电影企业经营资格准入暂行规定. Available at: www.sarft.gov.cn/art/2004/11/10/art_1583_26298.html (accessed 10 May 2016).

Law on Legislation (National People's Congress, Order of the President No. 31, 1 September 2000). 中华人民共和国立法法. Available at: http://english1.english.gov.cn/laws/2005-08/20/content_29724.htm (accessed 10 May 2016).

Measures for Control over Imported Films (Ministry of Culture and General Administration of Customs, 13 October 1981). 进口影片管理办法. Available at: www.sarft.gov.cn/art/2009/12/3/art_106_27237.html (accessed 10 May 2016).

Measures for Strengthening Administration of Cultural Products Import (MCP, Zhongxunfa [2005] No. 15, 28 April 2005) 中共中央宣传部、文化部、国家广电总局等关于加强文化产品进口管理的办法. Available at: www.pkulaw.cn (accessed 10 May 2016).

Measures for the Administration of Radio and Television Advertising (SARFT, Order No. 61, 1 January 2010). 广播电视广告播出管理办法. Available at: www.sarft.gov.cn/art/2009/9/10/art_1583_26310.html (accessed 10 May 2016).

Measures for the Administration of the Landing of Overseas Satellite Television Channels (SARFT, Order No. 27, 18 June 2004). 境外卫星电视频道落地管理办法. Available at: www.sarft.gov.cn/art/2004/8/1/art_1583_26284.html (accessed 10 May 2016).

National Human Rights Action Plan (State Council Information Office, June 2012). 国家人权行动计划. Available at: www.scio.gov.cn/zxbd/nd/2012/Document/1172889/1172889.htm (accessed 10 May 2016).

National Security Law (National People's Congress, 1 July 2015). 中华人民共和国国家安全法. Available at: www.npc.gov.cn/npc/xinwen/lfgz/flca/2015-05/06/content_1935766.htm (accessed 10 May 2016).

Ninth Five-Year National Economic and Social Development Plan and Outline of 2010 Visions at the 4th Plenum of the 8th National People's Congress (National People's Congress, 17 March 1996). 关于国民经济和社会发展"九五"计划和2010年远景目标建议. Available at: www.npc.gov.cn/wxzl/gongbao/2001-01/02/content_5003506.htm (accessed 10 May 2016).

Notice Concerning Improved Success in the New Era of Broadcast Television Connected Village Work (State Council, Guobanfa [2006] No. 79, 20 September 2006). 国务院办公厅关于进一步做好 新时期广播电视村村通工作的通知. Available at: www.pkulaw.cn (accessed 10 May 2016).

Notice of the General Office of the State Council on Dividing the Tasks for Implementation of the Plan for Institutional Reform and Functional Transformation of the State Council (State Council, Guobanfa [2013] No.22, 26 March 2013). 国办关于实施《国务院机构改革和职能转变方案》任务分工的通知. Available at: www.gov.cn/zwgk/2013-03/28/content_2364821.htm (accessed 10 May 2016).

Notice on Further Rectification of Illegal "Sex Medicine" and Venereal Disease Treatment Advertisements (SAIC, Gongshangchangzi [2007] No. 266, 2007). 关于进一步

Appendix I 215

治理整顿非法"性药品". 广告和性病治疗广告的通知. Available at: www.gov.cn/zwgk/2007-12/06/content_826562.htm (accessed 10 May 2016).

Notice on Further Strengthening the Administration of Broadcasting Advertisement (MRFT, Guangfabianzi [1997] No. 76, 19 February 1997). 关于进一步加强广播电视广告宣传管理的通知. Available at: www.hflib.gov.cn/law/law/falvfagui2/XZF/FLFG/WH%20TY/1086.htm (accessed 10 May 2016).

Notice on Further Strengthening the Administration of Radio and Television Advertisement Broadcasting (SARFT [2007] No. 74). 广电总局关于进一步加强广播电视广告播放管理工作的通知. Available at: www.pkulaw.cn (accessed 10 May 2016).

Notice on Issues concerning the Pilot Program for Convergence of Three Networks (State Council, 20 July 2010). 关于三网融合试点工作有关问题的通知. Available at: www.gov.cn/zwgk/2010-08/02/content_1669528.htm (accessed 10 May 2016).

Notice on Publication of Effective Radio, Film and Television Department Rules and Normative Documents (SARFT, 12 November 2012) 广电总局关于公布继续有效的广播影视部门规章和规范性文件目录的通知. Available at: www.sarft.gov.cn/art/2010/11/17/art_113_5343.html (accessed 29 July 2015).

Notice on the Issuance of the MRFT's Function, Organization and Staffing (State Council, Guobanfa [1994] No. 46, 23 March 1994). 国务院办公厅关于印发广播电影电视部职能配置、内设机构和人员编制方案的通知. Available at: www.gov.cn/zhengce/content/2010-11/15/content_7856.htm (accessed 10 May 2016).

Notice on the Issuance of the SAPPRFT's Function, Organization and the Staffing (State Council, Guobanfa [2013] No.76, 11 July 2013). 国务院办公厅关于印发国家新闻出版广电总局主要职责内设机构和人员编制规定的通知. Available at: www.gov.cn/zwgk/2013-07/17/content_2449645.htm (accessed 10 May 2016).

Notice on the Issuance of the SARFT's Function, Organization and Staffing (State Council, Guobanfa [1998] No. 92, 25 June 1998). 国务院办公厅关于印发国家广播电影电视总局职能配置、内设机构和人员编制方案的通知.. Available at: www.gov.cn/zhengce/content/2010-11/18/content_7733.htm (accessed 10 May 2016).

Notice on Strengthening the Governance of Press, Publication and Broadcasting (Zhongbantingzi [1996] No. 37, 14 December 1996). 中共中央办公厅、国务院办公厅关于加强新闻出版广播电视业管理的通知. Available at: www.szgm.gov.cn/szgm/132100/xwdt17/150043/151079/357156/index.html (accessed 10 May 2016).

Notice on Strict Prohibition of Advertisement Insertion during Program Transmission by Cable Television Network Operators (SARFT, 11 July 2008). 广电总局严禁有线电视网络机构在转播中插播广告. Available at: www.gov.cn/gzdt/2008-07/14/content_1044046.htm (accessed 10 May 2016).

Notice on Work Plan of Strengthening Rule of Law Government (SARFT, 11 November, 2010) 广电总局关于加强法治政府建设的工作规划. Available at: www.sarft.gov.cn/art/2010/11/25/art_113_5338.html (accessed 27 July 2015).

Opinion on Construction of Rule of Law Government (State Council, Guofa [2010] No.33, 10 October 2010). 国务院关于加强法治政府建设的意见. Available at: www.gov.cn/zwgk/2010-11/08/content_1740765.htm (accessed 10 May 2016).

Opinions on Earnestly Implementing the Separation of Broadcasting and Production (SARFT, Order No. 66, 27 August 2009). 关于认真做好广播电视制播分离改革的意见. Available at: http://media.people.com.cn/n/2015/1209/c401103-27907256.html (accessed 10 May 2016).

Opinions on Experimental Works of the Cultural System's Institutional Reform (Central Committee of CCP and State Council, 12 January 2006). 中共中央国务院发出深化文

216 *Appendix I*

化体制改革若干意见. Available at: http://news.xinhuanet.com/politics/2006-01/12/content_4044535.htm (accessed 10 May 2016).

Opinions on Improving Broadcasting and Film Industry Development (SARFT, 8 January 2004). 关于加快电影产业发展的若干意见. Available at: http://news.xinhuanet.com/zhengfu/2004-02/19/content_1322434.htm (accessed 10 May 2016).

Opinion on Strengthening the Construction and Governance of Broadcasting and Cable Network (State Council, Guobanfa [1999] No. 82, 13 September 1999). 关于加强广播电视有线网络建设管理意见的通知. Available at: www.chinaculture.org/gb/cn_zgwh/2004-06/28/content_53590.htm (accessed 10 May 2016).

Opinions on the Work of Deepening the Economic Reform in 2009 (State Council, Gufa [2009] No. 26, 19 May 2009). 关于2009 年深化经济体制改革工作意见. Available at: www.gov.cn/zwgk/2009-05/25/content_1323641.htm (accessed 10 May 2016).

Opinion Regarding Further Strengthening Internet Administration Work (SARFT, 8 May 2005). 关于进一步加强互联网管理工作的意见. Available at: www.pkulaw.cn (accessed 10 May 2016).

Outline of Cultural Development for the Eleventh Five-Year Plan (CCP and State Council, 13 September 2006). 国家"十一五"时期文化发展规划纲要. Available at: www.sdpc.gov.cn/fzgggz/fzgh/ghwb/gjjgh/200709/P020150630514110816419.pdf (accessed 10 May 2016).

Price Law (National People's Congress, Order of the President No. 92, 1 May 1998). 中华人民共和国价格法. Available at: www.gov.cn/banshi/2005-09/12/content_69757.htm (accessed 10 May 2016).

Principal Opinions on Experimental Works of Radio, Film and Television Conglomeration Development (SARFT, 17 November 2000). 广播电影电视集团化发展试行工作的原则意见.

Provisional Administrative Measures on Cable Television (MRFT, Order No. 2, 16 November 1990). 有线电视管理暂行办法. Available at: www.sarft.gov.cn/art/2009/12/3/art_1602_26268.html (accessed 10 May 2016).

Provisional Measures for the Administration of Examination and Approval of the Landing of Overseas Satellite TV Channels (SARFT, Order No. 8, 26 December 2001). 境外卫星电视频道落地审批管理暂行办法. Available at: www.gov.cn/gongbao/content/2002/content_61751.htm (accessed 10 May 2016).

Provisional Measures for the Administration of Television and Radio Advertisement Broadcasting (SARFT, Order No. 17, 1 January 2004). 广播电视广告播放管理暂行办法. Available at: www.pkulaw.cn (accessed 10 May 2016).

Provisional Provisions of Guangdong Province on Administration of Overseas Satellite Television Channels (The Yearbook of Guangdong, 2007). 广东省境外电视频道管理暂行规定.

Provisional Provisions on Supervision of Administrative License Implementation (SARFT, Order No. 24, 18 June 2004). 国家广播电影电视总局行政许可实施检查监督暂行办法. Available at: www.sarft.gov.cn/art/2004/6/20/art_1583_26282.html (accessed 10 May 2016).

Provisions on Internal Audition of Broadcasting and Film Organizations (SARFT, Order No. 46, 9 December 2004). 广播电影电视系统内部审计工作规定. Available at: www.sarft.gov.cn/art/2005/1/10/art_1583_26300.html (accessed 10 May 2016).

Provisions on Radio, TV and Film Legislative Procedures (SARFT, Order No. 23, 1 August 2004). 广播电影电视立法程序规定. Available at: www.sarft.gov.cn/art/2004/6/19/art_1588_26349.html (accessed 10 May 2016).

Appendix I 217

Public Order Penalty Law (State Council, Order of the President No. 38, 1 March 2006). 中华人民共和国治安管理处罚法. Available at: www.gov.cn/flfg/2005-08/29/content_27130.htm (accessed 10 May 2016).

Reform on Promoting "Separation of Broadcasting and Production" of Broadcasters (SARFT, 6 July 2009). 关于推进广播电视"制播分离"改革的征求意见稿（修改稿）. Available at: http://media.people.com.cn/n/2015/1209/c401103-27907256.html (accessed 10 May 2016).

Regulation on Production and Management of Radio and Television Programs (SARFT, Order No. 34, 20 August 2004). 广播电视节目制作经营管理规定. Available at: www.sarft.gov.cn/art/2004/8/20/art_1583_26290.html (accessed 10 May 2016).

Regulations on Protection of Radio and Television Facilities (State Council, Decree No. 295, 5 November 2000). 广播电视设施保护条例. Available at: www.sarft.gov.cn/art/2007/2/15/art_1602_26264.html (accessed 10 May 2016).

Regulation on the Protection of the Right to Network Dissemination of Information (State Council, Decree No. 468, 1 July 2006). 信息网络传播权保护条例. Available at: www.gov.cn/zwgk/2006-05/29/content_294000.htm (accessed 10 May 2016).

Rule the Country by Law, and Build a Socialist Country under the Rule of Law (CCP's National Congress, October 1997). 依法治国，建设社会主义法治国家. Available at: www.people.com.cn/GB/14576/15097/1912676.html (accessed 10 May 2016).

Several Regulations on Non-Public Capital's Entrance into the Cultural Industry (State Council, Guofa [2005] No. 10, 13 April 2005) 关于非公有资本进入文化产业的若干规定. Available at: www.gov.cn/gongbao/content/2005/content_64188.htm (accessed 15 December 2015).

Several Rules on Improving Economic Policy in Culture (State Council, Guofa [1996] No. 37, 5 September 1996). 国务院关于进一步完善文化经济政策的若干规定. Available at: www.seac.gov.cn/art/2011/1/19/art_59_108638.html (accessed 10 May 2016).

Some Opinions on Deepening the Reform of Press, Publication, Broadcasting and Film Industries (CCP, Zhongbanfa [2001] No. 17, 20 August 2001) 中共中央办公厅、国务院办公厅关于转发中央宣传部、国家广电总局、新闻出版总署关于深化新闻出版广播影视业改革的若干意见的通知. Available at: www.chinapublish.com.cn/cbfg/dlcbfg/zl/200701/t20070104_8339.html (accessed 10 May 2016).

State Council Forwarded the Notice Issued by the National Development and Reform Commission on Deepening the Reform of Economic System (State Council, Guofa [2009] No. 26, 19 May 2009). 国务院批转发展改革委关于2009年深化经济体制改革工作意见的通知. Available at: www.gov.cn/zwgk/2009-05/25/content_1323641.htm (accessed 23 November 2015).

State Council's Notice on "Overall Plan for Promoting Three Network Convergence" (State Council, Guofa [2010] No. 5, 21 January 2010). 国务院关于印发《推进三网融合总体方案》的通知. Available at: https://hk.lexiscn.com/law/law-chinese-1-2610409.html (accessed 10 May 2016).

Telecommunication Reform Plan (State Council, December 2001). 电信体制改革方案. Available at: http://news.xinhuanet.com/zhengfu/2002-05/17/content_397045.htm (accessed 10 May 2016).

(Tentative) Implementation Rules of Actively Propelling the Broadcasting Conglomeration Reform (SARFT, Guangfabanzi [2001] No. 1452, 13 December 2001). 国家广播电影电视总局关于积极推进广播影视集团化改革的实施细则（试行）. Available at: www.pkulaw.cn (accessed 10 May 2016).

The Eleventh Five-Year Plan (State Council, 16 March 2006). "十一五" 规划. Available at: www.gov.cn/ztzl/2006-03/16/content_228841.htm (accessed 10 May 2016).

218 *Appendix I*

The Party's Report Delivered at the Sixteenth Party National Congress (Central Committee of CCP, 8 November 2002). 全面建设小康社会, 开创中国特色社会主义事业新局面——在中国共产党第十六次全国代表大会上的报告. Available at: http://cpc.people.com.cn/GB/64162/64168/64569/65444/4429125.html (accessed 10 May 2016).

The Report Given by Hu Jintao at the Seventeenth National Congress of the CCP (Central Committee of CCP, 15 October 2007). 胡锦涛在中国共产党第十七次全国代表大会上的报告. Available at: http://cpc.people.com.cn/GB/104019/104099/6429414.html (accessed 10 May 2016).

The Thirteenth Five-Year Plan (State Council, 17 March 2016). 十三五规划. Available at: www.gov.cn/xinwen/2016-03/17/content_5054992.htm (accessed 10 May 2016).

The Timetable of Digitalization of Domestic Cable TV (SARFT, 10 June 2003). 我国有线电视向数字化过渡时间表. Available at: http://news.xinhuanet.com/zhengfu/2003-06/10/content_912322.htm (accessed 10 May 2016).

Three Network Convergence Promotion Plan (State Council, Guobanfa [2015] No. 65, 25 August 2015). 三网融合推广方案. Available at: www.pkulaw.cn (accessed 10 May 2016).

Tort Law (National People's Congress, Order of the President No. 21, 1 July 2010). 中华人民共和国侵权责任法. Available at: www.gov.cn/flfg/2009-12/26/content_1497435.htm (accessed 10 May 2016).

Urgent Notice on Strengthening the Administration of Television Advertisement Broadcasting (SARFT, Guangfabianzi [2002] No. 355, 30 April 2002). 国家广播电影电视总局关于切实加强电视广告播出管理的紧急通知. Available at: www.law-lib.com/law/law_view.asp?id=312721 (accessed 10 May 2016).

Urgent Notice on Strict Prohibition of Arbitrary Insertion and Over-broadcasting of Television Advertisements (SARFT, 23 August 1999). 关于坚决制止随意插播、超量播放电视广告的紧急通知. Available at: www2.jslib.org.cn/was5/web/detail?record=102&channelid=26662 (accessed 10 May 2016).

Working Plan for Pilot Sites of Three Network Convergence (sixth version). 国务院三网融合工作协调小组办公室关于三网融合试点工作有关问题的通知. Available at: www.pkulaw.cn (accessed 10 May 2016).

References

Ackerman B (2000) The new separation of powers. *Harvard Law Review* 113 (3): 633–729.

Administrative Procedure Law of the People's Republic of China (1989). Available at: www.china.org.cn/english/government/207336.htm (accessed 5 August 2015).

All about 3G (2009) Available at: https://razunitem.wordpress.com/2009/12/17/all-about-3g/ (accessed 23 November 2015).

All-China Journalists Association (2014) Chinese journalism development report. Available at: http://en.theorychina.org/chinatoday_2483/whitebooks/201504/t20150407_321 169.shtml (accessed 23 November 2015).

An interview with Yang Xingnong, the vice president of Shanghai Media Group: To reach the new high of conglomerate management work (集团经营工作实现跨越式发展——访传媒集团副总裁杨荇农) (2006). *Shanghai Media Group People (传媒人报)*, 8 May, 15 (1) (in Chinese).

AOL Time Warner (2001) AOL Time Warner signs historic reciprocal cable TV carriage agreement with PRC. Available at: www.timewarner.com/corp/newsroom/pr/0,20812,669028,00.html (accessed 19 September 2008).

Ash TG (2014) Welcome to China's political gamble of the century. *The Guardian,* 30 March. Available at: www.theguardian.com/commentisfree/2014/mar/30/china-political-gamble-of-century-president-xi-jinping (accessed 26 December 2015).

Bai Y (2011) SARFT's opinion on strengthening regulation of programs in satellite TV's general channels (广电总局下发加强电视上星综合频道节目管理意见). *Xinhua News Agency,* 25 October. Available at: www.gov.cn/jrzg/2011-10/25/content_1977909.htm (accessed 5 August 2015) (in Chinese).

Baldwin R and McCrudden C (1987) Regulatory agencies. In: Baldwin R and McCrudden C (eds.) *Regulation and Public Law.* London: Weidenfeld and Nicolson, 3–12.

Bao ZY (2004) The sixteenth central committee of the Chinese Communist Party: Formal institutions and factional groups. *Journal of Contemporary China* 13 (39): 223–256.

Barabantseva E (2012) In pursuit of an alternative model? The modernisation trap in China's official development discourse. *East Asia* 29: 63–79.

Barendt E (2007) *Freedom of Speech.* Oxford: Oxford University Press.

BBC News (2002a) Jiang's work report highlights, 8 November. Available at: http://news.bbc.co.uk/1/hi/world/asia-pacific/2419471.stm (accessed 29 April 2005).

BBC News (2002b) Jiang's message of change, 8 November. Available at: http://news.bbc.co.uk/1/hi/world/asia-pacific/2419907.stm (accessed 29 April 2005).

220 References

BBC News (2004) China's draft institutional amendments protect private property (中国宪法修正案保护私权), 8 March. Available at: http://news.bbc.co.uk/hi/chinese/news/newsid_3544000/35445712.stm (accessed 5 July 2005) (in Chinese).

Beland D and Yu KM (2004) A long financial march: pension reform in China. *Journal of Social Policy* 33 (2): 267–288.

Bell DA (2007) From Marx to Confucius: Changing discourses on china's political future. *Dissent* 54 (2): 20–28.

Bendix R (1962) *Max Weber: An Intellectual Portrait*. London: Methuen.

Bennett C and Howlett M (1992) The lessons of learning: reconciling theories of policy learning and policy change. *Policy Sciences* 25 (3): 275–294.

Blockson LC and Buren HJV (1999) *Strategic Alliances among Different Institutions: An Argument for Multi-Sector Collaboration in Addressing Societal Issues*. Washington, DC: Independent Sector Working Papers.

Born G and Prosser T (2001) Culture and consumerism: citizenship, public service broadcasting and the BBC's fair trading obligations. *Modern Law Review* 64: 657–687.

Brady AM (2006) Guiding hand: the role of the CCP Central Propaganda Department. *The Current Era, Westminster Papers in Communication and Culture* 3 (1): 58–77.

Brandt L and Rawski TG (2008) *China's Great Economic Transformation*. Cambridge: Cambridge University Press.

Brunswick Group (2013) Analysis of the decision on major issues concerning comprehensively deepening reform. Available at: www.brunswickgroup.com/media/229230/Brunswick-China-Analysis-CPC-Third-Plenary-Session-November-2013.pdf (accessed 26 December 2015).

Buckler S (2010) Normative theory. In: Marsh D and Stoker G (eds.) *Theory and Methods in Political Science*, 3rd edition. Hampshire: Palgrave Macmillan, 156–180.

Buckley C (2013) Chinese leader gets more sway on the economy and security. *New York Times*, 13 November. Available at: http://cn.nytimes.com/china/20131113/c13plenum/dual/ (accessed 26 December 2015).

Business Wire (2014) Star China's management team and China Media Capital to acquire 21st Century Fox's entire stake in Star China TV joint venture, 2 January. Available at: www.businesswire.com/news/home/20140102005296/en/Star-China's-Management-Team-China-Media-Capital (accessed 15 December 2015).

Cai MZ and Yang G (2004) The development of Guangdong's newspaper in the new era and reasons (论新时期广东报业的发展及其原因). *Journalism and Communication Review (*新闻与传播评论*)* 2003 (00): 222–235 (in Chinese).

Callamard A (2006) Development, poverty and freedom of expression. Paper presented at the UNESCO Conference on Freedom of the Media and Development, 3 May. Colombo, Sri Lanka.

Cao L *et al.* (1997) *Satellite Television Communication* (卫星电视传播). Beijing: Beijing Broadcasting Institute Press (北京: 北京广播学院出版社) (in Chinese).

CBN (China Business Network) (2003) *China Business Network Catalogue* (中国商务集团). Shanghai: SMG (in Chinese).

CBN officially launched (2003) 第一财经（China Business Network）正式启动. *Culture, Radio, Film and TV (*文化广播影视*)*, 7 July, 1 (in Chinese).

CCP (1991) Outline of the Eighth Five-Year Plan and Ten-Year Plan for Economic and Social Development (于国民经济和社会发展十年规划和第八个五年计划纲要的报告) (in Chinese).

CCP (1996a) CCP [1996] No. 37: General Office of the CCP Central Committee and General Office's Notice on Strengthening the Governance of Press, Publication and

References 221

Broadcasting. (中办厅字[1996]37号：中共中央办公厅、国务院办公厅关于加强新闻出版广播电视业管理的通知). Available at: www.chinalawedu.com/news/1200/22 598/22618/22868/2006/3/ya09961434316360022618-0.htm (accessed 13 January 2016) (in Chinese).

CCP (1996b) Resolution on Several Important Questions Concerning Strengthening Socialist Spiritual Civilization Construction (社会主义精神文明建设的几个重要问题) (in Chinese).

CCP (2000) Recommendations Concerning Drafting of the Tenth Five-Year Plan for a Citizens' Economy and Society (中共中央关于制定国民经济和社会发展第十个五年计划的建议) (in Chinese).

CCP (2001) CCP [2001] No. 17: General Office of the CCP Central Committee and General Office of the State Council's Notice on Forwarding Several Opinions of Propaganda Department of Central Committee, SARFT and State General Agency of Press and Publications about Deepening Reform of Press, Publication and Broadcasting. (中办发[2001]17号: 中共中央办公厅、国务院办公厅关于转发中央宣传部、国家广电总局、新闻出版总署关于深化新闻出版广播影视业改革的若干意见的通知) (in Chinese).

CCP (2004) CCP's Opinion on Further Strengthening Internet Administration Work (广电总局印发落实中办国办《关于进一步加强互联网管理工作的意见》实施细则的通知). Available at: www.cecc.gov/resources/legal-provisions/circular-regarding-detailed-implementing-regulations-of-the-opinion (accessed 27 July 2015) (in Chinese).

CCP (2005a) The Central Committee of the Communist Party of China to Develop the National Economy and Social Development of the Eleventh Five-year Planning Proposal (《中共中央关于制定国民经济和社会发展第十一个五年规划的建议》) (in Chinese).

CCP (2005b) CCP [2005] No. 27: Opinions on Further Strengthening the Rural Cultural Construction (关于进一步加强农村文化建设的意见). Normative document (in Chinese).

CCP (2006) CCP [2006] No. 19: Resolutions Concerning Several Important Issues on Construction of Socialist Harmonious Society (中共中央关于构建社会主义和谐社会若干重大问题的决定). Normative document (in Chinese).

CCP (2007) CCP [2007] No. 21: Several Views Concerning Public Cultural Service System Construction (关于加强公共文化服务体系建设的实施意见). Normative document (in Chinese).

CCP (2013) *Decision of the Chinese Communist Party Central Committee on Several Major Questions About Deepening Reform* (中共中央关于全面深化改革若干重大问题的决定). Available at: http://news.xinhuanet.com/politics/2013-11/15/c_118164235. htm (accessed 26 December 2015) (in Chinese).

CCP (2014) Main functions of Central Propaganda Ministry (中共中央宣传部主要职能). Available at: http://cpc.people.com.cn/GB/64114/75332/5230610.html (accessed 12 Oct 2014) (in Chinese).

CCP and State Council (2005) Several Views Concerning Deepening Cultural System Reform (中共中央 国务院关于深化文化体制改革的若干意见) (in Chinese).

CCP and State Council (2006) Outline of Cultural Development during the Eleventh Five-Year Plan (《国家"十一五"时期文化发展规划纲要》) (in Chinese).

CCP and State Council (2012) The Cultural Reform, Development and Plan for the National Twelfth Five-year Period (《国家"十二五"时期文化改革发展规划纲要》) (in Chinese).

222 References

CCP National Congress (2007) Harmonious society. The Seventeenth National Congress of the Communist Party of China. Available at: http://en.people.cn/90002/92169/92211/6274603.html (accessed 23 November 2015).

CCP Theoretical Bureau (2008) Facing Topical Theories (理论热点面对面). Xuexi Publication House and People's Publication House: Beijing (北京: 学习出版社，人民出版社) (in Chinese).

CCPLRO (Literature Research Office of CCP Central Committee 中共中央文献研究室) (2008) Summary of Important Speeches on Scientific Development View (科学发展观重要论述摘编). CCP Central Committee Literature Publication House: Beijing (北京: 中央文献出版社) (in Chinese).

CCTV (2002) The Dialogue Programme Team of Economic Department of the China Central Television Station (中央电视台经济部《对话》栏目组). *CCTV Dialogue (CCTV对话)*. HaiKou: Nanhai Publishing Co (海口:南海出版社). (in Chinese).

CCTV (2003) *Growth in the Market Competition (市场竞争中的成长)*. CCTV advertising department (中央电视台广告部) [Email] (accessed 12 September 2003) (in Chinese).

CCTV International (2005) SARFT energetically pushes forward connected village work (广电总局加大力度推进村村通广播电视工作). 18 September. Available at: www.cctv.com/news/china/20050318/102101.shtml (accessed 17 February 2011) (in Chinese).

CCTV Yearbook 1996 (中国中央电视台年鉴1996) (1997) Beijing: China Broadcasting Publishing House (北京: 中国广播电视出版社) (in Chinese).

Central Committee of CCP and State Council (2015) Opinions on Accelerating the Establishment of Modern System of Public Cultural Services (《中共中央办公厅、国务院办公厅关于加快构建现代公共文化服务体系的意见》) (in Chinese).

Central Propaganda Department (2009) Shanghai established supervision and management office of state-owned assets in culture field (上海市成立文化领域国有资产监督管理办公室) Available at: http://hxd.wenming.cn/whtzgg/2009-10/27/content_62610.htm (accessed 23 November 2015) (in Chinese).

Chan WK (2011) Network Governance in Chinese Educational Policy: the Case of Harbin State-owned Enterprise Schools. Paper Presented at AARE Annual Conference, Hobart.

Chao L (2009) China squeezes PC makers. *The Wall Street Journal*, 8 June. Available at: www.wsj.com/articles/SB124440211524192081 (accessed 24 December 2015).

Chen BH (2008) New thoughts on the net information for reconstruction of national identity at the transformation stage – based on Habermas' legitimacy theory (对社会转型期我国政治认同重构的新思考). *Journal of Shangrao Normal College (上饶师范学院学报)*, 28 (1) (in Chinese).

Chen DD (2014) 4 reasons Xi Jinping is a serious reformer. *The Diplomat*, 11 September. Available at: http://thediplomat.com/2014/09/4-reasons-xi-jinping-is-a-serious-reformer/ (accessed 26 December 2015).

Chen F (1997) Order and stability in social transition: neoconservative political thought in post-1989 China. *China Quarterly* 151: 593–613.

Chen H, Chen C and Li YW (2010) SARFT's main role and responsibilities in accelerating the three network convergence (广电在推动三网融合中的主要作用和任务——访国家广电总局科技司王效杰司长). *Radio and Television Information (广播电视信息)* 7: 11–13 (in Chinese).

Chen M and Hu X (2009) Retrospection of the reform of the management system of China's cultural institution in the past 30 years. In: Li J and Chen W (eds.) *Report on* the Development of China's Public Cultural Service 2009 (中国公共文化服务发展报告2009). Beijing: Social Sciences Academic Press (北京: 社会科学文献出版社), 54–62 (in Chinese).

Chen WX (2006) The essence of promoting "political civilization" in China: institution building. In: Zhong Y and Hua SP (eds.) *Political Civilization and Modernization in China: the Political Context of China's Transformation.* Singapore: World Scientific, 11–32.

Chen YF (2012) Removing online rumors needs regulation and self-regulation (铲除网络谣言需要自律和他律), *Sichuan United Front* (四川统一战线), 5: 22 (in Chinese).

Chin Y (2003) China's regulatory policies on transnational drama flow. *Media Development*, 3/2003, 17–22.

Chin YC (2003) The Nation-state in a globalising media environment: China's regulatory policies on transborder TV drama flow. *Javnost* 10 (4): 75–94.

Chin YC (2006) From the local to the global: local discourse and TV policies in China. Paper presented at the 2006 Internationalising Media Studies: imperative and impediments Conference, 15–16 September. University of Westminster, London.

Chin YC (2007) From the local to the global: China's TV policy in transition. In: Kops M and Ollig S (eds.) *Internationalization of the Chinese TV Sector.* Berlin: Lit Verlag, 221–240.

Chin YC (2011) Policy process, policy learning, and the role of the provincial media in China. *Media, Culture & Society* 33 (2): 193–210.

Chin YC (2012) Public service broadcasting, public interest and individual rights in China. *Media Culture & Society* 34: 898–912.

Chin YC (2013) Regulating social media, regulating life (and lives). *Rhodes Journalism Review* 33. Available at: www.rjr.ru.ac.za/rjrpdf/rjr_no33/Regulating_social-Media.pdf (accessed 13 January 2016).

Chin YC (2014) Privilege and public opinion supervision defences in China's right to reputation litigation, *Media and Arts Law Review* 19: 276–299.

Chin YC and Johnson, MD (2012) Public cultural service: new paradigms of broadcasting policy and reform in the People's Republic of China. In: Gregory Ferrell Lowe and Jeanette Steemers (eds.) *Regaining the Initiative for Public Service Media.* Sweden: NORDICOM, 149–166.

China Broadcasting Network Ltd (2014) Company profile (中国广播电视网络有限公司基本情况). Available at: www.cbn.cn/gsgk.html (accessed 23 November 2015) (in Chinese).

China Cable TV (2004) CCTV launched Pay TV channels today, Sichuan's subscription fee is the lowest one. *China Cable TV.* Available at: www.sarft.com/site/temp/show.htm?temp=T2001112940&id1=20040809a00060001 (accessed 9 August 2004) (in Chinese).

China Entrepreneur (2013) How Li Ruigang "play" well with Murdoch and his Sky TV (黎瑞刚如何玩转星空卫士，和默多克打成一片). 4 September. Available at: www.iceo.com.cn/renwu2013/2013/0904/270578.shtml (accessed 15 December 2015) (in Chinese).

China Mobile (2015) About China Mobile. Available at: www.chinamobileltd.com/en/about/milestones.php?year=2014 (accessed 23 November 2015).

China Radio and Television Yearbook (中国广播电视年鉴) (1997) Beijing: Beijing Broadcasting Institute Press. (in Chinese) (1997) Beijing: China Broadcasting Press (北京: 北京广播学院出版社) (in Chinese).

China Security Regulatory Commission (2015) Industry categorization result of listed companies for the third quarter of 2015 (2015年3季度上市公司行业分类结果). Available

224　*References*

at: www.csrc.gov.cn/pub/newsite/scb/ssgshyfljg/201510/W020151027378657037397.pdf (accessed 15 December 2015) (in Chinese).

Chovanec P (2011) Closing the gap between China's coast and interior. Available at: https://chovanec.wordpress.com/2011/01/13/closing-the-gap-between-chinas-coast-and-interior/ (accessed 18 December 2015).

Christopher P (1998) Murdoch steps down at Star TV satellite television: News Corp Chief surrenders chair after struggle to break into Chinese market. *Financial Times*, 2 September, 20.

CICC (2005) Company profile *(长城平台简介)*, 28 February. Available at: www.gw-tv.cn/ptjs_index.asp (accessed 16 November 2008) (in Chinese).

CNBC Asia (2003) CNBC Asia Pacific and Shanghai Media Group announce strategic partnership. Available at: www.cnbcasia.com/aboutcnbcasia/press20030410.asp (accessed 21 December 2004).

Constitution of the PRC (1954) Article 87. Promulgated by National People's Congress.

Constitution of the PRC (1975) Article 28. Promulgated by National People's Congress.

Constitution of the PRC (1978) Article 45. Promulgated by National People's Congress.

Constitution of the PRC (1982) Article 35, 41 and 47. Promulgated by National People's Congress.

Coonan C (2014) China's Shanghai Media Group merges subsidiaries to create internet giant. *Hollywood Reporter*, 24 November. Available at: www.hollywoodreporter.com/news/shanghai-media-creates-internet-giant-751814 (accessed 15 December 2015).

Coonan C (2015) China to clamp down on reality TV shows. *Hollywood Reporter.* Available at: www.hollywoodreporter.com/news/china-clamp-down-reality-tv-799433 (accessed 5 August 2015).

Couldry N (2012) *Media, Society, World: Social Theory and Digital Media Practice.* Cambridge: Polity.

Cox RW (1987) *Production, Power and World Order: Social Forces in the Marking of History.* New York: Columbia University Press.

Cox RW and Sinclair TJ (1996) *Approach to World Order.* Cambridge University Press.

CPS (Central Party School Project Team) (2005) To enhance reform and develop broadcasting industry. *Guidebook for Decision Making (决策参考)* 2005 (10): 36–41 (in Chinese).

Cui G and Liu QM (2000) Regional market segments of China: opportunities and barriers in a big emerging market. *Journal of Consumer Marketing* 17 (1): 55–72.

Cui M (2011) Officer big or law big: the introduction of CCP Central Committee's No. 64 Document (官大还是法大:中央64号文件出台始末). Available at: http://history.people.com.cn/GB/205396/15163570.html (accessed 9 July 2015) (in Chinese).

Curran J (2002) *Media and Power.* London: Routledge.

Curran J and Seaton J (2003) *Power without Responsibility.* London: Routledge.

Dahlgren P (2000) Media, citizenship and civic culture. In: Curran J and Gurevitch M (eds.) *Mass Media and Society.* 3rd edition. London: Arnold, 310–328.

Daugbjerg C (2003) Policy feedback and paradigm shift in EU agricultural policy. *Journal of European Public Policy* 10 (3): 421–437.

Deadline Hollywood (2012) It's Official: DreamWorks Animation Unveils China Joint Venture, 17 February. Available at: http://deadline.com/2012/02/its-official-dreamworks-animation-unveils-china-joint-venture-232568/ (accessed 15 December 2015).

Delegation of China Broadcast Television (2004) Investigation report on UK, Finland and France's digital broadcast television (英国、芬兰和法国数字广播电视考察报告). *Guidebook for Decision Making (决策参考)* 2004 (2): 23–27 (in Chinese).

References 225

Delegation of China Broadcast Television (2009) Report on Delegation of China Broadcast Television's visit to US, Mexico and Peru (中国广播电视代表团访问美国、墨西哥、秘鲁的情况). *Guidebook for Decision Making (决策参考)* 2009 (1): 30–35 (in Chinese).

Deng XP (1994) *Selected Works of Deng Xiaoping (邓小平文选)* 2: 236. Shanghai: Shanghai People's Publishing House (上海人民出版社) (in Chinese).

Derek S (2009) Deng undone: the costs of halting market reform in China. *Foreign Affairs* 88 (3). Available at: www.foreignaffairs.com/articles/china/2009-05-01/deng-undone-0 (accessed 24 December 2015).

Diao XS, Fan SG and Zhang XB (2003) China's WTO accession: impacts on regional agricultural income – a multi-region, general equilibrium analysis. *Journal of Comparative Economics* 31: 332–351.

Ding GG (2001) Deepening reform, enhancing the prosperous and healthy development of journalism, publication, broadcasting and film industries (深化改革，推动新闻出版广播影视业持续健康发展). *CCTV Yearbook 2002 (中国中央电视台年鉴2002)*. Beijing: CCTV, 5 (in Chinese).

Ding ZW (2004) Proposal on establishing a development department with new management system separating the institution and industry parts (关于建立事业和产业两分开的新型管理体制集团事业开发部的思考). *Guidebook for Decision Making (决策参考)* 2004 (7): 36–39 (in Chinese).

Dong J (2013) The comprehensive promotion of three network convergence in 2013 is impossible (三网融合2013年进入全面推广阶段被指不现实). Available at: www.newhua.com/2013/0106/191473.shtml (accessed 23 November 2015) (in Chinese).

Dong YY (1998) The rule of law road to political system reform (通过政治体制改革的法治之路). In: Dong YY and Shi BH (eds.) *Political China (政治中国)*. China Today Publisher (今日中国出版社), 57 (in Chinese).

Du N (2010) *Shadows of Traditions: Discourse Shifts on the Rule of Law and China's Modernity*. Unpublished PhD thesis. Carleton University Ottawa, Ontario.

Du XH and Chen L (2009) Analyze the separation of production and broadcasting through the transformation of Shanghai Media Group (由上海文广转企改制看制播分离之路). *Voice and Screen World (声屏世界)* [J] 12: 13–15 (in Chinese).

Du YH (2013) Capitalism and modernization in China. *Chinese Studies in History* 47 (2): 40–51.

D&R SARFT (Development and Research Centre, SARFT国家新闻出版广电总局发展研究中心) (2008) *Report on development of China's radio, film and television (中国广播电影电视发展报告)*. Beijing: Xinhua Press (北京: 新华出版社) (in Chinese).

Drucker SJ and Gumpert G (2010) Social media. In: Drucker SJ and Gumpert G (eds.) *Regulating Convergence*. New York: Peter Lang.

Dye TR (2008) *Understanding Public Policy*. 12th Edition. Upper Saddle River, NJ: Pearson/Prentice Hall.

Economic Observer (2003a) The breakthrough of local television, Li Ruigang one step advanced, 6 May. Available at: www.eobserver.com.cn/ReadNews.asp?NewsID=3897 (accessed 11 September 2004).

Economic Observer (2003b) The reform of Shanghai broadcasting, 11 October. Available at: www.eobserver.com.cn/ReadNews.asp?NewsID=6248 (accessed 11 September 2004).

Economist Intelligence Unit (2011) Consumer marketing: turfbattles. *Business China* 31 October, 4.

Emerson T (1977) Colonial intentions and current realities of the First Amendment. *University Of Pennsylvania Law Review* 125: 737–760.

226 References

Esarey A (2006) Speak no evil: mass media control in contemporary China. Freedom House. Available at: https://freedomhouse.org/sites/default/files/inline_images/Speak %20No%20Evil-%20Mass%20Media%20Control%20in%20Contemporary%20China. pdf (accessed 1 December 2014).

Evans D, Bratton S, and McKee J (2010) *Social Media Marketing: The Next Generation of Business Engagement.* Indiana: Sybex.

Fan M (2006) China's Party Leadership declares new priority: 'Harmonious Society'. *Washington Post,* 12 October. Available at: www.washingtonpost.com/wp-dyn/content/ article/2006/10/11/AR2006101101610.html (accessed 23 November 2015).

Fan XD (2015) The inside story of the billions integration of the media giant—Shanghai Media Group (传媒巨象转身记:上海文广千亿整合内幕). *Tencent Technology (*腾讯 科技*),* 17 March. Available at: http://tech.qq.com/a/20150317/010835.htm (accessed 15 December 2015) (in Chinese).

Fang K, Que ZM and Tan FB (1996) The features and development of Lingnan TV and radio culture (岭南广播电视文化的特色及发展). *South China Television Journal (*南 方电视学刊*)* 1996 (1): 1–55 (in Chinese).

Fang Z (2015) MIIT plans to manage three network convergence through information and communication administration bureau (工信部拟以信息通信管理局管理三网融合). Available at: www.dvbcn.com/2015/07/14-118438.html (accessed 23 November 2015) (in Chinese).

Featherstone M (1990) Global culture: an introduction. In: Featherstone M (ed.) *Global Culture.* London: Sage, 1–14.

Feintuch M and Varney M (2006) *Media Regulation, Public Interest, and the Law.* 2nd edition. Edinburgh: Edinburgh University Press.

Feng C, Lau TY, Atkin D and Lin C (2009) Exploring the evolution of digital television in China: an interplay between economic and political interests. *Telematics and Informatics* 26: 333–342.

Feng H and He K (2012) Decoding China's political future and foreign policy: an operational code analysis of Hu's and Wen's belief systems. In: Tzifakis Nikolaos (ed.) *International Politics in Times of Change.* Heidelberg: Springer, 135–152.

Feng XF and Zhang D (2008) China starts the fourth reform of telecommunication system (我国启动第四次电信体制改革). *China Economic Weekly* (中国经济周刊) 20: 10 (in Chinese).

Frater P (2014) China's BesTV and Oriental Pearl merge to create new media giant. *Variety,* 24 November. Available at: http://variety.com/2014/biz/asia/chinas-bestv-and-oriental-pearl-merge-to-create-new-media-giant-1201363369/ (accessed 15 December 2015).

Frater P (2015) Li Ruigang steps down as President of Shanghai Media Group. *Variety,* 5 January. Available at: http://variety.com/2015/biz/asia/li-ruigang-removed-as-chairman-of-shanghai-media-group-say-reports-1201392547/ (accessed 15 December 2015).

Freedman D (2002) Trade culture: an evaluation of the impact of current GATS negotiations on European broadcasting policy. Paper presented at the RIPE@2002 Conference, 17–19 January, Finland.

Freeman M (2002) *Human Rights: An Interdisciplinary Approach.* Cambridge: Polity Press.

Fulda A, Li YY and Song QH (2012) New strategies of civil society in China: a case study of the network governance approach. *Journal of Contemporary China* 21 (76): 675–693.

Gao S (2005) Developing digital television and strengthening broadcasting industry (发展数字电视和强化广播产业). *Guidebook for Decision Making (决策参考)* 2005 (10): 46–50 (in Chinese).

Garnham N (1990) *Capitalism and Communication: Global Culture and Economics of Information.* London: Sage.

Gearty C (2007) *Civil Liberties.* Oxford: Oxford University Press.

Gibbons T (1998) *Regulating the Media.* London: Sweet & Maxwell.

Giddens A (1990) *The Consequences of Modernity.* London: Polity Press.

Giddens A (1999) Comment: the 1999 Reith Lecture. New World Without End. *Observer,* 11 April, 31.

Greenawalt K (1980) Speech and crime. *American Bar Foundation Research Journal* 5 (4): 645–785.

Grindel M and Thomas JW (1989) Policy makers, policy choices, and policy outcomes. *Policy Sciences* 22: 213–248.

Guo Baogang (2010) From conflicts to convergence: modernity and the changing Chinese political culture. In: Zhong, Yang and Hua, Shiping (eds.) *Political Civilization and Modernization in China: The Political Context of China's Transformation.* Singapore: World Scientific, 69–74.

Guo KY (2001) Guo Kaiyong's speech given at 2001's working conference (在2001年工作会议上的讲话). *Culture, Radio, Film and TV (文化广播影视),* 5 February, 1 and 4 (in Chinese).

Guo RX, Gui H and Guo LC (2015) *Multiregional Economic Development in China.* Berlin: Springer.

Guo ZZ (1998) Historical legacy and contemporary explanation of European public service broadcasting (欧洲公共广播电视的历史遗产及当代解释). *Journal of International Communication* (国际新闻界) 1: 49–54 (in Chinese).

Guo ZZ (2003) Playing the game by the rules? Television regulation around China's entry into WTO. *Javnost/The Public* 10 (4): 5–18.

Guo ZZ (2004) *WTO, Media Industrialisation and Chinese Television.* Paper presented at the Transnational Media Corporations and National Media Systems: China after entry into the World Trade Organisation Conference, 17–21 May. The Bellagio Study and Conference Centre, Rockefeller Foundation, Italy.

Guo ZZ (2006) Public service broadcasting: between changed and unchanged (公共广播电视:变与不变之间). *Journalistic University (新闻大学)* 3 (in Chinese).

Hall P (1993) Policy paradigm, social learning, and the state. *Comparative Politics*: 25 (3): 275–296.

Hallin DC and Mancini P (2004) *Comparing Media Systems: Three Models of Media and Politics.* Cambridge: Cambridge University Press.

Ham C and Hill MJ (1993) *The Policy Process In the Modern Capitalist State.* New York: Harvester Wheatsheaf.

Hamm B (2001) A human rights approach to development. *Human Rights Quarterly* 23 (4): 1005–31.

Han DY (2005) An analysis of public interest in the constitutions (宪法文本中"公共利益"的规范分析). *Legal Forum (法学论坛)* 20 (1): 5–9 (in Chinese).

Han SS (2000) Shanghai between state and market in urban transformation. *Urban Studies* 37 (11): 2091–2112.

Hargrave AM and Shaw C (2009) *Accountability and the Public Interest in Broadcasting.* London: Palgrave Macmillan.

228 References

Harrison J and Woods LM (2001) Defining European public service broadcasting. *European Journal of Communication* 16: 477–504.

Hart CL (1997) Engagement or containment: a clear choice. In: Canyon AM (ed.) *Assessment of China into the 21st Century*. New York: Nova Science Publisher, 79–83.

Hays J (2008) China under Hu Jintao. Available at: http://factsanddetails.com/china/cat2/sub7/item75.html (accessed 24 December 2015).

He QL (2002) A historical turning point for Chinese reform: 1999–2001 (中国改革的历史转折:1999–2001). *21st Century Bimonthly (21世纪双月刊)* 2002 (70): 26–28 (in Chinese).

He X (2007) The public interest and state interest in public administration (公共管理中的公共利益和国家利益). *Journal of Chongqing University of Science and Technology* (Social Sciences Edition) (重庆大学学报社会科学版) 3: 18–19 (in Chinese).

Heclo H (1974) *Modern Social Politics in Britain and Sweden*. New Haven, CT: Yale University Press.

Hogan Lovells (2013) Will the merger of SARFT and GAPP end the turf war over control over the Internet? Available at: www.hoganlovells.com/files/Publication/9e7448a7-ea0c-4ed1-8b70-bc61da7648e5/Presentation/PublicationAttachment/f5997588-93f2-4bdd-bc31-ca3ce524e734/SHALIB01-%231083537.pdf (accessed 26 December 2015).

Holliday GD (1997) China and the World Trade Organization. In: Canyon AM (ed.) *Assessment of China into the 21st Century*. New York: NovacScience Publisher, 215–242.

Holmes L (1993) *The End of Communist Power*. Cambridge: Polity Press, 13 and 39.

Holmes L (1997) *Post-Communism: An Introduction*. Cambridge: Polity Press.

Hong Kong News Yahoo (2004) CCTV will launch Pay TV. *Yahoo Honk Kong*. Available at: http://hk.news.yahoo.com/040802/12/131gc.htm (accessed 2 August 2004).

Hu JT (2007) Report to the Seventeenth National Congress of the Communist Party of China, 15 October. Available at: http://news.xinhuanet.com/english/2007-10/24/content_6938749.htm (accessed 24 December 2015).

Hu JT (2012) Firmly march on the path of socialism with Chinese characteristics and strive to complete the building of moderately prosperous society in all respects. Report at the Eighteenth Party Congress. Available at: www.chinadaily.com.cn/china/2012cpc/2012-11/18/content_15939493.htm (accessed 7 July 2015).

Hu Y (1980) A look at American broadcasting (美国传播初探). *Modern Communication* (现代传播) 4: 93–97 (in Chinese).

Hu ZR (2003) The post-WTO restructuring of the Chinese media industries and the consequences of capitalisation. *The Public/Javnost* 10 (4): 19–36.

Hu ZR and Du X (2002) Governmental policies regulating the broadcasting media: from a comparative study. In: Yin, Hong and Li, Bin (eds.) *Globalization and the Mass Media: Clash, Convergence and Interaction (*全球化与大众传媒:冲突，融合与互动*)*. Beijing: Tsinghua University Press (北京: 清华大学出版社) (in Chinese).

Hu ZF, Wang K, Zhang X, Jin Y and Wang L (2008) Analysis of 2008's hot topics in television studies (2008年电视热点问题研究之分析). *Contemporary Cinema* (当代电影) 4: 40–48 (in Chinese).

Huang J, Wang B and Liu X (1996) IMI consumer behaviours and life patterns yearbook (Guangzhou Volume) IMI消费行为与生活形态年鉴(广州卷) [J] (in Chinese).

Huang SM and Ding JJ (1997) *Media Management and Study of Industrialization* (媒介经营与产业化研究). Beijing: Beijing Broadcasting Institute Press (北京: 北京广播学院出版社).

References 229

Huang SM and Wang LZ (eds.) (2003) *China TV report (2002–2003)* 中国数字电视报告 *(2002–2003)*. Beijing: Beijing Broadcasting Institute Press (北京: 北京广播学院出版社) (in Chinese).

Huang Y (2014) Transformation for state-owned Shanghai media. *China Daily*, 1 April. Available at: www.chinadaily.com.cn/business/2014-04/01/content_17394205.htm (accessed 15 December 2015).

Huang Y and Green A (2000) From Mao to the Millennium: 40 years of television in China (1958–98). In: French D and Richards M (eds.) *Television in Contemporary Asia*. New Delhi: Sage, 267–291.

Humphreys P (2010) Public policies for public service media: the UK and the German cases. Paper presented at the RIPE@2010 conference: Public Service Media After the Recession, 8–11 September. University of Westminster, London.

Huntington SP (1973). *Political Order in Changing Societies*. 7th edition. New Haven and London: Yale University Press, Chapter 1.

Hutzler C (2015) Despite slump, China's Xi Jinping pledges economic reforms. *The Wall Street Journal*, 22 September. Available at: www.wsj.com/articles/despite-slump-chinas-xi-pledges-economic-reforms-1442894460 (accessed 26 December 2015).

ICESCR (1976) *International Covenant on Economic, Social and Cultural Rights*. Available at: www.ohchr.org/EN/ProfessionalInterest/Pages/CESCR.aspx (accessed 14 January 2016).

Institute of Party Building of the Organization Department of the Central Committee of the Communist Party of China (2011) "The ABCs of the Communist Party of China" series – the present state structure and operation of party organizations. Available at: http://eg.china-embassy.org/eng/rdwt/P020110529735490640280.pdf (accessed 18 December 2015).

International Department of Central Committee of People's Republic of China (2008) China vows to press forward with economic reforms and opening-up. Available at: www.idcpc.org.cn/english/events/2008/201406/t20140617_2804.html (accessed 24 December 2015).

IOS (The Information Office of the State Council) (2009) *National Human Rights Action Plan of China* (2009–2010). Available at: http://news.xinhuanet.com/english/2009-04/13/content_11177126.htm (accessed 17 February 2011).

Jacques M (2005) The future is China's. *Guardian, G2*, 25 March, 6.

Jiang ZM (2002) Building a well-off society in an all-round way and create a new situation in building socialism with Chinese characteristics. Report delivered at the Opening of the Sixteenth CCP Congress, 8 November 2002. (全面建设小康社会，开创中国特色社会主义事业新局面——在中国共产党第十六次全国代表大会上的报告) Available at: http://news.xinhuanet.com/ziliao/2002-11/17/content_693542.htm (accessed 25 February 2016) (in Chinese).

John D, Zhao S, and Taffer A (2012) The China rising leaders project, Part 1: the Chinese Communist Party and its emerging next-generation leaders. *US–China Economic and Security Review Commission*.

Joseph F (2005) CCP launches campaign to maintain the advanced nature of party members. *China Leadership Monitor* 2005 (13): 1–10.

Keane M (2001) Broadcasting policy, creative compliance and the myth of civil society in China. *Media, Culture & Society* 23 (6): 783–798.

Kenis P and Schneider V (1991) Policy networks and policy analysis: scrutinizing a New analytical toolbox. In: Marin B and Mayntz R (eds.) *Policy Networks*. Frankfurt: Campus Verlag.

230 References

Kirst M and Jung R (1982) The utility of a longitudinal approach in assessing implementation. In: Williams W (ed.) *Studying Implementation*. Chatham, NJ: Chatham House, 119–148.

Kluver R (2005) US and Chinese policy expectations of the internet. *China Information* 19 (2): 299–324.

Kobayashi Y (2007) *The Impact of the World Trade Organization on the Chinese legal system. The Foundation of Law, Justice and Society in Collaboration with the Centre for Socio-legal Studies*. Oxford: University of Oxford.

Kroeber AR (2013) Xi Jinping's ambitious agenda for economic reform in China. Available at: www.brookings.edu/research/opinions/2013/11/17-xi-jinping-economic-agenda-kroeber#fn4 (accessed 26 December 2015).

Kwon S (2005) *Survival of the North Korean Regime and Changing Legitimation Modes*. The Mario Einaudi Center for International Studies Working Paper Series. Paper No. 07–05.

Kymlicka W and Norman W (1994) Return of the citizen: a survey of recent work on citizenship theory. *Ethics* 104: 352–381.

Lai HY, Wang ZX and Tok SK (2006) China's politics in 2006: harmony on the road to the Seventeenth Party Congress. Available at: www.nottingham.ac.uk/cpi/documents/briefings/briefing-17-china-politics-review-2006.pdf (accessed 24 December 2015).

Lampton D (2001) China's foreign and national security policy-making process. In: Lampton D (ed.) *The Making of Chinese Foreign and Security Policy in the Era of Reform*. Stanford: Stanford University Press, 1–38.

Lane RE (1979) Capitalist man, socialist man. In: Laslett P and Fishkin J (eds.) *Philosophy, Politics and Society*, 5th series. Oxford: Basil Blackwell, 57–77.

Lang J (2002) Analysis of the strategic model of China's media policy (中国媒体政策的策略模式研究). *Henan Social Science (河南社会科学)* 4: 94–97.

Lau TY, Feng GC, Atkin DJ and Lin CA (2008) Exploring the evolution of digital television in China. Paper presented at the Fifty-eighth Annual International Communication Association Annual Conference. Montreal, Canada, 22–26 May.

Law on Legislation (2000) Article 78 and 79. Promulgated by National People's Congress.

Lee CC (1980) *Media Imperialism Reconsidered: The Homogenizing of Television Culture*. Beverly Hills: Sage.

Lee CC (2000) State, capital, and media: the case of Taiwan. In: James Curran and Myung-Jin Park (eds.) *De-westernizing Media Studies*. London: Routledge.

Lee CC (2003) The global and the national of the Chinese media: discourses, market, technology, and ideology. In: Lee Chin-chuan (ed.) *Chinese Media, Global Context*. London: RoutledgeCurzon: 1–31.

Lee CC (2005) The conception of Chinese journalists: ideological convergence and contestation. In: de Burgh H. (ed.) *Making Journalists*. London: Routledge, 107–126.

Lee CC (2015) Local experiences, cosmopolitan theories: on cultural relevance in international communication research. In: Chin-Chuan Lee (ed.) *Internationalizing "International Communication"*. Ann Arbor: University of Michigan Press, 201–224.

Lee H (2010) Political institutionalization as political development in China. *Journal of Contemporary China* 19 (65): 559–571.

Lerner D (1958) *The Passing of Traditional Society: Modernising the Middle East*, 3rd printing. London: Collier-Macmillan Ltd

Levy T and Meyer D (2012) Challenges of network governance at the State Banks of China. *Journal of Contemporary China* 21 (75): 481–498.

References 231

Li DL (2015) My opinions on Press Law Legislation (新闻传播立法之我见). *Youth Journalist* (青年记者) 10: 15–16 (in Chinese).

Li KQ (2014) Report on the work of the government 2014. Available at: http://language.chinadaily.com.cn/news/2014-03/17/content_17350891.htm (accessed 26 December 2015).

Li LC (1998) *Centre and Provinces: China 1978–1993 Power as Non-zero-sum.* New York: Oxford University Press.

Li Q (2002) Modern state building in post-totalitarian state: the case of China. Paper presented at the conference *Modern State Structures in the Chinese World*, 10–12 May. London: The London School of Economic and Political Science.

Li RR (2003) Welcome to the website of the State-owned Assets Supervision and Administration Commission of the State Council (SASAC). Available at: http://en.sasac.gov.cn/n1461859/c1463753/content.html (accessed 15 December 2015).

Li S and Wei L (2011) Return to human orientation: route for China to secure human rights in the 21st century. *Human Rights* 10 (1): 17–20.

Li SM (2000) China's changing spatial disparities: a review of empirical evidence. In: Li SM and Tang WS (eds.) (2000) *China's Regions, Polity and Economy*. Hong Kong: The Chinese University of Hong Kong, 155–185.

Li TY (1995a) Speech given in the meeting with representatives of national broadcasting and film working conference. In: General Office of SARFT (2000) (ed.) *The Important Documents of Broadcasting and Film Work 1995* (广播影视工作重要文件汇编 1995). Beijing: SARFT, 252–260 (in Chinese).

Li TY (1995b) Speech given in the meeting with some staffs of CCTV. In: General Office of SARFT (2000) (ed.) *The Important Documents of Broadcasting and Film Work 1995* (广播影视工作重要文件汇编 1995). Beijing: SARFT, 261–264 (in Chinese).

Li W and Yan Z (2014). State-owned asset integration of Shanghai cultural sector (上海文化国资整合). *Shanghai State-owned Asset* (上海国资). 5: 031 (in Chinese).

Li X (2008) The paradox of western press freedom. In: Li B and Li M (eds.) *Expanded Reader of the Marxist Conception of the Media* (马克思主义新闻观拓展读本). Beijing: Tsinghua University Press (北京: 清华大学出版社), 7–10 (in Chinese).

Lian YM (ed.) (2002) *The Yellow Book of China's Figures* (中国数字黄皮书). Beijing: the China Contemporary Economic Publication House (北京: 中国时代经济出版社) (in Chinese).

Liang J and Yao C (2013) Communist Party of China in brief. *People's Daily Online*. Available at: http://english.cpc.people.com.cn/206972/206981/8188392.html (accessed 18 December 2015).

Liang LG (2002) The practice and explore of Guangdong's reform and opening up (广东改革开放的实践与探索). Available at: www.lmu.cn/sdh/llg/lw6.asp (accessed 4 January 2005) (in Chinese).

Liang P (2004) "Three representative" and broadcast television's "three attributes" ("三个代表"和广播电视的"三个属性"). *Guidebook for Decision Making* (决策参考) 2004 (3): 29–40 (in Chinese).

Lieberthal K (1997) Politics and economics in China. In: Canyon, AM (ed.) *Assessment of China into the 21st Century.* New York: Nova Science Publisher, 15–21.

Lieberthal K and Oksenberg M (1988) *Policy Making in China*, Princeton: Princeton University Press.

Lin AT (2010) Pilot programs on three network convergence failed, competition between different parties became fiercer (三网融合试点方案闯关失败 派系利益之争更趋尖锐). *IT Time Weekly* (IT时代周刊) 10: 52–53 (in Chinese).

232 *References*

Lin L (2015) China's reality shows must uphold 'socialist core values,' regulator says. *The Wall Street Journal*. Available at: http://blogs.wsj.com/chinarealtime/2015/07/23/chinas-reality-shows-must-uphold-socialist-core-values-regulator-says/ (accessed 5 August 2015).

Lin M (1999) *The Search for Modernity: Chinese Intellectuals and Cultural Discourse in the Post-Mao Era*. London: Macmillan.

Lin P (1990) Between theory and practice: the possibility of a right to free speech in the People's Republic of China. *Journal of Chinese Law*. 4: 257–276.

Lin QL (2014) Three major operators stripped away own signal resources and co-invested the new signal company (三大运营商合资成立铁塔公司 将剥离自身铁塔资源) *Beijing News*. Available at: http://finance.sina.com.cn/chanjing/cyxw/20140712/0230 19683415.shtml (accessed 23 November 2015) (in Chinese).

Linz JJ (1988) Legitimacy of democracy and socioeconomic system. In: Dogan M (ed.) *Comparing Pluralist Democracies: Strains on Legitimacy*. Boulder, Colorado: Westview Press, 65–113.

Lipset SM (1981) *Political Man: The Social Bases of Politics*. Baltimore: Johns Hopkins University Press.

Liu Binyan and Perry Link (1998) A Great Leap Backward?, *The New York Review of Books*. Available at: www.nybooks.com/articles/1998/10/08/a-great-leap-backward (accessed 12 January 2015).

Liu H (2003) Understanding the survival and development of the post-WTO broadcasters from Guangdong's practice. *South China Television Journal (南方电视学刊)*, 2003 (1): 23–26.

Liu S (2011) Structuration of information control in China. *Cultural Sociology* 5 (3): 323–39.

Liu XP and Xiao YF (2010) Changing of the radio and television industry under the separation of production and broadcasting (制播分离时代的广电产业变局). *Contemporary Literary Criticism* (当代文坛), 6: 147–149 (in Chinese).

Liu YL (2015) Reveal the picture of Li Ruigang's China Media Capital (揭秘黎瑞刚华人文化投资图谱). *Tencent Technology (腾讯科技)*. 20 July. Available at: http://tech.qq.com/a/20150720/004372.htm (accessed 15 December 2015) (in Chinese).

Lu D (2002) *The Crisis and a Change of China's TV Industry (中国电视产业的危机与转机)*. Beijing: Remin University Press (北京: 人民出版社) (in Chinese).

Lu D (2003) The decoding of China's television industry (中国电视产业大解码). *South China Television Journal (南方电视学刊)* 1: 11–27 (in Chinese).

Lu SG (2003) SMG signs up responsibility contract of fiscal assessment (SMG签署财政评估责任合同). *Culture, Radio, Film and TV (文化广播影视)*, 5 May, 1 (in Chinese).

Lu Y (1998) Controlled competition and coordinated development: a study of the reform model of Shanghai broadcasting industry (适度竞争、协调发展:上海广播电视改革模式探讨). *Journalism and Communication Study (新闻与传播研究)* 3 (in Chinese).

Lu Y (1999) *China's Broadcasting Industry development and challenges in the satellite age* (卫星时代中国大陆电视产业的发展与挑战). Taipei: Shin Ying Press. 台北:时英出版社.

Lubman S (1999) *Bird in a Cage: Legal Reform in China after Mao*. Stanford: Stanford University Press.

Luo W (2005) *Chinese Law and Legal Research*. Buffalo, New York: William S. Hein & Co.

Luo Y and Liu J (2006) The principles of public interest in journalism and communication (论新闻传播中的公共利益原则). *Journalism and Communication (新闻与传播研究)* 4: 14–16 (in Chinese).

References   233

Ma Eric Kit-wai (2000) Rethinking media studies: the case of China. In: Curran James and Park Myung-jin (eds.) *De-westernizing Media Studies*. London: Routledge, 21–34.

Ma K and Chao YS (eds.) (2002) *Transformation from Planned to Socialist Market Economic System (*计划经济体制向社会主义市场经济体制的转轨*)*. Beijing: People's Press (北京: 人民出版社) (in Chinese).

Mann M (2001) *State, Wars and Capitalism: Studies in Political Sociology*. Oxford: Blackwell.

Mao S (2009) Transformation and restructuring of China's cultural policy since reform. In: Li JY and Chen W (eds.) *Report on the Development of China's Public Cultural Service 2009 (*中国公共文化服务发展报告*2009)*. Beijing: Social Sciences Academic Press (北京: 社会科学文献出版社): 42–53 (in Chinese).

MCP (2005) No. 15 Measures for strengthening administration of cultural products Import (关于加强文化产品进口管理办法) (in Chinese).

McQuail D (1992) *Media Performance: Mass Communication and the Public Interest*. London: Sage.

McQuail D (2000) *McQuail's Mass Communication Theory*. 4th edition. Sage: London.

Mayfield A (2008) What is social media? iCrossing. Available at: www.icrossing.com/uk/ideas/fileadmin/uploads/ebooks/what_is_social_media_icrossing_ebook.pdf (accessed 13 January 2016).

Marshall TH (2009) Citizenship and social class. In: Manza J and Sauder M (eds.) *Inequality and Society*. New York: WW Norton and Co, 148–154.

Media (2001) China's broadcasting conglomeration reform before the WTO (加入WTO前中国广播影视的合并改革). *Media (*媒介*)* 2001(11): 1–21 (in Chinese).

Melkote SR (1991) *Communication for Development in the Third World: Theory and Practice*. London: Sage, 37–92.

MIIT and SARFT (2010) Questions and answers by MIIT and SARFT on three network convergence （工业和信息化部、国家广电总局有关负责人就推进三网融合相关工作答记者问）. *Cable Television Technology* (有线电视技术) 243: 1–2 (in Chinese).

MIIT and SARFT (2015) MIIT and SARFT's interpretation on *Three Network Convergence Promotion Plan* (工业和信息化部 新闻出版广电总局相关负责人解读《三网融合推广方案》). Available at: www.sarft.gov.cn/art/2015/9/22/art_113_28521.html (accessed 23 November 2015) (in Chinese).

Miller A (2008) China's new Party leadership. *China Leadership Monitor* 23: 1–10.

Ministry of Finance (1996) Ministry of Finance [1996] No. 469: Notice on Budget Management of Taxation on Cultural Institution Construction Fees (财政部关于开征文化事业建设费有关预算管理问题的通知). Normative document (in Chinese).

Minzner C (2013) What direction for legal reform under Xi Jinping. *The Jamestown Foundation*, 4 January. Available at: http://law.fordham.edu/28665.htm (accessed 11 March 2015).

Moore TG and Yang D (2001) Empowered and restrained. In: Lampton D (ed.) *The Making of Chinese Foreign and Security Policy in the Era of Reform*. Chicago, IL: Stanford University Press, 191–229.

Morgan B and Yeung K (2007) *An Introduction to Law and Regulation*. Cambridge: Cambridge University Press.

MRFT (1995) MRFT [1995] No. 757: Notice on issues regarding management of receiving foreign satellite television programmes. (广发社字[1995]757号: 关于接收境外卫星电视节目管理的有关问题的通知). Available at: www.chinalawedu.com/news/1200/22598/22619/22879/2006/3/cd148670951360021428-0.htm (accessed 12 January 2016) (in Chinese).

234 References

MRFT (1996) Several important problems and opinions about our country's present broadcasting development. *Guidebook for Decision Making (*决策参考*)* 1996 (10): 21–24 (in Chinese).

MRFT (1997a) To protect the systemic development of the broadcasting sector by law: the MRFT's official answers journalists' questions regarding to the release of *Regulations Governing the Administration of Radio and Television* (就《广播电视管理条例》的颁布施行广电部负责人答记者问). *Guidebook for Decision Making (*决策参考*)* 1997 (9): 6–8 (in Chinese).

MRFT (1997b) No. 76 Notice on further strengthening the administration of broadcasting advertisement (关于进一步加强广播电视广告宣传管理的通知) (in Chinese).

Mueller M (2004) *Ruling the Root: Internet Governance and the Taming of Cyber Space.* MIT: MIT Press.

Murdock G (2000) Money talks: broadcasting finance and public culture. In: Busombe E (ed.) *British Television: A Reader.* Oxford: Oxford University Press, 118–141.

Mustonen P (2009) *Social Media: A New Way to Success?* Turku: Turku School of Economics.

Nanfang Daily (南方日报) (2008) Guangdong's cable operators can insert advertisements into Hong Kong's television channels (广东有线在香港台插广告不违规). 15 July 2008, A09 (in Chinese).

Nash K (2009) Between citizenship and human rights. *Sociology* 43 (6): 1067–1083.

Nathan A (1989) *Chinese Democracy.* Berkeley: University of California Press.

Nathan A (2008) China's political trajectory: what are the Chinese saying? In: Cheng Li (ed.) *China's Changing Political Landscape.* Washington, USA: Brookings Institution Press, 25–43.

National Bureau of Statistics of China (2014) Statistical communiqué of the People's Republic of China on the 2013 National Economic and Social Development. Available at: www.stats.gov.cn/english/PressRelease/201402/t20140224_515103.html (accessed 23 November 2015).

National People's Congress (2004) The Constitution of the People's Republic of China. Available at: www.fdi.gov.cn/1800000121_39_1561_0_7.html (accessed 23 November 2015).

News of the Communist Party of China (n.d.) Main functions of Central Propaganda Department. Available at: http://cpc.people.com.cn/GB/64114/75332/5230610.html (accessed 23 November 2015).

Newscast of GDTV (24 August 2006) Available at: www.openv.com/play/GuangDongTV_20060824_51702_0.html (accessed: 18 January 2009).

Ngok K and Zhu G (2007) Marketization, globalization and administrative reform in China. *International Review of Administrative Sciences* 73 (2): 217–233.

Nie, J (2011): *Research of China's Media Self-regulation: Innovating Self-regulatory Mechanism of Beijing Association of Online Media* 《我国媒介自律模式研究:评北京网络媒体协会创新网络自律机制》, People's Tribune (《人民论坛》), 14: 220–221 (in Chinese).

NPC (1999) Article 14. In: Law of the People's Republic of China on Administrative Reconsideration. Adopted at the ninth Meeting of the Standing Committee of the Ninth National People's Congress on 29 April 1999 and promulgated by Order No. 16 of the President of the People's Republic of China on 29 April 1999. Available at: www.china.org.cn/china/LegislationsForm2001-2010/2011-02/14/content_21916122.htm (accessed 5 August 2015).

NPC (2003) Administrative License Law of the People's Republic of China (中华人民共和国行政许可法). Available at: www.lawinfochina.com/display.aspx?lib=law&id=3076&CGid= (accessed 28 August 2015) (in Chinese).

NPC (2004) Amendment to the Constitution of the People's Republic of China 中华人民共和国宪法修正案. (accessed 8 January 2016) (in Chinese).

NPC (2013) The Plan for State Council Restructuration and Function Transformation (国务院机构改革和职能转变方案). Available at: www.china.com.cn/news/2013lianghui/2013-03/14/content_28245220.htm (accessed 28 August 2015) (in Chinese).

Ollig S (2007) *Internationalization of the Chinese TV Sector,* Vol. 1. Münster: LIT Verlag.

Ong A (1997) Chinese modernities: narratives of nation and of capitalism. In: Ong A and Nonini DM (eds.) *Ungrounded Empires: The Cultural Politics of Modern Chinese Transnationalism.* London: Routledge, 171–202.

Orenstein D (2014) China's GDP growth has steep coastal costs. Available at: https://news.brown.edu/articles/2014/08/china (accessed 18 December 2015).

Oriental DreamWorks (2012) DreamWorks Animation looks east to establish leading China-focused family entertainment company. 17 February. Available at: www.oriental-dreamworks.com/dreamworks-animation-looks-east-establish-leading-china-focused-family-entertainment-company (accessed 15 December 2015).

Oriental DreamWorks (2015) About Oriental DreamWorks (关于东方梦工厂). Available at: www.oriental-dreamworks.com/zh/odw-guanyu-womende-dianying-zhizuoshi (accessed 15 December 2015) (in Chinese).

Osnos E (2013) Can China deliver the China dream(s)? *The New Yorker.* 26 March. Available at: www.newyorker.com/news/evan-osnos/can-china-deliver-the-china-dreams (accessed 26 December 2015).

Ou Nianzhong, Yu Ruijin, Zhang Zhongnan, Chen Huanxiang, and Yang Dejian (2006) *Globalization (*全球化*).* Guangzhou: Yangcheng Wanbao Press (广州: 羊城晚报) (in Chinese).

Pan W (2008) Superstition in democracy and direction of China's political reform. In: Li B and Li M (eds.) *Expanded Reader of the Marxist Conception of the Media (*马克思主义新闻观拓展读本*).* Beijing: Tsinghua University Press (北京: 清华大学出版社), 158–168 (in Chinese).

Peerenboom R (2001) *Let One Hundred Flowers Bloom, One Hundred Schools Contend: Debating Rule of Law in China.* University of California School of Law. Research Paper No. 02–14.

Peerenboom R (2002) *China's Long March Toward Rule of Law.* Cambridge: Cambridge University Press.

Peerenboom R (2006) A government of laws. In: Zhao S (ed.) *Debating Political Reform in China: Rule of Law vs. Democratization.* New York: Armonk.

Peerenboom R (2009) Middle income blues: East Asian model and implications for constitutional development in China. In: Balme S and Dowdle M (eds.) *Building Constitutionalism in China.* New York: Palgrave Macmillan, 77–98.

Peerenboom R (2014) Fly high the banner of socialist rule of law with Chinese characteristics! What Does the 4th Plenum decision mean for legal reforms in China? Available at SSRN: http://ssrn.com/abstract=2519917 or http://dx.doi.org/10.2139/ssrn.2519917 (accessed 11 March 2015).

Peng GB (2015) Foreign and domestic perspectives on Press Law Legislation (新闻传播立法的国外国内视角). Youth Journalist, 10: 26–27 (in Chinese).

236 References

Peng Z (1982) Report on the Draft of the Revised Constitution of the People's Republic of China. Report presented at the 5th meeting of the 5th National People's Congress in Beijing, 1982, 26 November.

People's Daily (2001) President Jiang Zemin meets Viacom Chairman. Available at: http://english.peopledaily.com.cn/english/200103/29/eng20010329_66365.html (accessed 17 September 2008).

People's Daily Online (2001) Li Langqing's letter to the national broadcasting and film working conference. 15 January. In: The Research office of CCTV (ed.) (2002) *CCTV Yearbook 2002 (*中国中央电视台年鉴*2002): 5–6 (in Chinese).

People's Daily Online (2002) CPC and state organs of the PRC. 7 February. Available at: http://english.people.com.cn/data/organs/home.html (accessed February 2002).

People's Daily Online (2004) The State Council. Available at: http://en.people.cn/data/organs/statecouncil.shtml (accessed 7 February 2004).

Perkins D (1997) Prospects for China's integration into the global economy. In: Canyon AM (ed.) *Assessment of China into the 21st Century*. New York: Nova Science Publisher, 49–58.

Perritt, Jr. Henry H and Clarke Randolph R (1998) Chinese economic development, rule of law, and the Internet. *Government Information Quarterly* 15 (4): 393–417.

Perry M (1984) Freedom of expression: an essay on theory and doctrine. *Northwestern University Law Review* 78 (5): 1137–1211.

Phillips T and Goodley S (2015) Xi Jinping plays down China's economic 'growing pains'. *Guardian*, 18 October. Available at: www.theguardian.com/world/2015/oct/18/xi-jinping-plays-down-chinas-economic-growing-pains (accessed 16 December 2015).

Phoenix (2000) *Phoenix Satellite Television Holdings Limited: Listing on the Growth Enterprise Market of The Stock Exchange of Hong Kong Limited*. Hong Kong: Phoenix.

Phoenix Net (2013) SARFT and GAPP merged to SAPPRFT. Available at: http://news.ifeng.com/mainland/special/2013lianghui/content-3/detail_2013_03/10/22931489_0.shtml (accessed 28 August 2015).

Pierson P (1993) When effect becomes cause. *World Politics* 45: 595–628.

Pitta A (2010) Using social media. *Journal of Consumer Marketing* 27 (5).

Potter B (2003) *The Chinese Legal System: Globalization and Local Legal Culture*. London: RoutledgeCurzon.

Prestinari P (1993) Structure of the European audiovisual sector. In: Pilati A (ed.) *Mind Media Industry in Europe*. London: John Libbey.

Price ME, Verhulst SG and Morgan L (2013) *Routledge Handbook of Media Law*. London: Routledge.

Qi Y (2006) Media's public nature and social responsibilities in a transitional society (社会转型期媒体的公共属性与社会责任). *China Radio and TV Academic Journal (*中国广播电视学刊*) 2006 (4): 20–21 (in Chinese).

Qian W (2002) *Politics, Market and Media: Research on the Institutional Transformation of China's Television (*政治,市场与电视制度-中国电视制度变迁史研究*). Zhengzhou: Henan People's Publishing House (郑州:河南人民出版社) (in Chinese).

Ranson S and Stewart J (1989) Citizenship and government: the challenge for management in the public domain. *Political Studies* 37 (1): 5–24.

Reed KM (2000) From the Great Firewall of China to the Berlin Firewall: the cost of content regulation on internet commerce. *Transnational Law* 13: 451.

Reeves G (1993). *Communication and the 'Third World'*. London and New York: Routledge.

Ren HJ (2011) New challenges of internet culture to political legitimacy (试论网络文化放大效应对政府合法性的新挑战). *Social Science Review (*社科纵横*)*, 11 (in Chinese).

Ren L and Ji G (2005) The term of public interest in law (论我国现行法律中的公共利益条款). *Journal of Nanhua University (social science edition)* (南华大学学报•社会科学版) 6 (1): 76–78 (in Chinese).

Ren Y (2005) On the two kinds of analytical approaches to policy networks and influences (政策网络的两种分析途径及其影响). *Chinese Journal of Public Management (*公共管理学报*)* 3: 55–60 (in Chinese).

Richard WS Wu and Grace LK Leung (2012) Implementation of three network convergence in China: a new institutional analysis. *Telecommunications Policy* 36 (10–11): 955–965.

Rogers E (1976) New perspective on communication and development: overview. In: Rogers E (ed.) *Communication and Development: Critical Perspectives.* London: Sage.

Ross L (2004) Rethinking government approvals: the New Administrative Licensing Law. *China Law and Practice*, Available at: www.chinalawandpractice.com/Article/1692779/Issue/8508/Rethinking-Government-Approvals-The-New-Administrative-Licensing-Law.html?ArticleId=1692779 (accessed 24 July 2015).

Sabatier PA (2007) The need for a better theory. In: Sabatier PA (ed.) *Theories of the Policy Process*, 2nd edition. Boulder, CO: Westview Press, 3–17.

SAIC (2007) No. 266 Notice on further rectification of illegal "sex medicine" and venereal disease treatment advertisements 关于进一步治理整顿非法"性药品" 广告和性病治疗广告的通知 (in Chinese).

Saich T (2001) *Governance and Politics of China.* New York: Palgrave.

SAPPRFT (2015a) SAPPRFT has introduced a series of regulatory documents leading legislative reform forward this year (新闻出版广电总局今年已出台一系列法规性文件以立法引领改革前进). Available at: www.gov.cn/xinwen/2015-03/12/content_2832729.htm (accessed 27 July 2015) (in Chinese).

SAPPRFT (2015b) The notice on strengthening management of the reality shows (总局发出《关于加强真人秀节目管理的通知》). Available at: www.sarft.gov.cn/art/2015/7/22/art_113_27532.html (accessed 5 August 2015) (in Chinese).

SAPPRFT (2015c) The notice on strengthening management of radio and television host and guests (国家新闻出版广电总局关于进一步加强广播电视 主持人和嘉宾使用管理的通知). Available at: www.sarft.gov.cn/art/2015/6/23/art_106_27265.html (accessed 5 August 2015) (in Chinese).

SAPPRFT (2015d) The structure of SAPPRFT (总局机构). Available at: www.sarft.gov.cn/col/col4/index.html (accessed 26 August 2015) (in Chinese).

SARFT (2001) The notice of state administration of radio, film and television (国家广播电影电视总局令). Available at: www.sarft.gov.cn/art/2001/5/22/art_1583_26277.html (accessed 24 July 2015) (in Chinese).

SARFT (2003a) Opinions on improving the broadcasting and film industry development (关于促进广播影视产业发展的意见). Available at: http://news.xinhuanet.com/newmedia/2004-02/20/content_1323651_2.htm (accessed 25 February 2016) (in Chinese).

SARFT (2003b) The summary of the broadcasting digital pay channel management meeting. Available at: www.sarft.gov.cn/manage/publishfile/35/1424.html (accessed 7 January 2004) (in Chinese).

SARFT (2004) Decree No. 39 of the SARFT: Administrative measures for the broadcast of audiovisual programs via the internet and other information networks (互联网等信息网络传播视听节目管理办法). Available at: www.sarft.gov.cn/art/2004/10/11/art_1583_26295.html (accessed 8 December 2014) (in Chinese).

238 *References*

SARFT (2004a) Regulation on production and management of radio and television programs (广播电视节目制作经营管理规定). Document No. 34 (国家广播电影电视总局令第34号). Available at: www.sarft.gov.cn/art/2004/8/20/art_1583_26290.html (accessed 15 December 2015) (in Chinese).

SARFT (2004b) Opinions on promoting the development of radio, film and television industry (关于促进广播影视产业的发展意见). Available at: www.china.com.cn/chinese/PI-c/495655.htm (accessed 15 December 2015) (in Chinese).

SARFT (2005) National radio, film and television working conference held in Hainan Bo'ao (全国广播影视工作会议在海南博鳌召开). *Guidebook for Decision Making (决策参考)* 2005 (1): 3–4 and 39 (in Chinese).

SARFT (2007a) Institution Table of Central Broadcasting Bureau (中央广播事业局机构简表). Available at: www1.sarft.gov.cn/articles/2007/09/02/20070908231035250793.html (accessed 17 July 2014) (in Chinese).

SARFT (2007b) The development of broadcasting and film institution (广播影视机构沿革). Available at: www.sarft.gov.cn/art/2015/6/2/art_7_711.html (accessed 14 August 2014) (in Chinese).

SARFT (2007c) Briefing on the progress of national cable TV's digitalization (全国有线电视数字化进展的情况通报). *Guidebook for Decision Making (决策参考)* 2007(4): 33–37 and 40 (in Chinese).

SARFT (2007d) Research report on the reform of Guangdong's Southern Media Group (广东南方报业传媒集团改革研究报告). *Guidebook for Decision Making (决策参考)* 2007(1): 34–38 (in Chinese).

SARFT (2008a) No. 63 Notice on 2008 Broadcasting Reform (广电总局办公厅关于印发《2008年广播影视改革工作要点》的通知). General Office, SARFT (in Chinese).

SARFT (2008b) Notice on strict prohibition of advertisement insertion during program transmission by cable television network operators (广电总局严禁有线电视网络机构在转播中插播广告) (in Chinese).

SARFT (2010a) Notice on work plan of strengthening rule of law government (广电总局关于加强法治政府建设的工作规划) Available at: www.sarft.gov.cn/art/2010/11/25/art_113_5338.html (accessed 27 July 2015) (in Chinese).

SARFT (2010b) SARFT's notice on publication of effective radio, film and television department rules and normative documents (广电总局关于公布继续有效的广播影视部门规章和规范性文件目录的通知). Available at: www.sarft.gov.cn/art/2010/11/17/art_113_5343.html (accessed 29 July 2015) (in Chinese).

SARFT (2015e) Opinions on earnestly implementing the separation of broadcasting and production (广电总局关于认真做好广播电视制播分离改革的意见). Available at: www.ytwgx.gov.cn/gbys/201508/t20150824_351873.htm (accessed 15 December 2015) (in Chinese).

SARFT and MII (2007) The Administrative Provisions on Internet Audio-Visual Program Service (《互联网视听节目服务管理规定》第56号) Available at: www.sarft.gov.cn/art/2007/12/29/art_1583_26307.html (accessed 27 July 2015) (in Chinese).

SARFT and Ministry of Finance (2014) China Broadcasting Television Network Limited Charter. 《中国广播电视网络有限公司章程》 Available at: http://wzb.mof.gov.cn/pdlb/gzdt/201404/t20140409_1065496.html (accessed 23 November 2015) (in Chinese).

SARFT Decree No. 8 (2001) Provisional measures for the administration of examination and approval of the landing of overseas satellite television channel (境外卫星电视频道落地审批管理暂行办法) (in Chinese).

SARFT Decree No. 17 (2003) Provisional measures for the administration of television and radio advertisement broadcasting (广播电视广告播放管理暂行办法) (in Chinese).

References   239

SARFT Decree No. 22 and No. 27 (2003 and 2004) Measures for the administration of landing of overseas satellite television channel (境外卫星电视频道落地管理办法) (in Chinese).

Sarti I (1981) Communication and cultural dependency: a misconception. In: McAnany EG, Schnitman J and Janus N (eds.) *Communication and Social Structure: Critical Studies in Mass Media Research*. New York: Praeger Publishers, 317–334.

Scannell P (2000) Public Service Broadcasting: the history of a concept. In: Buscombe E (ed.) *British Television: A Reader*. London: Clarendon Press, 45–62.

Schiller H (1970) *Mass Communications and American Empire*. New York: Augustus M. Kelley Publishers.

Science and Technology Division of SARFT (2004) The nation starts to promote integral transformation of cable TV from analogue to digital (我国开始全面推进有线电视从模拟向数字整体转换). *Guidebook for Decision Making (决策参考)* (2004) 5: 36–41 (in Chinese).

Shanghai Daily (2015) SMG president resigns to focus on PE investment. 6 January. Available at: http://china.org.cn/business/2015-01/06/content_34486003.htm (accessed 15 December 2015).

Shen H (2013) Sun Xupei: China missed the best time of introducing press law (孙旭培（上）:中国错过了新闻法出台的最佳时机). *New York Times Chinese*. Available at: http://cn.nytimes.com/china/20130628/cc28pressfreedom/ (accessed 6 August 2015) (in Chinese).

Shen HG (2015) Interpretation of the debates on 2015 Press Law Legislation (2015的中國新聞立法之爭解讀), *Media Digest* (4). Available: http://app3.rthk.hk/mediadigest/media/pdf/pdf_1427862758.pdf (accessed 10 December 2015) (in Chinese).

Shen K (2003) Is it the beginning of the era of the rule of the Constitution? Reinterpreting China's first constitutional case. *Pacific Rim Law and Policy* 12: 199.

Shen L (1998) To follow the conglomerate management road, and reach the new high of industry development: an interview with Ye, Zhikang, the head of Shanghai Broadcasting and Film Bureau (访上海文化广播影视集团总裁叶志康). *Shanghai Broadcasting Studies (上海广播电视学刊)* 1: 9–13 (in Chinese).

Shen L (2004) International cooperation and change of mass communication in China. In: *Transnational Media Corporations and National Media Systems: China after entry into the World Trade Organisation Conference*, The Bellagio Study and Conference Centre, Rockefeller Foundation, Italy, 17–21 May 2004.

Shen MC (2002) The "scale" and "diversity" of advertising management: an interview with Shen mingchang, the director of SMG's advertising center (访上海文广新闻传媒集团广告经营中心主任沈明昌). *Media (媒介)*, June, 50–53 (in Chinese).

Shi CS and Zhang JH (2007) *Public Service Broadcaster (公共电视)*. Wuhan, China: Wuhan University Press (武汉大学出版社) (in Chinese).

Shi CS and Zhuo L (2006) The public cultural service demand of public service television (公共电视的公共文化服务诉求). *China Radio and TV Academic Journal (中国广播电视学刊)* 2006 (12): 14–15 (in Chinese).

Shi L (2008) Expand the scope of citizens' right to bring an administrative suit (扩大公民提起行政诉讼的权利范围). *Legal System and Society (法制与社会)* 8: 34–36 (in Chinese).

Shue V (2004) Legitimacy crisis in China? In: Gries PH and Rosen S (eds.) *State and Society in 21st-century China*. London: RoutledgeCurzon, 24–49.

Sina News (2008) SARFT established a national radio and television. Available at: http://comment4.news.sina.com.cn/comment/skin/default.html?channel%20=gn&n%20ewsid=1-1-15323399&style=0 (accessed 4 September 2008).

240 References

Skocpol T (1979) *States and Revolutions: A Comparative Analysis of France, Russia, and China*. Cambridge: Cambridge University Press.

SMEG 2002 job summary and 2003 job arrangement (2003) SMEG2002年工作总结暨2003年工作安排. *Culture, Radio, Film and TV (文化广播影视)*, 20 January, 1–4 (in Chinese).

SMG (2015) Introduction of SMG (SMG简介). Available at: www.smg.cn/review/201406/0163874.shtml (accessed 15 December 2015) (in Chinese).

SMG's 2001 Year Report and 2002 Work Plan (2002). SMG2001年工作报告暨2002年工作计划). *Culture, Radio, Film and TV (文化广播影视)*, 28 February, 1–3 (in Chinese).

SohuNews (2008) Wang Huning: from young scholar to top think-tanker (王沪宁：青年学者到高层智囊). Available at: http://news.sohu.com/20081024/n260235669.shtml (accessed 9 February 2011) (in Chinese).

Song XW (1999) Why the illegal advertisement insertion can not be stopped? (违规插播广告为啥屡禁不止?) *China Business Monthly (中国经贸)* 1999 (10): 28–29 (in Chinese).

Sparks CS (1995) The future of public service broadcasting in Britain. *Critical Studies in Media Communication* 12 (3): 325–341

Sparks C (2004) The global, the local and the public sphere. In: Allen RC and Hill A (eds.) *Television Studies Reader*. London: Routledge, 139–150.

Sparks C (2008) Media systems in transition: Poland, Russia, China. *Chinese Journal of Communication* 1 (1): 7–24.

Sparks C with Reading A (1998) *Communism, Capitalism and the Mass Media*. London: Sage.

STAR (2001) STAR granted landing rights for a new channel in China. Available at: www.highbeam.com/doc/1G1-82472163.html (accessed 25 February 2016).

State Commission for Public Sector Reform (2015) Notice of State Commission for Public Sector Reform about Adjusting Relevant Responsibilities and Organizational Structures of MIIT (中央编办关于工业和信息化部 有关职责和机构调整的通知). Available at: www.miit.gov.cn/n11293472/n1459606/n11459642/11459720.html (accessed 23 November 2015) (in Chinese).

State Council (1991) Decree No. 31: Ministry of Culture report on views concerning several cultural institution economic policies. Normative document (国务院批转文化部关于文化事业若干经济政策意见报告的通知) (in Chinese).

State Council (1993) Decree No. 129 of State Council: Management and regulations on the ground receiving facilities of satellite television and broadcasting (国务院令第129号：《卫星电视广播地面接收设施管理规定》). Available at: www.gov.cn/fwxx/bw/gjgbdydszj/content_2262992.htm (accessed 12 January 2016) (in Chinese).

State Council (1994) Circular on the issuance of the MRFT's function, organization and the staff allocation (国务院办公厅关于印发广播电影电视部职能配置、内设机构和人员编制方案的通知). Available at: www.gov.cn/zhengce/content/2010-11/15/content_7856.htm (accessed 28 August 2015) (in Chinese).

State Council (1996) No. 37: Several rules on improving economic policy in culture (国务院关于进一步完善文化经济政策的若干规定) (in Chinese).

State Council (1997) Decree No. 228 of State Council: Broadcasting administrative regulation (国务院令228号：《广播电视管理条例》). Adopted at the 61st Executive Meeting of the State Council on 1 August 1997, and promulgated by Decree No. 228 of the State Council of the People's Republic of China on 11 August 1997. Available at: www.sarft.gov.cn/art/2003/10/21/art_1602_26263.html (accessed 17 July 2014) (in Chinese).

References 241

State Council (1998a) Circular on the issuance of the SARFT's function, organization and the staffing (国务院办公厅关于印发广播电影电视部职能配置、内设机构和人员编制方案的通知). Available at: www.gov.cn/zhengce/content/2010-11/18/content_7733.htm (accessed 28 August 2015) (in Chinese).

State Council (1998b) State Council [1998] 92: Regulations on SARFT's function disposition of internal organizations and personnel. (国办发[1998]92号: 国家广播电影电视总局职能配置内设机构和人员编制规定). Available at: www.gov.cn/zhengce/content/2010-11/18/content_7733.htm (accessed 23 November 2015) (in Chinese).

State Council (2001) Outline of cultural development programs during the national 'Tenth Five-Year Plan' (国家"十一五"时期文化发展规划纲要) (in Chinese).

State Council (2002) State Council [2002] No. 7: Guiding opinions on further strengthening grassroots cultural construction (关于进一步加强基层文化建设指导意见的通知) (in Chinese).

State Council (2005) State Council [2005] No. 10: Several regulations on non-public capital's entrance into the cultural industry (关于非公有资本进入文化产业的若干规定). Available at: www.gov.cn/gongbao/content/2005/content_64188.htm (accessed 15 December 2015) (in Chinese).

State Council (2006) State Council [2006] No. 79: Notice concerning improved success in the new era of broadcast television connected village work (国务院办公厅关于进一步做好 新时期广播电视村村通工作的通知) (in Chinese).

State Council (2008) Several policies on encouraging the development of cable TV industry (关于鼓励数字电视产业发展的若干政策). *Guidebook for Decision Making (*决策参考) 2008(3): 57–59 (in Chinese).

State Council (2009) State Council [2009] No. 26: State Council forwarded the notice issued by the National Development and Reform Commission on deepening the reform of economic system. (国发[2009]26号: 国务院批转发展改革委关于2009年深化经济体制改革工作意见的通知). Available at: www.gov.cn/zwgk/2009-05/25/content_1323641.htm (accessed 23 November 2015) (in Chinese).

State Council (2010a) State Council [2010] No. 5: State Council's Notice on "Overall Plan for Promoting Three Network Convergence" (国发[2010]5号: 国务院关于印发《推进三网融合总体方案》的通知) (in Chinese).

State Council (2010b) Notice of the Three Network Convergence Coordination Group Office under the State Council on Printing and Distributing the "Notice on Issues Concerning the Pilot Program for Convergence of Three Networks" (国务院三网融合工作协调小组办公室印发《关于三网融合试点工作有关问题的通知》) (in Chinese).

State Council (2012) State Council [2012] No. 184: State Council's reply on establishing China Broadcasting Television Network Limited (国函[2012]184号:《国务院关于组建中国广播电视网络有限公司有关问题的批复》) (in Chinese).

State Council (2013a) Scheme of institutional reform and function transformation of the State Council (《国务院机构改革和职能转变方案》). Available at: www.gov.cn/2013lh/content_2354443.htm (accessed 1 September 2014) (in Chinese).

State Council (2013b) Notice of the General Office of the State Council on dividing the tasks for implementation of the Plan for Institutional Reform and Functional Transformation of the State Council (国办关于实施《国务院机构改革和职能转变方案》任务分工的通知). Available at: http://news.xinhuanet.com/politics/2013-03/28/c_115200485.htm (accessed 17 July 2014) (in Chinese).

State Council (2013c) State Council [2013] No. 76: State Council on the issuance of notice on SAPPRFT's main functions, internal bodies and staffing. (国办发[2013]76号: 国务院办公厅关于印发国家新闻出版广电总局主要职责内设机构和人员编制规定的

242 *References*

通知). Available at: www.gov.cn/zwgk/2013-07/17/content_2449645.htm (accessed 24 August 2015) (in Chinese).

State Council (2014) Administrative regulations (行政法规). Available at: www.sarft. gov.cn/col/col1602/index.html (accessed 8 December 2014) (in Chinese).

State Council (2015) *Three Network Convergence Promotion Plan* (《三网融合推广方案》) Available at: www.gov.cn/zhengce/content/2015-09/04/content_10135.htm (accessed 23 November 2015) (in Chinese).

STS (2007) *The Southern Television Station.* Report presented at the National Forum of Presidents of Television Station 2007 (2007年全国电视台台长论坛), Beijing, China, 17–18 May 2008 (in Chinese).

Sun JZ (1995) Report given in the national broadcasting and film working conference (孙家正在全国广播电影电视工作会议闭幕式上的讲话). In: General Office of SARFT (2000) (ed.) *The Important Documents of Broadcasting and Film Work 1995* (广播影视工作重要文件汇编1995). Beijing: SARFT, 265–290 (in Chinese).

Sun JZ (1998) Report given in the national conference of chiefs of broadcasting bureaus (孙家正在全国广播电视(影视)厅(局)长会议上的报告). In: General Office of SARFT (2000) (ed.) *The Important Documents of Broadcasting and Film Work 1998* (广播影视工作重要文件汇编1998). Beijing: SARFT, 185–208 (in Chinese).

Supreme People's Court of China (2011) Supreme Court's interpretation on several issues regarding specific law application on hearing of criminal cases about destroying radio and television facilities and others《最高人民法院关于审理破坏广播电视设施等刑事案件具体应用法律若干问题的解释》(《刑法》第124条司法解释). *Baidu BaiKe.* Available at: http://baike.baidu.com/view/8437295.htm (accessed 31 July 2015) (in Chinese).

Sweet AS, Sandholtz W and Fligstein N (eds.) (2001) *The Institutionalization of Europe.* Oxford: Oxford University Press.

Swift A (2004) *Political Philosophy.* Cambridge: Polity.

Tamanaha BZ (2004) *On the Rule of Law: History, Politics, Theory.* Cambridge: Cambridge University Press.

Tang HF (2004) Policy network and policy consequence – the analysis of the changing allocation pattern in the rural taxation (政策网络与政策后果:中国的运用–对农村税费改革中利益分配关系变化的分析). *The Journal of CCP Zhejiang Provincial Party School* (中共浙江省委党校学报) 1: 31–36 (in Chinese).

Tang WS, Li SM and Kwok RYW (2000) Space, place and region and the study of contemporary China. In: Li SM and Tang WS (eds.) (2000) *China's Regions, Polity and Economy.* Hong Kong: The Chinese University of Hong Kong, 3–31.

Tanner MS and Green E (2007) Principals and secret agents. *China Quarterly* 191: 644–670.

Tian CM (1998) Speech given in the meeting with provincial radio and TV stations' chiefs (田聪明在省级电台电视台长会议上的讲话). In: General Office of SARFT (2000) (ed.) *The Important Documents of Broadcasting and Film Work 1998* (广播影视工作重要文件汇编1998). Beijing: SARFT, 244–250 (in Chinese).

Tian CM (2006) The inevitability of administration according to law (依法行政是必然趋势). *Guidebook for Decision Making* (决策参考) 2006 (3): 27–31 (in Chinese).

Tian J (2007) Speech given at the audiovisual meeting of national broadcasting system's rectification of unhealthy advertisement (田进在全国广播影视传媒机构和网络视听节目管理工作会议上的讲话). Available at: www.sarft.gov.cn/articles/2007/09/28/20 080205165058960769.html (accessed 11 December 2008) (in Chinese).

References 243

Tian J (2011) Deputy director of SARFT – Tian Jin's speech at China Content Broadcasting Network 2011 Theme Conference (国家广电总局副局长田进先生在CCBN2011主题报告会上讲话). *Radio and Television Information* 2011(4): 10–13 (in Chinese).

Tong G (2014) Conclusion speech at the 2014 National Radio, Film and TV Legal Work Training Class (在2014年全国广播影视法制工作骨干培训班上的总结讲话). Available at: www.sarft.gov.cn/art/2014/7/31/art_62_26110.html (accessed 27 July 2015) (in Chinese).

Tong ZW (2001) Some issues in judicial application of the Constitution (宪法司法适用研究中的几个问题). *Legal Science Monthly (法学)* 11: 4 (in Chinese).

The bureau hold a meeting to study, promote and execute the spirit of the fifteenth national congress (1997). 上海文化广播影视管理局组织会议学习、推进和贯彻十五大精神. *Radio, Film and TV (文化广播影视)*, 1 December, (in Chinese).

The Decision (2014). *The CCP Central Committee Decision Concerning Some Major Questions in Comprehensively Promoting Governing the Country According to Law.* Available at: www.gov.cn/xinwen/2014-10/28/content_2771714.htm (Chinese Version), https://chinacopyrightandmedia.wordpress.com/2014/10/28/ccp-central-committee-decision-concerning-some-major-questions-in-comprehensively-moving-governing-the-country-according-to-the-law-forward/ (accessed 9 March 2015) (English translation).

The Economist (2013a) Chasing the Chinese dream. 4 May. Available at: www.economist.com/news/briefing/21577063-chinas-new-leader-has-been-quick-consolidate-his-power-what-does-he-now-want-his (accessed 26 December 2015).

The Economist (2013b) Xi Jinping and the Chinese dream. 2 May. Available at: www.economist.com/news/leaders/21577070-vision-chinas-new-president-should-serve-his-people-not-nationalist-state-xi-jinping (accessed 26 December 2015).

The Establishment of Shanghai Culture, Radio, Film and TV Administrative Bureau (2000) 成立上海市文化广播影视管理局. *Radio, Film and TV* (文化广播影视), 25 April, 1 (in Chinese).

The Guardian (2003) Breakdown means no end in sight to Doha round. Larry Elliott and Charlotte Denny. 16 September. Available www.theguardian.com/world/2003/sep/16/politics.business (accessed 3 June 2010).

The Guardian (2015) The Guardian view on China under Xi Jinping: it prefers control to reform. *Guardian Editorial*. 10 August. Available at: www.theguardian.com/comment-isfree/2015/aug/10/the-guardian-view-on-china-under-xi-jinping-it-prefers-control-to-reform (accessed 26 December 2015).

The reply to the establishment of Shanghai Media & Entertainment Group (2001). 就成立上海文化广播影视集团的答复. *Culture, Radio, Film and TV* (文化广播影视), 15 May, 1 (in Chinese).

The Walt Disney Company (2014) The Walt Disney Company and Shanghai Media Group expand strategic entertainment alliance in China. 21 November. Available at: www.prnewswire.com/news-releases/the-walt-disney-company-shanghai-media-group-expand-strategic-entertainment-alliance-in-china-283447091.html (accessed 15 December 2015).

The World Bank (2015) Data: GDP growth. Available at: http://data.worldbank.org/indicator/NY.GDP.MKTP.KD.ZG?page=1 (accessed 24 December 2015).

The Yearbook of Guangdong (2007) Guangdong: Guangdong Yearbook publisher (广东:广东年鉴出版社) (in Chinese).

Thussu DK (2000) *International Communication.* London, Arnold.

TMT (2014) Official start of the merge of "small SMG" and "big SMG", and the concentration of power by Li Ruigang (大小文广合并正式启动，黎瑞刚集权). Available at:

244 References

http://tech.sina.com.cn/zl/post/detail/i/2014-03-31/pid_8445768.htm (accessed 15 December 2015) (in Chinese).

Tomlinson J (1997) Cultural globalization and cultural imperialism. In: Mohammadi A (ed.) *International Communication and Globalization*. London: Sage, 170–190.

Tomlinson J (1999) *Globalization and Culture*. Oxford, Polity.

Tracey M (1998) *The Decline and Fall of Public Service Broadcasting*. Oxford, Oxford University Press.

Tsang S (2009) Consultative Leninism: China's new political framework. *Journal of Contemporary China* 18 (62): 874.

Tylecote A and Cai J (2004) China's SOE reform and technological change: a corporate governance perspective. *Asian Business and Management* 3 (1): 57–84.

Tzifakis N (2011) *International Politics in Times of Change*. Berlin: Springer-Verlag Berlin Heidelberg Publisher.

Van Cuilenburg, Jan and McQuail, Denis (1998) Media policy paradigm shifts: in search of a new communication policy paradigm. In: Picard Robert G (ed.) *Evolving Media Markets: Effects of Economic and Policy Changes*. Finland: The Economic Research Foundation for Mass Communication, 57–80.

Walker R and Duncan S (2007) Policy evaluation. In: Bochel H and Duncan S (eds.) *Making Policy in Theory and Practice*. Bristol: The Policy Press, 169–187.

Wan Y, Ding N and Nan Y (2015) Interviews with Zhanjiang, Sun Xupeo: press law is expected to submit for consideration. (专访展江、孙旭培:新闻法有望提交审议). Available at: www.21ccom.net/articles/china/ggzl/20150310121967_all.html (accessed 26 December 2015) (in Chinese).

Wang F (1993) Speech given at the Nationwide Meeting of Heads of The Provincial and Municipal Television Stations (全国省市级电视台台长会议上的讲话). *Television Research* (电视研究) 2 (45): 8 (in Chinese).

Wang H (2008) The depoliticalisation of politics and the public nature of mass media. In: Li B and Li M (eds.) *Expanded Reader of the Marxist Conception of the Media* (马克思主义新闻观拓展读本). Beijing: Tsinghua University Press (北京: 清华大学出版社) (in Chinese), 11–39.

Wang H and Fu SM (2002) *WTO and China's Administrative Rule of Law Development* (WTO与中国行政法治建设). Beijing: Party School of CCP's Central Committee Press (北京: 中共中央党校出版社) (in Chinese).

Wang J, Lang JS and Deng WQ (2008) *Media Policy and Regulation* (传媒政策与法规). Beijing: China Broadcasting Publishing House (北京: 中国广播电视出版社) (in Chinese).

Wang JT (1998) Understanding the organisational reform from the relations between bureaus and stations (从局台关系理解机构改革). *Guidebook for Decision Making* (决策参考) 1998 (11): 17–21 (in Chinese).

Wang K (2003) New ideas of broadcasting development amid liberalisation of the Sky (自由化之下对于广播影视发展的新思考). *South China Television Journal* (南方电视学刊) 2003 (1): 19–22 (in Chinese).

Wang K (2014) *A Written Constitution without Functioning Constitutionalism – Analysis of Xi Jinping's 2012 Speech on Chinese Constitution, Coalition for Peace and Ethics*. Working Papers, No. 2/21.

Wang KM and Feng LY (2008) *Systematic Reformation of China's Broadcasting Industry—A New Model from Southern China* (中国广电体制改革——南方模式). Guangzhou: Guangdong Renmin Press (广州: 广东人民出版社) (in Chinese).

Wang S (2003) The problem of state weakness. *Journal of Democracy* 14 (1): 36–42.

Wang S (2015) Xi Jinping acts as the leader of four groups among over 22 central leading groups (中央领导小组逾22个 习近平任4小组组长). *The Beijing News (新京报)*, 31 July. Available at: http://news.china.com.cn/2015-07/31/content_36190622.htm (accessed 26 December 2015) (in Chinese).

Wang Sirui (1999) Today's neo-conservatism in China. *Beijing Literature* 1999 (3). Available at: www.bjsjs.net/news/news.php?intNewsId=69 (accessed 9 July 2005) (in Chinese).

Wang Y (2003) *Management and Administration of Media Group (*媒介集团经营与管理*)*. Huhehaote: Neimenggu University Press (呼和浩特: 内蒙古大学出版社) (in Chinese).

Wang YC (1999) The radicalism, conservatism and liberalism in 1990s' China (中国90年代的激进主义、保守主义和自由主义). Available at: www.literature.org.cn/Article.aspx?id=13837 (accessed 26 February 2016) (in Chinese).

Wang Z (2014) The Chinese dream: concept and context. *Journal of Chinese Political Science* 19 (1): 1–13.

Warner Bros. (2014) Shanghai Media Group and CMC Capital join forces with Warner Bros. Entertainment, RatPac Entertainment and WPP and plan to create global content investment fund. 14 October. Available at: www.warnerbros.com/studio/news/shanghai-media-group-and-cmc-capital-join-forces-warner-bros-entertainment-ratpac (accessed 15 December 2015).

Wasserstrom J (2015) Here's why Xi Jinping's 'Chinese Dream' differs radically from the American Dream. *Time Magazine*, 19 October. Available at: http://time.com/4077693/chinese-dream-xi-jinping/ (accessed 26 December 2015).

Weber I (2002) Reconfiguring Chinese propaganda and control modalities: a case study of Shanghai's television system. *Journal of Contemporary China* 11 (30): 53–75.

Weber I (2003) Localizing the global. *Gazette* 65 (3): 273–290.

Wei F (2014) Supervision of law enforcement should be a mainline for journalism and publishing legal work – interview with the SARPPFT deputy head Yan Xiaohong (执法监督应成新闻出版法制工作主线——访国家新闻出版广电总局副局长、国家版权局副局长阁晓宏). Available at: www.gapp.gov.cn/zt (accessed 31 July 2015) (in Chinese).

Wei P (2010) Discussion on the duplication of functions and multiple regulatory agencies between MIIT and SARFT – from the perspective of three network convergence (由工信部和广电总局的职能交叉和多头监管谈起——以三网融合与通信体制改革为视角). *Legal System and Society* 10 (1): 171–172 (in Chinese).

Wei R (2000) China's television in the era of marketisation. In: David F and Michael R (eds.) *Television in contemporary Asia*. New Delhi: Sage, 325–346.

Wei ZD and Chan JM (2000) Building a market-based party organ: television and national integration in China. In: David F and Michale R (eds.) *Television in Contemporary Asia*. New Delhi, Thousand Oaks and London: Sage, 233–263.

Wen JB (2006) Report on the work of the government (2006年国务院政府工作报告). Available at: www.gov.cn/test/2009-03/16/content_1260216.htm (accessed 24 December 2015) (in Chinese).

Wen JB (2007) Report on the work of the government (2007年国务院政府工作报告). Available at: www.gov.cn/test/2009-03/16/content_1260188.htm (accessed 24 December 2015) (in Chinese).

Wen YZ (2015) Three questions of press law legislation: does the boundary of communication already exist? (新闻立法三问:可否传播的界限不是已经有了吗). Available at: http://weiyongzheng.com/archives/33341.html (accessed 26 December 2015) (in Chinese).

246 References

Wieten J, Murdock G and Dahlgren P (eds.) (2000) *Television Across Europe: A Comparative Introduction*. London: Sage.

Williams, R. (1983). *Culture and Society, 1780–1950*. New York: Columbia University Press.

Wordometers (2015) China population. Available at: www.worldometers.info/world-population/china-population/ (accessed 18 December 2015).

WTO (2001) Report of the working party on the accession of CHINA. The World Trade Organization Website. Available at: http://preview.www.moftec.gov.cn/article/200207/20020700032358_1.xml (accessed 25 September 2002).

Wu B (2002) Economic transition and social transformation in the late 20th century China (二十世纪末中国的经济转轨和社会转型). *21st Century Bimonthly (21世纪双月刊)* 72: 4–22 (in Chinese).

Wu GG (2000) One head, many mouths: diversifying press structures in reform China. In: Lee CC (ed.) *Power, Money and Media: Communication Patterns and Bureaucratic Control in Cultural China*. Evanston, Illinois: Northwestern University Press, 45–67.

Wu GZ (2007) To prevent the corruption from its sources, and accelerate the construction of clean Party and battle on anti-corruption (拓展从源头上防治腐败工作领域, 深入推进党风廉政建设和反腐败斗争). *People's Daily*, 8 January, Beijing (in Chinese).

Wu LC and Wang Q (2015) Study on the insurance scope of national basic public cultural service directed by cultural rights (文化权利导向的国家基本公共文化服务保障范围研究). *China Social Science Network*. Available at: http://ex.cssn.cn/zzx/xsdj_zzx/wlc/201511/t20151103_2556706.shtml (accessed 23 November 2015) (in Chinese).

Wu RWS and Leung GLK (2012): A new institutional analysis. *Telecommunications Policy* 36 (10–11): 955–965.

Wu WP (1999) City profile Shanghai. *Cities* 16 (3): 207–216.

Xi JP (2012) Speech at a Congress marking the 30th anniversary of the current version of the Constitution (习近平在首都各界纪念现行宪法公布施行30周年大会上的讲话). Available at: http://cpc.people.com.cn/n/2012/1205/c64094-19793598.html (accessed 11 March 2015) (in Chinese).

Xi JP (2013a) An explanation of the Chinese Communist Party Central Committee *Decision on Several Major Questions About Deepening Reform* (习近平:关于《中共中央关于全面深化改革若干重大问题的决定》的说明). Available at: http://news.xinhuanet.com/politics/2013-11/15/c_118164294.htm (accessed 26 December 2015) (in Chinese).

Xi JP (2013b) General Secretary Xi Jinping's fifteen speeches systematically elaborate the Chinese Dream (习近平总书记15篇讲话系统阐述"中国梦"). Available at: http://theory.people.com.cn/n/2013/0619/c40531-21891787.html (accessed 26 December 2015) (in Chinese).

Xi JP (2014) Explanation on The CCP Central Committee *Decision Concerning Some Major Questions in Comprehensively Promoting Governing the Country According to Law* (关于《中共中央关于全面推进依法治国若干重大问题的决定》的说明). Available at: www.gov.cn/xinwen/2014-10/28/content_2771717.htm (accessed 11 March 2015) (in Chinese).

Xia B (1998) The dilemma of American public service broadcasting (美国公共电视的困境). *Chinese Television (中国电视)* 5: 157–159 (in Chinese).

Xia M (2008) *People's Congresses and Governance in China: Toward a Network Mode of Governance*. Oxford: Routledge.

Xia Q (2005) Public interest and broadcasting regulation in the US. *Journalism and Communication (新闻与传播研究)* 1: 54–61 (in Chinese).

References 247

Xian GE (1983) To reform of radio and television around propaganda: remember eleventh national radio and television work conference (以宣传为中心改革广播电视: 记第十一次全国广播电视工作会议). *The Press (*新闻战线*)* 5: 13 and 18 (in Chinese).

Xian TL (2002) *China's Party-state Government and Market (*中国政党政府与市场*)*. Beijing: Economic Daily Publishing House (北京: 经济日报出版社) (in Chinese).

Xiao SW (2009) Chinese academics' major opinions and comments on public interest (我国学术界关于公共利益的主要观点及评介). *Journal of Yunnan University, Law Edition*, (云南大学学报, 法学版) 122 (16): 30–36 (in Chinese).

Xiao Y (2007) The proposing, formation and development of governing according to law strategies (依法治国基本方略的提出、形成和发展) Available at: http://theory. people.com.cn/GB/49169/49171/6384817.html (accessed 8 August 2014) (in Chinese).

Xie WJ (2001) Conservatism thought trend of China in the 1990s. 20世纪90年代中国的保守主义思潮. *Journal of the Party School of the Central Committee of China Communist Party*. 中共中央党校学报. 5 (3): 103–109 (in Chinese).

Xinhau Net (2006) The history of Xinhua News Agency (新华社的历史沿革). Available at: http://news.xinhuanet.com/newmedia/2006-11/01/content_5277627.htm (accessed 12 July 2014) (in Chinese).

Xinhua News (2011) Beijing Municipal's Certain Provisions on the Administration of Micro-Blog Development 《北京市微博客发展管理若干规定》, 16 December. Available at: http://news.xinhuanet.com/legal/2011-12/16/c_111249899.htm (accessed 20 December 2012) (in Chinese).

Xinhua News Agency (2007) National Corruption Prevention Bureau established. 13 September. Available at: www.china.org.cn/english/government/224301.htm (accessed 24 December 2015).

Xinhua News Agency (2010) Wen Jiabao chaired the State Council's Executive Meeting and decided to accelerate three networks convergence (温家宝主持国务院常务会, 决定加快推进三网融合). *People's Daily*, 14 January, 001 (in Chinese).

Xinhua News Agency (2011) Han Chinese population in China's population drops: census data, 28 April. Wang GQ (ed.). Available at: http://news.xinhuanet.com/english2010/china/2011-04/28/c_13849933.htm (accessed 18 December 2015).

Xinhua News Agency (2012) China issues first public services plan. 19 July. Available at: www.china.org.cn/china/2012-07/19/content_25950483.htm (accessed 23 November 2015).

Xinhua News Agency (2013a) Communiqué of the Third Plenum of the Eighteenth CCP Central Committee (中国共产党第十八届中央委员会第三次全体会议公报). Wang MM (ed.), 12 November. Available at: http://news.xinhuanet.com/politics/2013-11/12/c_118113455.htm (accessed 26 December 2015) (in Chinese).

Xinhua News Agency (2013b) Youth urged to contribute to realization of "Chinese Dream". Available at: www.china.org.cn/china/2013-05/05/content_28731285.htm (accessed 26 December 2015).

Xiong Q and Zhu Z (2005) The State interest and public interests (国家利益和公共利益–从我国高等教育公共政策的视角). *Contemporary University Education (*现代大学教育*)* 2: 1–4 (in Chinese).

Xu F (2008) 2008 Chinese television research report (2008年中国电视研究报告). Available at: http://chinamediaresearch.cn/article.php?id=6060 (accessed 26 February 2016) (in Chinese).

Xu GC (1998) Speech given in the national meeting of the chiefs of provincial TV and radio stations (徐光春在全国省级电台、电视台台长会议上的讲话). In: General

248 *References*

Office of SARFT (2000) (ed.) *The Important Documents of Broadcasting and Film Work 1998* (广播影视工作重要文件汇编*1998*). Beijing: SARFT, 251–263 (in Chinese).

Xu GC (2000a) Speech given at the national radio and television propaganda and chiefs of two stations meetings (徐光春在全国广播电视宣传工作暨省级电台、电视台台长会议上的讲话). In: General Office of SARFT (2001) (ed.) *The Important Documents of Broadcasting and Film Work 2000* (广播影视工作重要文件汇编*2000*). Beijing: SARFT, 439–454 (in Chinese).

Xu GC (2000b) Speech given at the national meeting of the chiefs of Broadcasting and Film Bureaus (徐光春在全国广播影视局长会议上的讲话). In: General Office of SARFT (2001) (ed.) *The Important Documents of Broadcasting and Film Work 2000* (广播影视工作重要文件汇编*2000*). Beijing: SARFT, 459–478 (in Chinese).

Xu GC (2001) Speech given at the national meeting of the chiefs of Broadcasting and Film Bureaus (徐光春在全国广播影视局长会议上的讲话). In: General Office of SARFT (2002) (ed.) *The Important Documents of Broadcasting and Film Work 2001* (广播影视工作重要文件汇编*2001*). Beijing: SARFT, 523–543 (in Chinese).

Xu GC (2002a) Conclusion speech given at the national meeting of the chiefs of Broadcasting and Film Bureaus (徐光春在全国广播影视局长会议闭幕式上的讲话). *Guidebook for Decision Making* (决策参考) 2002 (9): 1–7 (in Chinese).

Xu GC (2002b) WTO and the reform of audio-visual industry (WTO与广播影视业改革). Available at: www.people.com.cn/GB/paper79/6821/664666.html (accessed 13 January 2016) (in Chinese).

Xu GC (2003a) *The Outline History of PRC's Broadcast Media* (中华人民共和国广播电视简史). Beijing: China Broadcast Media Publishing House (北京: 中国广播电视出版社) (in Chinese).

Xu GC (2003b) Speech given at the Working Conference of the Heads of National Broadcasting and Film Bureaus (徐光春在全国广播影视局长座谈会上的讲话). *Guidebook for Decision Making* (决策参考) 2003 (9) (in Chinese).

Xu GC (2004a) Vigorously promote the reform and development of radio, film and television (大力推进广播影视改革发展). *Guidebook for Decision Making* (决策参考) 2004 (8): 3–14 (in Chinese).

Xu GC (2004b) Vigorously promote the digitalization of cable TV with joint force, and the pragmatic spirit (形成合力，求真务实，大力推进有线电视数字化). *Guidebook for Decision Making* (决策参考) 2004 (5): 8–18 (in Chinese).

Xu GC (2004c) Speech at the planning conference of national movie and television cartoon work and cartoon theme (在全国影视动画工作暨动画片题材规划会上的讲话). *Guidebook for Decision Making* (决策参考) 2004 (7): 1–7 (in Chinese).

Xu GC (2004d) Speech at the meeting of SARFT's implementation of Administration Licensing Law. *Guidebook for Decision Making* (决策参考) 2004 (3): 1–3 (in Chinese).

Xu S (2009) Promoting reading for everyone, constructing a literate China – report on 2008 'reading for everyone' activities (2008年全民阅读活动情况调查报告). In: Li J and Chen W (eds.) *Report on the Development of China's Public Cultural Service (2009)* (中国公共文化服务发展报告*2009*). Beijing: Social Sciences Academic Press (北京: 社会科学文献出版社), 135–144 (in Chinese).

Xu XY (2008) History and reflection on China Telecommunication reform (中国电信体制改革历程及其反思). *Modern Transmission* 1: 16–19 (in Chinese).

Xu ZF (2013) The sentences are about reform, the words have intensity: Authoritative discussion on studying the implementation of the spirit of the Third Plenum of the Eighteenth Party Congress (句句是改革 字字有力度权威访谈·学习贯彻十八届三中

全会精神). *People's Daily*, 15 November, 2. Available at: http://paper.people.com.cn/rmrb/html/2013-11/15/nw.D110000renmrb_20131115_1-02.htm (accessed 26 December 2015) (in Chinese).

Xue HK and Jiang YL (2010) Incrementalism and the reform of China Telecommunication (渐进主义与中国电信体制改革). *China CIO News* (信息系统工程) 3: 133–135 (in Chinese).

Yan LQ (2000) China. In: Gunaratne SA (ed.) *Handbook of the Media in Asia*. New Delhi: Sage, 497–526.

Yan MN (1998) *Protection of Free Flow of Information and Regulation of Transfrontier Television: Case Studies of Western Europe and China*. Doctoral dissertation, University of Essex.

Yang B (2009) Perfecting the rural broadcast television public service system – an analysis of the case of Sichuan (健全农村广播电视公共服务体系——基于四川省的案例分析). *Jiangnan Nationalities University Journal (Humanities and Social Sciences Edition)* 西南大学学报（人文社科版）1: 179–184 (in Chinese).

Yang C (2008) The three stages of Chinese broadcasting public service system construction (中国广播电视公共服务的三个历史阶段). *Modern Communication* (现代传播) 1: 123–124 (in Chinese).

Yang DL (2003) China in 2002: leadership transition and the political economy of governance. *Asia Survey* 43 (1): 25–40.

Yang FC (2002) *The Introduction of Chinese Government (*中国政府概要*)*. Beijing: Beijing University Press (北京: 北京大学出版社) (in Chinese).

Yang G (2008) Political participation. In: Yu KP (ed.) *China's Political Reform Towards Good Governance 1978–2008 (*中国治理变迁30年*)*. Beijing: Social Sciences Academic Press (北京: 社会科学文献出版社), 55–82 (in Chinese).

Yang M (2009) The practice and developing model of China's broadcasting public service. In Li J and Chen W (eds.), *Report on China's Cultural Public Service Development 2009 (*中国公共文化服务发展报告2009*)*. Beijing: Social Sciences Academic Press (北京: 社会科学文献出版社), 123–134 (in Chinese).

Yang Q (2014) SMG denies the rumor of Li Ruigang's resignation (SMG否认黎瑞刚辞职传闻). *Tencent Finance (*腾讯财经*)*. 26 December. Available at: http://finance.qq.com/a/20141226/051945.htm (accessed 15 December 2015) (in Chinese).

Yang ZY (2008) From "blocking order" to understand the administration according to law. ("封杀令"看依法行政). *China Reform (*中国改革*)* 5: 71–73 (in Chinese).

Ye ZK (2001) Ye Zhikang's speech given at 2001's bureau's working conference (叶志康在2001年上海文化广播影视管理局工作会议上的讲话). *Culture, Radio, Film and TV (*文化广播影视*)*, 5 February, 1–3 (in Chinese).

Ye ZK (2002a) Speech given in SMEG's 2002 working conference (Summary). 叶志康在上海文化广播影视集团2002年工作会议上的讲话). *Culture, Radio, Film and TV (*文化广播影视*)*, 28 February, 1 and 3 (in Chinese).

Ye ZK (2002b) SMEG's 2001 Annual Report and 2002 Work Plan (上海文化广播影视集团2001年工作报告暨2002年工作计划). *Culture, Radio, Film and TV (*文化广播影视*)*, 4 February, 1–3 (in Chinese).

Ye ZK (叶志康) (2003) Promote the spirit of the OTV, create a new prospect of Shanghai's Broadcasting (弘扬东方卫视精神，创上海广播电视新辉煌). *Shanghai Broadcasting Studies (*上海广播电视学刊*)*. OTV 10 Year Anniversary Special Issue (东方卫视10周年特刊): 2–5 (in Chinese).

Yu B, Jiang H and Guo Q (2003) Thinking of the central, provincial, municipal and county levels' radio and television development (中央、省、市、县四级广播电视发

展定位的思考). *Radio and Television Information* (广播电视信息) 2003 (6): 22–23 (in Chinese).

Yu GM (2002) *The Analysis of the Changing Environment of the Mass Media* (解析传媒变局). Guangzhou: Nanfang Daily Press (广州: 南方日报出版社). (in Chinese).

Yu Y (2006) Institutional origins of the disorder of advertisement broadcasting (广告无序播放的体制根源). *News Circle* (新闻界) 6: 113–114.

Yuan L, Wang YL and Wang JC (2011) *Analysis of Three Networks Convergence Based on Policy Network Theory.* In: Business Computing and Global Informatization (BCGIN) 2011 International Conference 142 (145): 29–31.

Yuan Q and Xiang LX (2006) Public service television is inevitable (公共电视，势在必行). *Modern Communication* (现代传播) 5: 121–123 (in Chinese).

Yuan Y (2014) Li Ruigang: Merge the "small SMG" and "big SMG" with Internet mindset (黎瑞刚: 以互联网思维整合大小文广). *Asian Business Leader* (东方企业家), [J] 1 (in Chinese).

Zeng JH (2014) The debate on regime legitimacy in China: Bridging the wide gulf between Western and Chinese Scholarship. *Journal of Contemporary China* 23 (88): 612–635.

Zhang D (2010) Protection of non-political speech in China (论我国非政治性言论自由的保障). *Charming China* (魅力中国) 06: 61 (in Chinese).

Zhang GT (2008) The basic implications of broadcast television public service (广播电视公共服务的基本内涵). *Modern Communication* (现代传播) 1: 119–121 (in Chinese).

Zhang HT (2003) Speech given at the meeting of national cable digital broadcasting and film services experimental works (张海涛在全国有线数字电视试点工作现场会上的讲话). *Guidebook for Decision Making* (决策参考) 2003 (8): 1–8 (in Chinese).

Zhang HT (2004a) Speech at the on-site meeting of the national cable TV pilot work (张海涛在全国有线数字电视试点工作现场会上的讲话). *Guidebook for Decision Making* (决策参考) 2004 (9): 4–8 (in Chinese).

Zhang HT (2004b) Speech at the national conference of cable TV toll administration work (在全国有线电视收费管理工作座谈会上的讲话). *Guidebook for Decision Making* (决策参考) 2004 (7): 18–21 (in Chinese).

Zhang HT (2006) Strengthen the wireless coverage and ensure the public service of rural broadcasting television (加强无线覆盖，确保农村广播电视公共服务). *Guidebook for Decision Making* (决策参考) 2006 (10): 16–22 (in Chinese).

Zhang HT (2007a) Promote the technological and career development of radio, film and television greatly with unified thinking and joint force (统一思想，形成合力，推动广播影视科技和事业发展上一个大台阶——在总局科技委第七届四次会议上的讲话). *Guidebook for Decision Making* (决策参考) 2007 (3): 45–58 (in Chinese).

Zhang HT (2007b) Speech at the 2007 China Content Broadcasting Network (CCBN). (在2007年中国国际广播电视信息网络展览会主体报告会上的讲话). *Guidebook for Decision Making* (决策参考) 2007 (5): 31–42 (in Chinese).

Zhang HT (2007c) Speech at the theme conference of the sixteenth Beijing International Radio, Television and Film Equipment Exhibition (在第十六届北京广播电影电视设备展览会主体报告会上的讲话). *Guidebook for Decision Making* (决策参考) 2007 (10): 4–12 (in Chinese).

Zhang HT (2009) Study and practice scientific development model and propel the technical and industrial development of the broadcasting system. Speech delivered at National Broadcasting Technical Conference (深入学习实践科学发展观 推动广播影视科技和事业建设又好又快发展——张海涛在全国广播影视科技工作会议上的讲话). *Guidebook for Decision Making* (决策参考) 2209 (3): 10–20 (in Chinese).

References 251

Zhang J, Mao S, and Zhang X (2009). Reform pragmatically, move forward our nation's public culture under the guidance of the scientific development concept. In: Li J and Chen W (eds.) *Report on the Development of China's Public Cultural Service 2009 (*中国公共文化服务发展报告*2009)*. Beijing: Social Sciences Academic Press (北京: 社会科学文献出版社), 1–20 (in Chinese).

Zhang JW and Lou CW (2007) The research of policy networks on the real estate marco-control (房地产宏观调控之政策网络研究). *Journal of Northeastern University (Social Science)* 东北大学学报（社会社科版）9 (4): 341–344 (in Chinese).

Zhang L (2006) Discussion of the applicability of normative documents (浅谈规章以下规范性文件的适用). China Court. Available at: http://old.chinacourt.org/html/article/200611/27/225053.shtml (accessed 5 August 2015) (in Chinese).

Zhang LL (2006) Behind the 'Great Firewall': decoding China's internet media policies from the inside. *The International Journal of Research into New Media Technologies* 12 (3): 271–291.

Zhang LP (2008) On legality and validity of administrative decisions (行政决策中的合法性及有效性分析). *Journal of Henan Police College* 21 (5): 96–100 (in Chinese).

Zhang WW (2000) *Transforming China: Economic Reform and Its Political Implications.* London: Macmillan Press.

Zhang YJ (2003) *China's Emerging Global Businesses: Political Economy and Institutional Investigations.* New York: Palgrave Macmillan.

Zhang YN (2001) Analysing 2000 Shanghai TV Rating (2000年上海电视收视率分析). *Shanghai Broadcasting Studies.* 03/04: 31–33 (in Chinese).

Zhang YR (1992) Comments on the significant changes of Western European broadcasting (评西欧广播电视体制的重大变化). *China Radio and Television Academic Journal (*中国广播电视学刊*)* 1992 (2): 104–108.

Zhang ZF (2008) Important contradictions and issues encountered in the construction of Beijing's broadcast television public service system (北京市广播电视公共服务体系建设面临的主要矛盾与问题). *Modern Communication* (现代传播) 1: 127–128 (in Chinese).

Zhang ZL (2002) Behind the Figures: The Case Study of STV's Sports Channel (数字的背后——上海电视台体育频道收视率个案分析). *Shanghai Broadcasting Studies.* 03/04: 55–59 (in Chinese).

Zhao DX (2001) *The Power of Tiananmen: State-Society Relations and the 1989 Beijing Student Movement.* Chicago: The University of Chicago Press.

Zhao H (2011) Disputes sound media integration death knell. *Caixin Online*, 12 April. Available at: http://english.caixin.com/2011-04-12/100247201.html (accessed 23 November 2015).

Zhao K (1998a) Several thoughts about the Shanghai's broadcasting and film industries towards 21 century (关于上海广播影视产业迈向21世纪的几点思考). *Shanghai Broadcasting Studies (*上海广播电视学刊*)* 1: 3–8 (in Chinese).

Zhao K (1998b) The exploration of the development strategy and management mode of Shanghai's Broadcasting and Film Sectors (上海广播影视行业发展策略与管理模式探究). *Radio, Film and TV (*广播影视*)*, 5 December, 2 (in Chinese).

Zhao S (2004) Circular about the meeting of heads of national broadcasting and film bureaus (赵实在全国广播影视局长会议上的讲话). *Guidebook for Decision Making (*决策参考*)* 2004 (8): 15–27 (in Chinese).

Zhao S (2006) Strengthening administration according to law, serving harmonious development and compressively advancing radio, film and television legal work (强化依法行政, 服务和谐发展, 全面提高广播影视法制工作水平). Available at: www1.sarft.

252 References

gov.cn/articles/2006/11/24/20070910152550670177.html (accessed 27 July 2015) (in Chinese).

Zhao SS (2010) The China model: can it replace the Western model of modernization? *Journal of Contemporary China* 19 (65): 419–436.

Zhao SS (2011) *In Search of China's Development Model: Beyond the Beijing Consensus.* New York: Routledge.

Zhao SS (2014) *Debating Political Reform in China: Rule of Law vs. Democratization.* New York: Routledge.

Zhao YZ (1998) Public Interest, Democracy, and Marketization of American and European Broadcasting (公众利益、民主与欧美广播电视的市场化). *Journalism and Communication (*新闻与传播研究*)* 2: 25–44 (in Chinese).

Zhao, YZ (2003) Transnational capital, the Chinese State, and China's communication industries in a fractured society. *Javnost-The Public* 10 (4): 53–74.

Zheng HT, De Jong M and Koppenjan J (2010) Apply policy network theory to policy-making in China: the case of urban health insurance reform. *Public Administration* 88 (2): 398–417.

Zheng J (2013) Analyze the financial road of media groups through Shanghai Media Group (从SMG看传媒集团的金融路线). *China Culture (*中国文化报*).* 10 August. Available at: http://epaper.ccdy.cn/html/2013-08/10/content_103515.htm (accessed 15 December 2015) (in Chinese).

Zheng YN (1999) *Discovering Chinese Nationalism in China: Modernization, Identity, and International Relations.* Cambridge: Cambridge University Press.

Zheng YN (2006) Explaining the sources of de facto federalism in reform China: inter-governmental decentralization, globalization, and central-local relations. *Japanese Journal of Political Science* 7 (2): 101–126.

Zheng YN, Wang ZX and Lye LF (2005) China political review 2005: Promoting a harmonious society to cope with a crisis of government. China Policy Institute. Briefing Series, Issue 3. Available at: www.nottingham.ac.uk/cpi/documents/briefings/briefing-3-china-political-review-2005.pdf (accessed 24 December 2015).

Zhou R (2006) Broadcasting CunCunTong construction: history, present and future (广电村村通建设历史、现状和未来). *Modern Communication* (现代传播) 5: 45–49 (in Chinese).

Zhou Y (2007) *A Study on Formation of the Industrial Policy of Digital TV in China (*中国数字电视产业政策的形成研究*).* Beijing: China Communication University Press (中国传媒大学出版社).

Zhu H (2002) Outline of the speech given in the broadcasting and film reform workshop (朱虹在广播影视改革研讨会上的讲话摘要). *Guidebook for Decision Making (*决策参考*)* 2002 (3): 23–26 (in Chinese).

Zhu H (2003) China's entry to the WTO and protection of broadcasting copyrights (中国加入世贸组织与广播电视版权保护). *Guidebook for Decision Making (*决策参考*)* 2003 (4): 18–21 (in Chinese).

Zhu H (2004a) Strengthening rule of law at broadcasting sector, improving broadcasting media's reform and development (法制建设与广播影视改革发展). *Guidebook for Decision Making (*决策参考*)* 2004 (2): 34–39 (in Chinese).

Zhu H (2004b) Reform and development of China's radio, film and television industry (中国广播影视业的改革与发展). *Guidebook for Decision Making (*决策参考*)* 2004 (7): 22–32 (in Chinese).

Zhu H (2004c) Strengthen China's radio, film and television industry through reform and development (靠改革发展壮大中国广播影视业——国家广电总局新闻发言人朱虹

答美国《华尔街日报》记者问). *Guidebook for Decision Making (*决策参考*)* (2004) 9: 9–13 (in Chinese).

Zhu H (2006) Digitalization of China's cable television has stepped into the new stage of comprehensive promotion (我国有线电视数字化已进入全面推广的新阶段). *Guidebook for Decision Making (*决策参考*)* 2006 (7): 10–13 (in Chinese).

Zhu JF (2002) The Challenge – WTO and China's TV (WTO与中国电视). *TV Research (*电视研究*)* 147, 7–9 (in Chinese).

Zhu RJ (2001) Report on the Outline of 10th Five-year Plan on National Economic and Social Development (关于国民经济和社会发展第十个五年计划纲要的报告). Presented at the Fourth meeting of the 9th National People's Congress, Beijing (在第九届全国人民代表大会第四次会议上) (in Chinese). Available at: www.gov.cn/english/official/2005-07/29/content_18334.htm (accessed 7 July 2010).

Zhu YL (2002) Zhu Yonglei (朱咏雷). *Media (*媒介*)*, January, 16–27 (in Chinese).

Zhu YP (2008) Housing problem and solution in China (中国住房领域的问题与出路:政策网络的视角). *Wuhan University Journal (Philosophy & Social Sciences)* 武汉大学学报（哲学与社会科学版） 61 (3): 345–350.

Zong M (2006a) Speech given by Zong Ming at the 2006 annual work conference (宗明在集团2006年度工作会议上的讲话). *Shanghai Media Group People (*传媒人报*)*, 25 May, 26 (in Chinese).

Zong M (2006b) Abstract of the speech given by Zong Ming at the meeting of integration of TV news and entertainment resources, and the mobilization of comprehensive reform of HR management (宗明在电视新闻、娱乐资源整合暨人力资源管理综合改革动员大会上的讲话（摘要）). *Shanghai Media Group People (*传媒人报*)*, 20 April, 5 (in Chinese).

Zuo XL and Wang YL (2003) CCTV reform brings in new competition (央视改革引发新竞局中国电视面临"大洗牌"–对省级电视台发展战略的新思考). *South China Television Journal (*南方电视学刊*)* 4: 24–27. (in Chinese).

Index

Page numbers in *italics* denote tables, those in **bold** denote figures.

accountability 32–3, 54, 55, 56–7, 69, 205
Administrative Licensing Law 50–1, 69, 70–1, 77, 181
Administrative Litigation Law (1987) 66, 74, 75
Administrative Measures for the Broadcast of Audiovisual Programs via the Internet or Other Information Networks 51
Administrative Penalties Law (1996) 66
Administrative Provision for the Internet Audio-Video Program Service (SARFT and MIIT) 119
Administrative Provisions on Internet Audio-Visual Program Service (SARFT and MII) 70
Administrative Provisions on Online Publishing Service (SAPPRFT and MIIT) 70, 73
Administrative Reconsideration Law (1990) 66, 74
administrative regulation 51–2; administration according to law and its limits 72–5; court actions 74; rule according to the law 65–72
Administrative Regulations on Radio and Television 67
Administrative Supervision Law (1990) 66
advertising 81–2, *81*, 90, 139, 155, *156*; regulation of TV advertising 179–80, 180–1, 182–3, 188–9
Advertising Law 183
agriculture 30
Anti-Online Rumor Website 56
authoritarianism 13, 28, 134

BAR *see Broadcasting Administrative Regulations* (BAR)

Barabantseva, Elena 14, 15
Bennett, C 174
BIA 55–6
British Broadcasting Corporation (BBC) 145
Broadcasting Administrative Regulations (BAR) 42–3
broadcasting media 40–58; administrative regulation 51–2; broadcasting authority, history of 40–4; broadcasting related laws 50–1, *50*; from a command to a consensus mechanism 54–6; Constitution 49–50; department rules 52–3; domestic law 49; factors influencing the structure of 3–4; international law 48; local government, role of in the media policy-making process 171–90; network governance 55; normative documents and written comments 53–4, 67, 70; normative requirements of 16–17; regulatory areas 68–9; regulatory instruments of SAPPRFT 48; rule according to the law in broadcasting regulation 65–72; social media 54–5; *see also* public service broadcasting; television policy

Cai J 27
CBN *see* Chinese Business Network (CBN)
CCP Central Committee Decision Concerning Some Major Questions in Comprehensively Promoting Governing the Country According to Law (CCP CC) 64, 65–6
CCTV *see* China Central Television (CCTV)

Index 255

censorship 55, 77, 91, 94, 99, 101, 103, 181–2
Central Broadcasting Department (CRD) 41
central government *see* political system and reform
central leading small groups 37
Central Organization Department (COD) 46
Central Propaganda Department *see* Ministry of Central Propaganda (MCP)
Central Radio Administrative Office (CRAO) 40
central-local relationship *see* political system and reform
Chan Ye Hua concept 89–90, 92, 93, 95, 96
Channel Young 192–3
China: Constitution 5, 15–16, 38, 49–50, 63, 64–5, 67, 76, 128, 129, 130, 134, 205; overview of 19–20; political landscape 149
China Central Television (CCTV) 79, 83, 178, 185, 202
China Media Capital (CMC) 166, 193; CMC Creative Fund 167
China Radio, Film and Television Group 100
China TV Report 100
China United Network Communications Ltd (China Unicom) 116
Chinese Business Network (CBN) 165–6
Chinese Communist Party 2, 4, 25, 38; Central Committee (CC) 5, 79; decision-making process 54, 68, 73; institution-building 15; leadership reform 31–2, 63–4; and neo-conservatism 13, 203–9; official ideology on development 14; organization of 20–1, **21**; party-state power structure 21–3, **22**; political economy and television policy from the late 1990s *194–200*; and political reform 13–14; political status 191; and the public interest 129–30; role in overseas satellite television policy formulation 179–80; social learning role 182–8; "stability overwhelms everything else" policy 28; "Three Represents" idea 28–9
Chinese Dream concept 35–6
Chinese Government Legislative Information Network – Public Consultation System 70
Chinese People's Political Consultative Congress (CPPCC) 37

Circular on the Outline of the Report on Broadcasting Work (CCP CP) 41–2
citizenship 127–9
CMC *see* China Media Capital (CMC)
CNBC Asia Pacific 164–5
COD *see* Central Organization Department (COD)
communism: and legitimation 60–1; and the nature of transformation 3–5
Confucianism 10, 14
conglomerates 100, 103
Connected Village Project (CVP) 137, 138–9, 142
corporate governance 27, 39n6
corruption 23, 28, 38, 62, 71, 130
Cox, Robert 106
CPPCC *see* Chinese People's Political Consultative Congress (CPPCC)
CRAO *see* Central Radio Administrative Office (CRAO)
CRD *see* Central Broadcasting Department (CRD)
cultural essentialism 11, 205, 209
cultural public service policy 124, 135–8

DBTA *see* departments of broadcasting and television administration (DBTA)
decentralization: fiscal and administrative power 6; and globalization 9–10; intergovernmental decentralization 7; of state capitalism 7; television 82–4
Decision Concerning Some Major Questions in Comprehensively Promoting Governing the Country According to Law (CCP) 50
Decision of the First Session of the Twelfth National People's Congress on the Plan for State Council Restructuration and Function Transformation (NPC) 47
Decision on Important Issues of the Reform and Development of SOEs (CCP CC) 26
Decision on Several Major Questions About Deepening Reform (CCP) 34–5
Decision to Comprehensively Promote Administration According to Law (State Council) 66
Decisions on the Reform of Economic Institution (CCP CC) 26
Decree No. 22 (SARFT) 181
Decree No. 27 (SARFT) *see Measures for the Administration of the Landing of Foreign Satellite Television Channels*, Decree No. 27 (SARFT)

256 Index

Democratic Progressive Party (DPP) 94
Deng Xiaoping 15, 20, 41, 60–1, 61, 88
departments of broadcasting and television
 administration (DBTA) 43
Dewey, John 13
Ding Guangen 94–5
Ding JJ 90
Document No. 17 (2001) 95
Document No. 17 (CCP) 100
Document No. 82 (State Council) 100
Dong Jun 122
double consciousness concept 11
DPP *see* Democratic Progressive Party
 (DPP)
DreamWorks 166–7
Dye, TR 175

Economic Observer 164, 165
economic reform and transition 6, 7–8, 13;
 central-local relationship 1, 3, 5–8, 17,
 23, 24–5, 201–2; China, overview of
 19–20; Chinese Communist Party
 organization 20–1, **21**; Chinese Dream
 concept 35–6; deepening reform with no
 political priority 36–7; economic
 transition since 1978 25–6; economy
 and politics under the Hu-Wen
 administration 30–4; economy, state-
 owned enterprises reform and politics
 1997–2003 26–30; internalization of the
 economy 29–30; party-state power
 structure 21–3, **22**; and the political
 system 19–39; regional disparities 23–4;
 scientific development and a
 harmonious society 33–4; and television
 broadcasting 102–6; tightened political
 control and administrative reform 31–3;
 Xi Jinping and Li Keqiang
 administration 34–5
Eleventh National Broadcasting Working
 Meeting (1983) 41
equity funds 166
Establishment of Social Market Economy
 (Third Plenary of the Fourth National
 Party Congress) 26

Falun Gong movement 94
federalism 6–7, 17n3
Feng Ninyi 185
Film Promotion Law 69
Four Cardinal Principles 61
Four No Changes principle 98, 103
freedom of expression 49–50, 76, 132,
 133–4

Gao Shuxun 186
GAPP *see* General Administration of Press
 and Publication (GAPP)
Garnham, Nicholas 208
GATS *see General Agreement on Trade in
 Services* (GATS)
GDP *see* gross domestic product (GDP)
General Administration of Press and
 Publication (GAPP) 76–7
General Agreement on Trade in Services
 (GATS) 104, 108, 206
Giddens, Anthony 9–10, 206
Gilroy, Paul 11
globalization 9–10, 31, 104, 205–6; global
 capitalism 203–9
Gong Xueping 149–50
Grindel, M 179
gross domestic product (GDP) 24, 31, 102
Guangdong *see* local media policy,
 Guangdong
Guidebook of Decision 185
Guo Baogang 14

Hall, P 174, 175, 189
Ham, Christopher 87–8
harmonious society idea 33–4, 36, 205
He Qinglian 4
Hill, Michael 87–8
Holmes, Leslie 60, 61
Hongbin Liu 183–4
Howlett, M 174
Hu Jintao 14, 16, 30–4, 63, 182–3
Hu Qiaomu 77
Huang Shengmin 89–90, 95
human rights 72, 133, 134–5, 205
Huntington, Samuel 15

ICCPR *see International Covenant on
 Civil and Political Rights* (ICCPR)
ICCSCR *see International Covenant on
 Economic, Social and Cultural Rights*
Implementation Outline (State Council)
 66, 69
Implementation Rules (SARFT) 100
*Instruction of the CCP's Central
 Committee on Strong Guarantee of
 Criminal Law and Criminal Litigation
 Law's Effect Implementation* (CCP CC)
 62
*International Covenant on Civil and
 Political Rights* (ICCPR) 48
*International Covenant on Economic,
 Social and Cultural Rights* (ICESCR)
 48, 135

Index   257

internet 31, 55–6, 70, 118–19

Jenkins, WI 88
Jiang Weimin 157–8
Jiang Zemin 28–9, 62–3, 96, 178

Keman Wang 183–4, 185

law: administration according to law and
its limits 72–5; administrative regulation
51–2; broadcasting related laws 50–1,
50, 59; court actions 74; domestic law
49; international law 48; press law 75–7;
rule according to the law in broadcasting
regulation 65–72; rule of law 15–16, 28,
29, 59, 62–5; and state legitimacy 59–78
*Law on Protection of the Broadcasting and
Film Program Transmission* 69
Law on Supervision 32
Legislation Law 16
legitimacy 59–78, 132; administration
according to law and its limits 72–5;
court actions 74; Four Cardinal
Principles 61; legitimation 60–1;
political legitimacy 59–62; press law
75–7; rule according to the law in
broadcasting regulation 65–72; rule of
law, development in China 62–5; Three
Supremes notion 65
Lerner, Daniel 8–9, 208
Li Chang Chun 185
Li Danling 77
Li Keqiang 34–5, 36–7
Li Qiang 25
Li Rangang 160
Li Ruigang 163, 164, 165, 166, 167
Li Ruihuan 29
Li Tieying 88, 89
liberalism and liberalization 9, 13, 89, 92,
94–5, 104–6, 108, 125, 127–8, 129,
132–3, 151, 203–4, 206
licensing 59, 60–1, 70–1, 74
Lieberthal, Kenneth 7–8
Lin Min 11, 12
Ling Gang 162–3
Linz, Juan J 60
Lipset, Seymour Martin 60
Liu Binjie 76, 77
Liu Qibao 47
Liu Yunshan 47
local government *see* political system and
reform
local media policy, Guangdong 171–90;
China's foreign TV policies 177–8;

China's media policy process
conceptualization 172–4; Guangdong
province and its TV market landscape
178; overseas satellite television policy
formulation 179–80; policy learning and
the Chinese policy-making process
176–7; policy learning concept 173–5;
regulatory enforcement, supervisory
discretion and policy implementation
180–2; roles of the Party, provincial
media and officials in social learning
182–8
Lu Ye 151
"Lust, Caution" (film) 74, 75

Macau Asia Satellite Television (MASTV)
187
McQuail, Denis 16, 17
Marshall, TH 127
MASTV *see* Macau Asia Satellite
Television (MASTV)
MCP *see* Ministry of Central Propaganda
(MCP)
MCP (98) No. 1 (MCP) 92
*Measures for the Administration of the
Landing of Foreign Satellite Television
Channels*, Decree No. 27 (SARFT) 181,
184
*Measures on Radio, Film and Television
Administrative Reconsideration*
(SARFT) 71
MIIT *see* Ministry of Industry and
Information Technology (MIIT)
Ministry of Central Propaganda (MCP) 41,
46–8, 68, 70, 79, 92, 93, 94, 183, 187
Ministry of Industry and Information
Technology (MIIT) 31, 113–15, **113,
114**, 117, 119–20, 201
Ministry of Information Industry of China
70
Ministry of Radio, Film and Television
(MRFT) 41, 42, 43, 67, 84, 88, 89,
90–1, 99, 115; downgrading of 91–2
modernization: Chinese conceptualization
and interpretations of 10–16; debates on
8–10; dominant modernization paradigm
and its constrainment on China 14–15;
and globalization 9–10; institution-
building 15; of the media 203–9; neo-
conservatism 12–13, 203–9; scientific
development 14–15; and Westernization
10–12; Westernization development
paradigm 8–9
Moore, TG 177

258 *Index*

National Broadcasting and Film Working Conference 43–4
National Development and Reform Commission (NDRC) 117
National Human Rights Action Plan of China (2009–2010) 133, 134–5, 205
National People's Congress (NPC) 16, 19, 37, 44, 49, 76
NDRC *see* National Development and Reform Commission (NDRC)
neo-conservatism 12–13, 203–9
Ninth Five Year Development Plan 88
Ninth Five Year National Economic and Social Development Plan and Outline of 2010 Visions (NPC) 63
nomenklatura appointment system 46–7, 114
normative documents 53–4, 67, 70
Notice of the General Office of the State Council on Dividing the Tasks for Implementation of the Plan for Institutional Reform and Functional Transformation of the State Council (State Council) 47–8
Notice on Deepening Telecommunication Reform 117
Notice on Dividing the Tasks for Implementation of the Plan for Institutional Reform and Functional Transformation of the State Council (State Council) 44
Notice on the issuance of the MRFT's function, organization and staffing (State Council) 47
Notice on the Issuance of the SAPPRFT's Function, Organization and the Staffing (State Council) 48
Notice on the issuance of the SARFT's function, organization and staffing (State Council) 47
Notice on Issues concerning the Pilot Program for Convergence of Three Networks (State Council) 120
Notice on Work Plan of Strengthening Rule of Law Government (SARFT) 69
NPC *see* National People's Congress (NPC)

Office of the Communications Authority (Ofca) 120
Online News and Information Council 56
Opinion on Construction of Rule of Law Government (State Council) 69
Opinion Regarding Further Strengthening Internet Administration Work (CCP) 70

Opinions on Earnestly Implementing the Separation of Broadcasting and Production (SARFT) 160
Opinions on Experimental Works of the Cultural System's Institutional Reform (CCP) 97–8
Opinions on Experimental Works of the Cultural System's Institutional Reform (National Broadcasting and Film Working Conference) 43–4
Opinions on Improving Broadcasting and Film Industry Development (SARFT) 98–9, 100–1
Opinions on promoting the development of radio, film and television industry (SARFT) 160
Opinions on the Work of Deepening the Economic Reform in 2009 (NDRC) 118
Outline of Cultural Development for the Eleventh Five Year Plan (State Council) 48, 127, 135–8
Overall Plan for Promoting Three Network Convergence (State Council) 118

Passing of Traditional Society, The (Lerner) 8–9
Peng Guibing 77
Peng Zhen 128, 129
political system and reform 13–14, 19–39; central-local relationship 1, 3, 5–8, 17, 23, 24–5, 201–2; China, overview of 19–20; Chinese Communist Party organization 20–1, **21**; Chinese Dream concept 35–6; deepening reform with no political priority 36–7; economic transition since 1978 25–6; economy and politics under the Hu-Wen administration 30–4; economy, state-owned enterprises reform and politics 1997–2003 26–30; internalization of the economy 29–30; party-state power structure 21–3, **22**; political legitimacy 59–62; political stability 7, 15, 28, 61, 191, 193; regional disparities 23–4; scientific development and a harmonious society 33–4; tightened political control and administrative reform 31–3; Xi Jinping and Li Keqiang administration 34–5
Press Law of the PRC 77
Press Law Research Office 76–7
privatization 26–7
propaganda 40, 41, 46–8, 68, 88, 138
Propaganda Leading Small Group 47
protectionism 25, 38, 177, 203

Provincial Measures for the Administration of Examination and Approval of the Landing of Overseas Satellite TV Channels (SARFT) 183
Provincial Provisions of Guangdong Province on Administration of Overseas Satellite Television Channels 181
Provision on SARFT's functions, internal organs and staffing (State Council) 115–16
Provisional Provisions on Supervision of Administrative License Implementation (SARFT) 71
"Provisional Regulation on the Party and Government Resignation" (CCP CC) 32
Provisions on Radio, TV and Film Legislative Procedures (SARFT) 71
public opinion 134, 192, 204
public service broadcasting 124–46; Beijing Television Station (BJTV) 143; citizenship 127–9; commercialization and socialist spiritual civilization 138–40; comparison with the BBC 145; Connected Village Project (CVP) 137, 138–9, 142; cultural public service policy 124, 127, 135–8; defining the public interest 127–31; depoliticization of public interest 143–4; finance and income 137–8, *138*, 139, 141–2; future development of 145; governance and regulation 142–3; improved protection of individual rights 144; infrastructure expansion 140–1; normative concept of 125; normative functions 131–5; policy implementation 140–3; public service concept 7, 48; public service frameworks in Europe and China 125–7; Tibet-Xinjiang Project (TXP) 138–9; *see also* broadcasting media

Qi Ye Hua concept 93
Qi Yongfeng 131–2, 133

Radio and Television Shanghai (RTS) 161
Radio Department (RD) 40–1
RatPac Entertainment 167
RD *see* Radio Department (RD)
Reeves, Geoffrey 207
Reform on Promoting "Separation of Broadcasting and Production" of Broadcasters (SARFT) 160
Regulation on production and management of radio and television programs (SARFT) 160

Regulations Governing the Administration of Radio and Television 91
Report to Further Strengthen and Improve Radio, Film and TV Work (MRFT) 88, 89
Rogers, Everett 9
RTS *see* Radio and Television Shanghai (RTS)
rule of law 15–16, 28, 29, 59, 62–5; administration according to law and its limits 72–5; and broadcasting regulation 65–72

SAPPRFT 2, 37, 40, 44–6, **45**, 47, 48, 52, 53, 66–7, 68, 69, 70, 73, 74, 202; and MIIT 113–15, **113**, **114**, 201
SARFT *see* State Administration of Radio, Film and Television (SARFT)
SARS *see* Severe Acute Respiratory Syndrome (SARS) crisis
Sarti, Ingrid 206, 207
SASAC *see* State-owned Assets Supervision and Administration Commission (SASAC)
scientific development concept 14–15; and a harmonious society 33
Several Important Problems about Our Country's Present Broadcasting Development (MRFT) 90–1
Several regulations on non-public capital's entrance into the cultural industry (State Council) 160
Severe Acute Respiratory Syndrome (SARS) crisis 32
SGAPP *see* State General Agency of Press and Publications (SGAPP)
Shanghai Culture, Radio, Film and TV Bureau 152–3, *153*
Shanghai Gang 149
Shanghai Media and Entertainment Group (SMEG) 153–4, 157, 162–3, 167–8, 192–3, 201
Shanghai Media Group (SMG) 154–5, *154*, 157–9, 160–3, 164, 165, 168, 202
Shanghai Oriental Pearl New Media Co. 163
Shanghai Radio, Film and TV Bureau 152
Shanghai State-owned Assets Supervision and Administration Commission (SASAC) 162, 168
Shanghai television *see* television policy
Shen Li 165–6
Shen Mingchang 155
Sina Weibo 55

260 *Index*

SMEG *see* Shanghai Media and Entertainment Group (SMEG)
SMG *see* Shanghai Media Group (SMG)
social learning 172, 174–5, 182–8
social media 54–5
SOE *see* state-owned enterprises (SOEs)
Southern Media Group 185
Southern Television Station (STS) 182, 184, 185
Sparks, Colin 3–5, 17, 193
Standing Committee of the National People's Congress 6, 76
Star China 166
State Administration of Press, Publication, Radio, Film and Television *see* SAPPRFT
State Administration of Radio, Film and Television (SARFT) 43, 67, 69–70, 71, 73, 74, 79, 91–2, 98, 100, 119–20, 122, 160, 161, 163, 182; digitalization plan 101, 110; and overseas satellite television policy formulation 179–80, 183–4; policy formulation procedure 176; *Provision on SARFT's functions, internal organs and staffing* (State Council) 115–16; "reaching out" project 95–6, 106, 178, 203; regulation of TV advertising 180–1
State Compensation Law (1994) 66
State Council 5, 19–20, 22, 44, 57n4, 66, 67, 69, 84, 91; control of 46–8
State General Agency of Press and Publications (SGAPP) 95
State Statistic Bureau 28, 61–2, 84
State-owned Assets Supervision and Administration Commission (SASAC) 113, 191
state-owned enterprises (SOEs) 26–9, 35, 38, 39n5, 162
Strengthening the Governance of Press, Publication and Broadcasting (CCP/State Council) 99
Sun Jazheng 89
Sun Xupei 77

Tang Wei 75
Telecommunication Reform Plan (State Council) 117
telecommunications 116–21, 122
television policy 147–70, 171–90; 1990s television 79–86; advertising *81*, 90–1, 179–80, 180–1, 182–3, 188–9; cable television 83–4, 84–5; censorship 91, 103, 181–2; channel specialization

155–7, *156*, 168; Channel Young 157–9, **159**, 192–3; decentralized television sector and chaotic television market 82–4, *83*; development before 1996 in Shanghai and the "controlled competition" model 149–52, *150*; developments after 1996 in Shanghai 152–7, *153*; digitalization 101, 110–12, 177; domestic political economy and international communication order 102–6, *105*; features of, from the 1980s to mid-1990s 80, *80*; finance and income 155, *156*; foreign TV policies 177–8; Four No Changes principle 98, 103; Guangdong province and its TV market landscape 178; internationalization 164–8; marketization of 81–2, 86; media conglomeration in Shanghai 152; media policy process conceptualization 172–4; merger of OTV, STV, cable TV and conglomeration since 2001 in Shanghai 153–5, *154*; modernization of 203–9; network convergence 112–13; network convergence policy, key stages of 121–2; number of channels 99–100; overseas satellite television policy formulation 179–80, 183–8, 189, 202, 203–4; overseas television channels (OTvC) 172, 174; party-state television policy since 1996 87–8; pay TV 101, 111–12; policy and political economy from the late 1990s *194–200*; policy and transformation 191–4, 201; policy between 1996 and 2003 87–109; policy between 2004 and 2015 110–23; policy learning and the Chinese policy-making process 176–7; policy learning concept 173–5; political independence from government 208; quasi-market and dual system phase 2001 94–9; re-centralization, conglomeration, de-regulation and digitalization after 1996 99–101; "reaching out" project 95–6, 106, 178, 203; *Regulations Governing the Administration of Radio and Television* 91; regulatory enforcement, supervisory discretion and policy implementation 180–2; roles of the Party, provincial media and officials in social learning 182–8; SAPPRFT, MIIT and network convergence 113–15, **113, 114**; separation of broadcasting and production in Shanghai 160–3; set top boxes (STB) 111; Shanghai television

147–70, 193, 201–2; state regulation and local commercial concern 84–5; structure of TV 8, 79; three network convergence development 115–21; traditional phase of the national television policy 1996–1997 89–91; trans-border satellite flows 84–5, 86; transitional phase of the national television policy 1998–2000 91–4; *see also* broadcasting media; public service broadcasting
Third Plenary of the Fourteenth National Party Congress 26
Thirteenth Five Year Plan of China 36
Thomas, JW 179
Three Network Convergence Coordination Group Office 120
Three Network Convergence Promotion Plan (State Council) 122
Three Supremes notion 65
Tian Congming 66, 92–3
Tian Jing 120–1
Tibet-Xinjiang Project (TXP) 138–9
Timetable of Digitalization of Domestic Cable TV, The (SARFT) 110
Tomlinson, John 10, 208
Tong Gang 66
transformation, nature of, in the communist state 3–5, 17, 191–4, 201
Tylecote, A 27

UN Committee on Economic, Social and Cultural Rights (CESCR) 135
unemployment 28, 61–2

Walt Disney Company 167
Wang Jianjun 163, 167
Wang Xiaodong 205–6
Wang Xiaojie 121
Wang Xixin 74
Warner Bros. Entertainment 167
Weber, Max 60
Wen Jiabao 30–4, 66
Wen Yongzheng 77
Westernization 8–9; and modernity 10–12; rationalist philosophy 13; Western centralism 11

Work Plan 2010 70
Working Plan for Pilot Sites of Three Network Convergence (SARFT and MIIT) 119–20
World Trade Organization (WTO) 27, 28, 29, 38, 94, 104–5, *105*, 106, 108, 206
WPP 167
WTO *see* World Trade Organization (WTO)
Wu Bangguo 148
Wu Guangzheng 182–3
Wu Lengxi 41
Wuxi Broadcasting Group 100

Xi Jinping 16, 34–6, 37, 65, 205
Xiao SW 128
Xie Wujun 13
Xinhua News Agency (XNA) 40
XNA *see* Xinhua News Agency (XNA)
XNCR *see* Yanan Xinhua Radio Station (XNCR)
Xu Guangchun 42, 92, 93–4, 96, 98, 157

Yan Xiaohong 71
Yanan Xinhua Radio Station (XNCR) 40
Yang D 177
Yang Mingpin 137
Yang Weimin 34
Yang Xingnong 159
Ye Zhikang 151, 157

Zhan Jiang 77
Zhang Haitao 101, 138
Zhang LP 73–4
Zhang Yongjin 29, 106
Zhao Dinxing 60
Zhao Kai 151–2
Zhao Suifu 176
Zhao Suisheng 13–14, 15
Zheng Yongnian 6, 7, 201
Zhou Y 177
Zhu Hong 68, 99, 101
Zhu Rongji 28, 29
Zhu Yonglei 155, 157
Zou Jiangxing 120

Taylor & Francis eBooks

Helping you to choose the right eBooks for your Library

Add Routledge titles to your library's digital collection today. Taylor and Francis ebooks contains over 50,000 titles in the Humanities, Social Sciences, Behavioural Sciences, Built Environment and Law.

Choose from a range of subject packages or create your own!

Benefits for you
- Free MARC records
- COUNTER-compliant usage statistics
- Flexible purchase and pricing options
- All titles DRM-free.

REQUEST YOUR FREE INSTITUTIONAL TRIAL TODAY

Free Trials Available
We offer free trials to qualifying academic, corporate and government customers.

Benefits for your user
- Off-site, anytime access via Athens or referring URL
- Print or copy pages or chapters
- Full content search
- Bookmark, highlight and annotate text
- Access to thousands of pages of quality research at the click of a button.

eCollections – Choose from over 30 subject eCollections, including:

Archaeology	Language Learning
Architecture	Law
Asian Studies	Literature
Business & Management	Media & Communication
Classical Studies	Middle East Studies
Construction	Music
Creative & Media Arts	Philosophy
Criminology & Criminal Justice	Planning
Economics	Politics
Education	Psychology & Mental Health
Energy	Religion
Engineering	Security
English Language & Linguistics	Social Work
Environment & Sustainability	Sociology
Geography	Sport
Health Studies	Theatre & Performance
History	Tourism, Hospitality & Events

For more information, pricing enquiries or to order a free trial, please contact your local sales team:
www.tandfebooks.com/page/sales

The home of Routledge books

www.tandfebooks.com